Teaching

Theory
into Practice

Allan C. Ornstein

LOYOLA UNIVERSITY OF CHICAGO

ALLYN AND BACON
Boston   London   Toronto   Sydney   Tokyo   Singapore

Series Editor: *Virginia Lanigan*
Production Administrator: *Marjorie Payne*
Editorial Assistant: *Nicole De Palma*
Cover Administrator: *Linda Knowles*
Composition/Prepress Buyer: *Linda Cox*
Manufacturing Buyer: *Louise Richardson*
Editorial-Production Service: *Raeia Maes*
Cover Designer: *Suzanne Harbison*
Marketing Manager: *Ellen Mann*

© 1995 by Allyn & Bacon
A Simon & Schuster Company
Needham Heights, Mass. 02194

Library of Congress Cataloging-in-Publication Data

Teaching : theory into practice / Allan C. Ornstein.
       p.   cm.
    Includes bibliographical references and index.
    ISBN 0-205-15778-5
    1. Teaching   I. Ornstein, Allan C.
  LB1025.3.T438   1995
  371.1'02—dc20   94-27202
                                                                         CIP

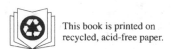

This book is printed on
recycled, acid-free paper.

Printed in the United States of America

10 9 8 7 6 5 4 3 2 1   99 98 97 96 95 94

Contents

Preface

Teaching: Theory into Practice is intended to give students some exposure to various aspects of teaching that have relevance for understanding what teach ers do and how they think when they teach. The book was created to help students reflect on teaching both in a theoretical and practical sense. We try to answer five basic questions: What is effective teaching? What teaching procedures facilitate learning and under what conditions? How do cultural, linguistic, and reflective practices influence teacher beliefs and behaviors? What social and political forces impact on teaching? And how can teachers influence the social and political order?

In trying to answer these basic questions, I have enlisted a large group of experts who have diverse viewpoints and who recommend diverse methods of teaching. Some of the authors stress cognition and teaching, some are more behavioristic, and still others are humanistic and existentialist. Some of the contributors use quantitative approaches, others rely on qualitative approaches, and still others attempt to incorporate both approaches. A few of the authors are scientific in their views about teaching, others view teaching as a craft, and still others view teachers as reconstructionists and critical pedagogists.

My purpose as editor was to invite authorities in the field of teaching, with different philosophical and political positions, to contribute their latest thoughts on the research and practice of teaching. The decision was made to request that the contributors avoid statistical analysis, research jargon, and "metatalk"—that is, the language scholars use when they talk to other scholars and that confuses most other readers. The contributors were instructed to examine a major concept, trend, or essential aspect of teaching and to cover it in such a way that beginning and experienced teachers alike could understand and make use of that concept in their own teaching practice. Because of the expertise of the authors, the chapters should present important methods and offer new ways to analyze the research and practice of teaching.

To be sure, some relevant chapters appear in every reader, but to the best of my knowledge nowhere else is there a similar collection of timely and original works on teaching and learning. Nowhere has such a large number of authorities in the field been asked by one editor to contribute their ideas for teachers or for those studying to be teachers. Herein lies the purpose of the book.

This book does not attempt to duplicate the publications about research on teaching of the American Association of Colleges for Teacher Education, American Educational Research Association, American Psychological Association, or the National Society for the Study of Education. Contributors to these publications detail research methodology and generate esoteric conversations among scholars. This book, however, is written for practitioners to understand and to use in their everyday teaching experiences. In most other books of readings, scholars of this caliber write to other scholars to bolster their careers.

To help acquaint the reader with the authors, each contributor is introduced by a short personal biography and photograph. To help the reader understand the theory of teaching, I have asked the authors to integrate practical elements throughout their discussions and to include a "Theory into Practice" section at the end of their respective chapters. Finally, each chapter ends with a short summary and five or six discussion or overview questions to help focus on main ideas.

Before concluding, I want to extend my thanks to all the contributors who met a tight schedule and put forth their time and effort to help complete this project. I am indebted to the editor at Allyn and Bacon, Virginia Lanigan, who had sufficient faith in the project, and the publisher who permitted these original papers to be reprinted as a book. I want to thank Kenneth Jerick, Illinois State University, who wrote the Instructor's Manual that accompanies this book.

I also want to thank the reviewers of the manuscript: Greg Bryant, Towson State University; Hal Funk, Southwest Missouri State University; and Michael Meloth, University of Colorado.

A.C.O.

Contributors

Frances S. Bolin, *Teachers College, Columbia University*

Kathy Carter, *University of Arizona*

Marilyn Cochran-Smith, *University of Pennsylvania*

Lyn Corno, *Teachers College, Columbia University*

Philip A. Cusick, *Michigan State University*

Walter Doyle, *University of Arizona*

Carolyn M. Evertson, *Peabody College, Vanderbilt University*

Henry A. Giroux, *Pennsylvania State University*

Gary A. Griffin, *University of Arizona*

Martin Haberman, *University of Wisconsin, Milwaukee*

Simon Hooper, *University of Minnesota*

Dona M. Kagan, *University of Alabama*

Susan Laird, *University of Oklahoma*

Thomas J. Lasley, *University of Dayton*

Susan L. Lytle, *University of Pennsylvania*

Linda Mabry, *University of Washington*

Thomas J. Matczynski, *University of Dayton*

Carla Meister, *Aurora Public Schools and University of Illinois, Urbana-Champaign*

Allan C. Ornstein, *Loyola University of Chicago*

John E. Penick, *University of Iowa*

Linda Post, *University of Wisconsin, Milwaukee*

Catherine H. Randolph, *Peabody College, Vanderbilt University*

Lloyd P. Rieber, *University of Georgia*

Mark Riney, *University of Arizona*

Barak V. Rosenshine, *University of Illinois, Champaign*

Robert E. Slavin, *Johns Hopkins University*

Robert E. Stake, *University of Illinois, Champaign*

Bruce W. Tuckman, *Florida State University*

Hersholt C. Waxman, *University of Houston*

Herbert J. Walberg, *University of Illinois, Chicago*

Edward A. Wynne, *University of Illinois, Chicago*

Part I

The Science and Art of Teaching

The science of teaching attempts to systemize teaching—how to define it, identify it, measure it, and evaluate it. Two schools of thought emerge: The minority group, once the majority view, maintains that research on teaching is inclusive and so complex that it is nearly impossible to agree on what effective teaching is. Since the mid-1970s, the majority view contends that the principles and practices of good teaching can be agreed upon: Based on the proper statistical methods and analysis, we can identify and evaluate teacher effectiveness. These researchers provide the groundwork for what is called "process-product" research, which identifies relationships between teacher processes (what teachers do) and teacher products (student learning outcomes).

The science of teaching tends to be analytical, denotive, and prescriptive; it is based on observing and measuring behaviors of teachers and students. The evaluation instruments for assessing teachers are varied and include rating scales, observational techniques, and personality inventories. The method for assessing student outcomes or learning is based on standardized tests, usually in reading or mathematics. The belief is, according to the majority of researchers, that teachers do make a difference and that a knowledge base involving the methods and effects of teaching can be taught to beginning teachers.

The art of teaching deals with feelings, attitudes, and values. It emphasizes human relationships and creative and imaginative thinking and it enables the learner to be recognized as a worthwhile and experiencing person. The emphasis is on processes of teaching, not on products or outcomes, and the language or description of the teaching process is not conducive for empirical research. The teacher is viewed as an artist, composer, or actor in a supporting or facilitating role—like an orchestra leader, acting director, or coach—not as a scholar, problem solver, or taskmaster, that is, someone who controls or manages students.

Part I begins with a chapter by Allan Ornstein, who examines the historical and philosophical considerations in determining teacher effectiveness. A number of important issues are discussed: Is teaching an art or a science? How do we categorize, observe, and measure teaching? What measurement techniques should be used for assessing teaching, and under what conditions? What groups are the best raters and/or observers of teachers: students, parents, other teachers, supervisors, or researchers? Should research focus on generic principles of teaching or specific content- and grade-related principles of teaching? The author ends with fourteen recommendations for improving research on teachers.

Francis Bolin, in Chapter 2, examines "Teaching as a Craft." She maintains that teaching is neither science nor art, although it borrows from both. For her, teaching involves human encounters and interactions between the teacher and students. She evokes the metaphor of a craft, which Dewey did some ninety years ago, and refers to teaching as a skillful and caring occupation, and a process that involves imaginative and meaningful engagements with students. By looking at the relationship between subject matter and pedagogy, we gain further insight into teaching as a craft. Good teachers are excited about what they teach and are ex-

cited when students learn the subject material. Pedagogy is a form of presentation—illustrated by the way the teacher moves about, utilizes various resources, balances time among students, and makes students come alive when learning the subject.

In Chapter 3, Herbert Walberg summarizes and synthesizes research in the twin areas of teaching and instruction. He examines various teaching methods, instructional plans, student grouping patterns, and early intervention programs—explaining what techniques and combinations work. Walberg pays special attention to cues, engagement, corrective feedback and reinforcement, explicit teaching and comprehension teaching, mastery learning, adaptive instruction, and cooperative learning, among other techniques. He ends with a discussion on how to train teachers to be more effective through practice, audio-feedback, observations and modeling, and coaching.

The next chapter by Bruce Tuckman discusses the competent teacher: what it means to be competent and how to measure competency. Tuckman maintains there are two basic principles for determining teacher competency: on the basis of student performance and on the basis of judgments of or about teachers. He looks at four broad areas in which *teacher attitudes* are critical to teacher effectiveness: teaching efficacy, locus of control, expectations, and enthusiasm. Afterwards, he examines five broad areas of *teacher behavior* critical to teacher effectiveness: planning, instructing, communicating, managing, and evaluating.

Chapter 5 describes the use of classroom observation methods to investigate processes and behaviors that occur in classrooms. Hersholt Waxman briefly summarizes research from the last two decades that has employed systematic classroom observation techniques to investigate effective teaching at the elementary, middle, and high school levels. Some of the criticisms and cautions related to the use of structured observation techniques are also examined. Three specific areas where systematic classroom observation has been found to be especially useful for educational practice are highlighted in this chapter: (1) the improvement of teachers' classroom instruction based on feedback from individual classroom profiles, (2) the investigating of instructional inequities for different groups of students, and (3) the improvement of teacher education programs.

Allan C. Ornstein

Allan C. Ornstein is professor of education at Loyola University of Chicago, and author of more than 375 articles and twenty-seven books. A native New Yorker, with a doctorate from New York University, he still favors that slight eastern accent, although he has lived in Chicago for the last twenty-five years—specifically in Winnetka, Illinois, where he lives with his wife, Valerie, and their three children, Joel, Stacey, and Jason.

Home life and work life are, according to this professor, "100 percent separate." They are divorced from one another. "I don't bring my professional problems home." Yet, he does bring a bit of home into his office. Photographs he took of his children, more than 40 in total, cover his office wall.

A professor at Loyola since 1972, Ornstein has opened up the ninth floor at 7:30 A.M. most mornings for as long as he can remember. He attributes his extensive writing to his ability to organize both himself and his thoughts to stay focused. "I structure my ideas in my head before anything ever goes on paper so I know exactly where I'm going. I can also sense when I'm drifting, and make cor-

rections at the early stages to avoid off-task time."

Ornstein is beginning to slow down. No longer is he producing three books a year; today, he is down to one or two. Instead of consulting, whereby he has chalked up more than seventy-five jobs for government and education agencies (such as the U.S. Courts, Educational Testing Service, American Federation of Teachers, and National Education Association), he now spends his nonprofessorial time golfing with his adolescent and teen kids, and skiing out West (the Tetons in Jackson Hole, Wyoming, is his favorite place). He also manages to coach the hometown kids in baseball and basketball and claims to have fielded a winning baseball team every year for the last six years by spending more time with the less proficient half of the team than the better half and building team morale, while his counterparts usually devote more attention to the stars and build a team around their stars. He maintains that this has implications for classroom teachers: how they organize academic time, whom they spend their time with, and how they develop classroom rapport and cooperation.

1 ❧

Historical and Philosophical Considerations in Determining Teacher Effectiveness

Allan C. Ornstein

It is not an exaggeration to say that the literature on teaching is a morass of ill-defined and changing concepts. Investigators have examined teacher personalities, traits, behaviors, attitudes, values, abilities, competencies, methods, and many other characteristics. A host of measuring instruments have been employed: personality tests, attitudinal scales, observation instruments, rating scales, check-lists, bipolar descriptors, and closed- and open-ended written statements. The results of teaching have been studied in terms of student achievement, adjustment, attitudes, skills, and creativity. Despite all this activity and thousands of studies conducted in the last fifty years, common denominators and agreed-upon generalizations are hard to come by; hence, few agreed-upon facts concerning teacher effectiveness have been established (Borich, 1986; Ornstein, 1986a, 1990).

Confusion over terms, measurement problems, and the complexity of the teaching act are major reasons for the negligible results in judging teacher effectiveness. The studies themselves are often confirmations of common sense (a "democratic" teacher is an effective teacher) or are contradictory ("direct" behaviors are effective; "indirect" behaviors are effective), or the contexts within which the studies take place have little bearing on classroom setting, subject, or grade level of the individual teacher.

Because we are unable to agree on or precisely define what a good teacher is, we can use almost any definition, so long as it makes sense or seems logical. Despite the elusive and complex nature of teaching, research on teaching should continue with the hope it can be better understood. This chapter, then, is concerned with the understanding of teacher effectiveness—and with some of the theoretical issues related to defining effective teaching.

THE SCIENCE AND ART OF TEACHING

One problem with determining teacher effectiveness is that we cannot agree on whether teaching is a science or an art. Some readers may say that this is a hopeless dichotomy, because the real world rarely consists of neat packages or either/or situations. Gage (1978) uses this distinction between teaching as a science and as an art to describe the elements of predictability in teaching and what constitutes "good" teaching. A science of teaching is possible, he contends, because it "implies that good teaching will some day be attainable by closely following vigorous laws that yield high predictability and control." Teaching is more than a science, he observes, because it also involves "artistic judgment about the best ways to teach" (p. 17). When teaching leaves the laboratory or textbook and goes face to face with students, "the opportunity for artistry expands enormously." No science can prescribe successfully all the twists and turns as teaching unfolds, or as teachers respond with "judgment, sudden insight, sensitivity, and agility to promote learning" (p. 15). These are expressions of art that depart from the rules and principles of science.

Is such a limited scientific basis of teaching even worthwhile to consider? Yes, but the practitioner must learn as a teacher to draw not only from his or her professional knowledge (which is grounded in scientific principles), but also from a set of personal experiences and resources that are uniquely defined and exhibited by the teacher's own personality and "gut" reaction to classroom events that unfold (which form the basis for the art of teaching). For Jackson (1990), the hunches, judgments, and insights of the teacher, as he or she responds spontaneously to events in the classroom, are as important as, and perhaps even more important than, the science of teaching.

To some extent, the act of teaching must be considered intuitive and interactive, not prescriptive or predictable. According to Eisner (1983), teaching is based primarily on feelings and artistry, not scientific rules. In an age of science and technology, there is a special need to consider teaching as an "art and craft." Eisner condemns the scientific movement in psychology, especially behaviorism, and the scientific movement in education, especially in school management, as reducing the teaching act to trivial specifications. He regards teaching as a "poetic metaphor," more suited to satisfying the soul than informing the head, more concerned with the whole than with a set of discrete skills or stimuli. Our role as teachers, he claims, should not be that of a "puppeteer," an "engineer," or a manager; rather, it is "to orchestrate the dialogue [as the conductor of a symphony] moving from one side of the room to the other" (p. 8). The idea is to perceive patterns in motion, to improvise within the classroom, and to avoid mechanical or prescribed rules.

Rubin (1985) has a similar view of teaching—that effectiveness and artistry go hand in hand. The interplay of students and teacher is crucial and cannot be predetermined with carefully devised strategies. Confronted with everyday problems that cannot be easily predicted, the teacher must rely on intuition and on "insight acquired through long experience" (p. 61). Rubin refers to such terms as "with-it-ness," "instructional judgments," "quick cognitive leaps," and "informal guesses" to explain the difference between the effective teacher and the ineffective teacher. Recognizing limits to rationality, he claims that for the artistic teacher a "feel for what is right often is more productive than prolonged analysis" (p. 69). In the final analysis, Rubin compares the teacher's pedagogy with the "artist's colors, poet's words, sculptor's clay, and musician's notes" (p. 60)—in all of which a certain amount of artistic judgment is needed to get the right mix, medium, or blend.

Blending Science and Art

The more we consider teaching as an art, packed with emotions, feelings, and excitement, the more difficult it is to derive rules or generalizations. If teaching is more of an art than a science, then principles and practices cannot be easily codified or developed in the classroom or easily learned by others. Hence, there is little reason to offer methods courses in education to teachers. If, however, teaching is more of a science, or at least partly a science, then pedagogy is predictable to that extent; it can be observed and measured with some accuracy, and the research can be applied to the practice of teaching (as a physician applies scientific knowledge to the practice of medicine) and also learned in a university or on the job (Gage & Berliner, 1989; Ornstein, 1989, 1991).

But a word of caution is needed. The more we rely on artistic interpretations or on old stories and accounts about teachers, the more we fall victim to fantasy, wit, and romantic rhetoric, and the more we depend on hearsay and conjecture rather than on social science or objective data in evaluating teacher competency. On the other hand, the more we rely on the scientific interpretations of teaching, the more we overlook those commonsense and spontaneous processes of teaching, and the sounds, smells, and visual flavor of the classroom. The more scientific we are in our approach to teaching, the more we ignore what we cannot accommodate to our empirical assumptions or principles. What sometimes occurs, according to Eisner (1993) and Peshkin (1993), is that the educationally significant but difficult to measure or observe is replaced by what is insignificant but comparatively easy to measure or observe.

It is necessary to blend artistic impressions and relevant stories about teaching, because good teaching involves emotions and feelings, with the objectivity of observations and measurements and the precision of language. There is nothing wrong with considering good teaching to be an art, but we must also consider it to lend itself to a prescriptive science or practice. If it does not, then there is little assurance that prospective teachers can be trained to be effective teachers—told what to do, how to instruct students, how to manage students, and so forth—and educators will be extremely vulnerable to public criticism and to people outside the profession telling them how and what to teach.

True knowledge of teaching is achieved by practice and experience in the classroom. It deals with beliefs, values, and attitudes—with people and not statistics. The knowledge that teachers come to have the most faith in and use most frequently to guide their teaching is what works for them, not necessarily what theory or research says.

Thus, the real value of scientific procedures may not be realized in terms of research or theoretical "generalizations" that can be translated into practice. Research may have limited potential for teachers, but it can help them become aware of the problems and needs of students. Scientific generalizations and theories may not always be applicable to specific teaching situations, but such propositions can help in the formulation of a reliable and valid base for teaching in classrooms. Scientific ideas can serve as a starting point for discussion and analysis of the art of teaching.

THE CRITERION PROBLEM

Among the reams of empirical research on teaching, there are two basic parts to the investigation. Consideration must be given to the *criterion*, that is the behavior(s) we are categorizing, observing, and/or measuring; and the type of *measurement*, that is the instrument or test we use to obtain data that is usually in the form of some assessment of processes or outcomes.

The criteria, that is the behaviors or characteristics we are analyzing, represent the starting point of the vast majority of studies. But the research has produced an endless list of terms and is based primarily on the knowledge, interest, and purposes of the investigators. Even when there is agreement on terms, the definitions and usages often vary. For example, a "direct" teacher in the classic study of Ryans (1960) is related to the way a teacher manages the classroom, whereas in the study by Flanders (1965) it refers to teacher talk. Our inability to agree on what criteria to study, and what specific behaviors to observe or measure, has confused researchers and has prevented us from building a science of teaching.

When we classify someone as a "democratic" or "authoritative" teacher, or someone as "creative" or "routine," it means different things to different researchers and practitioners. The words *democratic* or *creative* are being used to convey meaning, but the meaning for each of us is based on our prior experiences and thought patterns—which in turn are embedded in cultural meaning, professional judgment, and personal factors such as gender, ethnicity, age, and education. Thus when we communicate with each other and think there is agreement, the meaning may vary—and often does.

According to Bowers and Flinders (1990), words are used to convey messages, but they are not neat, precise containers into which meaning is put, nor do they correspond to the same entities among different people. When words are understood as metaphors, they can be viewed as helping to interpret meaning. Yet, there is often a lack of precision or agreement of what we really mean, because language is somewhat imprecise. (Perhaps this is one reason why we have so many attorneys.)

Perhaps the only chance for precision and agreement deals with obvious teacher behaviors. For example, a "friendly" or "warm" teacher indicates a "good" or "effective" teacher, and "hostile" or "cold" behavior (the opposite teacher type) connotes a "poor" or "ineffective" teacher. But even here, when we are dealing with the so-called obvious, there may be difficulty in agreeing on what we mean by friendly or hostile. What may be construed as friendly by one person may be construed as unfriendly by another, especially in context with culture, gender, ethnicity, and so on. Does a wink always connote friendly behavior? Certainly the context is important, but can we always agree on the context? Or are we talking about a blink, not a wink? It is acceptable for a teacher to wink (or blink) at most students. Certainly gender is a factor, but so is age and a host of other previous interactions between the parties.

Thus, even when we think there is agreement on "good" teacher behavior, it is wrong to assume that there is commonly agreed-upon meaning regarding the words used to describe such behavior. Teacher behavior—concepts and definitions—has different meanings among different groups, especially among students, teachers, supervisors, researchers, and so on—in part because of their different roles—as well as within the same groups, in part because of cultural and linguistic contexts.

Although it is essential to agree on the criteria for investigating what teachers do, and how they do it, there are literally thousands of descriptive words that may be used to describe and classify teacher behavior. Actually, the more behaviors or categories we use, despite their presumed independence, the more often they are related logically or statistically: overlapping increases, while mutual exclusiveness decreases. However, when teacher behaviors are decreased, the findings become more oversimplified, and less worthwhile data are forthcoming. A balance is needed in terms of sufficient teacher behaviors, but where that balance lies is subjective and relative to the views of the researcher.

The use of predetermined behaviors and categories has also been criticized as being mechanistic and providing no convincing evidence that the actual classroom processes coincide with the behaviors or categories, or that the items being investigated actually lead to desired outcomes. It is true, according to Needels and Gage (1991), that predetermined behaviors do not give as rich an account as ethnography or qualitative research can provide, for the behaviors represent an abstraction from a host of classroom events and interactions. But they provide the framework for making generalizations and interpreting observational data within the context described.

In the final analysis, it is inappropriate to ask whether a system of teacher behaviors is a true classification. The most we can hope is that the selection and classification of teacher behaviors is wise and useful, and the methods for establishing them are reliable and valid—bearing in mind that these conditions will never be fully satisfied by any investigation. Then we might ask whether the teacher behaviors we have selected correlate with learning outcomes, and to what extent and under what conditions.

THE MEASUREMENT PROBLEM

In addition to the limitations of finding an acceptable and valid criterion, researchers do not agree on how to measure teacher behaviors or what methods to use to determine the relative merits or effectiveness of these behaviors. Methods for measuring teacher behavior generally fall into three broad areas: (1) student tests of achievement (or behavior), (2) rating forms, and (3) observation and instruments.

Student Tests

Beyond the usual discussion of reliability and validity of standardized tests, the use of standardized tests for assessing learning outcomes related to teacher behavior is flawed by another problem: Changes in posttest scores over short periods of time (say one term or year) are usually unreliable.

Magnitude of differences among tests tends to be small, and it is difficult to obtain reliable scores (or accurate changes in performance) when the magnitude of differences remains small. Factors pertaining to guessing, coaching, regression effect, and test administration are magnified when differences in performance are compared over short periods of time and when converting raw scores to grade equivalent scores; for example, three or four items answered right or wrong on a typical standardized test (usually consisting of thirty to fifty questions) can change the outcomes one-half to one year when changing the raw score to grade equivalents. These changes in scores may have nothing to do with teaching or learning, but more with the testing factors above.

Most reliable changes in test outcomes do not reflect the effects of teachers but more potent factors such as parents, home life, peers, television viewing habits, and a host of other school- and test-related factors. A teacher may be quite effective but not obtain proper results because students lack motivation or interest in learning because home life is disruptive or they don't eat or sleep properly, or because the school is poorly organized. The effects of one teacher may even be neutralized by another teacher or by the parents of the child.

The student tests we use in conjunction with determining teacher effectiveness measure only a small portion of the expected outcomes of learning. The focus is usually on knowledge, not problem solving, creativity, moral education, aesthetic appreciation, love of country, social and personal development, and so on. The fact is, a teacher can teach toward the test, constantly review and drill tiny facts, administer small quizzes to encourage memorization of information— and students would probably show significant gains in posttest scores. Reviewing, practicing, drilling, and breaking down tasks into step-by-step procedures, monitoring student work, providing feedback, and instructing students in test procedures—all of which deal with compliance and completion of low-level academic work—have become recommended behaviors. Asking divergent questions or requiring students to think and discuss ideas is deemphasized and even considered wasteful by some authorities of teacher behavior.

Achievement tests may be valid for assessing the abilities of a student in relation to a larger group, but they do not accurately measure changes in learning, nor do they approximate good teacher behavior. We possess no simple, direct way of correlating teacher behavior with changes in student achievement, even with reliable and valid tests. The outcomes usually have little to do with the performance of the teacher; rather they are the result of a host of other social and cultural factors.

Rating Forms

Rating forms probably represent the most common technique for measuring teacher behavior. A large number of rating instruments have been used, with a wide range of reliability and validity. A large portion are home-made, stemming from doctoral dissertations and supervisors' files, and are more appropriate for a particular study or school. On a typical form, students, other teachers, supervisors, administrators, or researchers may rate the teacher's abilities or performance. However, research data suggest that different groups markedly disagree in their judgments of identifying good teachers (Light, 1973; Ornstein, 1976, 1990; Popham, 1993). This is not surprising, given that people are handicapped by their own personal biases and beliefs of what is or what should be a good teacher; moreover, different groups possess different experiences and perceive the social world differently. They also have a different knowledge base or understanding of teaching ("pedagogical knowledge") and the subject field ("content knowledge").

The rater is also human, and a host of contaminating factors affect his or her rating. On a more technical level, ratings are distorted by the (1) "halo effect," where the rater evaluates or reacts to each item in the direction of the general impression of the teacher, (2) "error of leniency," a tendency of the rater to rate low or high, no matter what the reason, (3) "error of central tendency," whereby the rater reluctantly offers extreme judgments about others (teachers), and (4) "constant error," whereby the rater tends to rate others in the opposite direction to his or her attitudes and behaviors. (For example, the business-like rater tends to rate the teacher as less business-like, or the non-business-like rater tends to rate the teacher as more business-like.) Other factors affecting raters include (1) sex, (2) race (ethnicity), (3) age, (4) intelligence, (5) understanding of directions, (6) understanding of purpose, (7) sufficient time to complete the ratings, (8) possession of traits measured, and (9) different criteria raters employ for assessing the same trait or behavior (Ornstein, 1976, 1986b).

The teacher-raters' reference group (usually based on gender, ethnicity, or religion) is also a factor, whether the reference group is perceived as different or the same. Sometimes raters possess two different attitudes—one for friends and relatives, the other for formal questionnaires. Raters are not always motivated or honest; moreover, because raters are human, they offer imperfect judgments; they remain susceptible to selective perceptions, memory, and lack of sensitivity to importance or significance.

Actually, students are the best raters of teachers, because they see them over an extended period of time and under varied circumstances. Their sample size is larger (say an N of 30 in one class) compared to a supervisor or researcher (an N of 1), and therefore, the data are more reliable. Students are the consumers of education, and their feelings and attitudes (even if misguided) directly influence learning and are therefore more important than teachers', supervisors', or researchers' feelings and attitudes. Regardless of how knowledgeable the other raters are, they can be easily misled or fooled by infrequent observations of the teacher, and by virtue of the teacher putting on an act. Moreover, there is no sure way of offsetting the personal biases of one rater; however, extreme scores of students are theoretically neutralized in a large sample.

We frequently dismiss student raters on the basis of their immaturity. The fact is that they tend to be the most difficult raters to please, since they have high expectations of their teachers to teach them and are required to sit in their seats daily for an extended period of time. Although their view of good teaching may not coincide with the view of professionals, they tend to be more honest than adult raters (who sometimes have hidden agendas), and their perceptions (right or wrong) are important since they interact with learning outcomes.

Observation and Instruments

In actual practice, observation of teacher behavior is costly and time consuming. The high number of interpersonal interchanges in the classroom, some 200 to 250 in one hour, is germane and subsequently limits the person attempting to discern the context of the teacher's behavior. Human overload limits the observer, and he or she can perceive only a fraction of what actually transpires and without guarantee that the perceptions of these swift and complex interchanges are accurate. Moreover, the numerous problems of rating teachers apply to observing them; in effect, the observer falls into the category of a rater.

Other limitations exist: (1) observer reliability, (2) the teacher tends to put on an act while being observed, (3) the presence of the observer creates a "Hawthorne effect"—namely, the teacher and students are aware of a study or another person in the room and their behaviors change, and (4) the observer becomes influenced by his or her own values and interpretations of what constitutes a good teacher. Even the position of the observer is a fact to consider. If he or she sits in the back of the room, he sees a number of heads and shoulders, which partially block his vision of the students. If the observer positions herself in the side or front of the room, she accentuates her presence and increases the likelihood of behavioral changes among students.

There are three common observational techniques: categorical checklists, specimen record techniques, and open-ended forms. With the *categorical checklist,* the observer emphasizes a number of specific teacher or student behaviors. Scoring occurs at intervals, usually within time units or on a continuum suggesting "excellent" to "poor." This process ignores the richness of the interaction process. In using the *specimen record technique,* the observer focuses on a specific person (teacher or student) and records all things the person says or does. As a main limitation, the observer ignores the rest of the classroom that still impacts on the behavior of the observed individual. Also, the descriptions usually avoid interpretive or explanatory remarks and interactions often essential in fully understanding the intent and effects of behavior. With the *open-ended form,* the observer may concentrate on whatever she wants to write about or describe—ranging from the evenness (or unevenness) of the window shades to the teacher's attire. At the end of the session or day, the observer summarizes her data in journalistic style and frequently holds a postevaluation conference with the teacher. This method (along with rating scales) is frequently used in schools. Although potentially rich in narration, open-ended procedures constitute perhaps the most unreliable and invalid observational technique. The observer goes into the room with a host of biases and preconceived attitudes about the teacher. Since no controls or checklists exist to focus on or use as a guide during the observation, the observer enjoys more latitude to see what he or she wants or expects to see.

Actually, each of us possesses a preferred set of biases, and regardless of the observational technique, we tend to concentrate on favored items and by-pass others. Although we might point out that we can solve some of the above problems by playing back visual and auditory tapes, mechanical problems and recording costs do not make the mechanized approach as attractive as it might first seem. Moreover, the recordings that the observer produces and replays filter through his eyes and ears; therefore, they still incorporate and reflect most of the above contaminating factors.

CONTENT VERSUS PROCESS

Early humanistic educators, such as Maslow and Rogers, wrote extensively for the need of teachers to be process oriented rather than content oriented in their approaches. This means being less concerned about the content of Whitman's poems and the battles of World War II and more concerned about how students feel about these subjects. It means spending less time on right answers and asking why?, how?, and what if?

Critics argue that process-product research rarely examines teacher behavior in relation to subject matter, grade level, or student characteristics. For example, not only do "warm" teacher behaviors or "direct" teacher behaviors have different meanings among different investigators, but also the same teacher (that is, the warm teacher) would have different effects with different subjects such as reading, math, and history; with first graders, sixth graders, and twelfth graders; as well as with low-income and middle-income students; high achievers and low achievers; boys and girls; and so on (Ornstein, 1986b; Needles & Gage, 1991). Making such distinctions is not always the intent of researchers who usually seem content with examining generic teaching principles and methods. To be sure, it is difficult and even misleading to build a science of teaching based on broad dimensions of teaching without considering specialized content or subject matter, grade levels, and students.

Whereas one group of investigators argues that failure to control accurately for these particular constructs and their interaction effects leads to inappropriate research findings and misleading data for teachers, others argue that these constructs entail a diversity of specifics as to defy worthwhile quantification. If we were to break down teacher behaviors into precise agreed-upon constructs by a host of subject, grade, and student variables, the number of behaviors and their relationships would vastly increase to the point of trivia. Generalizations would be hard to come by, and we would become bogged down in a maze of interactions and multiple relationships beyond use for most readers. How far we carry out our analysis would depend on our knowledge and purposes, but we would enter into a hall of mirrors whereby only a few could cope and make sense of the data.

There is disagreement, also, about what effects a teacher is called upon to produce. Should a teacher's effectiveness be defined in terms of long-range or short-term goals, broad educational goals or specific outcomes? Should a teacher be called upon for equal behaviors or outcomes with all types of subjects, grades, and students—or should differences be allowed in reading, math, or art (certain subjects may be more difficult to effect changes in achievement over similar periods of time); with sixth graders or tenth graders (it is more difficult to effect changes in achievement for older students; thus a two-year reading deficit for a tenth-grade student provides a more difficult change problem than does a sixth-grade class with the same reading deficit); and with the disadvantaged, handicapped, average, or high-achieving student.

In studies of teacher effectiveness, standardized tests are extensively used to measure learning outcomes. These tests tend to be reliable and valid for measuring student achievement at a given point in time, and in an age of state-mandated tests they are being used more regularly than in previous years. They usually have high *curriculum* validity and are predictive of academic success. The trouble is that they often do not reflect what is taught in the classroom. These tests are designed to measure cumulative achievement or knowledge of content. They have inadequate *instructional* validity (what the teacher has stressed at the classroom level for the school semester), or for measuring what students have learned over a short period of time (Ornstein, 1986b).

There is disagreement about what effects a teacher is called upon to produce. Should a teacher's effectiveness be determined in terms of the skills and facts students master, or should the behaviors and categories correspond with more complex levels of achievement—high-order skills (such as problem solving, critical thinking, metacognition, and so on)—and advanced knowledge of content (such as understanding, in-depth or "thick" knowledge, and expertise)? Assessing high orders of achievement has gained recent attention among cognitive psychologists. However, these views of learning add greater complexity to our observations, testing instruments, and correlational designs. These high-order skills, according to researchers (Cole, 1990; Ennis, 1990), are more diffuse and abstract than the skills and facts of subject matter, and arise out of several different contexts that are not easy to systematize. Whereas skills and facts can be assessed with little ambiguity, even listed and directly taught, critical thinking and metacognitive thinking strategies are not easy to break down, isolate, and measure.

Whereas today most educators advocate high-order thinking, some critics, such as Hirsch (1987), would argue that by emphasizing generic thinking skills we lose sight of important content that needs to be taught as a foundation for learning. Knowing the items on Hirsch's list of 5,000 important dates, people, and places means more than facts; rather using knowledge to understand why events occur, what the relationship of these events is, and how these events impact on our society. Similarly, Ravitch (1992) argues for a common curriculum in terms of history, literature, and art, which binds us as a nation and helps foster national standards for purposes of testing. She ignores process and argues for content that teaches children what we as Americans have in common, and to teach specific knowledge and skills necessary for citizenship, work, health, and continued education.

Content Versus Pedagogy

In the mid-1980s, Schulman (1986, 1987) introduced the phrase "pedagogical content knowledge" that sparked a host of articles and books concerning teachers' knowledge of their content or subject field. He argues that content had been ignored during the years of "process-product" researchers of teaching and by cognitive psychologists—who have stressed generic teaching principles at the expense of content knowledge. In Schulman's model of teaching, teachers need pedagogical knowledge as well as knowledge of the subject they are teaching, including the most useful forms of representation of ideas, analogies, and explanations, and an understanding of what makes learning of specific topics easy or difficult.

A number of researchers now suggest we analyze and dissect teacher behavior in terms of knowledge of subject, namely in ways that represent content in appropriate and engaging ways to enhance student comprehension (Livingston & Borko, 1989; Ferman-Nemser & Parker, 1990). In this connection, teaching preparation programs have reduced general method courses (whereby generic teaching principles are now taught in courses such as introduction to education and education psychology), and increased special method or content method courses. This is a return to the post-Sputnik era, when there was a similar effort to stress subject matter and beef up the curriculum.

From the focus on content evolves forms of constructivism such as those ideas underlying critical pedagogists, poststructuralists, feminist theorists, and reconstructionists—all of whom deal in political and "emancipatory" knowledge. It is a way of challenging researchers who maintain that "objective" truths exist or that through logic or rational thinking we can arrive at authoritative knowledge. Constructionism recognizes the subjectivity of knowledge, that teaching and learning are colored by class, caste, gender—as well as our prior experiences— and explicit power relations of the pedagogical situation (O'Laughlin, 1992).

It is argued that schools are middle-class institutions that deny students who are other than middle class opportunities to speak in their own discourse, to introduce opposing views, or to question the process by which "official" knowledge is produced. Teachers become, unwittingly, agents of the system in this process to the extent that they are unconscious of the power relations embedded in schools, and to the extent that their own values, culture, and language oppose or even suppress those of their students.

"Emancipatory knowledge," "critical pedagogy," and "constructivist teaching" are new metaphors that are central to teaching and cannot take place unless teachers become conscious of the need to create a new dialogue with their students: whereby they openly examine their inner thoughts and feelings and act out their visions of a better, more democratic and egalitarian world (Giroux, 1990,

1991; Pinar, 1992). Although some of this "emancipatory knowledge" may be considered as rhetoric, the need for face-to-face relationships, honest dialogue, and authentic encounters between teachers and students is long needed. There is a history in our classrooms, where students' feelings and voices have been repressed—under the guise of teaching the facts, and nothing but the facts, and shaping up students in ways to control them and to pass on the cultural heritage of the larger society.

But this new pedagogy goes for naught if in our haste to engage students in critical inquiry we hastily codify and analyze it. We are dealing with authentic experiences, personal encounters, and in-depth feelings that take time to surface and talk about and cannot easily be treated in terms of neat boxes or checklists. Real teaching is not mechanistic, but involves aesthetic, emotional, and even passionate interactions between teachers and students, and demands new ways of thinking about conducting and interpreting research on teaching.

Traditional research on teaching respects quantitative designs and methods, and quickly synthesizes these human experiences to make it clinical, objective, and distant so it is easy to categorize and assess. Nonetheless, classroom participants must tell their own stories in their own ways, and this takes time and patience. It also means understanding how our own cultural biases, personal patterns of thought, and research language is used to communicate with others.

Most of this new way of looking at knowledge and dealing with human encounters challenges the scientific-rational approach to teacher behavior, as well as the traditional view of research as culturally neutral and objective. The common method of analyzing teaching follows a behaviorist mold, steeped in the theories of Thorndike and Skinner. It focuses on those patterns and responses which can be easily categorized, observed, and measured.

Not only is much of this past research criticized as technocratic, but also as male dominated and control dominated. For example, the research on teaching in the 1970s and 1980s sought to show that teachers do make a difference in learning outcomes, and emphasized structured, monitored, and organized behaviors—routine and order—as effective. Female-oriented behaviors, such as caring, nurturing, and empathy, were rarely equated with effective teaching (see Gilligan, 1982; Noddings, 1992). The connection between scientific-rational behavior and gender is also related to the practice of equating effective teaching with the exercise of teacher power and control through classroom management techniques. This concept of effective teaching highlights the current teaching models of Brophy, Doyle, Evertson, and Good. For a teacher to surrender power, or to lose control in the classroom, is to become an ineffective teacher.

BEYOND EFFECTIVE TEACHER RESEARCH

A good deal of effective teaching may not directly correlate with student performance measured by achievement tests. For some observers, good teaching and learning involves such intangibles as values, experiences, insights, and appreciation—the "stuff" that cannot be easily observed or measured. Teaching and learning is an "existential" encounter, a philosophical process involving creative ideas and inquiries that cannot be easily quantified.

We might add that much of teaching involves caring, nurturing, and valuing behaviors—attributes not easily assessed by evaluation instruments. Teaching also deals with hunches and intuitive judgments that teachers make as classroom events and interactions unfold. These events and interactions are rapid and complex, and the teachers' behaviors and responses are not preplanned—nor can they easily be categorized or made to fit into a measurable unit of some evaluation instrument.

Teaching is a complex holistic enterprise, and trying to slice, isolate, or categorize it into a set of recommendations or a hierarchy of principles or methods may not be realistic. It may be the best that researchers can offer as they struggle to define good teaching, but all these codified and observed behaviors are nothing more than an abstraction of the teaching-learning process. The principles or methods evolving from the events and interactions of the classroom rarely consider prior classroom experience, teacher-student thoughts and feelings, and other context variables.

What is not measurable goes unnoticed in a process–product-oriented teaching model. By breaking down the teaching act into behaviors, competencies, or criteria that can be defined operationally and quantified, educators overlook the hard-to-measure aspects of teaching, the personal and humanistic aspects of teaching. To say that excellence in teaching only involves measurable behaviors and outcomes is to miss a substantial part of teaching—what some aforementioned educators refer to as artistry or drama. It can be argued, too, that teacher behaviors that correlate with measurable outcomes often lead to rote learning, drill, and automatic responses.

In their attempts to observe and measure what teachers do and to detail whether students improve their test performance, our research models tend to ignore the learners' imaginations, dreams, hopes, and aspirations—how teachers influence these hard-to-define but very important aspects of the students' lives. The chief variable in correlating teaching with learning outcomes is knowledge of facts, as evidenced by scores on achievement tests and at the expense of critical thinking, problem solving, creativity, and so on (Ornstein, 1989, 1991).

Good teachers know, although they may not be able to prove it, that good teaching is really about the capacity to accept, understand, and appreciate students on their terms and through their world; making students feel good about themselves; having positive attitudes; and getting fired up with enthusiasm and a cheerful presence.

These are basically fuzzy qualities that the scientific theories and paradigms of effective teaching tend to overlook. Indeed, teachers who place high priority on humanistic and affective practices, and on the personal and social development of their students, are not really interested in devoting much time to the empirical or behavioral literature, or in teaching small pieces of information that can be measured and correlated with their own teaching behaviors.

Teachers who are confident about themselves are not overly concerned about their evaluation ratings, or even what the research has to say about their teacher achieving and average students unaffected but yields big benefits on talented students and on attitudes toward the subject matter. In elementary schools, the grouping of students with similar reading achievement but from different grades yields substantial effects. Within-class grouping in mathematics yields worthwhile effects, but generalized grouping does not.

Tutoring, because it gears instruction to individual or small-group needs, yields big effects on both tutees and tutors. It yields particularly large effects in mathematics, perhaps because of the subject's well-defined scope and organization.

In whole-group instruction, teachers may ordinarily focus on average or low-achieving students to ensure that they master the lessons. But when talented students are freed from repetition and slow progression, they can proceed quickly. Grouping may work best when students are accurately grouped according to their specific subject-matter needs rather than IQ, demeanor, or other irrelevant characteristics.

Social Environment

Cooperative learning programs delegate some control of the pacing and methods of learning to student groups of two to six members who work together (and sometimes compete with other groups within classes). Their success may be attributable to relief from exclusively teacher-to-student interaction of whole-group teaching; the time freed for interactive engagement of students (highest in two-person teams); and the opportunities for targeted cues, engagement, correctives, and reinforcement. As in comprehension teaching, the acts of cooperative tutoring or teaching may encourage students to think about subject matter organization and productive time allocation.

Classroom Morale   Many correlational studies suggest that classroom morale is associated with achievement gains, greater subject matter interest, and the worthy end of voluntary participation in nonrequired subject-related activities. Morale is assessed by asking students to agree or disagree with such statements as, "Most of the students know each other well," "The class members know the purpose of the lessons."

Students who perceive the morale as friendly, satisfying, goal-directed, and challenging, and the classroom as having the required materials, tend to learn more. Those who perceive student cliques, disorganization, apathy, favoritism, and friction learn less. The research, though plausible, lacks the causal confidence and specificity of control-group experiments on directly alterable methods discussed elsewhere in this chapter.

TEACHING SPECIAL POPULATIONS

We can gain insights from programs outside the usual scope of elementary and secondary classrooms.

behaviors. How does the profession reconcile the fact that so many competent teachers consider teacher research as "irrelevant and counterintuitive" to their own practice of teaching? Why do we often hear the complaint: "That's all good theory, but it does not work in practice"?

Teaching is a people industry, and people (especially young people) perform best in places where they feel wanted and respected. To be sure, it is possible for a teacher to "disengage" or "disinvite" students by belittling them, ignoring them, undercutting them, comparing them to other siblings or students, or even yessing them (failing to hold them accountable for the right answer), and still perform high on other discrete competencies or behaviors associated with the teacher as a technician: "The teacher came to class on time." "The teacher's objectives were clearly stated." "The teacher checked homework on a regular basis." "The teacher's expectations were clearly stated." "The teacher graded quizzes on a timely basis," and so on.

Such a checklist or behaviorist approach is common today, as we search for a research-based model of what is a "good" or "effective" teacher. This mentality can make us technically right but can never really describe good teaching. This mentality coincides with the bureaucratic process, where rules, regulations, and checklists prevail. Also, teachers who lack maturity or a balanced perspective, who are ill at ease with personal and authentic encounters, or who get carried away with the power relationship of teaching, often hide behind these procedures—and even say they are doing an "excellent" job in teaching. They find similar reasons to blame students if they fail: The student did not come to class on time, the student missed two homework assignments, the student did not follow the directions on the test, the student wrote his assignment and was told that it had to be typed, and so on. But these processes miss the essence of classroom teaching, where feelings, attitudes, and imagination are crucial and should take precedence over tiny measurable pieces of behavior, information, or rules that sometimes border on silliness and trivia. Of course, some of the research that often characterizes good teaching is reasonable and warranted, but most of this "wisdom" is old hat and what experienced teachers already know.

Humanistic Teaching

The focus of teacher research should be on the learner, not on the teacher; on the feelings and attitudes of the student, not on knowledge and information (since feelings and attitudes will eventually determine what knowledge and information are sought after and acquired); and on long-term development and growth of the students, not on short-term objectives or specific teacher tasks. But if teachers spend more time on learners, on their feelings and attitudes, as well as on social and personal growth, teachers may be penalized when cognitive outcomes (little pieces of information) are correlated with their behaviors.

Students need to be encouraged and nurtured by their teachers, especially when they are young. They are too dependent on approval from significant adults—first their parents, then their teachers. Parents and teachers need to help young children and adolescents establish a source for self-esteem by focusing on their strengths, supporting them, discouraging negative self-talk, and helping them take control of their lives and live within the context of their own culture and values.

People (including young people) with high self-esteem achieve at high levels, and the more one achieves, the better one feels about oneself. The opposite is also true: Students who fail to master the subject matter, get down on themselves and eventually give up. Students with low self-esteem give up quickly. In short, student self-esteem and achievement are directly related (Ames, 1990; Corno, 1992). If we can nurture students' self-esteem, almost everything else will fall into place, including achievement scores and academic outcomes.

This builds a strong argument for creating success experiences for students to help them feel good about themselves. The long-term benefits are obvious: The more students learn to like themselves, the more they will achieve; and the more they achieve, the more they will like themselves. But that's down the road; that takes time, that's nurturing for future benefits; that does not show up on a standardized test within a semester or school year; and it doesn't help the teacher who is being evaluated by a content- or test-driven school administrator. It certainly does not benefit the teacher who is being evaluated for how many times he or she attended departmental meetings, whether the shades in the classroom were even, or whether his or her instructional objectives were clearly stated.

It is obvious that certain behaviors contribute to good teaching. The trouble is that there is little agreement on exactly what behaviors or methods are most important. There are some teachers who gain theoretical knowledge of "what works," but are unable to put the ideas into practice. Some teachers act effortlessly in the classroom and others consider teaching a chore. All this suggests that teaching cannot be described in terms of a checklist or a precise model. It also suggests that teaching is a humanistic activity that deals with whole people (not tiny behaviors or competencies) and how people (teachers and students) develop and behave in a variety of classroom and school settings.

While the research on teacher effectiveness provides a vocabulary and system for improving our insight into good teaching, there is a danger that it may lead to some of us becoming too rigid in our view of teaching. Following only research on teaching effectiveness can lead to too much emphasis on specific behaviors that can be easily measured or prescribed in advance—at the expense of ignoring humanistic behaviors that cannot easily be measured.

Most teacher evaluation instruments tend to deemphasize the human side of teaching, because it is difficult to measure. In an attempt to be scientific, to predict and control behavior, and to assess group patterns, we sometimes lose sight of affective behaviors. Although some educators have moved to a search for humanistic factors that influence teaching, we continue to define most teacher behaviors in terms of behaviorist and cognitive factors.

In providing feedback and evaluation for teachers, many factors need to be considered so the advice or information does not fall on deaf ears. Teachers appreciate feedback processes whereby they can improve their teaching, so long as the processes are honest and fair and are professionally planned and administered;

so long as teachers are permitted to make mistakes; and so long as more than one model of effectiveness is considered so that they can adopt recommended behaviors and methods that fit their personality and philosophy of teaching.

Teachers must be permitted to incorporate specific teacher behaviors and methods according to their own unique personality and philosophy; to pick and choose from a wide range of research and theory; and to discard other teacher behaviors that conflict with their own style, without fear of being considered ineffective. Many school districts, even state departments of education, have developed evaluation instruments and salary plans based exclusively on prescriptive and product-oriented behaviors. Even worse, teachers who do not exhibit these behaviors are often penalized or labeled as "marginal" or "incompetent" (Holdzkom, 1987, 1991; Milner, 1991; Ornstein, 1988, 1991). There is an increased danger that many more school districts and states will continue to jump on this bandwagon and make decisions based on prescriptive teacher research without recognizing or giving credibility to other teacher behaviors or methods.

THEORY INTO PRACTICE

Teacher behaviors are indications of teachers' abilities to perform various tasks. Examining such behavior in a systematic and scientific way in the classroom should provide the most relevant data regarding their success or competency. The list of suggestions below provides practical methods that may be used to advance the research on teaching, as well as the direction in which teacher effectiveness research might be improved.

1. We need to put more research effort into assessing the behaviors and skills needed by beginning teachers, and to be clear on the kinds of teachers we are trying to develop at teacher preparation institutions. We need to assess the mental processes or thoughts of teachers, to clarify and analyze specific teaching situations, and to provide opportunities for such teachers to reflect upon and analyze their own behaviors.

2. We need teachers who are motivated to improve and believe that they can make a difference in the lives of their students, in their schools and communities.

3. We need to move beyond the familiar studies that compare teacher behaviors (methods), and address more sophisticated questions such as similarities and differences in the effects of behavior A or B (or method A or B) with different students under different conditions—particularly as they relate to various subjects and grades.

4. Many investigators have focused on classifying and analyzing teacher behavior, giving little consideration to the behavioral patterns of the students—and their effects on teachers. Although one can understand why the methodological approaches have focused on teachers, student behaviors deserve greater emphasis. More attention should also be paid

to whether significant teacher-student interaction patterns can be replicated.

5. A further shortcoming of teacher behavior research has been the focus on verbal behavior without considering such nonverbal behaviors as facial expressions, gestures, and physical proximity. These nonverbal behaviors may very well affect the classroom climate and the behavior of learners.

6. Also, we need to promote caring, supporting, and empathetic teacher behaviors, to encourage teachers to serve the best interests of their students, and to treat children (youth) as children (youth)—that is, with respect, trust, care, and love. Rather than promote these behaviors as part of women's traditional culture or associate them as part of maternal thinking, as feminists do, we need to treat them as appropriate behaviors for all teachers—just like we need to break down the old male view that teaching (or caring for children) is the kind of work appropriate for women.

7. Differences between short- and long-term effects should be clarified. Different teacher behaviors or methods may have different effects on students over different periods of time—that is, in terms of student retention, success rates, and low- and high-order learning patterns.

8. Previous teacher behavior research has focused on teacher-student interaction during whole-group instruction and teacher-dominated recitations. Yet, students in most classrooms spend more than half their time in class engaged in seatwork or individualized activities. This is especially the case at the elementary school level. We need more information on the kinds of seatwork that are appropriate and on how teachers can effectively present individualized work to students.

9. Little is known about effective remedial instruction, too, yet increasingly teachers are required to remediate students' learning difficulties. This is involving more teacher time and more students, especially in reading and mathematics. (These are the very same subjects and test scores studied by teacher behavior researchers in their attempt to make generalizations about the field.) Henceforth, we need to focus on various remedial practices: to what extent they are effective, and with what type of students and under what conditions.

10. Pedagogical knowledge, along with subject-specific teacher behaviors, needs to be studied and understood by researchers and teachers. Although this teacher knowledge opens new forms and ways of assessing what teachers do when they teach content, there is the danger that it can lead to trivia and hard-to-generalize information. The question that needs to be answered is: Is it more important to extrapolate across subjects than within subjects, and for what subjects and grade levels?

11. The research has not always been related to actual classroom practice, and many teachers have complained that the research is too theoretical to be of practical value. Nonetheless, theoretical constructs are needed both to identify existing teacher behaviors and to predict their effects on learners. We need to combine good theory with practice.

12. New technologies offer new opportunities for research. For instance, tape-recording devices can record classroom behavior in ways that allow more meticulous analysis. Another promising approach is micro-teaching, the analysis of much smaller time segments of teacher behavior.

13. Family relationships are the key to learning and the heart of life, yet researchers on teaching give them peripheral consideration or ignore them entirely because of class, ethnic, and gender sensitivity. We need to raise questions about teenage pregnancy, one-headed households, women who work, and latchkey children—and their effects on learning. These are high-inference variables that correlate with achievement and need to be incorporated in our studies and recommendations for improving education. How frank we can be in our public discussion of these matters is still another issue that needs to be addressed.

14. The research on teaching cannot assume a simple causal relationship between teacher behaviors and learning, or assume that what is observed are main behaviors affecting student learning. Many factors in the students' lives, and many hard-to-measure variables, affect learning. Moreover, what we observe may mean one thing for the teacher, another for the student, and yet another for the researcher. Our prior experiences, as well as age, IQ, social class, ethnicity, and gender, do affect what we observe and how we interpret it.

SUMMARY

Few, if any, activities are as crucial in schooling as teaching; and, as elusive and complex as teaching may be, research toward understanding it must continue. The problem, however, is that most of the research on teaching is not read by the most important group, teachers, who can and should benefit from knowing, understanding, and integrating the concepts and principles of the research.

It is obvious that certain behaviors contribute to good teaching. The trouble is that there is little agreement on exactly what behaviors or methods are most important. Some teachers will learn most of the rules about good teaching, yet be unsuccessful. Other teachers will break the rules of "good" teaching, yet be profoundly successful. All this suggests that teaching is more art than science and practice is more important than theory.

In recent years, teacher behavior research has raised concerns about pedagogical and content knowledge, as well as concerns about culture, gender, and language. Little of this new information has been integrated into research on teaching, especially that guided by traditional designs or methodology.

Most teacher evaluation processes do not address the question of how to change teacher behavior. The developers of evaluation instruments assume that once they have discovered what ought to be done, teachers will naturally do what is expected. If our purpose is to change or improve the practices of teachers, then it is necessary to come to grips with teachers' beliefs and attitudes and with their concepts of "good" or "effective."

References

Ames, C. (1990). "Motivation: What Teachers Need to Know." *Teachers College Record* 91 (Spring): 409–421.

Borich, G. D. (1986). "Paradigms of Teacher Effectiveness Research." *Education and Urban Society* 18 (February): 143–167.

Bowers, C. A., and D. J. Flinders (1990). *Responsive Teaching.* New York: Teachers College Press, Columbia University.

Cole, N. S. (1990). "Conceptions of Educational Achievement." *Educational Researcher* 19 (April): 2–7.

Corno, L. (1992). "Encouraging Students to Take Responsibility for Learning and Performance." *Elementary School Journal* 93 (September): 69–83.

Eisner, E. W. (1983). "The Art and Craft of Teaching." *Educational Leadership* 40 (January): 4–13.

Eisner, E. W. (1993). *The Educational Imagination*, 3rd ed. New York: Macmillan.

Ennis, R. H. (1990). "The Extent to Which Critical Thinking Is Subject-specific." *Educational Researcher* 19 (May): 13–16.

Ferman-Nemser, S., and M. B. Parker (1990). "Making Subject Matter Part of the Conversation in Learning to Teach." *Journal of Teacher Education* 4 (May–June): 32–43.

Fisher, C. W., D. C. Berliner, and N. N. Filby (1978). *Teaching and Learning in Elementary Schools.* San Francisco: Far West Laboratory for Educational Research and Development.

Flanders, N. A. (1965). *Teacher Influence, Pupil Attitude, and Achievement.* Washington, D.C.: U.S. Government Printing Office.

Flanders, N. A. (1970). *Analyzing Teaching Behavior.* Reading, MA: Addison-Wesley.

Gage, N. L. (1978). *The Scientific Basis of the Art of Teaching.* New York: Teachers College Press, Columbia University.

Gage, N. L., and D. C. Berliner (1989). "Nurturing the Critical, Practical, and Artistic Thinking of Teachers." *Phi Delta Kappan* 71 (November): 212–214.

Gilligan, C. (1982). *In a Different Voice.* Cambridge, MA: Harvard University Press.

Giroux, H. A. (1990). "Curriculum Theory, Textual Authority, and the Role of Teachers as Public Intellectuals." *Journal of Curriculum and Supervision* 5 (Summer): 361–383.

Giroux, H. A. (1991). "Curriculum Planning, Public Schooling, and Democratic Struggle." *NASSP Bulletin* 75 (February): 12–25.

Hirsch, E. D. (1987). *Cultural Literacy: What Every American Needs to Know.* Boston: Houghton Mifflin.

Holdzkom, D. (1987). "Appraising Teacher Performance in North Carolina." *Educational Leadership* 44 (April): 40–44.

Holdzkom, D. (1991). "Teacher Performance Appraisal in North Carolina." *Phi Delta Kappan* 72 (June): 782–785.

Jackson, P. W. (1990). *Life in Classrooms*, 2nd ed. New York: Teachers College Press, Columbia University.

Light, R. J. (1973). "Issues in the Analysis of Qualitative Data," in R. M. Travers, ed., *Second Handbook of Research on Teaching.* Chicago: Rand McNally, pp. 318–381.

Livingston, C., and H. Borko (1989). "Expert-novice Differences in Teaching." *Journal of Teacher Education* 40 (September–October): 36–42.

Medley, D. M., H. Cooker, and R. S. Soar (1984). *Measurement-based Evaluation of Teacher Performance.* New York: Longman.

Middleton, S. (1993). *Educating Feminists.* New York: Teachers College Press, Columbia University.

Milner, O. (1991). "Suppositional Style and Teacher Evaluation." *Phi Delta Kappan* 72

(February): 464–467.

Needels, M. C., and N. L. Gage (1991). "Essence and Accident in Process-product Research on Teaching," in H. C. Waxman and H. J. Walberg, eds., *Effective Teaching: Current Research.* Berkeley, CA: McCutchan, pp. 3–31.

Noddings, N. (1992). *The Challenge to Care in Schools.* New York: Teachers College Press, Columbia University.

O'Laughlin, M. (1992). "Engaging Teachers in Emancipatory Knowledge Construction." *Journal of Teacher Education* 43 (November–December): 336–346.

Ornstein, A. C. (1976). "Can We Define a Good Teacher?" *Peabody Journal of Education* 53 (April): 201–207.

Ornstein, A. C. (1986a). "Research on Teaching." *Education and Urban Society* 18 (February): 176–181.

Ornstein, A. C. (1986b). "Teacher Effectiveness: Current Research and Issues." *Education and Urban Society* 18 (February): 168–175.

Ornstein, A. C. (1988). "The Evolving Accountability Movement." *Peabody Journal of Education* 65 (Spring): 12–20.

Ornstein, A. C. (1989). "Theoretical Issues Related to Teaching." *Education and Urban Society* 22 (November): 95–104.

Ornstein, A. C. (1990). "A Look at Teacher Effectiveness Research." *NASSP Bulletin* 74 (October): 78–88.

Ornstein, A. C. (1991). "Teacher Effectiveness Research: Theoretical Considerations," in H. C. Waxman and H. J. Walberg, eds., *Effective Teaching: Current Research.* Berkeley, CA: McCutchan, pp. 63–80.

Peshkin, A. (1993). "The Goodness of Qualitative Research." *Educational Researcher* 22 (March): 23–29.

Pinar, W. F. (1992). "Dreamt into Existence by Others: Curriculum Theory and School Reform." *Theory into Practice* 31 (Summer): 228–235.

Popham, W. J. (1993). *Educational Evaluation,* 3rd ed. Boston: Allyn and Bacon.

Ravitch, D. (1992). "A Culture in Common." *Educational Leadership* 49 (December–January): 8–11.

Rubin, L. J. (1985). *Artistry in Teaching.* New York: Random House.

Ryans, D. G. (1960). *Characteristics of Teachers.* Washington, D.C.: American Council on Education.

Schulman, L. (1986). "Those Who Understand: Knowledge Growth in Teaching." *Educational Researcher* 15 (March): 4–14.

Schulman, L. (1987). "Knowledge and Teaching: Foundations of the New Reform." *Harvard Educational Review* 57 (February): 1–22.

Discussion Questions

1. What are the differences between teacher characteristics, teacher competencies, and teacher effects? What characteristics, competencies, and effects do you consider important to assess?

2. Recall two or three of your favorite teachers. Compare their characteristics, as you remember them. Were their emphases or strengths related to teaching content, classroom management, or humanistic qualities?

3. What measurement problems would you improve in order to assess good teaching?

4. As a teacher, would you rather be evaluated by your students, colleagues, supervisor or principal, or a researcher from outside the school? Defend your choice.

5. How can you as a teacher reconcile content validity of standardized tests with instructional validity? Do you teach how to take tests, toward the test, or test without worrying about results? Defend your choice.

6. How can teachers integrate content knowledge in the subject with pedagogical knowledge of teaching? What is the value of content knowledge, or a content methods course, when teachers are already well prepared in the subject matter?

Frances S. Bolin

"I decided to teach for very selfish reasons," says Frances Bolin. "I was a dabbler—I have always loved visual art, music, and theater. I was fascinated by psychology. I wanted to do something that would be meaningful and fun. Teaching brought all my interests together."

Frances began her teaching career in 1964 in Seattle, Washington, and then taught in Portland, Oregon; Nashville, Tennessee; and Baltimore, Maryland. She taught all the elementary grades, except the sixth grade, and "loved every minute of it." But her interest moved from wanting to invest in teaching content to a concern for the children with whom she worked. "I learned about some of the inequities in our society from the children I taught—beautiful children who were full of imagination and dreams, who wanted to say 'yes' to life, but to whom so much of life said, no. I kept wondering where I could make the most difference for children and the question eventually led me into teacher education."

Bolin's schooling matches the places she has taught. She graduated from the University of Washington, Seattle, with a degree in elementary education, did a Master of Arts in early childhood education at Vanderbilt University in Tennessee, and graduate studies in educational leadership at the University of Maryland and Johns Hopkins University. Eventually, she completed her doctorate in curriculum theory and practice at Teachers College, Columbia University, where she is currently an associate professor and co-director of the Preservice Program in Childhood Education.

Frances recalls many of her favorite professors at Teachers College including Dwyne Huebner, Philip Phenix, Arno Bellack, and Maxine Greene. "I am fortunate enough to have had many favorite teachers along the way. They were all interesting, knowledgeable, and caring people. My idea of an 'effective' teacher encompasses all of these qualities." Her outlook is positive and she advises that teachers need to be sensitive to all of the possibilities, to imagine a better world for children, to have fun along the way, and to periodically borrow from Winston Churchill: "Never give up. Never give up. Never, never give up."

2 🐚

Teaching as a Craft

Frances Schoonmaker Bolin

Is teaching an art? This is a persistent and important question. Some people believe teaching is an art, but others, with equal conviction, claim it is a science. These differences of opinion have historical antecedents that have left an enduring mark on our work as teachers. In this chapter, I discuss the art of teaching. I do so in the firm belief that teaching is not an art, any more than it is a science, although teaching borrows from both. Teaching involves relationships around knowing, doing, and discovering that are embedded in an ethic of caring. I begin by briefly looking at the question of teaching as art or science. Then I focus on how art, as a metaphor, informs teaching practice. Finally, I look at teaching as craft-art. In doing so, I draw upon anecdotes from my own experience as a teacher, supervisor, and teacher educator and upon work on the ethic of caring.

THE SAME OLD QUESTIONS

Around the turn of the century, the needs of a dynamic, growing society were placing new demands on teachers and schools. Waves of immigration brought cultural diversity into many communities. Changes in attendance laws brought more students into schools for longer periods, resulting in a shortage of qualified teachers. At the same time, advances in the new field of psychology, particularly child development and psychology of learning, brought into question the classical, taken-for-granted subjects that had been the mainstay of the curriculum (see Kliebard, 1986; Cremin, 1964).

A new concern for children's health and welfare emerged during this period. Joseph Mayer Rice, pediatrician and school reformer, conducted a study of American public schools in the late 1800s, visiting thirty-six cities (Rice, 1893). Rice was outraged by the insensitivity of schools to the needs of children. In a series of articles that appeared in *The Forum,* an influential journal of the period, Rice called attention to conditions in schools. And it was teachers who received the brunt of Rice's criticism.

A Science of Teaching

Unprecedented advances were being made in science and the application of technology to the solution of human problems. Educators, eager to identify with the blossoming field of science, hoped for greater efficiency and effectiveness in teaching. Many, like Rice, assumed there was a "best" way to produce learning in students, calling for the discovery of standard practices that could be learned by all teachers. Research on teaching began to be written and spoken about in scholarly circles.

Enthusiasts, such as Rice, seemed unaware of the limitations and potential for negative consequences of scientific discovery. Furthermore, many activities that passed for science were little more than slavish adherence to routine or efforts to count and measure every aspect of teaching. This activity was spurred on by the development of educational testing and measurement, which offered potential for linking the best teaching practices with student outcomes. A "science" of teaching began to develop. It presumed a separation between curriculum and instruction. The curriculum was to be developed by experts in content and pedagogy. Teaching was an instructional problem, and it could be considered quite apart from what was being taught (Bolin & Panaritis, 1992).

These events changed the nature of teaching in this country for the rest of the century. The character, knowledge, and expertise of the teacher had always been central to public education. No longer content to leave what was taught to the teacher, special interest groups lobbied to see that the curriculum contained their vision of what was worth knowing and doing (Kliebard, 1986).

A Difference of Opinion

There were those who held a different opinion about the nature of teaching. John Dewey (1929) pointed out that if he were forced to choose, he would have to side with those who see teaching as an art, but science and art are not in opposition in education:

> Education is by its nature an endless circle or spiral. It is an activity which *includes* science within itself. In its very process it sets more problems to be further studied, which then react into the educative process to change it still further, and thus demand more thought, more science, and so on, in everlasting sequence. (p. 77)

The teacher was to have knowledge and expertise in subject matter, human development, and pedagogy. These were tools for active and intelligent engagement in scientific inquiry into one's own practice. Dewey (1904) believed that those who master technique may appear to have an advantage in their first year or two of teaching, but they will not be as effective in the long run as teachers who learn how to think about their work and hold an experimental attitude.

The argument over teaching as science versus art persisted. It had not been settled when Gilbert Highet wrote *The Art of Teaching*, published in 1950. Highet argued:

> I believe that teaching is an art, not a science. It seems to me very dangerous to apply the aims and methods of science to human beings as individuals, although a statis-

tical principle can often be used to explain their behavior in large groups and a scientific diagnosis of their physical structure is always valuable. But a "scientific" relationship between human beings is always distorted. . . . Teaching involves emotions, which cannot be systematically appraised and employed, and human values, which are quite outside the grasp of science. (p. vii)

N. L. Gage attempted to put the argument to rest in a series of essays delivered in 1977 and published as *The Scientific Basis of the Art of Teaching*. Like Dewey, Gage saw teaching as an art that relies on science. Gage (1978, 1984) distinguished between "a scientific basis for the art of teaching" and a science of teaching. He (1984) asks:

What does it mean to speak of an "art" of teaching? Teaching is an instrumental or practical art, not a fine art aimed at creating beauty for its own sake. As an instrumental art, teaching is something that departs from recipes, formulas, or algorithms. It requires improvisation; spontaneity; the handling of hosts of considerations of form, style, pace, rhythm in [complex] ways. . . . (p. 4)

The nature of teaching is an important question that will undoubtedly resurface from time to time. There are still those who believe that teaching is essentially an applied science. They are convinced that we have isolated the variables that differentiate effective from ineffective teachers. To them, learning to teach is a process of becoming increasingly skilled in applying proven techniques in a wide array of situations. Ideas about the nature of teaching are tied to basic beliefs about what it means to be human, what is important, and how we come to know (Bolin, 1987b).

Neither and Both

Whether teaching is art or science is probably not a fruitful question. Perhaps teaching is neither art nor science and is at the same time *both* art and science. What could I mean by such a confusing and contradictory statement?

In the first place, teaching is not one of the fine arts such as dance, drama, music, or painting. Nor is it a science such as physics, biology, or astronomy. Teaching is about human relationships in a way that neither art nor science deals with human relationships. While it is true that there is a social dimension to art (people have to be able to see, hear, or somehow experience it), art is not social in the way that teaching is social. Science, too, is social in that it is aimed toward human understanding and social ends. But even science that is directed toward ending human suffering, or understanding how people communicate, is not social in the same way that teaching is social. One can say that teaching is neither art nor science.

At the same time, both "good art" and "good science" are very much like "good teaching." They are the result of imagining and exploring. The artist explores and depicts what is imagined. The scientist, too, searches for the imagined. Novelty, new ways of seeing the world may come, but not so much from procedures or data itself, but from the mental leaps or inferences the artist or the scientist makes with procedure, material, or data. Art compels us to look at or experience the familiar in a new way. It involves imagination and discovery. So does science. These are all characteristics of good teaching. In this sense, teaching is both art and science. One can learn a great deal about teaching by examining its relationship to either. But I am concerned here with the art of teaching.

THINKING ABOUT TEACHING AS ART

We may liken the work of the teacher to that of the storyteller who must thoroughly know his or her story, the audience, and be skillful with the use of voice, gesture, intonation, pause, and the like. Or we may think of the teacher as a great choreographer who works with music, set, light, dancers, and costume to create something imagined. Each of these furnishes us with a metaphor for teaching.

When we use art or some form of art as a metaphor for teaching, we have in mind a particular notion of art. Yet, when it comes to declaring what we mean by art, it is often hard to articulate a coherent definition. Gage (1984) referred to art as any complex process or procedure that makes the process resistant to systematic formula. For most people, it seems to be much easier to recognize instances of art than to identify the criteria by which some works are judged as good art and others are not. At the very least, we know what we like and do not like. And usually, we accept as art some of what we do not like because it seems to meet inner criteria which we affirm—even though we cannot quite say what it is we are affirming.

This is not unlike the dilemma we face in understanding good teaching. There are many acceptable forms of teaching practice: Some teachers approach their work in a very technical manner. They use a variety of activities and experiences to achieve specific objectives. Others are more "free flowing." They have an idea or theme in mind and activities and events emerge. Teachers may be effective and skillful (or ineffective and inept) at any form of practice. But what do we mean by a good teacher?

When we attempt to answer this question by isolating the things teachers do, or by coming up with a list of steps that ought to be in every good lesson, we find that one can perform all of the steps and still fail to meet some intangible criterion that seems to transcend all of the parts we have isolated. Like the child who has skillfully completed a "paint by number" masterpiece, all of the parts are filled in as directed, but a work of art has not been produced.

Beauty in Teaching

A work of art is associated with beauty. We often think of the arts as those things designed to be viewed, read, or heard with an appreciation for their beauty. Teaching, too, may be viewed, "read," or heard with such an appreciation for beauty. A great deal has been learned about teaching by thinking of it as art (see Eisner, 1979).

When we describe something as beautiful it is in reference to some relevant value criterion. Yet, many artistic works were not created with this intention in mind, even though they evoke an aesthetic response. This is true of teaching, too. An act of teaching may occur in order to achieve a purpose quite apart from beauty; yet we might be touched by its aesthetic beauty, as occurred in the following episode:

> A friend has just spent a week as Head in her new school. "You *must* come to visit my school. I have some teachers who are just phenomenal. I was watching a teacher who was so skillful! She was moving students into and out of groups and experiences. The only word I could think of was 'beautiful'! At a certain point I forgot what she was trying to teach, I was in awe of the way she was working."

Perhaps it is not what the teacher intends that makes his or her work an art, but how it affects our experience. So a teaching act, episode, or career that functions to evoke an aesthetic response may be akin to a work of art.

Good Teaching

But what of the relevant value criteria that may be applied to teaching as an art? The history of research on teaching is crowded with discussion and disagreement over the criteria by which to judge teaching. Since the 1920s, A. S. Barr (1961) was impressed by the fact that competent observers who observed the same teacher simultaneously could disagree about the quality of teaching that was witnessed. The very things that captured the imagination of some observers were troubling and bothersome to others. Yet anyone who has taught for long knows that administrators and supervisors vary enormously in what they consider to be appropriate and effective teaching, as the following illustrates:

> When I took a job in another state I was very careful to find out what was expected. I felt competent and professional, after seven years of teaching, but I'd just finished graduate work in early childhood education and I wanted to teach in a school that was "child centered." Even though the principal and I used the same words in my interview, we weren't thinking alike.
>
> My first clue was when the Assistant Principal began to be a regular in my room. She thought nothing of interrupting. "Ms. Bolin is not new to teaching, but she is new in our school. She doesn't know how we do things here," she announced to my first graders.
>
> "These children should know phonics," she said. I used what we now call a "whole language" approach to reading. But, I thought it would be a challenge to meet her requirements without compromising what I thought was appropriate. Her reaction was, "Well, they know their letters, but you are teaching them in the wrong order."
>
> It didn't get better. She said that I just wasn't "working out." She demanded that I produce a copy of every worksheet (ditto) I'd asked the children to do. (I wasn't using the commercial materials she had given me.) She sternly scrutinized each worksheet—worksheets that I had made with specific student interests and needs in mind. "Well, they're okay," she grudgingly admitted, "But children's names should be written on the top!"

At the most fundamental level, we differed over what was good teaching practice.

The search for the criteria of effective teaching has been a long one. Many researchers have hoped to link teacher interventions with student performance outcomes, assuming that effective teaching should yield some kind of measurable change in students.

It is certainly fair to ask if the art of teaching is related to results or outcomes. (Could teaching be artfully done without regard to student learning? Could teaching be an art when students failed to learn what was taught?) But while there are some researchers who believe they have isolated the crucial teacher behaviors that produce particular gains in student achievement, many educators would disagree. They would argue that it is not the things that teachers do in themselves that make great teachers, but the intangible something that transcends all of the variables—the way they craft their practice.

TEACHING AS CRAFT

When we talk about teaching as art, we are usually referring to the craft dimension of art. Alan Tom (1984) talks about teaching as a *moral craft*. By this, Tom seems to mean that teaching involves "craft knowledge," which includes both mechanical skill and analytic knowledge, and which focuses on both right conduct and what is of value. The teacher should be able to apply mechanical and analytic abilities to specific situations. Herbert Kohl (1984) refers to a number of skills such as "teaching sensibility," or the ability to focus students in their growth; keeping one's ego out of the way; and management as the craft of teaching.

We often think of craft art as useful art, forming objects to be used in everyday life. There is a purpose for the object beyond its beauty; its beauty brings us pleasure, though the object serves a useful function.

Teachers intend to convey or introduce students to subject matter. They desire to help students develop the tools to be life-long learners. This may be done in such a way as to evoke an aesthetic response. That is, it opens teacher and student to new possibilities; it sparks imagination and wonder. It has a transcendent quality, a beauty of its own. It is nonetheless useful and practical. Masterful crafting requires execution based on an awareness of the beautiful. This seems to me to be something that is missing in the way Tom, Kohl, and others have used craft in relation to teaching.

Teaching combines sounds, visual responses, colors, movements, textures, and words from the page as well as spoken words. There are dimensions of teaching that deal with space, sequences of events in time and movement—even in the most predictable classroom where desks are arranged in rows and the teacher is at the front of the room. Aspects of teaching, like a painting, must be apprehended as a whole, though they may be entered one piece at a time in order to understand them.

Perhaps anyone, given time, could generate a list of ways in which teaching is a form of craft art. Instead of trying to exhaust the similarities, it seems more useful to think about the nature of craft and what it may mean to teachers to know their work as craft.

The Nature of Craft

Craft is associated with skilled work involved in creating art. It requires both knowledge and practice. The word *craft* has evolved from the early 1200s, when it referred to skilled occupation. It was associated with apprenticeship to a master artist. Craft referred to a kind of perfection, strength, and virtue in execution based on an awareness of beauty. At the same time, craft was also used to describe a magical device, spell, or enchantment—activities that also required dedication and skill. Knowledge, skill, strength, and virtue are embedded in the meaning of craft. In the craft of teaching, each of these is an essential dimension.

Dewey (1904) evokes a craft image when he describes soul action, or the bringing together of subject, knowledge of human growth and development, and pedagogy in such a way that the inner life of the child is illuminated. One can imagine skillful work, beauty, and the magical.

In understanding a work of art, whether a fine art or craft, we often speak of characteristics such as subject, representation, meaning, and sensuous values. In teaching, we often talk about the relationship between subject matter and pedagogy. By looking at subject matter and pedagogy in relation to characteristics of art, we gain insight into the craft of teaching.

Subject—What Is It About?

We may ask what a work of art is about, its subject. The subject may be seen as a theme, plot, or a big idea that is explicit or to be discovered. Not all works of art have a subject. In craft art we may confuse subject for function; for example, we may look at a jug and see it as something in which to store water. Yet its subject may have to do with an underlying concept that is presented in the form of a jug which happens to be useful. Art may be nonrepresentational. Theme may not be an underlying idea or subject, but a repeated pattern of colors or sounds.

To be a teacher, one must have something to teach. Subject for the teacher may be academic content or a skill. It will not be the actual mastery of a subject that makes teaching it an art. Subject must be crafted so that it is satisfying in itself, yet remains open to discovery, dreaming, movement, and surprise. The teacher who not only knows but continues to explore, imagine, and wonder is developing his or her craft. It is not necessary that the teacher know more than the students, although the teacher must be knowledgeable. Rather, it is necessary that the teacher remain excited by learning and discovery and capable of finding out new sources of knowledge. In this way, leadership may be offered, even to the student who far surpasses his or her teacher in actual mastery of subject. I learned this early in my teaching career:

> A group of my fifth graders want to learn about astronomy. I have noticed that they have found just about everything in our school library on the subject. Their desks and cubbies are stuffed with books, papers, articles on stars, planets, galaxies, nova and super nova. I see them poring over materials during free periods. I'm pleased that they have developed this interest. But they ask if we can study astronomy in class. I can find the big dipper on a clear night—that is about the extent of my knowledge

in astronomy. I must confess this to them. We will meet to decide how we can learn more, how to involve their classmates, how we might organize for learning, and what resources are available to us.

The study that emerged was not altogether successful when measured in terms of the amount of new knowledge gained by the interest group—though they learned a great deal. But it was enormously successful when seen in light of their sense of effectiveness, responsibility, and self-direction, and discovery of new sources of knowledge.

The teacher needs to recognize limits, however. One might mislead or misinform. There are limits of subject matter, too. Disciplines of knowledge are ways of organizing and understanding the world; representations of things in the world rather than the truth of the world. There are many ways of knowing. Taking a course out of one's field—as when the biology teacher studies drama, music, mathematics, another language, or painting—is a way of opening one's vision and gaining new insight into one's own subject.

Like art, teaching, too, may be nonrepresentational. Themes may not be found in a subject, but in the patterns that emerge from the experiences of students within an environment for learning. A. S. Neill's *Summerhill* (1960) comes to mind. Neill wrote:

> We set out to make a school in which we should allow children freedom to be themselves. In order to do this, we had to renounce all discipline, all direction, all suggestion, all moral training, all religious instruction. . . . All it required was what we had—a complete belief in the child as a good, not an evil, being. For almost forty years, this belief in the goodness of the child has never wavered; it rather has become a final faith. (p. 4)

Those who want the teacher to be "teaching something" may find it hard to accept a nonrepresentational approach by the teacher, just as it is difficult for some people to appreciate "art that doesn't look like anything."

Pedagogy—How Is It Presented?

The common dictionary definition of *pedagogy* is the art or science of teaching—teaching methods. One could focus an entire discussion of the art of teaching around methods.

A beginning teacher wants "tricks of the trade." These provide a sense of security. It is false security, however, because there are few "tricks of the trade" that will work in any situation. Of far more value than a collection of "how to's" will be the ability to study a situation, notice what students care about and what is important to them, and invent appropriate practices. This comes from habits of mind more than from methods.

Form, unity, and diversity are elements of art and of skilled pedagogy. Just as art must have some aesthetically satisfying form—harmony, pattern, or design—so must teaching. The crafting of a lesson gives it form: It is organized and there is an interrelationship of parts. It hangs together; there is unity. Diverse elements result in satisfaction, not confusion.

Monotony and confusion are said to be enemies of art. They are no less enemies of teaching. In art, interest and unity are maintained through contrast among parts, transitions, theme and variation, and restraint. These principles have analogs in pedagogy. A lesson or learning experience, a series of classes, a day, a learning strand, requires contrast, transitions, theme, and variation as well as restraint.

In art, we often speak of the sensuous values in a work. We find delight in texture, color, or tone. It is not the object in itself, but its presentation that engages us. In a sense, pedagogy is presentation. One might watch a teacher move from whole class to small groups, balance time with individuals and groups, utilize a variety of technologies in ways that are delightful to the observer and engaging to students—as when the school head, quoted earlier, stood in awe of one of her faculty. The sensuous quality of teaching makes it alive to students and vividly recalled. Can we speak of a lesson as having texture? Color? Tone? Sensuous pedagogy invites imaginative engagement through emotions, touch, taste, sight, smell, and sound. Students bring their whole selves to learning, as in this recollection of a seventh grade experience:

> We were studying Greek mythology and we had to tell a myth any way we chose, like writing, picturing, in a poem, through drama. I decided to tell the story of Persephone. I didn't want to just tell the story, I decided to be Persephone. So I got a blanket, turned off the lights, and pulled the window shades. I sat in the big rocker in our classroom and had everyone gather around my feet, sitting on the floor. I held the silence of the room for a brief moment before I began my tale. Everyone was spellbound as I took them through the gates of Hades. When it was over they just sat there for a few minutes as if they didn't want to break the spell. My teacher said, "Wow," and hugged me.

When this future teacher talks about teaching, she talks about making experience vivid for her students.

The challenge of pedagogy is in the crafting—bringing art, science, intuition, and skill to bear in the creating of something that can become transcendent, or reach into the limitless range of possibilities and relationships. It requires the ability to plan and construct with ingenuity and dexterity. It involves a constant working at, adjusting, imagining, and adjusting again until the thing seems right.

TEACHING AS CARING CRAFT

Artists often speak of seeing a work within a piece of wood, marble, or clay. They enter and bring the vision out of the material at hand. This is part of the craft of teaching, as well. The teacher attempts to enter into a situation and see it in a new way. The good teacher not only tries to find out what students need to know, but what they want to know. The most skillfully crafted lesson or experience is always contingent on a number of unpredictables, particularly the student who may or may not be ready or willing to participate. Coming to the situation completely prepared and allowing a creative reconstruction to occur requires receptivity and engrossment. These are characteristics of the ethic of caring. Here, I agree with Nel Noddings (1984) that a pedagogy of caring is more important than a pedagogy of method, though method is important. Noddings speaks of caring in terms of *receptivity, engrossment,* and *reciprocity.* When I think of a caring pedagogical craft, the words hope, empathy, respect, wonder, awe, and reverence come to mind. These are characteristics that Philip Phenix (1974) referred to as "dispositions" of transcendence; dispositions evoked in a caring pedagogy.

Receptivity

Noddings (1984) talks about "feeling with" the other as a characteristic of caring. This requires a receptivity, or taking the other into oneself. Hope moves us forward, toward the other.

Emily Dickinson wrote

Hope is the thing with feathers
That perches in the soul,
And sings the tune without the words,
And never stops at all.

Hope encourages receptivity. We open to the possibilities brought by students, by materials at hand, by the day. Phenix (1974) spoke of "awareness," or a pre disposition to relate, pointing out that the student will not "learn effectively in the absence of a hospitable openness to the world and to those who assist him in establishing satisfying relationships with it" (p. 330).

James is staring out the window. I am annoyed that he is not attending to the task at hand. I ask what he is doing. "I am thinking about things," James tells me. His seriousness reaches me and my irritation dissolves. I have to honor this. Why wouldn't I want him to think about things? But suppose he is daydreaming? James, too, is responsible for what happens in his learning. When he gets stuck he must be involved in figuring out what is keeping him from wanting to know. When he is thinking about things that are more important than the agenda I had planned, I need to figure out how to provide space for him in meeting both agendas or in creating a new, mutually shared agenda.

Receptivity is the basis of empathy. One takes in the reality of the other as if it were one's own.

Engrossment

With empathy comes respect. We see our students as people who have ideas about what is important, good ideas. Sometimes their ideas about importance are better than ours. But we must listen and notice or we will not know this. Noddings (1984) says:

Caring involves stepping out of one's own personal frame of reference into the other's. When we care, we consider the other's point of view, his objective needs, and what he expects of us. Our attention, our mental engrossment is on the cared-for, not on ourselves. Our reasons for acting, then, have to do both with the other's wants and desires and with the objective elements of his problematic situation. (p. 24)

When one becomes deeply engrossed in another, open to his or her needs and possibilities, understanding with empathy—this is when one experiences a sense of wonder, awe, and reverence (Phenix, 1974). Reverence borrows from theological vocabulary; Phenix describes it as "a recognition of one's participation in transcendence as a surprising and continually renewed gift, in contrast to the view of one's existence as a secure possession and as an autonomous achievement" (p. 332).

Teaching requires tools, skills (the ability to read, write, and reason well), and the ability to plan and to present material in a variety of ways. But a pedagogy of caring suggests that one must not let the tools get in the way of the exploration, or become the thing. Skilled teacher artisans are able to leave the lesson behind, drop the plan, and entertain another set of goals when the situation requires it. They begin with careful regard for the rules, structure, or plan. This is also true of open, progressive, or nontraditional approaches to teaching, which, like nonrepresentational art, are not without regard for "the rules of practice."

> Jill, my student teacher, has been in my classroom for three weeks. She has been assisting and observing. I am aware that she is not used to first graders and that she is uncomfortable in our "open" classroom. But she seems to have a remarkable capacity for suspending judgment. I know she is studying us, trying to figure things out. Then, when we are meeting for routine planning, she bursts out, "I get it, I've finally figured it out. I thought this was an unstructured classroom. It wouldn't work without structure! I think this is the most structured classroom I have ever been in. I am just now seeing it."

Jill has become engrossed in the classroom and opened herself to a new way of knowing. She now sees rules where she saw randomness. One must be deeply immersed in rules of practice and thoroughly understand the nuances of learning in order to rearrange them productively.

Admittedly, there are exceptions—the natural who is able to inspire students with little if any preparation as a teacher, just as the natural artist may be able to produce a masterpiece with little formal training. But most masterpieces are produced after long and arduous study in the techniques and disciplines of an art form. Rules of practice are important.

Wonder, awe, and reverence seem far removed from basics, such as computation and literacy. The idea that the teacher should be most concerned with teaching basic skills is impoverished, according to Noddings (1984):

> Among the intangibles that I would have my students carry away is the feeling that the subject we have struggled with is both fascinating and boring, significant and silly, fraught with meaning and nonsense, challenging and tedious, and that whatever attitude we take toward it, it will not diminish our regard for each other. The student is infinitely more important than the subject. (p. 20)

In a pedagogy of caring, one respects the personal meaning that each student draws from experiences shared together.

Reciprocity

In art one often addresses the question of meaning. What is a work about? What is the theme? What is the thesis? What is the intended effect on the audience? Works of art may have effects from which meanings may be drawn, but meaning is elusive in art. It is often elusive in teaching as well. Yet it is personal meaning that most motivates us to receive. Phenix often commented that "education should nourish being." Teachers "are creators and bearers of meaning. Our work is to empower students to find their own personal meaning" (Bolin, 1987a, p. 219).

Personal meaning will likely be derived by teacher and students through relationships of receiving and responding that occur around struggles to know. One can learn in a variety of ways; but when one learns with and from a teacher, one has entered into a unique human relationship. Henri Nowen (1972) likened the teacher to a gift giver, pointing out that a gift is not complete until it is received. This places the teacher in an interdependent relationship with the student. Noddings (1984) describes reciprocity as a responsiveness. The student responds freely in his or her own way.

One enters a work of art imaginatively and receptively, and while one may not agree with the meaning the artist ascribes to the work, or fully understand the work, one is able to set aside preconceived notions of what "ought to be" and engage with what the artist has presented. One then experiences satisfaction. I assume this to be the case in teaching. As a teacher, one is receptive to students. The meaning the teacher derives from engagement will not be the same as for students. Students will be free to draw their own unique meanings and satisfactions. The process, in continuous cycle, involves receptivity, engrossment, and responsiveness.

THE MAGIC IN CRAFT

All of us can remember at least some magical moments in our experience as students. Any good teacher seems to be part magician, inviting students to explore the mystery and wonder of a portion of the universe. We do not like to think of teaching in terms of deception and deceit, however. Yet these are elements of magic.

Most people who choose to teach are at least relatively wholesome and balanced people. There will always be those exceptions, charlatans, who disappoint and alarm us by their abuses of power or reprehensible actions toward themselves, students, or other teachers. These are rare, sensational instances.

No teacher is without temptation to misuse power over students, however (see Kohl, 1984; Jersild, 1955; and Bolin, 1987a). Usually, power is abused in benign ways. For example, we may try to entice students into learning without regard for their perspective or manipulate them into giving us the responses we want.

Part of our pledge as teachers is to accept the ethical and moral responsibility of power. As teachers we are privy to a great deal of knowledge about our students and about how to motivate and manipulate children. We are never free of the temptation to humiliate or hurt a student who challenges us, or to get even with a student who has made us feel stupid. To teach is to invite people in, to ask them to participate in a conversation, to be involved in an adventure. It is tempting to invite students in to comfort and care for our own ego needs. The natural bonding that occurs between student and teacher can become a form of bondage. And we see teachers who so tie a group of students to themselves that the students seem unable to bond with other teachers.

Most of us care most of the time. But teachers who care are sometimes employed in schools that are uncaring places. Schools are not intentionally uncaring. The problem is that structures of schooling can deny the teacher's own actions and intentions. Teachers find, for example, that just about the time they get to know students, the year is over and the students are promoted. They find that they have to teach in ways that are uninteresting, unchallenging, and un-rewarding in order to please administrators who are, themselves, acting in a rule-governed way in order to meet the demands of a test-driven system. Teachers and administrators too often find that paperwork and procedures seem to be more important than students. Greed and hoarding of knowledge and materials seem to be critical to survival—a departing teacher's room will be stripped of paper, textbooks, and supplies because these are so scarce. The new teacher who faces the empty supply closet will have to bear up under it and learn cunning solutions. A beginning teacher described the following:

> I got into my room the week before school started. It was completely empty. I mean, there were desks and that is it! There wasn't a scrap of anything to work with, no chalk, no nothing—not even textbooks. People were friendly, but when I asked about supplies they acted kind of vacant. The Assistant Principal told me that in the middle of September I would have some discretionary money that I could spend on supplies. In the meantime? Well, I went out and bought supplies out of my own pocket.
>
> Then when the kids came, this one teacher was so nice. She asked me about each of the kids and how they were doing. I thought, "How helpful!" Then I found out that she wanted to know who the smart kids were—because she had them all transferred into her class in exchange for kids she didn't want to work with! I've heard of "Paying your dues," but I couldn't believe this was really happening!

Teachers sometimes feel forced to use their craft in other dark ways: to manipulate students to perform when the supervisor or administrator is in the room so they can demonstrate all of the points on the checklist by which they are being evaluated, whether these particular points make any sense in terms of their students; to teach materials that are inappropriate, silly, or trivial; to keep their own situation as calm and unchaotic as possible, even if it means controlling and manipulating their students.

Where there is overcrowding, lack of community support, emphasis on test scores, unmotivated students, apathetic or burned-out colleagues, and indiffer-ent administrators, teachers resort to survival. But they do so at a cost. Teach-ers experience widespread feelings of loneliness, hopelessness, and disenchantment with teaching. Often they blame students for being poorly motivated, or parents for not caring. They blame other teachers for not doing an adequate job.

Teachers, like others in our society, have internalized a kind of public mindset that imagines teaching to be for people who have no other options or who are not too bright. Most teachers are thoughtful and bright people; often they distance themselves from this internalized image of teaching and speak disrespectfully of their colleagues and of the profession. Like the parent who has been a battered child, they "batter" other teachers.

THEORY INTO TEACHING

The craft of teaching includes owning one's whole capacities as a person and choosing how to be. It requires learning subject and pedagogy, remaining open to exploring the boundaries of learning, and holding an experimental mindset. The craft of teaching involves owning one's own darker inclinations and capacities with compassion. In an exceptionally helpful book, *When Teachers Face Themselves*, Arthur Jersild (1955) points out how important it is to know and accept one's feelings and needs:

> . . . to go all out, to *feel for* others (as distinguished from going through the motions of *doing* for others), to *feel with* others (as distinguished from going through the motions of *cooperating* with them), it is essential that the teacher draw upon his own capacity for feeling. And he can do this only if he respects his feelings and is at home with them, if he accepts them as part of himself. This means self acceptance, which involves compassion for oneself. (p. 133)

Compassion involves answering that part of the self that calls us to connect to beauty and goodness. It involves answering that natural part of the self that desires to connect to and care for others. When teachers band together to perfect their craft, they can be a powerful and positive force for changing schools so that they can be communities of caring. Many of the schools that are experimenting with alternative models of governance, new classroom structures, and the like are guided by teachers whose compassion for self and others has challenged them to face and change structures that are indifferent and uncaring.

SUMMARY

I have suggested that teaching is neither art nor science, but a relationship embedded in caring. It is the relationship between one who knows, and knows how to find out, and others who are learning. Teaching shares many characteristics of art, particularly craft art. To be most successful, I believe, teaching needs to be characterized by the qualities that are present in caring relationships: receptivity, engrossment, and reciprocity.

When this happens, teaching, like skilled craft art, can be both beautiful and functional.

References

Barr, A. S., et al. (1961). *Wisconsin Studies of the Measurement and Prediction of Teacher Effectiveness: A Summary of Investigations.* Madison, WI: Dembar Publications.

Bolin, F. S. (in press). *Hope Is the Thing with Feathers: Poetry of Emily Dickinson for Young People.* New York: Magnolia.

Bolin, F. S. (1987a). "Teaching as a Self-Renewing Vocation," in F. S. Bolin and J. M. Falk, eds., *Teacher Renewal: Professional Issues, Personal Choices.* New York: Teachers College Press, Columbia University, pp. 217–230.

Bolin, F. S. (1987b). "The Teacher as Curriculum Decision Maker," in F. S. Bolin and J. M. Falk, eds., *Teacher Renewal: Professional Issues, Personal Choices.* New York: Teachers College Press, Columbia University, pp. 92–108.

Bolin, F. S. and P. Panaritis (1992). "Searching for a Common Purpose: A Perspective on the History of Supervision," in C. D. Glickman, ed., *Supervision in Transition.* Alexandria, VA: ASCD, pp. 30–43.

Cremin, L. A. (1964). *The Transformation of the School.* New York: Vintage Books, Random House.

Dewey, J. (1904). "The Relation of Theory to Practice in Teaching," in C. A. McMurry, ed., *The Relation of Theory to Practice in the Education of Teachers* (Third Yearbook of the National Society for the Scientific Study of Education, Part I). Chicago: University of Chicago Press, pp. 9–30.

Dewey, J. (1929). *The Sources of a Science of Education.* New York: Horace Liveright.

Eisner, E. W. (1979). *The Educational Imagination.* New York: Macmillan.

Gage, N. L. (1978). *The Scientific Basis of the Art of Teaching.* New York: Teachers College Press, Columbia University.

Gage, N. L. (1984). *Hard Gains in the Soft Sciences: The Case of Pedagogy.* Bloomington, IN: Phi Delta Kappa.

Highet, G. (1950). *The Art of Teaching.* New York: Vintage Books.

Jersild, A. T. (1955). *When Teachers Face Themselves.* New York: Teachers College Press, Columbia University.

Kliebard, H. M. (1986). *The Struggle for the American Curriculum, 1893–1958.* Boston: Routledge & Kegan Paul.

Kohl, H. (1984). *Growing Minds: On Becoming a Teacher.* New York: Harper & Row.

Neill, A. S. (1960). *Summerhill: A Radical Approach to Child Rearing.* New York: Hart.

Noddings, N. (1984). *Caring: A Feminine Approach to Ethics and Moral Education.* Berkeley: University of California Press.

Nouwen, H. (1972). *Creative Ministry.* New York: Doubleday.

Phenix, P. (1974). "Transcendence and the Curriculum," in W. Pinar, ed., *Curriculum Theorizing: The Reconceptualists.* Berkeley, CA: McCutchan, pp. 321–340.

Rice, J. M. (1893). *The Public School System of the United States.* New York: Century.

Tom, A. R. (1984). *Teaching as a Moral Craft.* New York: Longman.

Discussion Questions

1. Describe the best teacher you have had in any of your school experiences. Why do you think of this person as your best teacher?

2. This chapter takes the position that teaching is neither art nor science, but borrows from both of these disciplines. Take the position that teaching is either an art or a science. On what grounds can you defend the position you have chosen?

3. What do you believe to be the most essential characteristics of a good teacher? Which characteristics might be considered artistic in some way?

4. Compare teaching to an art form. What art form did you choose, and why?

5. How would you redesign schools to support teaching as a caring craft? What changes in classrooms, school organization, and the like would you make?

6. Describe an experience you have had in school that was both beautiful and functional.

Herbert J. Walberg

Herbert J. Walberg was awarded a Ph.D. in educational psychology by the University of Chicago in 1964. He has held research appointments at that university, the University of Wisconsin, and the Educational Testing Service, and taught at Harvard University. In 1984 Dr. Walberg was appointed Research Professor of Education—one of four such research professors at the University of Illinois at Chicago—whereby he was nominated by faculty colleagues and appointed by the university president and board of trustees for distinguished contributions to research.

Herb's main research interest is the educational promotion of human learning and talent. He has written or edited forty-six books and sixty-seven chapters, four encyclopedia articles, twenty-three pamphlets and monographs, and about 350 research papers. They concern such topics as causes and effects of learning; institutional and personal productivity; the encouragement of excellent performance; teaching and instructional effectiveness; family, peer-group; national comparisons of achievement; educational measurement and evaluation; and statistical analysis and computer processing.

Much of Walberg's research has appeared in psychological journals, and he has presented more than 100 research papers at scientific meetings in Australia, England, Denmark, France, Germany, Israel, Singapore, Sweden, and the United States.

On a personal level, he says his favorite place to visit is Japan because, as he puts it, "My wife is Japanese and I find the Japanese culture fascinating." Walberg has also written frequently for widely circulated journals such as *Daedalus*, *Educational Leadership*, *Kappan*, and *Nature*, and for many newspapers such as the *Chicago Tribune*, *Wall Street Journal*, and the *Washington Post*. Also, he often gives testimony in federal district courts, the U.S. Senate, House of Representatives, and federal task forces and agencies.

In 1985 Walberg was appointed by the U.S. Secretary of Education, William Bennett, to a blue-ribbon task force on federal priorities for educational research. He helped to plan, write, and edit *What Works: Research About Teaching and Learning*, and with 1.2 million printed copies, it turned out to be one of the most widely circulated government reports.

Obviously, Herb is on the professional fast-track. But he also spends considerable time on his indoor skiing exerciser and stairclimber, running, climbing, perspiring, and working out some of his best theories on education. Although not one for idle chit-chat, his advice for young teachers is: "Be cognizant of Oscar Wilde's advice who claimed two great disappointments in life: not getting what you want and getting it." Well, I hope that chit-chat sunk in.

3 ❧

Productive Teaching

Herbert J. Walberg

A key question of research on teaching is what best promotes learning. During the twentieth century, thousands of studies have been devoted to this question. Investigators typically ask one group of teachers to use a particular teaching method, then compare their students' learning on achievement tests and other measures with a "control group" of students that have taught by conventional methods. This scientific approach follows from the pragmatic philosophy of William James and John Dewey and from the experimental psychology of Edward Thorndike.

It would be a major effort to read the thousands of studies. So, my colleagues and I have used statistical techniques to summarize findings. In 1984, I began by summarizing the results of nearly 3,000 studies that had been analyzed (Walberg, 1984). In 1987, an Australian-U.S. team assessed 134 summaries of 7,827 field studies and several large-scale U.S. and international surveys of learning (Fraser, Walberg, Welch, & Hattie, 1987). We updated this work twice (Walberg, 1986; Waxman & Walberg, 1991), and in 1993, we compared these results to those summarized in 179 authoritative reviews and the ratings of 61 research experts (Wang, Haertel, & Walberg, 1993). This chapter provides a compact summary of the findings on elementary and secondary school students.

I begin with the effects of the psychological elements of teaching and then discuss methods and patterns of teaching—all of which can be accomplished by a single teacher without unusual arrangements and equipment. Then I turn to systems of instruction that require special planning, student grouping, and materials. The remaining results concern special students and techniques, and effects of training on teachers. (In the references are articles on special techniques most appropriate for specific subjects such as reading and science.)

The compilation of effects allows us to compare teaching methods with one another—including some effective ones that are no longer popular. We can see that some techniques have enormous effects, while others confer only trivial advantages. In practice, however, we might attain results half or twice as good as indicated by the research. Success depends on care in implementation, the extent to which methods are appropriate for personal and school philosophies, and other factors.

PSYCHOLOGICAL ELEMENTS OF TEACHING

A little history will help us understand the evolution of psychological research on teaching. Psychologists have often emphasized thought, feeling, or behavior at the expense of one another, even though educators require balance. Today, thinking or cognition is sovereign in psychology, but a half century ago, behaviorists insisted on specific operational definitions—a standard still required.

In particular, Yale psychologist Neal Miller (1941), stimulated by Edward L. Thorndike and B. F. Skinner, wrote about cues, responses, and positive reinforcement, especially in psychotherapy. Later Dollard and Miller emphasized three components of teaching—cues, engagement, and reinforcement—similar to input, process, and output in physiology. Their influential conception stimulated research on what teachers do rather than their age, experience, certification, college degrees, and other characteristics not connected with what their students learn.

The behavioral model emphasized the quality of instructional cues impinging on the learner, the learner's active engagement in the process, and reinforcement or rewards that encourage continuing effort over time. Bloom (1976) recognized, however, that learners may fail the first time or even repeatedly in cycles of cues and effort; if they make no progress, they may practice incorrect behavior, and they cannot be reinforced. Therefore, he introduced the ideas of feedback to correct errors and frequent testing to check progress. Bloom also emphasized engaged learning time and stressed that some learners require much more time than others. Mastery effects are among the largest estimated. The underlying research has been unusually rigorous and well controlled. Even though the research was conducted in school classes, the investigators helped to ensure precise timing and deployment of the elements in short-term studies, usually less than a month. Similar effects are difficult to sustain for long time periods.

Elements of Mastery Learning

Cues show what is to be learned and explain how to learn it. Their quality can be seen in the clarity, salience, and meaningfulness of explanations and directions provided by teachers, instructional materials, or both. Ideally, as the learners gain confidence, the salience and numbers of cues can be reduced.

Engagement is the extent to which learners actively and persistently participate until appropriate responses are firmly entrenched in their repertoires. Such participation can be indexed by the extent to which teachers engage students in overt or covert activity—indicated by the absence of irrelevant behavior, concentration on tasks, enthusiastic contributions to group discussion, and lengthy study.

Corrective feedback remedies errors in oral or written responses. Ideally, students waste little time on incorrect responses, and teachers rapidly detect and remedy difficulties by reteaching or alternate methods. When necessary, they also provide additional time needed for practice.

The immense effort elicited by athletics, games, and other cooperative and competitive activities illustrates the power of immediate and direct *reinforcement* and shows how some activities are intrinsically rewarding in themselves. By comparison, classroom reinforcement may seem crass at times.

The usual classroom reinforcers are acknowledgment of correctness and social approval, say, in the form of a smile or praise. More unusual reinforcers include contingent activity—for example, allowing a music lesson or other enjoyable activity for 90 percent correctness on a math test. Other reinforcers are tokens or check marks accumulated for steps accomplished and later exchanged for tangible reinforcers such as cookies, trinkets, or toys.

In special-education programs, students have been reinforced not only for achievement but also for minutes of reading, attempts to learn, and accuracy of task performance in special programs. When the environment can be rigorously controlled, and when teachers are able to gear reinforcement to performance accurately, as in programs for unruly or emotionally disturbed students, the results have been impressive. Improved behavior and achievement, however, often fail to extend past the period of reinforcement or beyond the special environment.

Educators ordinarily confine reinforcement to marks, grades, and awards because they must assume that students work for intangible, long-term goals such as pleasing parents, further education, adult success, and (we hope) for the ultimate aim of education—the intrinsic reward of learning itself. Even so, when corrective feedback and reinforcement are clear, rapid, and appropriate, they can powerfully affect learning by signaling what to do next without wasting time. In ordinary classrooms, then, the chief value of reinforcement is in providing information rather than incentive.

Methods of Teaching

Psychological elements undergird many teaching methods and the design of instructional media. By improving the affective or informational content of cues, engagement, correctives, and reinforcement, they have shown a range of effects from small to enormous—though generally not as big as short-term highly controlled studies of the pure elements.

Cues

Advance organizers are brief overviews that abstractly relate new concepts or terms to previous learning. They are effective if they bridge new to old learning. Those spoken by the teacher or graphically illustrated in texts work best.

Adjunct questions alert students about key questions to answer, particularly in texts. They work best on questions repeated on posttests, and moderately well on questions related to the adjuncts. As we might expect, however, adjunct questions distract attention away from incidental material that might otherwise be learned.

Goal setting sets forth objectives, guidelines, methods, or standards for learning. Like adjunct questions, goal setting sacrifices incidental for intended learning.

Pretests are benchmarks for determining how much students learn from various methods of teaching. Psychologists have found, however, that pretests can have positive cuing effects if they show students what will be emphasized by instruction and on posttests.

Several principles follow from these results: To concentrate learning on essential points and save time, as in training, remove elaborations and extraneous oral and written prose. To focus learners on selected questions or teach them to find answers in elaborated prose, as in textbooks, use adjunct questions and goal setting. To encourage acquisition of as much undifferentiated material as possible, as in college lecture courses, assign big blocks of text and test students on randomly selected points. Although the means may seem clear, consensus about educational purposes may be difficult.

Clarity at the onset saves time and helps learners to see things the teacher's way; but it deters autonomy and deep, personal insights. At one ancient extreme, Zen masters ask novitiates about the sound of one hand clapping and wait a decade or two for an answer.

Engagement

High expectations transmit teachers' standards of learning and performance. These may function as both cues and incentives for students to engage actively with extended effort and perseverance.

Frequent tests increase learning through increased effort and feedback. Their effects are larger, however, on quiz performance than on final examinations.

Questioning also appears to work by engagement and may encourage deeper thinking, as in Plato's accounts of Socrates. Questioning has bigger effects in science than in other subjects. *Wait time*, allowing students several seconds to reflect rather than the usual one second, leads to longer and better answers.

Correctives and Reinforcement

Corrective feedback remedies errors by reteaching by the same or a different method. It has moderate effects that are somewhat higher in science, perhaps because science may offer more conceptual than memory challenge when compared with other subjects.

Homework by itself constructively extends engagement or learning time. Correctives and reinforcement in the form of grades and comments on homework raise its effects dramatically.

Praise has a small, positive effect. For young or disturbed children, praise may lack the power of tangible and token reinforcers used in psychological experiments. For students able to see ahead, grades and personal standards may be more powerful reinforcers than momentary encouragement. Praise may be under- or over-supplied; it may appear demeaning or sardonic; and it may pale in comparison with the incentives afforded by youth culture in the form of cars, clothes, dating, and athletics.

None of this is to say that encouragement, incentives, and good classroom morale should be abandoned: Honey is better than vinegar. As cognitive psychologists point out, the main classroom value of reinforcement may lie in its information for the student about progress rather than its power to reward.

Patterns of Teaching

As explained previously, methods of teaching enact or combine more fundamental psychological elements. By further extension, patterns of teaching integrate elements and methods of teaching. These more inclusive formulations follow the evolution of psychological research on education: Behavioral research evolved in the 1950s from psychological laboratories to short-term, controlled experiments on one element at a time in classrooms. In the 1970s, educational researchers tried to find patterns of effective practices from observations of ordinary teaching.

Thus, behaviorists traded educational realism for theoretical parsimony and scientific rigor; later psychologists preferred realism until their insights were experimentally confirmed. Fortunately, the results from both approaches appear to converge. It seems possible, moreover, to incorporate the work of cognitive psychologists of the 1980s into an enlarged understanding of teaching.

Explicit Teaching

Explicit teaching can be viewed as traditional or conventional whole-group teaching done well. Since most teaching has changed little in the last three-quarters of a century (Hoetker & Ahlbrand, 1969) and may not change substantially in the near future, it is worthwhile knowing how the usual practice can excel. Since it has evolved from ordinary practice, explicit teaching is easy to carry out and does not disrupt conventional institutions and expectations. It can, moreover, incorporate many previously discussed elements and methods.

N. L. Gage, Donald Medley, and others (see Waxman & Walberg, 1991, for extended discussion) employed "process-product" investigations of the association between what teachers do and how much their students learn. The various contributors do not completely agree about the essential components of explicit teaching, and they refer to it by different names such as explicit, process-product, direct, active, and effective teaching. Moreover, the contributors weigh their own results heavily; but Rosenshine, as a long-standing and comprehensive reviewer, has taken an eagle's eye view of the results (see Chapter 8 in this book).

In his early reviews of correlation studies, Rosenshine discussed the traits of effective teachers including clarity, task orientation, enthusiasm, and flexibility, as well as their tendencies to structure their presentations and occasionally use student ideas. From later observational and control-group research, Rosenshine identified six phased functions that correlated with learning outcomes: (1) daily review, homework check, and, if necessary, reteaching; (2) rapid presentation of new content and skills in small steps; (3) guided student practice with close teacher monitoring; (4) corrective feedback and instructional reinforcement; (5) independent practice in seatwork and homework with a more than 90 percent success rate; and (6) weekly and monthly reviews.

Comprehension Teaching

The descendants of Aristotle and the Anglo-American traditions of Bacon, Locke, Thorndike, and Skinner objected to philosophical "armchair" opinions; mid-century behaviorists, particularly John Watson, constructively insisted on hard empirical facts about learning. But they also saw the child's mind as a blank tablet, and seemed to encourage active teaching and passive acquisition of isolated facts. Reacting to such atomism, cognitive psychologists revived research on student-centered learning and "higher mental processes," in the tradition of Plato, Socrates, Kant, and Piaget. In American hands, however, this tradition had the potential for vacuity and permissiveness, as in the extremes of the "progressive education" movement of the 1930s.

Oddly, the Russian psychologist Lev Vygotsky (1978) hit on an influential compromise: Emphasizing the two-way nature of teaching, he identified a "zone of proximal development" extending from what learners can do independently, to the maximum they can do with the teacher's help. Accordingly, teachers should set up "scaffolding" for building knowledge but should remove it when it becomes unnecessary. In mathematics, for example, the teacher can give hints and examples, foster independent use, and then remove support. This approach is similar to the "prompting" and "fading" of behavioral cues and to common sense, but it sufficed to revive interest in transferring some autonomy to students.

In the 1980s, cognitive research on teaching sought ways to encourage self-monitoring, self-teaching, or "meta-cognition" to foster independence. Skills were important, but the learner's monitoring and management of them have primacy, as though the explicit teaching functions of planning, allocating time, and reviewing are partly transferred to learners.

Pearson (1985), for example, outlined three phases: (1) *modeling*, where the teacher exhibits the desired behavior; (2) *guided practice*, where students perform with help from the teacher; and (3) *application*, where students perform independently of the teacher—much like explicit teaching functions. Pallincsar and Brown (1984), moreover, described a program of "reciprocal teaching" to foster comprehension by having students take turns in leading dialogues on pertinent features of the text. By assuming planning and executive control ordinarily exercised by teachers, students learn planning, structuring, and self-management. Perhaps that is why tutors learn from teaching, and why we say that to learn something well, teach it.

Comprehension teaching encourages readers to measure their progress toward explicit goals. If necessary, they can reallocate time for different activities. In this way, self-awareness, personal control, and positive self-evaluation can be enlarged (Haller & Walberg, 1992).

OPEN EDUCATION

In the late 1960s, open educators enlarged autonomy in primary grades by enabling students to join teachers in planning educational purposes, means, and evaluations. In contrast to teacher- and textbook-centered education, students were given voice in what to learn—even to the point of writing their own texts to share with one another. Open educators tried to foster cooperation, critical thinking, constructive attitudes, and self-directed life-long learning. Open educators revived the spirit of the New England town meeting, Thoreau's self-reliance, Emerson's transcendentalism, and Dewey's progressivism. Their ideas also resonate with the late Carl Roger's "client-centered" psychotherapy that emphasizes the "unconditional worth" of the person.

Giaconia and Hedges' (1982) synthesis of 153 studies showed that open education had worthwhile effects on creativity, independence, cooperation, attitudes toward teachers and schools, mental ability, psychological adjustment, and curiosity. Students in open programs had less motivation for grade grubbing, but they differed little from other students in actual achievement, self-concept, and anxiety.

Giaconia and Hedges, however, found that open programs were more effective in producing the nonachievement outcomes—attitudes, creativity, and self-concept—and sacrificed some academic achievement on standardized measures. These programs emphasized the role of the child in learning, use of diagnostic rather than norm-referenced evaluation, individualized instruction, and manipulative materials, but not three other components thought by some to be essential to open programs—multiage grouping, open space, and team teaching.

Giaconia and Hedges speculated that children in the most extreme open programs may do somewhat less well on conventional achievement tests because they have little experience with them. At any rate, it appears that open classes enhance several nonstandard outcomes without detracting from academic achievement unless they are radically extreme.

INSTRUCTIONAL SYSTEMS

All the techniques discussed thus far can be planned and executed by a single teacher, perhaps with some extra effort, encouragement, or training but without unusual preparation and materials. In contrast, instructional systems require special arrangements and planning, and they often combine several components of instruction. Moreover, they tend to emphasize adaption of instruction to individual students rather than student adaption to a fixed pattern of teaching such as explicit whole-group instruction. A little history will aid our understanding of current systems.

Mastery Learning

Mastery learning combines the psychological elements of instruction and suitable amounts of time. Formative tests are employed to allocate time and guide reinforcement and corrective feedback. Mastery programs have yielded substantial effects. The largest come from programs that establish a criterion of 95 to 100 mastery and require repeated testing to mastery before allowing students to proceed to additional units (which yielded gigantic effects of one standard deviation). Mastery yielded larger effects on less able students, and reduced the disparities in performance to 82 percent of control groups.

The success of mastery learning is attributable to several features: The Kuliks (1986), for example, found that when control groups were provided feedback from quizzes, the mastery group's advantage was smaller. Mastery, as Bloom (1976) pointed out, takes additional time (in the range of 10 to 100 percent more than conventional instruction). Mastery studies that provided equal time for mastery and control groups showed a very small advantage for mastery learning on standardized tests. The advantage, however, was moderate on experimenter-made, criterion-referenced tests for nine equal-time studies. These results illustrate the separate contribution of cues, feedback, and time components of mastery learning.

Mastery learning yielded larger effects in studies of less than a month's duration than those lasting more than four months. Retention probably declines sharply no matter what the educational method, but the decline can be more confidently noted about mastery since it has been more extensively investigated.

Adaptive Instruction

Developed by Robert Glaser and Margaret Wang, adaptive instruction now combines mastery, cooperative, open education, tutoring, computer, and comprehension approaches into a complex system to tailor instruction to individual and small-group needs. It includes managerial steps executed by a master teacher including planning, time allocation, task delegation to aides and students, and quality control. It is a comprehensive program for the whole school day rather than a single method that requires simple integration into one subject or into a single teacher's repertoire. Its achievement effects are substantial, but its broader effects are probably underestimated since adaptive instruction aims at diverse ends including student autonomy, intrinsic motivation, and teacher and student choice that are poorly indicated by the usual outcome measures.

Computer-assisted Instruction

Ours may be the age of computers; computers have already shown substantial effects on learning. With hardware costs declining and software increasing in sophistication, we may hope for still more as computers are better integrated into school programs.

Computers show the greatest advantage for handicapped students, probably because they may be more adaptive to their special needs; computers may also be more patient, discreet, nonjudgmental, or even encouraging about their progress. Perhaps for the same reasons, computers generally have bigger effects in elementary schools than in high schools and colleges.

Another explanation, however, is plausible: Elementary schools provide less tracking and differentiated courses for homogeneous groups. Computers may adapt to larger within-class differences among elementary students by allowing them to proceed at their own pace without invidious comparisons.

Simulations and Games

Without the computer's help, simulations and games can require active, specific learner responses and may strike a balance between vicarious book learning and the dynamic, complicated, and competitive "real world." Their interactiveness, speed, intensity, movement, color, and sound add interest and information to academic learning. Without gearing to educational purposes, however, they can also waste time, as in arcade games.

STUDENT GROUPING AND MORALE

Teaching students what they already know and what they are yet incapable of learning is equally wasteful—perhaps even harmful to motivation. For this reason, traditional whole-class teaching of heterogeneous groups can present serious difficulties and inefficiency, often unacknowledged in our egalitarian age. Outside universities, however, most educators recognize that it is difficult to teach arithmetic and trigonometry at the same time. (Even some English professors might balk at teaching phonics and deconstructionism simultaneously.) If we want students to learn as much as possible rather than make them all alike, we need to consider how they are grouped, and try to help the full range.

Grouping

Acceleration programs identify talented youth (often in mathematics and science), and group them together or with older students. Such programs provide counseling, encouragement, contact with accomplished adults, grade skipping, summer school, and the compression of the standard curriculum into fewer years. The effects are huge in elementary schools, substantial in junior high schools, and moderate in senior high schools. The smaller effects at advanced levels may be attributable to the smaller advantage of acceleration over tracking and differentiated course placement practiced in high schools.

The effects of acceleration on educational attitudes, vocational plans, participation in school activities, popularity, psychological adjustment, and character ratings were mixed and often insignificant. These outcomes may not be systematically affected in either direction.

Ability grouping is based on achievement, intelligence tests, personal insights, and subjective opinions. In high school, ability grouping leaves low-

Early intervention programs included educational, psychological, and therapeutic components for handicapped, at-risk, and disadvantaged children from one to sixty-six months of age. The immediate and large outcome advantages declined rapidly and disappeared after three years.

Preschool programs also showed initial learning effects that were unsustained. It appears that young children can learn more than is normally assumed; but, like other learners, they can also forget. The key to sustained gains may be sustained programs and effective families, not one-shot approaches.

Handicapped students classified as mentally retarded, emotionally disturbed, and learning disabled have been subjects in research that has several important implications: When they serve as *tutors* of one another and younger students, handicapped students can learn well—a finding similar to those in comprehension monitoring and tutoring studies of nonhandicapped children showing beneficial effects of teaching on tutors. "Handicapped" students, moreover, are often spuriously classified, and we may underestimate their capacities.

Mainstreaming studies show that mildly to moderately handicapped students can prosper in regular classes and thereby avoid the stereotyped, invidious "labeling" often based on misclassifications. *Psycholinguistic training* of special-needs students yields positive effects; it consists of testing and remedying specific deficits in language skills.

Shortcuts: At the request of the U.S. Army, the National Academy of Sciences evaluated exotic techniques for learning and performance enhancement described in popular psychology and presumably being exploited in California and the U.S.S.R. (Druckman & Swets, 1988). Little or no evidence, however, was found for the efficacy of

learning during sleep

mental practice of motor skills

"integration" of left and right brain hemispheres

parapsychological techniques

biofeedback

extrasensory perception

mental telepathy

"mind over matter" exercises

"neurolinguistic programming," in which instructors identify students' modes of learning and mimic students' behavior as they teach

The Greeks found no royal road to geometry: Even kings, if they desired mastery, had to sweat over Euclid's elements. Perhaps brain research will eventually yield an elixir or panacea. But, for proof, educators should insist on hard data in refereed scientific journals.

TEACHING TEACHERS

Programs to help teachers in their work have had substantial effects—notwithstanding complaints about inservice sessions. Do physicians complain about the medical care they get?

Microteaching

Developed at Stanford University in the 1960s, microteaching is a behavioral approach for preservice and inservice training that has substantial effects. It employs explanation and modeling of selected teaching techniques; televised practice with small groups of students; discussion, correctives, and reinforcement while watching playbacks; and recycling through subsequent practice and playback sessions with new groups of students.

Inservice Education

Inservice teacher education also proves to have substantial effects. Somewhat like the case of physician training, the biggest effects are on teacher knowledge, but effects on classroom behavior and student achievement are also big.

For inservice training, authoritative planning and execution seem to work best; informal coaching by itself seems ineffective. Instructor responsibility for design and teaching of the sessions works better than teacher presentations and group discussions. The best techniques are observation of classroom practices, video-audio feedback, and practice. The best combination is lecture, modeling, practice, and coaching. The size of the training group ranging from tutoring to greater than sixty makes no detectable difference.

Some apparent effects may be attributable to participant selectivity rather than superior efficacy: Federal, state, and university sponsored programs appear more effective than locally initiated programs. Competitive selection of participants and college credit apparently work better as incentives than extra pay, certificate renewal, and no incentives. Independent study seems to have larger effects than workshops, courses, mini-courses, and institutes.

THEORY INTO PRACTICE

Much of this chapter concerns theories and practices of teaching as well as the research on which they are based. Still, it is worthwhile before concluding to indicate the several steps teachers can employ in making use of the theories and research in their practical work:

1. Think about the comparative effects of the various teaching methods and arrangements in relation to your philosophy and ideals of education, your personal experiences as a teacher and student, the purposes and circumstances of the school in which you teach (or will or would like to teach), and the propensities of your students and colleagues. Think about which

methods suit you best but may not be best for the circumstances, and about those most often used but unsuitable in your view.

2. Given these considerations, tentatively select methods that seem most appropriate. Ideally, they should have large effects, suit your views well, and be adaptable to the students and school setting.

3. Read more about these methods in the references given at the end of this chapter and in other works on teaching research and practice. Pay particular attention to writings on the suitability of each method for different subjects, students, and conditions. Analyze the particular requirements for using each method effectively, wisely, and well. If in doubt, begin again at the first step.

4. Employ the most suitable method. This may take several weeks or months to give it a fair test.

5. Carefully evaluate the chosen method from its inception. Are students stimulated by the experience? Are they learning as much as possible? What are your colleagues' reactions?

At each step, teachers may find it useful to discuss the various considerations with their principals, supervisors, mentors, colleagues, and students. Together with such discussion, the five steps can be central to professional development since they concern the planning, execution, and evaluation of the defining acts of education—teaching and learning.

SUMMARY

Psychological research provides estimates of the effects of teaching methods on learning. Effective methods may be identified from the psychological elements of teaching, open education, learning systems, student grouping, techniques for special populations, and the teaching of teachers.

Some practices may be costly—not in dollars but in new or complicated arrangements that may be difficult for some teachers and schools to begin and continue. Thus, the estimates of effects are only one basis for decision making. Psychology alone cannot suffice to prescribe practices, since different means bring about different ends. Educators must choose among student-, teacher-, and curriculum-direction of effort; facts and concepts; breadth and depth; short- and long-term ends; academic knowledge and real-world application; equal opportunity and equal results; and Plato's triumvirate of thinking, feeling, and acting. Once these choices are made, the estimates of effects can provide one of the bases for choosing the most productive practices.

References

Bloom, B. S. (1976). *Human Characteristics and School Learning.* New York: McGraw-Hill.

Druckman, D., and J. A. Swets (1988). *Enhancing*

Human Performance. Washington, D.C.: National Academy Press.

Fraser, B. J., H. J. Walberg, W. W. Welch, and J. A.

Hattie (1987). "Syntheses of Educational Productivity Research." *International Journal of Educational Research* 11: 73–145 (whole issue).

Giaconia, R. M., and L. V. Hedges (1982). "Identifying Features of Effective Open Education." *Review of Educational Research* 52: 579–602.

Haller, E., and H. J. Walberg (1992). "Meta-Cognition." *International Encyclopedia of Education: Research and Studies: Second Supplement and Second Edition.* Oxford, England: Pergamon Press.

Hoetker, J., and W. P. Ahlbrand (1969). "The Persistence of the Recitation." *American Educational Research Journal* 6: 145–167.

Miller, N., and J. Dollard (1941). *Social Learning and Imitation.* New Haven: Yale University Press.

Pallincsar, A. M., and A. Brown (1984). "Reciprocal Teaching of Comprehension Fostering and Comprehension Monitoring Activities." *Cognition and Instruction* 1: 117–176.

Pearson, D. (1985). "Reading Comprehension Instruction: Six Necessary Steps." *Reading Teacher* 38: 724–738.

Peterson, P. L., and H. J. Walberg, eds. (1979). *Research on Teaching.* Berkeley, CA: McCutchan.

Vygotsky, L. (1978). *Mind in Society.* Cambridge, MA: Harvard University Press.

Walberg, H. J. (1984). "Improving the Productivity of America's Schools." *Educational Leadership* 41 (8): 19–27.

Walberg, H. J. (1986). "Synthesis of Research on Teaching," in M. C. Wittrock, ed., *Handbook of Research on Teaching.* New York: Macmillan.

Walberg, H. J. (1990). "Productive Teaching and Instruction: Assessing the Knowledge Base." *Phi Delta Kappan* 71: 470–478.

Wang, M. C., G. D. Haertel, and H. J. Walberg (1993). "Toward a Knowledge Base for School Learning." *Review of Educational Research* 63: 365–376.

Waxman, H. C., and H. J. Walberg (1991). *Effective Teaching: Current Research.* Berkeley, CA: McCutchan.

Discussion Questions

1. Are the various teaching methods equally applicable to the several school subjects such as reading, mathematics, physical education, and art?

2. Which methods require the most preparation on the part of teachers?

3. Why is explicit teaching by far the most prevalent form of teaching? What are its advantages and disadvantages?

4. Is it the teacher's job to bring all students up to a minimum standard or to encourage all students to learn as much as they can, despite the fact that some will do much better than others?

5. Why is it difficult to begin and sustain innovative teaching methods such as open education and computer-assisted instruction in schools?

6. What factors, other than the quality of teaching, affect how much students learn?

Bruce W. Tuckman

Bruce W. Tuckman is professor of educational research and coordinator of the educational psychology program at Florida State University in Tallahassee, Florida. He earned his Ph.D. in psychology from Princeton University in 1963, doing part of his work under the direction of Robert M. Gagné. Dr. Tuckman is a Fellow of the American Psychological Association, and a Charter Fellow of both the American Psychological Society and the American Association of Applied and Preventative Psychology. In addition to his numerous articles, he has authored a number of books including *Conducting Educational Research*, *Testing for Teachers*, and *Educational Psychology: From Theory to Application*.

For fun, Bruce jogs six miles or more a day, runs numerous marathons, and reads "high brow" novels such as *All the Pretty Horses* and *White Noise*. Although he claims to have no plans to cut back his exercise and pursue more leisurely sports such as swimming or golf, I wouldn't be too sure since Bruce lives in the sunshine state.

Last year, Tuckman was awarded the "University Teaching Award" by Florida State University. He believes that teachers should be experts in what they teach and should combine good organizational skills with instructional activities and discussion. "Planning and preparation are also important ingredients for good teaching," he adds.

His advice to new teachers is threefold: "Believe in yourself, come to class prepared, and try different approaches to learn what works best." He recalls his own efforts at maturing as a teacher: "It took me several years of looking in the mirror and facing myself." Right now, Bruce's latest personal teaching discovery is to give students small quizzes on a frequent basis. "This encourages them to come to class prepared and makes subsequent instruction more meaningful."

4 🐌

The Competent Teacher

Bruce W. Tuckman

What does it mean to be a "competent" teacher? In general, it means to be satisfactorily skilled and able at teaching, but saying that is not particularly illuminating of the issue, because it immediately gives rise to another question. We must now ask what it means to be "skilled" and "able" and what constitutes a "satisfactory" amount. Clearly, defining or describing the "competent " teacher is neither an easy nor an obvious task.

However, providing such a definition or description is an important task for both the training and the evaluation of teachers. In order to train teachers, we must have some definite objectives in mind, things we would like them to know or do or believe, so that we can have a target around which to build our training. Furthermore, in order to evaluate the effectiveness or competence of teachers, we must determine exactly what we expect of them.

Where shall these statements of teacher competencies come from, what shall they be, and how will their presence be determined? These are the questions that this chapter will address. Shall they come from each individual teacher, each specifying the competencies that he or she would like to achieve, or perhaps from a representative group of teachers, representing those competencies they can agree on? Or maybe they should come from students, or from principals, or perhaps from parents? Better yet, should they come from research, the collection of data about what works in classrooms, and what does not work? But then we have to decide upon a criterion for determining what "works."

Defining teaching competence is a puzzle or enigma, and that is likely why no one has arrived at the definitive answer. We will look at a number of possible components including (1) attitudes and beliefs, (2) behavioral competencies, (3) subject-matter competencies, and (4) teaching styles, and see how each contributes to the idea of the competent teacher. But first, let us consider the ways in which people have tried to define or describe teaching competence.

DETERMINING THE CRITERIA OF TEACHING COMPETENCE

There are basically two ways to define a competent teacher. One is on the basis of judgments of or about a teacher. The second is on the basis of the performance of the students that are taught by the teacher. Because the second seems more objective, we will begin with it first.

Measuring the Product of Teaching

If the purpose of teaching is to teach, then its effectiveness should be reflected by how much students learn. If we want to measure a teacher's effectiveness or competence, we should only need to measure how much his or her students learn; the more learned, the better the teaching. Moreover, if we want to identify the ways that competent teachers teach, then we should observe the teaching techniques of those teachers whose students learn the most and see exactly what they do that sets them off from their peers.

In fact, so-called process-product research used that very approach (Good & Brophy, 1991; Porter & Brophy, 1988; Evertson et al., 1993; to name only a few of the many sources). Using scores attained on standardized achievement tests by students in a given teacher's class, while controlling for the prior scores of the same students, teachers were compared, and those presiding over classes showing greater gains were distinguished from those presiding over classes showing lesser gains. In a sense, the "proof of the pudding" is in the results ("the tasting"). In fact, a considerable amount of what we know about teaching competence has come by this route. A sample list of effective instructional techniques identified through process-product research is shown in Table 4.1.

But there are problems with this approach, chief among them being the measure of student achievement. The widespread use of standardized achievement tests is mainly restricted to the elementary grades, and mainly to the subject areas of mathematics and reading/language arts. And even within these areas, more than one test is used and none totally mirrors the material a given teacher is trying to teach. Hence, the test as the measure of the target of teaching is not entirely accurate. Entire topics, areas, subjects, and even domains may be excluded from the measurement of student outcomes. (For example, the criterion measure includes *no* aspect of emotional or attitudinal growth in students, nor does it include thinking or problem-solving skills.)

This shortcoming does not render the entire approach useless, but it is a limiting factor. If it were possible to measure a wider variety of student outcomes in an equivalent way across classrooms using tests that were not only well-constructed but that equally fit the objectives of each classroom, then this approach for evaluating teaching competence or for identifying specific teaching competencies would be more universally accepted. However, such measurement is not even remotely possible without a national standardization of curriculums at all levels of instruction, and that eventuality is neither likely nor, in the eyes of most, desirable. Therefore, we must look carefully for the overlapping findings from studies using this approach, and avoid overgeneralizing any unique results.

Table 4.1 Summary of Key Direct Instructional Techniques

Task	Behaviors
Daily review (first 8 minutes except Mondays)	1. Review the concepts and skills associated with the homework 2. Collect and deal with homework assignments 3. Ask several mental computation questions

Development (about 20 minutes)	1. Briefly focus on prerequisite skills and concepts
	2. Focus on meaning and on promoting student understanding by using lively explanations, demonstrations, process explanations, illustrations, and so on
	3. Assess student comprehension by
	   a. Using process-product questions (active interaction)
	   b. Using controlled practice
	4. Repeat and elaborate on the meaning portion as necessary

Seatwork (about 15 minutes)	1. Provide uninterrupted successful practice 2. Momentum (keep the ball rolling), get everyone involved, then sustain involvement 3. Alerting—let students know their work will be checked at the end of the period 4. Accountability—check the students' work
Homework assignment	1. Assign on a regular basis at the end of each math class except Friday's 2. Should involve about 15 minutes of work to be done at home 3. Should involve one or two review problems

Special reviews	1. Weekly review/maintenance
	   a. Conduct during the first 20 minutes each Monday
	   b. Focus on skills and concepts covered during the previous week
	2. Monthly review/maintenance
	   a. Conduct every fourth Monday
	   b. Focus on skills and concepts covered since last monthly review

Based on Good, Grouws, and Ebermeier, 1983.

Judging the Process of Teaching

Because teaching is a human act, and is considered by many to be as much an art as a skill, the specification of exact teaching competencies is likely to depend on human judgment. Hence, the alternative to the first approach is to try to build some consensus about what teaching behaviors, characteristics, and styles represent effective or competent teaching, based on the judgments of various constituencies as to what good teaching is. When groups or organizations wish to

Table 4.2 Competencies and Skills Required for Teacher Certification in Florida

1. Applies knowledge of physical, social, and academic developmental patterns and of individual differences to meet the instructional needs of all students in the classroom and to advise students about those needs.

2. Enhances students' feelings of dignity and self-worth and the worth of other people: those from other ethnic, cultural, linguistic, and economic groups.

3. Arranges and manages the physical environment to facilitate instruction and ensure student safety.

4. Recognizes overt signs of severe emotional distress in students and demonstrates awareness of appropriate intervention and referral procedures.

5. Recognizes signs of alcohol and drug abuse in students and demonstrates awareness of appropriate intervention and referral procedures.

6. Recognizes the overt physical and behavioral indicators of child abuse and neglect and knows the rights and responsibilities regarding reporting and how to interact appropriately with a child after a report has been made.

7. Formulates a standard for student behavior in the classroom.

8. Deals with misconduct, interruptions, intrusions, and digressions in ways that promote instructional momentum.

9. Determines the entry level knowledge/skills of students for a given set of instructional objectives using diagnostic tests, observations, and student records.

10. Identifies long-range goals for a given subject area.

11. Constructs and sequences related short-range objectives for a given subject area.

12. Selects, adapts, and/or develops instructional materials for a given set of instructional objectives and student learning needs.

13. Selects/develops and sequences learning activities that are appropriate to instructional objectives and student needs.

14. Uses class time efficiently.

15. Communicates effectively using verbal and nonverbal skills.

16. Creates and maintains academic focus by using verbal, nonverbal, and/or visual motivational devices.

17. Presents forms of knowledge such as concepts, laws, and law-like principles, academic rules, and value knowledge.

18. Presents directions appropriate for carrying out an instructional activity.

19. Stimulates and directs student thinking and checks student comprehension through appropriate questioning techniques.

20. Provides appropriate practice to promote learning and retention.

21. Relates to students' verbal communications in ways that encourage participation and maintain academic focus.

22. Uses feedback procedures that give information to students about the appropriateness of their response(s).

23. Conducts reviews of subject matter.

24. Constructs or assembles classroom tests and tasks to measure student achievement of objectives.

25. Establishes a testing environment in which students can validly demonstrate their knowledge and skills and receive adequate information about the quality of their test performance.

26. Utilizes an effective system for maintaining records of students and class progress.

27. Uses computers in education.

Based on Florida Department of Education, 1993.

determine the competencies that teachers should possess, they typically seek input from teachers, school administrators, and teacher educators. Input from parents and students may also be sought. The result is a list like the one shown in Table 4.2, representing the skills and competencies required for teacher certification in the state of Florida.

The judgment process can be expected to yield a variety of lists of teaching competencies, depending upon who is asked and exactly how the question is put. However, as the range of teachers to which any list of competencies is expected to apply becomes broader, the nature of the items on the list can be expected to become broader as well. Thus, the list in Table 4.2 includes considerably broader and less specific items than the one in Table 4.1, reflecting the greater specificity (or perhaps increased narrowness, depending on one's perspective) of the process-product approach. In judging any such list, one must take into account the procedure that was used to generate it.

We will now turn to the specific areas of competence that distinguish the competent teacher.

COMPETENCIES IN ATTITUDES AND BELIEFS

It may sound odd to talk about teachers having attitudes and beliefs that represent competencies, but indeed we often distinguish teachers on the basis of how they regard students and their teachability, both as individuals and collectively. Let us look at four areas in which teacher attitudes and beliefs are regarded as critical to their effectiveness.

Teaching Efficacy

The concept of self-efficacy, as developed by Bandura (1977, 1986), refers to a person's self-perceived capacity to perform a task or carry out a plan of action to deal with a situation. Self-efficacious people believe they have the ability to succeed, while those lacking in self-efficacy do not share this same belief. Teaching efficacy refers to teachers' beliefs about their capacity to affect student performance (Ashton, 1984; Dembo & Gibson, 1985; Greenwood et al., 1990).

Efficacious teachers believe that (1) good teachers can affect students regardless (or in spite of) the circumstances of their home environment, and (2) by trying hard, they, personally, can reach even the most difficult students (Ashton & Webb, 1986). The first factor is sometimes referred to as general teaching efficacy and the second as personal teaching efficacy.

Why is it necessary for a competent teacher to have teaching efficacy? Because, as Ashton (1984) has found, teachers who have it think and do different things in the classroom than teachers who do not have it. Specifically, teachers with teaching efficacy (1) find teaching meaningful and rewarding rather than frustrating and discouraging, (2) expect student success, rather than failure, and tend to get it, (3) look inward for student failure rather than blaming it on students, (4) set goals and develop strategies for themselves and students rather than ignoring these important success-seeking activities, (5) feel good about themselves and their students rather than constantly complaining, (6) feel in control and influential rather than at a loss, and (7) not only share their goals with students but involve students in setting them (Ashton, 1984).

In addition, teachers with strong efficacy beliefs have been shown to elicit greater achievement from their students (process-product) than teachers without strong efficacy beliefs (Ashton, Webb, & Doda, 1983; Ashton & Webb, 1986). Ashton, Webb, and Doda (1983) also showed that at the challenging junior high school level, teachers with strong efficacy beliefs maintained high academic standards, had clear expectations, concentrated on academic instruction, maintained student on-task behavior, and demonstrated "with-it-ness," that quality of seeming to have "eyes in the back of their heads."

Therefore, the competent teacher must be a self-believer, a person who believes that teachers in general and he or she in particular can make a difference in the lives of students. Teachers with this belief have a greater likelihood of succeeding than teachers who believe otherwise.

Locus of Control

Locus of control refers to the location or source of the causes a person perceives for his or her own behavior and the outcomes or reinforcements that result (Rotter, 1966). These causes can be *internal,* or come from within, such as one's own ability or the effort or strategy one adopts in dealing with a situation. Or the causes can be perceived as *external,* or coming from outside oneself, such as fate, luck, or the influence of others. People with an internal locus of control believe their reinforcements are contingent on their own behavior, while those with an external locus of control believe their reinforcements are contingent on forces outside of themselves (Rotter, 1966).

How do competent teachers fall on this attitudinal variable? Murray and Staebler (1974) found that teachers with an internal locus of control, those who believed that people determined their own outcomes, obtained greater student progress in the classroom than teachers with an external locus of control, those who believed that fate or others determined their outcomes. Moreover, internal teachers were less vulnerable to burn-out than external teachers. Rose and

Medway (1981) also found that a more internal locus of control was associated with a lesser degree of perceived stress than a more external locus of control.

Therefore, competent teachers believe that people are responsible for their own outcomes, a generalized belief that obviously contributes to the belief, described above, that they can make a difference in the lives of their students.

Teacher Expectations

While self-efficacy refers to teachers' expectations about their own effectiveness or ability to succeed, expectations here refers to teachers' belief about the ability of students to succeed. This belief is important because it gives rise to what has been called the *self-fulfilling prophecy*, the tendency for teachers' expectations for students' performance to be borne out by students' actual performance, often as a function of the communication of that expectation from teacher to student.

Good (1987) and Good and Brophy (1991) have documented the differences in the way many teachers communicate with high versus low achievers, thereby sending the message of their expectations. In contrast to their treatment of high achievers, teachers often do the following to low achievers: (1) wait less time for them to answer questions, (2) interrupt them more, (3) criticize them more and praise them less, (4) react more often to their responses with indifference, (5) pay less attention to them, (6) call on them less often, (7) interact with them less in private, (8) seat them farther away, and (9) demand less from them.

Given that the above behaviors are likely to limit the effectiveness of teachers, it is important for teachers to have positive expectations for all students, regardless of their achievement history. Competent teachers need to adopt teaching approaches that are consistent with their positive expectations, and that do not discriminate against so-called low achievers, in order to break the self-fulfilling low achievement cycle.

Competent teachers also need to monitor or be aware of their communications with students and the messages that they send. Teachers who do not monitor themselves are much more likely to convey their expectations to students (Sullins, Friedman, & Harris, 1985).

Teacher Enthusiasm

The last teacher attitude is enthusiasm, affecting the degree to which a teacher likes to teach and invests emotional energy in the teaching process. Clark, Boyer, and Corcoran (1985) used the term *vitality* to describe a positive, intangible quality of teachers that led to positive production, sustained commitment, and dedication to beliefs that produce action. Such a quality is related to personal job satisfaction (Lortie, 1975). It is also related to the willingness to take the risks that are required by discovery learning (Robinson, Noyes, & Chandler, 1989).

Enthusiasm or vitality may be a key emotional ingredient of teaching competence. Sederberg and Clark (1990) discovered that teachers high in vitality reported high energy, an internal driving force, "dedication, a missionary zeal, obsession, passion, and consuming" desire in describing their feelings toward teaching (p. 8). Gorham and Zakahi (1990) found that teachers who enjoyed teaching were more likely to react positively to student performance than teachers who did not enjoy teaching, and that this behavior tended to improve the performance of students.

Enthusiasm, like the other affective characteristics described above, seems to be an important part of good teaching. Not only is it important for a new or prospective teacher to start out enthusiastically, by virtue of the desire to become a teacher, but that enthusiasm must be maintained, even in the face of difficulty and occasional failure. Teachers who lose their enthusiasm are likely to lapse into a state of helplessness, thereby reducing their competence to a low level.

BEHAVIORAL COMPETENCIES

To be a competent teacher, one must demonstrate specific teaching behaviors in a range of teaching functions such as planning, instructing, communicating, managing, and evaluating. We shall examine each of these areas in turn.

Planning

Most models of teaching effectiveness cite planning as an important ingredient, with the lesson plan being the primary manifestation. A lesson plan typically includes the following: (1) objectives, (2) motivational strategy, (3) content outline, (4) specification of teaching methodologies (including activities), (5) materials and media, (6) summaries and reviews, and (7) assignments (for example, homework) (Board of Education of the City of New York, 1986). In other words, planning means deciding what you are going to do before you do it. It may also include evaluation.

A competent teacher, therefore, develops a lesson plan prior to teaching a lesson, and that lesson plan includes objectives, content, skills, materials, methods, assignments, and evaluation or some similar or equally complete representation of coverage. The adequacy of the plan could be determined by examining it and looking at its specifics.

Instructing

Instructing is a major aspect of teaching (probably the "most" major), in that it represents the methods and activities teachers use to promote learning in students. All specifications of teacher competencies place heavy emphasis on instructing. How does the competent teacher instruct?

According to secondary school principals (as reported by Arnn & Mangieri, 1988), there are nine effective teacher competencies that fall into the area of instructing. These are described as follows:

1. Keeping the classroom and the students *on task*, meaning academically engaged.

2. Carrying out *direct instruction,* including setting goals, assessing student progress, and making presentations of assigned work. (Also, see Table 4.1 for a description of direct instruction.)

3. *Pacing* the lesson and its difficulty level to the students' abilities and interests.

4. Providing the students with *feedback.*

5. *Asking questions* at different levels and using them appropriately in the lesson.

6. Allocating instructional *time* to fit the lesson.

7. Adapting the teaching method to fit the situation.

8. Employing *organized instructional activities.*

9. Covering the *material* that it is necessary to cover.

The Florida Performance Measurement System, an approach based on process-product research, includes the following ten indicators of effective instruction: (1) beginning instruction promptly; (2) handling material in an orderly manner; (3) orienting students to classwork and maintaining an academic focus; (4) conducting beginning and ending reviews; (5) asking single, factual questions, and questions requiring analysis or reasons; (6) recognizing student responses, amplifying them, and giving corrective feedback; (7) giving specific academic praise; (8) providing for practice; (9) giving directions, assignments, checking comprehension of assignments, and giving feedback; and (10) circulating among and assisting students. It also lists the following four indicators of effective presentation of subject matter: (1) treating attributes, examples, and nonexamples; (2) discussing cause and effect, using linking words, and applying a law or principle; (3) stating and applying an academic rule; and (4) developing criteria and evidence to support a value judgment.

Both approaches are reasonably specific to direct instruction. If one wanted to describe instructional competencies at a high level of generality, they would be restricted to using the technique that fits the students and the situation, using a variety of techniques and adjusting when necessary, presenting information in a clear and concise manner, and using questioning effectively.

Communicating

Communication can take both verbal and nonverbal forms. Within verbal communication, we refer to how teachers transmit information to students. Bellack (1966) identified four verbal behaviors of teachers which he termed (1) structuring, which is primarily procedural, (2) soliciting, or asking questions, (3) responding to student responses, and (4) reacting to other than student responses. Effective teachers use these behaviors, primarily in cycles, proceeding from the first to the last. Most of teachers' verbal communications are oriented toward content, and most of those toward the transmission of facts.

However, there is another distinctly different aspect of teacher communication that has to do with the emotional nature of what teachers say. Ginott (1972) calls communication between teacher and student that is harmonious and authentic, and where words fit feelings, *congruent* communications. Congruent communicators use a language of acceptance that accepts a child's situation. Incongruent communicators use a language of rejection that derogates and degrades a child's character and personality. For example, upon entering the art classroom and seeing a jar of spilled paint, a teacher communicating congruently might say: "I see the paint spilled. We need a rag to clean it up." A teacher communicating incongruently might say: "Why are you so clumsy and careless?"

Communicating verbally involves both sending and receiving messages. Schmuck and Schmuck (1992) suggest that in sending a message, competent communication involves (1) making clear statements (short and understandable), (2) describing one's own behavior, (3) describing one's own feelings, and (4) aiming statements at the level and nature of one's audience. In receiving a message, they suggest (1) paraphrasing what you have heard, (2) describing others' behavior (rather than their character), and (3) checking impressions to see if you are accurately perceiving the message-sender's feelings.

Nonverbal communication in teaching often refers to the choices you make and the emotions you exhibit, particularly the students you choose for different activities and how you react to their performance. To be competent is to be fair; to react to students based on their actual performance and not on their past performance or on what you think their current performance will be. Good and Brophy (1991) reported that teachers reacted differently to students on whom they had called to answer questions depending on whether or not they believed students to be able to perform well. If teachers anticipated good performance from students, they were more likely to react positively, coach them, and wait longer for them to answer than if they anticipated poor performance. In so doing the teachers communicated their feelings indirectly, without actually spelling them out verbally, and perhaps without intending to do so.

Regardless of their intentions, when teachers communicate negative expectations to students through such "causal messages" as facial expressions, hesitation, avoidance, assigning blame, displays of anger, unsolicited and unneeded help, and assignment of easy tasks, they are causing the students who receive these messages to believe that they are lacking in the ability to succeed (Graham & Weiner, 1983). To avoid this tendency, teachers should be (1) mindful or aware of discrepancies in their behavior between different students, so that they can adjust it, and (2) uniformly accepting and encouraging of all students.

Managing

Teachers must also be competent classroom managers, since ideally they must maintain the interest and involvement of twenty-five to thirty children or young adults over an extended period of time. They must also minimize disruptions so that the time spent by students engaged in the learning process can be maximized. How do successful classroom managers behave, or, put differently, what *management functions* do successful classroom managers perform? Doyle (1986) has identified the following sixteen:

1. Establishing classroom activities—defining the order early.

2. Rules and procedures—focusing particularly on potentially disruptive behavior.

3. Academic work and activities—these are governed by procedures for maintaining a group focus and avoiding disruptions.

4. Routines—making the context of instruction stable and predictable.

5. Enacting processes—specifying when and what student talk is permitted.

6. Hidden curriculum—emphasizing following directions, accepting responsibility, and working diligently.

7. Monitoring—watching everything (groups, behavior, pace) and reacting quickly.

8. Maintaining group lessons—keeping everybody involved.

9. Seatwork—using it; monitoring it.

10. Transitions—without losing momentum.

11. Engaged time—routines help maximize this.

12. Cueing—verbal and nonverbal messages or signals.

13. Maintaining academic work—breaking down big tasks into smaller ones.

14. Cooperative learning teams—small group work.

15. Subject matter as procedure—practice and drill assignments that can be carried out one after another.

16. Teacher expectations—using ability grouping to help activities flow.

Competent classroom managers maintain their poise and dignity; they stay calm and businesslike and avoid talking too much. But they do expect order, attention, and rule following, and they act quickly and with determination to maintain control and overcome disruptions when they do occur.

Evaluating

To be considered competent, a teacher must know how to evaluate students, since evaluation is an important and frequent duty a teacher performs. Since most evaluation of student achievement is based on test performance, a competent teacher must be able to construct tests, to improve tests once constructed, and to score tests—all three activities being done in such a way as to enhance the validity and reliability of the results.

To construct tests, teachers must be able to (1) prepare a content outline, (2) write objectives in measurable terms, (3) construct test items that fit both the content outline and the objectives, and (4) validate that each item indeed reflects the action called for in the matching objective (Tuckman, 1988). Teachers must also be able to follow the rules of writing good short-answer test items (Tuckman, 1992).

To score tests, teachers must be familiar with scoring approaches, with the pitfalls or traps that make scoring inaccurate, and with ways of overcoming these potential influences. For example, teachers should know to cover the name of the student writing the answer, to randomize the order in which answers are read, and to read answers more than once (Tuckman, 1992). Teachers must also know how to use their results to improve their existing tests, and to improve their own ability to construct and score tests.

Evaluating also requires that teachers know how to interpret standardized test scores so that they can (1) communicate them to parents, (2) use them to help individual students, and (3) use them to help improve their own instruction. Also, since evaluating means grading, teachers must know about norm-referencing and criterion-referencing, and how to convert test scores into grades.

Finally, teachers must know about evaluative techniques other than formal testing, so that they can use them with their students. Teachers must know how to collect observational data, how to evaluate performance, how to judge thinking skills, how to judge projects, and how to assess behavior. Many of the same rules that govern test construction and scoring can be brought to bear in using these other approaches.

SUBJECT-MATTER COMPETENCIES

In addition to knowing how to teach, being a competent teacher requires knowing what you teach. It also requires a general subject-matter competency that is often referred to as literacy.

Literacy

Competent teachers should be expected to have general knowledge, as well as be able to read, write, and compute well. They should be familiar with basic facts in science and in the political realm including current events. Regardless of what a teacher teaches, these basic literacy skills can be expected to apply. Without them, a teacher will have difficulty communicating, formulating lessons, and establishing credibility. Literacy and teaching competence seem to be closely related in that the former is a prerequisite for the latter.

Knowing Your Subject

Teachers should have expertise in the subject or subjects they teach. To teach art history, one must know art history. So too with grammar, algebra, the political structure of South American countries, and so on. It would seem a truism, and in little need of elaboration, to say that teachers must know what they teach.

TEACHING STYLE

Tuckman (1974, 1991) has described a model of teaching that reflects the interpersonal style or manner by which the teacher relates to the teaching environment and the students in it. The model reflects the personal constructs the teacher uses to manage the teaching/learning environment, and contains five dimensions that are described below. The instrument for measuring interpersonal style, *The Tuckman Teacher Feedback Form*, appears in Table 4.3. It is a set of thirty scales, each anchored at its ends by a pair of bipolar adjectives, chosen to define the meaning of a particular aspect of teaching style. The individual bipolar scales cluster into the five major dimensions that follow.

Organized Demeanor

Competence in this area means being organized, efficient, orderly, clear, in control, confident, and aware. The *organized* teacher functions in a managerial way by being completely prepared for the teaching task. Writing objectives and planning, as described earlier, are ways the organized teacher prepares to deal with a lesson and the students to which it is to be taught.

Dynamism

Competence in this area means being outgoing, bubbly, lively, aggressive, outgoing, and independent. The *dynamic* teacher uses energy, force, charisma, and what was earlier called enthusiasm or vitality, to control the attention of students and enable them to focus on what is being taught. In some ways the dynamic teacher is like an actor playing a teaching role on the classroom "stage."

Flexibility

Competence in this area means being flexible, sensitive, easygoing, and lenient, or being inclined on occasion to let things go their own way. The *flexible* teacher knows when to change or to allow rules to be broken in order to keep the instructional process flowing in the classroom.

Warmth and Acceptance

Competence in this area means being warm, accepting of others, caring, likeable, patient, polite, and modest. The *warm and accepting* teacher is a "humanist," influencing student behavior by developing relationships and providing support. Being this way means using congruent communication, as previously described. Warm and accepting teachers make personality work as an aid to teaching.

Table 4.3 The Tuckman Teacher Feedback Form

Person Observed _____ Observer _____

Date _____

TUCKMAN TEACHER FEEDBACK FORM (STUDENT EDITION)

MY TEACHER IS

1	DISORGANIZED	①	②	③	④	⑤	⑥	⑦	ORGANIZED
2	CLEAR	①	②	③	④	⑤	⑥	⑦	UNCLEAR
3	AGGRESSIVE	①	②	③	④	⑤	⑥	⑦	SOFT-SPOKEN
4	CONFIDENT	①	②	③	④	⑤	⑥	⑦	UNCERTAIN
5	COMMONPLACE	①	②	③	④	⑤	⑥	⑦	CLEVER
6	CREATIVE	①	②	③	④	⑤	⑥	⑦	ORDINARY
7	OLD FASHIONED	①	②	③	④	⑤	⑥	⑦	MODERN
8	LIKEABLE	①	②	③	④	⑤	⑥	⑦	"STUCK UP"
9	EXCITING	①	②	③	④	⑤	⑥	⑦	BORING
10	SENSITIVE	①	②	③	④	⑤	⑥	⑦	ROUGH
11	LIVELY	①	②	③	④	⑤	⑥	⑦	LIFELESS
12	ACCEPTS PEOPLE	①	②	③	④	⑤	⑥	⑦	CRITICAL
13	SNOBBY	①	②	③	④	⑤	⑥	⑦	MODEST
14	CONFUSED	①	②	③	④	⑤	⑥	⑦	ORDERLY
15	STRICT	①	②	③	④	⑤	⑥	⑦	LENIENT
16	IN CONTROL	①	②	③	④	⑤	⑥	⑦	ON THE RUN
17	TRADITIONAL	①	②	③	④	⑤	⑥	⑦	ORIGINAL
18	WARM	①	②	③	④	⑤	⑥	⑦	COLD
19	RUDE	①	②	③	④	⑤	⑥	⑦	POLITE
20	WITHDRAWN	①	②	③	④	⑤	⑥	⑦	OUTGOING
21	EASYGOING	①	②	③	④	⑤	⑥	⑦	DEMANDING
22	OUTSPOKEN	①	②	③	④	⑤	⑥	⑦	SHY
23	UNCHANGEABLE	①	②	③	④	⑤	⑥	⑦	FLEXIBLE
24	QUIET	①	②	③	④	⑤	⑥	⑦	BUBBLY
25	AWARE	①	②	③	④	⑤	⑥	⑦	FORGETFUL
26	"NEW IDEAS"	①	②	③	④	⑤	⑥	⑦	SAME OLD THING
27	IMPATIENT	①	②	③	④	⑤	⑥	⑦	PATIENT
28	UNCARING	①	②	③	④	⑤	⑥	⑦	CARING
29	DEPENDENT	①	②	③	④	⑤	⑥	⑦	INDEPENDENT
30	UNPLANNED	①	②	③	④	⑤	⑥	⑦	EFFICIENT

Creativity

Competence in this area means being creative, exciting, clever, original, modern, and having new ideas. The *creative* teacher does things differently, perhaps unconventionally, in order to help students learn. Often, the environment is arranged creatively so that students can discover what is to be learned rather than having it told to them.

THEORY INTO PRACTICE

An important question being asked today is how we can tell whether or not a teacher is competent. Let us suggest some possible answers to this question based on what has been presented in this chapter.

Measure Student Achievement

As was suggested at the beginning of the chapter, competent teachers cause students to learn. Therefore, to measure teacher competence just measure student learning. As was said earlier, there may not be a way to perform this measurement that is sufficiently valid and reliable. Where comparable standardized tests are regularly given to students, as in the elementary grades, this approach could be employed. Teachers whose students show sufficient achievement gains from year to year would be considered competent.

This approach would probably win few friends among teachers. Many are the vicissitudes that affect student performance, only one of which is the teacher. Holding the teacher accountable for something that is the product of many forces seems somewhat unfair.

Test the Teachers

Subject-matter knowledge and literacy can be tested, and typically are, as prerequisites to getting a certificate to teach. Attitudes and beliefs are also testable, but these tests are subject to distortion by respondents who choose to be careful not to show themselves in a "poor" light. Beyond these, teachers may be tested on their knowledge of how to teach, but knowing how to do something and actually being willing and able to do it are not the same thing. One can describe in detail how to hit a golf ball or perform a complex dive, but not be able to do either in a skillful way. Similarly, a teacher may be able to tell you how a difficult classroom situation should be handled but, when faced with one, reacts in a completely different manner. Testing for knowledge clearly has its limitations in assessing teaching competency.

Ask the Students

At the college level it is common to ask students to evaluate teachers, and their input is often quite legitimate and revealing. However, the questions asked will have an effect on the answers. Most student rating forms ask about organization and enthusiasm, but not about the creativity required to depart from the traditional lecture format. In addition, student judgments tend to reflect popularity and grade expectations. Teachers who expect more of their students often get lower ratings than those whose requirements are easier to meet. Finally, younger students would be less able to render an accurate and useful judgment than older ones, so the approach has limited practicality. Student judgments may be a necessary part of the evaluation, but they certainly are not sufficient in themselves.

Observe the Teachers

To evaluate many aspects of teaching, it probably has to be observed. But this too poses problems. Who shall observe? What shall they look for? How can we be sure that they really saw it? These three questions immediately come to mind. Moreover, it would be a costly and time-consuming process that requires paid, trained observers and multiple observations to be done right. Think of the performance ratings made in athletic events: figure skating, diving, synchronized swimming, and gymnastics, to name a few. Despite the number of judges and their level of expertise, controversy about their judgments seems to be the rule rather than the exception. Therefore, even the observational approach, despite potentially being the best, would have its limitations.

Ask the Right People

With all its failings, this is the way teaching competence is most often judged. We ask the principal, the assistant principals, the department heads, other teachers, even parents, and when we consistently hear the same names, we conclude that those are the most competent teachers. That is a far cry from where we started out, measuring student achievement, but it is the way the culture of teaching, like many other professional cultures (for example, law, medicine), works. We obviously have a long way to go before we can adequately assess teaching competence.

SUMMARY

The criteria of teaching competence have been determined by two methods. The first, called the process-product approach, identifies teachers whose students have shown the greatest achievement test gains, and then observes them to see what teaching behaviors they use. The alternative method relies on judgments, often by school administrators, teacher educators, or groups of teachers themselves.

Teaching competency covers a variety of aspects of teachers and the ways they teach. One aspect of teaching competency is in terms of attitudes and beliefs that teachers hold. Competent teachers believe in teaching efficacy; believe they can have an impact on student learning even among the most difficult students. They also have an internal locus of control, or the belief that what happens to them is caused by factors internal to themselves, such as ability or effort.

Third, they have positive expectations about their students, that is, they believe their students can succeed. Fourth, they believe teaching to be exciting and fulfilling, which makes them enthusiastic teachers.

Competent teachers also behave in competent ways. These behavioral competencies can be found in the planning that they do thoroughly; in the instructing that they do in direct and appropriate form, being both clear and concise; in their communicating that is congruent, authentic, and includes positive rather than negative messages; in their managing that effectively keeps students on task and minimizes disruptions; and in their evaluating that includes well-written, well-scored tests, and other forms of performance assessment.

Competent teachers are also literate, meaning they can read, write, and compute, and have basic knowledge in science and social science, and subject-matter knowledgeable, meaning they are expert in the content they teach. As regards their interpersonal style, they are organized, dynamic, flexible, warm and accepting, and creative.

There are a number of ways we can determine whether a teacher is competent. These include measuring the achievement of their students, testing them, asking their students, observing them, or asking their administrators, colleagues, and the parents of the students they teach. Each of these approaches introduces a bias or inaccuracy into the process, but so far no one has been able to come up with the perfect way.

References

Arnn, J. W., and J. N. Mangieri (1988). "Effective Leadership for Effective Schools: A Survey of Principal Attitudes." *NASSP Bulletin* 72: 1–7.

Ashton, P. T. (1984). "Teacher Efficacy: A Motivational Paradigm for Effective Teacher Education." *Journal of Teacher Education* 35: 28–32.

Ashton, P. T., and R. B. Webb (1986). *Making a Difference: Teachers' Sense of Efficacy and Student Achievement.* New York: Longman.

Ashton, P. T., R. B. Webb, and N. Doda (1983). "A Study of Teachers' Sense of Efficacy." Final Report. Gainesville, FL: University of Florida (ERIC # ED 231 834).

Bandura, A. (1977). "Self-Efficacy: Toward a Unifying Theory of Behavioral Change." *Psychological Review* 84:191–215.

Bandura, A. (1986). *Social Foundations of Thought and Action: A Social Cognitive Theory.* Englewood Cliffs, NJ: Prentice Hall.

Bellack, A. A. (1966). *The Language of the Classroom.* New York: Teachers College Press, Columbia University.

Board of Education of the City of New York (1986). *Getting Started in the Elementary School: A Manual for New Teachers,* rev. ed. New York: New York City Board of Education.

Clark, S. M., C. M. Boyer, and M. Corcoran (1985). "Faculty and Institutional Vitality in Higher Education," in S. M. Clark and D. R. Lewis, eds., *Faculty Vitality and Institutional Productivity: Critical Perspectives for Higher Education.* New York: Teachers College Press, Columbia University, pp. 1–24.

Dembo, M. H., and S. Gibson (1985). "Teachers' Sense of Efficacy: An Important Factor in School Improvement." *Elementary School Journal* 86:173–184.

Doyle, W. (1986). "Classroom Organization and Management," in M. C. Wittrock, ed., *Handbook of Research on Teaching,* 3rd ed. New York: Macmillan, pp. 392–431.

Evertson, C., et al. (1993). *Classroom Management for Elementary Teachers,* 3rd ed.

Englewood Cliffs, NJ: Prentice Hall.

Florida Department of Education (1993). *Competencies and Skills Required for Teacher Certification in Florida,* 3rd ed. Tallahassee, FL: Department of Education.

Ginott, H. (1972). *Teacher and Child.* New York: Macmillan.

Good, T. L. (1987). "Two Decades of Research on Teacher Expectations." *Journal of Teacher Education* July–August: 32–47.

Good, T. L., and J. E. Brophy (1991). *Looking in Classrooms,* 5th ed. New York: Harper-Collins.

Good, T. L., D. Grouws, and H. Ebermeier (1983). *Active Mathematics Teaching.* New York: Longman.

Gorham, J., and W. R. Zakahi (1990). "A Comparison of Teacher and Student Perceptions of Immediacy and Learning: Monitoring Process and Product." *Communication Education* 39: 354–368.

Graham, S., and B. Weiner (1983). "Some Educational Implications of Sympathy and Anger from an Attributional Perspective," in R. Shaw and M. Farr, eds., *Cognition, Affect, and Instruction.* Hillsdale, NJ: Lawrence Erlbaum, pp. 199–221.

Greenwood, G. E., S. F. Olejnik, and F. W. Parkay (1990). "Relationships Between Four Teacher Efficacy Belief Patterns and Selected Teacher Characteristics." *Journal of Research and Development in Education* 23: 102–106.

Lortie, D. C. (1975). *Schoolteacher: A Sociological Study.* Chicago: University of Chicago Press.

Murray, H. B., and B. K. Staebler (1974). "Teacher's Locus of Control and Student Achievement Gains." *Journal of School Psychology* 12: 305–309.

Porter, A. C., and J. E. Brophy (1988). "Synthesis of Research on Good Teaching." *Educational Leadership* 45: 74–85.

Robinson, W. P., P. Noyes, and P. Chandler (1989). "Motivational and Attitudinal Predictors of Judged Quality of Novice Primary Teachers." *Teaching and Teacher Education* 5: 179–187.

Rose, J. S., and F. J. Medway (1981). "Measurement of Teachers' Beliefs in Their Control Over Student Outcome." *Journal of Educational Research* 74: 185–190.

Rotter, J. B. (1966). "Generalized Expectancies for Internal versus External Control of Reinforcement." *Psychological Monograph* 80, whole no. 609.

Schmuck, R. A., and P. A. Schmuck (1992). *Group Processes in the Classroom,* 6th ed. Dubuque, IA: Wm. C. Brown.

Sederberg, C. H., and S. Clark (1990). "Motivation and Organizational Incentives for High Vitality Teachers: A Qualitative Perspective." *Journal of Research and Development in Education* 24: 6–13.

Sullins, E. S., H. S. Friedman, and M. J. Harris (1985). "Individual Differences in Expressive Style as a Mediator of Expectancy Communication." *Journal of Nonverbal Behavior* 9: 229–238.

Tuckman, B. W. (1974). "The Application of Psychological Constructs," in R. T. Hyman, ed., *Teaching: Vantage Points for Study,* 2nd ed. Philadelphia: Lippincott, pp. 295–307.

Tuckman, B. W. (1988). *Testing for Teachers,* 2nd ed. San Diego, CA: Harcourt Brace Jovanovich.

Tuckman, B. W. (1991). "Derivation and Description of an Interpersonal Construct Model of Teaching to Help Student Teachers Self-actualize." Paper presented at annual meeting of the American Educational Research Association, Chicago.

Tuckman, B. W. (1992). *Educational Psychology: From Theory to Application.* Fort Worth, TX: Harcourt Brace.

Tuckman, B. W., and D. S. Yates (1980). "Evaluating the Student Feedback Strategy for Changing Teacher Style." *Journal of Educational Research* 74: 74–77.

Discussion Questions

1. Should teachers be held accountable for how much students learn? If you believe they should, to what extent should they be? If you believe they should not, explain why not.

2. Look at Table 4.2, the list of twenty-seven teaching competencies. In your estimation, which are the ten most important? How would you justify your choices?

3. What can be done in schools to help teachers believe they can make a difference in the lives of their students? Can anything be done to increase the enthusiasm of experienced teachers?

4. What do you think is the best way to determine a teacher's competency in planning, communicating, instructing, managing, and evaluating? Should it be determined, and if so, by whom?

5. How would you describe yourself on the five dimensions of teaching style described by Tuckman? What steps can you take to change or improve yourself on any of the five?

Hersholt C. Waxman

Hersholt C. Waxman is the associate dean for research in the College of Education and associate professor in curriculum and instruction at the University of Houston. He is also a senior research associate at the National Research Center on Education in the Inner Cities. Dr. Waxman is a former president of the Southwest Educational Research Association and a recent recipient of the Distinguished Alumni Award from the College of Education at the University of Illinois at Chicago, where he received his Ph.D. in 1982. After obtaining his Ph.D., Hersh received a postdoctorate fellowship at the Learning Research and Development Center at the University of Pittsburgh. He joined the faculty at the University of Houston in 1983 and received the University of Houston Teaching Excellence Award in 1988.

Hersh has conducted many field-based studies in the areas of classroom instruction, teacher education, school effectiveness, classroom learning environments, student learning, instructional technology, and students at risk. He has written over 100 chapters and articles in those areas. He has recently co-edited four books: *Leadership, Equity, and School Effectiveness* (Sage, 1990), *Effective Teaching: Current Research* (National Society for the Student of Education, 1991), *Students at Risk in At-Risk Schools* (Corwin, 1992), and *Research Approaches on Technology and Teacher Education* (Association for the Advancement of Computer Education, 1993).

Hersh has previously taught elementary and middle school in the Chicago public schools, and in the past ten years he has worked collaboratively with many school districts in the Houston metropolitan area. His five-year-old son, David, attends kindergarten at Hairgrove Elementary School and his wife, Yolanda, is an associate professor in education at the University of Houston—Clear Lake. For fun Hersh and his family enjoy attending the University of Houston's football games and then eating fajitas at Ninta's restaurant.

Over the past fifteen years, Hersh and his colleagues have been involved in many national, regional, and local research projects that have used classroom observations. One day he plans to write a book describing some of the best teachers he has observed. For Waxman, an effective teacher is someone "who motivates students, engages in active teaching, and encourages high-level thought processes among his or her students."

5 ❧

Classroom Observations of Effective Teaching

Hersholt C. Waxman

This chapter describes the use of classroom observation methods to investigate processes and behaviors that actually occur in classrooms. The chapter briefly summarizes research from the last two decades that has employed systematic classroom observation techniques to investigate effective teaching at the elementary, middle, and high school levels. Three specific areas where systematic classroom observation has been found to be especially useful for educational practice are highlighted: (1) the improvement of teachers' classroom instruction based on feedback from individual classroom profiles, (2) the investigation of instructional inequities for different groups of students, and (3) the improvement of teacher education programs. Some of the criticisms and cautions related to the use of structured observation techniques are also described. Finally, a recent example of how feedback from classroom observational data can be used by teachers to improve their instruction is described.

Descriptions of Systematic Classroom Observation

One area that has important implications for the improvement of teaching and student learning is the use of classroom observation methods to investigate processes and behaviors that actually occur in classrooms. In the last three decades, there has been a great deal of research that has employed systematic classroom observation techniques in order to investigate effective teaching at the elementary, middle, and high school levels (Brophy & Good, 1986; Stallings & Mohlman, 1988). Medley (1982) defines systematic classroom observation as a "scheme that specifies both the events that the observer is to record and the procedure to be used in recording them" (p. 1842). Generally, the data that is collected from this procedure focuses on the frequency with which specific behaviors or types of behaviors occurred in the classroom and the length of time they occurred. There are several elements that are common to most observational systems: (1) a purpose for the observation, (2) operational definitions of all the observed behaviors, (3) training procedures for observers, (4) a specific observational focus, (5) a setting, (6) a unit of time, (7) an observation schedule, (8) a method to record the data, and (9) a method to process and analyze data (Stallings & Mohlman, 1988).

Prior to the use of systematic observational methods, research on effective teaching typically consisted of subjective data based on personal and anecdotal accounts of effective teaching (Nuthall & Alton-Lee, 1990). In order to develop a scientific basis for teaching, researchers began to use the more objective and reliable measures of systematic classroom observation. In the past three decades, several hundred different observational systems have been developed and used in classrooms (Anderson & Burns, 1989). Similarly, there have been hundreds of studies that have used classroom observation systems during the past three decades.

There are several types of observational procedures or techniques that have been used to examine effective teaching (for example, charts, rating scales, checklists, and narrative descriptions), but systematic classroom observation based on interactive coding systems has been the most widely used procedure or research method. These interactive coding systems allow the observer to record nearly everything that students and teachers do during a given time interval (Stallings & Mohlman, 1988). These interactive systems are very objective and typically do not require the observer to make any high inferences or judgments about the behaviors they observe in the classroom. In other words, such low-inference observational systems provide specific and easily identifiable behaviors that observers can easily code (Stodolsky, 1990).

Some of the major strengths of using classroom observation are that they (1) permit researchers to study the processes of education in naturalistic settings, (2) provide more detailed and precise evidence than other data sources, and (3) can be used to stimulate change and verify that the change occurred (Anderson & Burns, 1989). The descriptions of instructional events that are provided by this method have also been found to lead to improved understanding and better models for improving teaching (Copley & Williams, 1992, 1993; Good & Biddle, 1988).

A final strength of this research method is that the findings from these observational studies have provided a coherent, well-substantiated knowledge base about effective instruction. Many of the reviews and summaries of the classroom observation research have consistently found that a number of classroom behaviors significantly relate to students' academic achievement (Brophy & Good, 1986; Rosenshine, 1987; Walberg, 1986, 1991). Several aspects of classroom instruction such as (1) conducting daily reviews, (2) presenting new material, (3) conducting guided practice, (4) providing feedback and correctives, (5) conducting independent practice, and (6) conducting weekly and monthly reviews have been found to be significantly related to students' academic achievement

(Rosenshine, 1987). In other words, research using classroom observations has provided a substantial knowledge base that has allowed us to better understand effective teaching.

PURPOSES OF CLASSROOM OBSERVATION

Classroom observation has many valid and important educational purposes. For example, it has been used to evaluate programs and, more specifically, to evaluate the fidelity or degree of implementation of a program (Stallings & Freiberg, 1991). It has been used in school effectiveness studies to investigate observable differences between effective and ineffective schools (Teddlie, Kirby, & Stringfield, 1989). This section summarizes three of the most important purposes or areas where systematic classroom observation has been widely used. These major purposes are (1) the improvement of classroom instruction, (2) the detection of inequities in classroom instruction, and (3) the improvement of teacher education programs. The following subsections describe each of these purposes.

Improving Teaching

One of the traditional problems hindering teachers' effectiveness has been the lack of valid and accurate information that teachers could use to facilitate their professional growth (Johnson, 1974). Many teachers, even experienced ones, are not always aware of the nature of their interactions with individual students (Doyle, 1979). Consequently, one of the most important purposes of systematic classroom observation is to improve teachers' classroom instruction (Stallings & Freiberg, 1991; Stallings, Needels, & Stayrook, 1979). Feedback from individual classroom profiles derived from systematic observations has been found to help teachers understand their own strengths and weaknesses and has consequently enabled them to significantly improve their instruction. One of the important practical implications of using systematic classroom observations is that they provide teachers with feedback that allows them to see their own instructional strengths and weaknesses. Through feedback, teachers can become aware of how their classroom functions and thus bring about changes they desire (Brophy, 1979; Stallings, Needels, & Sparks, 1987). This process typically involves having trained observers systematically observe teachers and students in their classrooms and subsequently provide teachers with information about their instruction in clinical sessions. This approach is based on the assumption that teachers value accurate information that they can use to improve their instruction.

There is growing evidence that feedback from systematic observations can be used to improve teaching (Stallings & Freiberg, 1991). Several studies have found that teachers could positively change their attitudes and behaviors toward pupils after receiving feedback from classroom observations (Ebmeier & Good, 1979; Good & Brophy, 1974; Good & Grouws, 1979; Stallings, 1980). Good and Brophy's (1974) "Treatment Study" exemplifies this type of research. In that study, teachers were given feedback based on forty hours of classroom observation. As a result of this "one-shot" interview where feedback was given, teachers' interaction patterns changed, and their attitudes toward individual students changed too. Stallings (1980), Ebmeier and Good (1979), and Good and Grouws (1979) have utilized similar strategies in other projects. In those studies, teachers were presented with individual feedback regarding their classroom instruction and then were found to change their behavior in desirable ways. All these studies have found that teachers can improve their classroom instruction given appropriate feedback and suggestions for improvement.

The overall findings from this research clearly suggest that feedback from classroom observations is a viable and effective mechanism for providing teachers with the information they need about their classroom behavior. This feedback is intended to create what Heider (1958) calls an "imbalance" in teachers' perceptions of their own behaviors. This imbalance exists whenever teachers find out that their attitudes or perceptions of their teaching differ from those of trained observers. Teachers in such a state of "imbalance" are motivated to do something about their behavior in order to restore themselves to a balanced condition (Gage, 1972). A similar notion is that self-awareness increases teachers' control of their actions and the possibility that they will modify them (Feiman, 1981). Consequently, the use of feedback from classroom observations appears to be a potent strategy that can improve conditions in specific classrooms and schools. A more specific example of how this strategy can be used will be described later in the Theory into Practice section of this chapter.

Identifying Instructional Inequities

A second area where systematic classroom observation has been found to be beneficial is in investigating instructional inequities for different groups of students. Classroom observation can answer some important questions like, are some students being treated differently in the classroom, and does that explain why some students learn more than others? Often this issue has been defined as differences in opportunity to learn or inequitable allocation of instruction. Another way of asking this question is, to what extent is there variation in the quality and quantity of instruction that students experience in school, and does that variation explain inequality in educational outcomes?

Several studies have found that some groups or types of students are treated differently by teachers in classrooms and that these inequitable patterns of teacher-student interaction in classrooms result in differential learning outcomes for students (Fennema & Peterson, 1987). There have been many studies, for example, that have found gender imbalances in teachers' interaction patterns in the classroom. Brophy and Good's (1974) review of the research found that consistent sex differences exist in teachers' interaction patterns in the classroom. Boys typically have been found to receive more praise and criticism in the classroom than girls. They also found that teachers have more behavioral, procedural, and academic interactions with boys than with girls. Boys have also been found to ask more questions in the classroom, and teachers have been found to ask boys more questions.

Other studies have looked at both sex- and ethnic-related differences in the classroom. Hart (1989) examined the relationship between teacher-student interaction and mathematics achievement by race and sex. She found that (1) white and black male students had more classroom interactions than students from other groups, (2) there was a disparity in the type of interaction between white and black students, and (3) boys were involved in more public interactions with teachers than girls. In other words, it appears that patterns of teacher-student interaction may be influenced not only by the sex of the student, but also by the ethnicity of the student.

The findings from these classroom observational studies have important policy implications for schools. If differential classroom behaviors are found to exist by sex and ethnicity, policy makers may need to specifically examine the quality and quantity of classroom instruction for some groups of students and determine if appropriate instructional improvements are needed. Future studies may also want to examine teachers' expectations and/or the classroom behavior of teachers to see if they impact the classroom behavior of individual students.

Improving Preservice Teacher Education Programs

While there are conflicting findings regarding the research on the effects of early field experiences (Waxman & Walberg, 1986), there is some evidence that systematic classroom observation is an effective component of preservice teacher education programs (Freiberg & Waxman, 1988a; Merkley & Hoy, 1992–93; Timm & Marchant, 1992; Waxman, Rodriguez, Padron, & Knight, 1988). Systematic observation of classroom teachers provides prospective teachers with the opportunity to actually observe specific teaching behaviors that are emphasized in their teacher education courses. It allows prospective teachers the opportunity to integrate what they are learning in their teacher education courses with the realities of the classroom. Furthermore, such focused observations allow prospective teachers to see how classroom instruction can differentially influence student behavioral and affective outcomes.

Waxman, Rodriguez, Padron, and Knight (1988) illustrated how the use of systematic classroom observation can be an important component of teacher education programs. Not only did the prospective teachers in the study observe some of the teaching skills that were emphasized in their teacher education courses, but they also observed how those instructional behaviors differentially affected student outcomes. Merkley and Hoy (1992–93) found that observation improved preservice teachers' ability to describe selected classroom teaching behaviors and cite significantly more examples than students in the control group that received a traditional lecture and written material about a classroom lesson.

Systematic classroom observation can provide a common language for describing effective teaching. Such observations enable prospective teachers to focus on specific teaching skills that they have been learning about in their pedagogy courses. Many of the prospective teachers in the Waxman et al. (1988) study, for example, indicated that the systematic observations were the most beneficial aspect of the course for them. They also reported that their observations helped them become more aware of the social reality of teaching from the teacher's perspective.

Another area where systematic classroom observation can help prospective teachers is during the student teaching phase. Freiberg, Waxman, and Houston (1987) used systematic classroom observation to provide feedback to student teachers. In their experimental study, one group of student teachers received traditional supervision from a university supervisor, a second group of student teachers received the traditional supervision and systematic feedback about their classroom instruction from the Stallings Observational System (SOS), and the third group of student teachers received the systematic feedback, engaged in self-analysis, and received feedback from their peers. At the end of the student-teaching semester, student teachers who engaged in the self-analysis and collegial feedback significantly improved their classroom instruction in desired directions, while the student teachers in the other two groups did not improve their instruction. The implications from this study clearly suggest that when student teachers receive systematic feedback about their classroom instruction, engage in discussions about their instruction with their peers and supervisors, and conduct further self-analyses of their own teaching, they are likely to improve their instruction. The findings from this study also suggest that systematic feedback alone may not be sufficient to improve the instruction of student teachers.

LIMITATIONS OF CLASSROOM OBSERVATION

While the previous sections highlighted some of the important purposes of classroom observation, there have also been several criticisms and cautions related to the use of structured observation techniques (Evertson & Green, 1986; Galton, 1988). In the following sections, the criticisms and limitations of using structured observation techniques are categorized into two subsections: (1) Methodological and Pragmatic Concerns, and (2) Theoretical and Epistemological Criticisms. This section also includes a brief discussion of the implications of classroom observation and some new directions.

Methodological and Pragmatic Concerns

Most observational techniques have many limitations. Some of these concerns or limitations are related to methodological issues that can interfere with the drawing of valid conclusions. Other concerns are more pragmatic and focus on the practicality of conducting observational research.

One of the primary methodological concerns or source of invalidity that needs to be addressed regarding the use of systematic observational techniques relates to the obtrusiveness of the technique. Observer effects may occur due to the fact that teachers and students are aware that their behaviors are being observed. This may result in reactive effects such as evaluation apprehension or socially desirable responding that can interfere with the drawing of valid inferences about what normally occurs in the classroom.

There are other methodological concerns that are related to the actual amount of time that is necessary to obtain a valid observation, as well as the appropriate number of observations that are required to obtain reliable and valid measures of instruction. Similarly, there are a number of methodological concerns related to the analyses of data. Most of these concerns address the issue of what appropriate level of analysis (for example, student, the class, or students within class) should be used when analyzing the observation data.

Another concern related to prior classroom observation research is that it has typically been generic (that is, generalizing across grade levels and content areas), rather than focused on a given grade level and/or subject area (Anderson & Burns, 1989; Gage, 1985; Needels & Gage, 1991; Ornstein, 1991). Similarly, the content of the lesson is often neglected as well as the quality of the interaction that is being recorded (Anderson & Burns, 1989).

One of the primary pragmatic concerns of observation research is that it is costly because it requires extensive training as well as time for someone to actually do the observations. Some training programs for observers, for example, require as much as seven full days of intensive training before the observations are conducted in classrooms (Stallings & Freiberg, 1991). Gaining access to schools and classrooms to conduct observations is another serious concern. Many school districts are reluctant to allow researchers to observe in their schools because they feel it would be too disruptive to the learning environment.

A final pragmatic concern relates to the misuse of classroom observation data. Classroom observation can be very useful as a formative evaluation procedure, but it should not be used to provide summative decisions such as whether or not a teacher should be dismissed or rehired. Similarly, classroom observation should not be tied to summative decisions like salary increases. Unfortunately, several school districts and state departments of education have misused this observational research and translated findings into specific rules or standards that they have used in developing evaluation instruments (Ornstein, 1991). These misuses are more "accidents" of the research, however, than problems associated with the "essence" of the research (Needels & Gage, 1991).

Theoretical and Epistemological Criticisms

Although observational research has produced a substantial body of research findings, there is still a lack of consensus or lack of confidence regarding the research (Nuthall & Alton-Lee, 1990). In addition to the previously discussed methodological and pragmatic concerns, there have been many theoretical and epistemological criticisms of classroom observational process-product research (Doyle, 1977; Evertson & Green, 1986; Fenstermacher, 1978; Galton, 1988; Popkewitz, Tabachnick, & Zeichner, 1979; Winne & Marx, 1977; Winne, 1987). Several critics, for example, have argued that this research is devoid of theory or is atheoretical, and consequently cannot explain why some instructional behaviors impact student outcomes. There are also similarly related concerns about why some variables are selected to be observed, while others are not. Because there is no model or theory behind the research, critics argue that there is no justification for the selection of variables nor meaningfulness associated with the interpretation of results. They further argue that the selection of events or behaviors may not be clear to anyone except the observer. In other words, these critics argue that this research paradigm has not dealt with the theoretical assumptions of why a particular style of teaching or set of instructional variables influences student learning.

Popkewitz, Tabachnick, and Zeichner (1979) argue that process-product research has a behaviorist orientation that maintains that "it is possible to identify, control, and manipulate specific outcomes of teaching by altering selected aspects of a teacher's overt behavior." They contend that teaching is seen in this perspective, "as the sum of discrete behaviors and a change in one or several of these behaviors is assumed to affect the quality of teaching as a whole" (p. 52). Their most strenuous argument, however, concerns the notion that these teaching behaviors "are often viewed independent of the curricular context with which the techniques are associated" (p. 52). In other words, they are concerned that observers generally focus on isolated behaviors without concern for the preceding and subsequent behaviors that they feel provide the context and meaning of the behavior.

The previously mentioned criticisms, however, do not necessarily detract from the value and utility of the observational method. As previously discussed, many of these criticisms are "accidents" or incidental aspects of some observational research. Gage and Needels (1989), Needels and Gage (1991), and others, for example, have refuted many of these criticisms and have provided several examples of how observation research has contributed to instructional theories. Medley (1992) has also argued that the previous methodological limitations of observational research have been greatly reduced in recent years. Nevertheless, observational research can be improved, and the next section addresses some ways the research paradigm can be strengthened.

Implications for Future Study

Although research on classroom observation has made significant progress over the past three decades, there are still additional areas that need further investigation. In order to capture all the processes and nuances that occur in classrooms, triangulation procedures are needed to collect data from multiple perspectives (Evertson & Green, 1986). Collecting multiple measures or indicators of classroom processes may help alleviate some of the concerns and criticisms of observational research and provide us with a more comprehensive picture of what goes on in classrooms. Student and teacher self-report survey and interview data, as well as more qualitative, ethnographic data (for example, extensive field notes), could all be used to help supplement classroom observation data.

Another area that may improve the research in the field and improve student learning in schools is the use of newer and better analytic techniques. Although some techniques such as causal modeling have been widely used in education, there have been few applications using classroom observation data to analyze effective teaching. Causal modeling techniques such as LISREL have promise because they address the issues of measurement as well as examine the structural relationships among variables (Hayduk, 1987; Loehlin, 1987). Furthermore, such causal modeling techniques force researchers to develop and test theories or conceptual models of classroom processes, which has been one of the major criticisms of this research paradigm. Other techniques such as hierarchical linear models (HLM) similarly hold promise because they allow researchers to investigate hypotheses about the effects of within- and between-school or class factors on teachers' or students' behavior in the classroom (Bryk & Raudenbush, 1989; Raudenbush & Bryk, 1989; Raudenbush & Willms, 1991; Rowan, Raudenbush, & Kang, 1991). These new analytic procedures allow us to conceptualize the research on effective teaching differently and thus develop new ways of thinking about educational phenomena.

Although the findings summarized by the current observational research in the field suggest several consistent relationships between classroom instruction and students' outcomes, further correlational, longitudinal, and especially experimental research is needed to verify these results. Other research questions that still need to be investigated in this area include examining (1) the ideal or optimal levels and ranges of student and teacher behaviors that should exist in various classrooms, (2) whether there are content area differences or other contextual variables that influence students' or teachers' behaviors, (3) whether there are differential classroom interaction effects among student subgroups or characteristics such as sex, ethnicity, grade, and achievement level, (4) if teacher characteristics such as training and experience influence classroom instruction, and (5) what other variables or factors influence classroom teaching. More studies are also needed to examine how teaching influences students' cognitive learning strategies and higher-level thinking. Similarly, more observation instruments that emphasize inquiry-based or constructivist learning environments need to be developed and validated. Since observational research has not been able to explain how students cognitively interact with process variables (Winne, 1987), further research may need to specifically focus on students' cognitive operations and observations of students' responses. Finally, studies should attempt to replicate some of the previous studies in other settings, especially in inner-city settings where many more students are at risk of dropping out and not furthering their education. These and similar issues still need to be examined so that we can continue to understand and improve classroom instruction.

THEORY INTO PRACTICE

As previously discussed, there are several areas in the study of classroom observation that hold promise for improving education. The following section describes one specific program of research where systematic classroom observations were used to help improve the education of students in inner-city schools. This example will illustrate (1) the type of observational data that can be collected from classrooms, and (2) how teachers view the feedback from that data.

In response to the great challenges and opportunities of education in the inner cities, the National Research Center for Education in the Inner Cities (CEIC) was established by Temple University, in collaboration with the University of Illinois at Chicago and the University of Houston. CEIC is supported by a five-year cooperative agreement with the Office of Educational Research and Improvement (OERI) of the U.S. Department of Education as one of OERI's network of national research and development centers. CEIC consists of three research and development programs (the family, the school, and the community), and an outreach program for dissemination and utilization. The interdisciplinary teams of CEIC researchers engage in a number of different studies such as exemplary practices, longitudinal studies, and field-based experiments.

In one of the major studies that focuses on improving classroom instruction in inner-city classrooms, CEIC researchers have systematically observed elementary, middle, and secondary schools in Houston and Philadelphia. Information on classroom processes were obtained through observations of selected categories of student and teacher behaviors that have been found to be characteristic of effective classroom and instructional learning environments. Two separate observation instruments were used: (1) the Classroom Observation Schedule (COS), and (2) the Teacher Roles Observation Schedule (TROS).

The COS (Waxman, Wang, Lindvall, & Anderson, 1988a) is a systematic observation schedule designed to document observed student behaviors in the context of ongoing classroom instructional-learning processes. Individual students are observed with reference to (1) their interactions with teachers and/or peers and the purpose of such interactions, (2) the settings in which observed behaviors occur, (3) the types of materials with which they are working, and (4) the specific types of activities in which they engage. Four students from each class were randomly selected (stratified by sex and ethnicity, if possible). Each student was observed for ten thirty-second intervals during each of the two data collection periods.

The TROS (Waxman, Wang, Lindvall, & Anderson, 1988b) was used to observe teacher behaviors in the context of ongoing classroom instructional-learning processes. Teachers were observed with reference to (1) their interactions with students, other teachers, or aides; (2) the settings in which observed behaviors occurred; (3) the types of content with which they were working; and (4) the specific types of behaviors they were using. Each teacher was observed for ten thirty-second intervals at two separate times during each data collection period. Both instruments have been found to be reliable and valid. The median interrater reliability (Cohen's Kappa) for the COS is .94, and .96 for the TROS.

In the present study, approximately eight to ten teachers in each school were observed twice during the school year. In addition to aggregating the data across all schools (by grade level), each school was provided with an individual school profile. These school profiles were individually presented to each school. The school means for each of the indicators on both of the observation instruments were presented along with the overall school district mean value, which allowed each school to compare their school means to the district's average. In most cases, school meetings were held where all the teachers and administrators received the profiles and discussed the implications. Tables 5.1 and 5.2 illustrate sample school profiles that were disseminated to each school.

Table 5.1   CEIC—School Profile
Clinton Elementary School—Student Observation

INTERACTIONS

Variables	Your School Mean %	All Elem. Schools Aggregated Mean %
A. No interaction/independence	52.73	59.48
B. Interaction with teacher	39.07	33.40
C. Interaction with support staff	0.00	0.02
D. Interaction with other students	8.08	7.06
E. Interaction with others (not students)	0.10	0.01

ACTIVITY TYPES

Variables	Your School Mean %	All Elem. Schools Aggregated Mean %
A. Teacher assisted activity	99.76	99.85
B. Student selected activity	0.23	0.14
1. Working on written assignments	9.52	19.55
2. Interacting	5.00	6.74
3. Watching or listening	60.83	53.03
4. Reading	3.45	8.82
5. Getting/returning materials	1.90	2.77
6. Coloring, drawing, painting, etc.	1.07	0.46
7. Working with manipulative materials/equip.	10.83	4.55
8. Presenting/acting	1.42	0.78
9. Tutoring peers	0.00	0.18
10. Not attending to task	3.33	4.08
11. Other	4.04	3.21

Note: More than one activity may be coded during one observation.

SETTING

Variables	Your School Mean %	All Elem. Schools Aggregated Mean %
A. Whole class	80.23	78.19
B. Small group	13.09	12.20
C. Individual	6.66	9.60

MANNER

Variables	Your School Mean %	All Elem. Schools Aggregated Mean %
A. On task	95.11	94.48
B. Waiting for teacher's help	0.23	0.30
C. Distracted	2.97	3.45
D. Disruptive	1.19	0.84
E. Other	0.47	0.90

TABLE 5.2   CEIC—School Profile
Clinton Elementary School—Teacher Roles Observation

INTERACTION

Variables	Your School Mean %	All Elem. Schools Aggregated Mean %
A. No interaction	2.31	4.60
B. Interaction with other adults	0.27	0.36
C. Interaction with student(s)/instructional	81.88	85.69
D. Interaction with student(s)/managerial	15.15	8.82
E. Interaction with student(s)/personal	0.37	0.50

SETTING

Variables	Your School Mean %	All Elem. Schools Aggregated Mean %
A. Teacher's desk	1.94	3.79
B. Student's desk	1.29	1.73
C. Small group	7.03	8.48
D. Whole class	75.74	69.36
E. Traveling	11.75	14.75
F. Other (specify)	2.22	1.86

PURPOSE OF INTERACTION

Variables	Your School Mean %	All Elem. Schools Aggregated Mean %
A. Praise	18.93	13.39
B. Correction	23.33	15.54
C. Feedback	18.14	14.70
D. Teacher support	6.96	6.03
E. Task orientation	28.59	23.65

NATURE OF INTERACTION[1]

Variables	Your School Mean %	All Elem. Schools Aggregated Mean %
A. Questioning	40.46	48.58
B. Explaining	68.24	69.30
C. Cueing or promoting	13.98	13.43
D. Demonstrating	10.27	10.63
E. Modeling	3.42	3.99
F. Commenting	47.77	31.91
G. Listening	11.94	9.08

Note[1]: More than one activity may be coded during one observation.

Feedback from these profiles was used to stimulate dialogue and discussion about instructional strengths and weaknesses in the school. The profiles also helped initiate discussion about specific instructional areas that needed to be improved in the school. In Clinton Elementary School (Table 5.1), for example, students were found to be generally on task (95%), working in whole class settings (80%), and most often involved in watching or listening activities (61%). During the feedback session, teachers immediately expressed concern about the amount of time students in their school were involved in watching or listening, especially since this amount of time was much greater than that of other elementary schools in the district (53%). On the other hand, teachers at Clinton Elementary School were pleased that students in their school were found to use manipulative materials about twice as much as other schools, while they worked much less on written assignments (10%), about half as much as other schools in the district. They explained that they were consciously trying to move away from the traditional instructional activities (that is, written assignments) and move toward more constructivist activities (that is, working with manipulative materials). Clinton teachers also admitted that they needed to reduce the amount of whole class instruction that was occurring in their school, but overall, they were encouraged with their school profile and felt that it provided them with sufficient feedback that they could build on.

It should be pointed out again that these profiles provided some guidelines for practice; they were not attempts to tell teachers what to do. These profiles provide teachers with concepts and criteria that they can use to reflect about their own teaching (Nuthall & Alton-Lee, 1990). We did not view the feedback session as one where we would apply our research findings into specific rules or guidelines for teachers to follow. Rather, the observational feedback was intended to be used as a guide for teachers where they and their colleagues could reflect about their practices on their own and decide what action to take. Inservices, workshops, formalized staff development programs, and university courses are some of the possibilities that teachers could choose if they wanted us to continue to collaborate with them in order to help them improve their instruction.

SUMMARY

In summary, it appears that systematic classroom observations are useful for (1) improving teachers' classroom instruction, (2) identifying subgroup differences in classroom behavior and inequitable opportunities to learn among students, and (3) improving the preparation of prospective teachers. Classroom observation data, however, has some limitations. It is costly because it requires extensive training as well as time for someone to actually do the observations. Furthermore, there are some validity concerns related to the obtrusiveness of the technique and the actual amount of time and number of observations to obtain a valid measure of the classroom. Finally, there are concerns related to the instrumentation involved in classroom observations. Do the classroom observation instruments currently used in the field capture the important instructional variables that we should be looking at? There have been other theoretical and epistemological criticisms of classroom observational research, but these concerns appear to be more "accidental" or incidental features of the research rather than the true "essence" of the research.

Finally, it is important to point out again that no one data source or methodology will sufficiently answer all our critical educational questions. Multiple measures or indicators of instruction are needed to help us capture a more comprehensive picture of what goes on in classrooms. Student and teacher self-report survey and interview data, as well as more qualitative ethnographic data (for example, extensive field notes), could all be used to help supplement classroom observation data. In conclusion, classroom observation is a powerful research methodology that can be used for several important educational purposes. Combined with some of the other research methods previously described, it can be used to help us improve educational processes.

References

Anderson, L. W., and R. B. Burns (1989). *Research in Classrooms: The Study of Teachers, Teaching, and Instruction.* Oxford, England: Pergamon Press.

Brophy, J. E. (1979). "Using Observation to Improve Your Teaching" (occasional paper no. 21). East Lansing, MI: Michigan State University, Institute for Research on Teaching.

Brophy, J. E., and T. L. Good (1974). *Teacher-student Relationships: Causes and Consequences.* New York: Holt, Rinehart and Winston.

Brophy, J. E., and T. L. Good (1986). "Teacher Behavior and Student Achievement," in M. C. Wittrock, ed., *Handbook of Research on Teaching,* 3rd ed. New York: Macmillan, pp. 328–375.

Bryk, A. S., and S. W. Raudenbush (1989). "Toward a More Appropriate Conceptualization of Research on School Effects: A Three-level Hierarchical Linear Model, " in R. D. Bock, ed., *Multilevel Analysis of Educational Data.* San Diego: Academic Press, pp. 159–204.

Copley, J. V., and S. E. Williams (1992). "The Use of Classroom Observations in Technology and Education Research," in D. Carey, R. Carey, D. A. Willis, and J. Willis, eds., *Technology and Teacher Education Annual 1992.* Charlottesville, VA: Association for the Advancement of Computing in Education, pp. 381–385.

Copley, J. V., and S. E. Williams (1993). "Systematic Classroom Observations of Technology Use," in H. C. Waxman and G. W. Bright, eds., *Approaches to Research on Teacher Education and Technology.* Charlottesville, VA: Association for the Advancement of Computing in Education, pp. 113–122.

Doyle, W. (1977). "Paradigms for Research on Teacher Effectiveness," in L. S. Schulman, ed., *Review of Research in Education,* vol. 5. Itasca, IL: Peacock, pp. 163–198.

Doyle, W. (1979). "Making Managerial Decisions in Classrooms," in D. L. Duke, ed., *Classroom Management.* Chicago: National Society for the Study of Education, pp. 42–74.

Ebmeier, H., and T. L. Good (1979). "The Effects of Instructing Teachers About Good Teaching on the Mathematics Achievement of Fourth-grade Students." *American Educational Research Journal* 16: 1–16.

Evertson, C., and J. Green (1986). "Observation vs. Inquiry and Method," in M. C. Wittrock, ed., *Handbook of Research on Teaching,* 3rd ed. New York: Macmillan, pp. 162–207.

Feiman, S. (1981). "Exploring Connections Between Different Kinds of Educational Research and Different Conceptions of Inservice Education." *Journal of Research and Development in Education* 14 (2): 11–21.

Fennema, E., and P. L. Peterson (1987). "Effective Teaching for Girls and Boys: The Same or

Different?" in D. C. Berliner and B. V. Rosenshine, eds., *Talks to Teachers*. New York: Random House, pp. 111–125.

Fenstermacher, G. (1978). "A Philosophical Consideration of Recent Research on Teacher Effectiveness," in L. S. Schulman, ed., *Review of Research in Education*, vol. 6. Itasca, IL: Peacock, pp. 157–185.

Freiberg, H. J., H. C. Waxman, and W. R. Houston (1987). "Enriching Feedback to Student-teachers through Small Group Discussion." *Teacher Education Quarterly* 14 (3): 71–82.

Freiberg, H. J., and H. C. Waxman (1988). "Alternative Feedback Approaches for Improving Student Teachers' Classroom Instruction." *Journal of Teacher Education* 39 (4): 8–14.

Gage, N. L. (1972). *Teacher Effectiveness and Teacher Education*. Palo Alto, CA: Pacific.

Gage, N. L. (1985). *Hard Gains in the Soft Science: The Case of Pedagogy*. Bloomington, IN: Phi Delta Kappa.

Gage, N. L., and M. C. Needels (1989). "Process-product Research on Teaching? A Review of Criticisms." *Elementary School Journal* 89: 253–300.

Galton, M. (1988). "Structured Observation Techniques," in J. P. Keeves, ed., *Educational Research, Methodology and Measurement: An International Handbook*. Oxford, England: Pergamon Press, pp. 474–478.

Good, T. L., and B. Biddle (1988). "Research and the Improvement of Mathematics Instruction: The Need for Observational Resources," in D. Grouws and T. Cooney, eds., *Research Agenda for Mathematics Education: Effective Mathematics Teaching*. Reston, VA: National Council of Teachers of Mathematics, pp. 114–142.

Good, T. L., and J. Brophy (1974). "Changing Teacher and Student Behavior: An Empirical Investigation." *Journal of Educational Psychology* 66: 390–405.

Good, T. L., and D. Grouws (1979). "The Missouri Mathematics Effectiveness Project: An Experimental Study in Fourth-grade Classrooms." *Journal of Educational Psychology* 71: 355–362.

Hart, L. E. (1989). "Classroom Processes, Sex of Students, and Confidence in Learning Mathematics." *Journal for Research in Math-ematics Education* 20: 242–260.

Hayduk, L. A. (1987). *Structural Equation Modeling with LISREL*. Baltimore: Johns Hopkins University Press.

Heider, F. (1958). *The Psychology of Interpersonal Relationships*. New York: Holt, Rinehart and Winston.

Johnson, D. W. (1974). "Affective outcomes," in H. J. Walberg, ed., *Evaluating Educational Performance*. Berkeley, CA: McCutchan, pp. 99–112.

Loehlin, J. C. (1987). *Latent Variable Models: An Introduction to Factor, Path, and Structural Analysis*. Hillsdale, NJ: Lawrence Erlbaum.

Medlcy, D. M. (1982). "Systematic Observation," in H. E. Mitzel, ed., *Encyclopedia of Educational Research*, 5th ed. New York: The Free Press, pp. 1841–1851.

Medley, D. M. (1992). "Structured Observation," in M. C. Alkin, ed., *Encyclopedia of Educational Research*, vol. 4. New York: Macmillan, pp. 1310–1315.

Merkley, D. J., and M. P. Hoy (1992-93). "Observation as a Component in Teacher Preparation." *National Forum of Teacher Education Journal* 2: 15–21.

Needels, M., and N. L. Gage (1991). "Essence and Accident in Process-product Research on Teaching," in H. C. Waxman and H. J. Walberg, eds., *Effective Teaching: Current Research*. Berkeley, CA: McCutchan, pp. 3–31.

Nuthall, G., and A. Alton-Lee (1990). "Research on Teaching and Learning: Thirty Years of Change." *The Elementary School Journal* 90: 546–570.

Ornstein, A. C. (1991). "Teacher Effectiveness Research: Theoretical Considerations," in H. C. Waxman and H. J. Walberg, eds., *Effective Teaching: Current Research*. Berkeley, CA: McCutchan, pp. 63–80.

Popkewitz, T. S., R. Tabachnick, and K. Zeichner (1979). "Dulling the Senses: Research in Teacher Education." *Journal of Teacher Education* 30: 52–60.

Raudenbush, S. W., and A. S. Bryk (1989). "Quantitative Models for Estimating Teacher and School Effectiveness," in R. D. Bock, ed., *Multilevel Analysis of Educational Data*. San Diego: Academic Press, pp. 205–232.

Raudenbush, S. W., and J. D. Willms, eds. (1991). *Schools, Classrooms, and Pupils: International Studies of schooling from a Multilevel Perspective.* San Diego: Academic Press.

Rosenshine, B. V. (1987). "Explicit Teaching," in D. C. Berliner and B. V. Rosenshine, eds., *Talks to Teachers.* New York: Random House, pp. 75–92.

Rowan, B., S. W. Raudenbush, and S. J. Kang (1991). "School Climate in Secondary Schools," in S. W. Raudenbush, and J. D. Willms, eds., *Schools, Classroom, and Pupils: International Studies of Schooling from a Multilevel Perspective.* San Diego: Academic Press, pp. 203–223.

Stallings, J. A. (1980). "Allocated Academic Learning Time Revisited, or Beyond Time on Task." *Educational Researcher* 9 (11): 11–16.

Stallings, J. A., and H. J. Freiberg (1991). "Observation for the Improvement of Teaching," in H. C. Waxman and H. J. Walberg, eds., *Effective Teaching: Current Research.* Berkeley, CA: McCutchan, pp. 107–133.

Stallings, J. A., and G. G. Mohlman (1988). "Classroom Observation Techniques," in J. P. Keeves, ed., *Educational Research, Methodology, and Measurement: An International Handbook.* Oxford, England: Pergamon Press, pp. 469–474.

Stallings, J., M. C. Needels, and G. M. Sparks (1987). "Observation for the Improvement of Student Learning," in D. C. Berliner and B. V. Rosenshine, eds., *Talks to Teachers.* New York: Random House, pp. 129–158.

Stallings, J. A., M. C. Needels, and N. Stayrook (1979). *How to Change the Process of Teaching Basic Reading Skills at the Secondary School Level.* Menlo Park, CA: SRI International.

Stodolsky, S. S. (1990). "Classroom Observation," in J. Millman and L. Darling-Hammond, eds., *The New Handbook of Teacher Evaluation: Assessing Elementary and Secondary School Teachers.* Newbury Park, CA: Sage, pp. 175–190.

Teddlie, C., P. C. Kirby, and S. Stringfield (1989). "Effective versus Ineffective Schools: Observable Differences in the Classroom." *American Journal of Education* 97: 221–236.

Timm, J. T., and G. J. Marchant (1992). "Using a Structured Observational Instrument in Observational Settings in Teacher Education." *Teaching Education* 5: 65–70.

Walberg, H. J. (1986). "Synthesis of Research on Teaching," in M. Wittrock, ed., *Handbook of Research on Teaching,* 3rd ed. New York: Macmillan, pp. 214–229.

Walberg, H. J. (1991). "Productive Teaching and Instruction: Assessing the Knowledge Base," in H. C. Waxman and H. J. Walberg, eds., *Effective Teaching: Current Research.* Berkeley, CA: McCutchan, pp. 33–62.

Waxman, H. C., J. Rodriguez, Y. Padron, and S. Knight (1988). "The Use of Systematic Classroom Observations during Field Experience Components of Teacher Education Programs." *The College Student Journal* 22: 199–202.

Waxman, H. C., M. C. Wang, M. Lindvall, and K. A. Anderson (1988a). *Teacher Roles Observation Schedule Technical Manual,* rev. ed. Philadelphia: Temple University, Center for Research in Human Development and Education.

Waxman, H. C., M. C. Wang, M. Lindvall, and K. A. Anderson (1988b). *Classroom Observation Schedule Technical Manual.* Pittsburgh: University of Pittsburgh, Learning Research and Development Center.

Winne, P. H. (1987). "Why Process-product Research Cannot Explain Process-product Findings and a Proposed Remedy: The Cognitive Mediational Paradigm." *Teaching and Teacher Education* 3: 333–356.

Winne, P. H., and R. W. Marx (1977). "Reconceptualizing Research on Teaching." *Journal of Educational Psychology* 69: 668–678.

Discussion Questions

1. What are some of the strengths or advantages of using classroom observation data?

2. How can classroom observation improve classroom instruction?

3. How can classroom observation data help us uncover inequities in the opportunities students have to learn?

4. How can classroom observation improve the training of prospective teachers?

5. What are some of the limitations of using classroom observation data?

6. What additional types of data (that is, either student or teacher behaviors) would you like to see included in the profiles reported in Tables 5.1 and 5.2?

Part II

Teaching and Learning

The teaching act involves some teacher behavior and transfer of information to the learner. The behavior may be verbal or nonverbal; the transfer takes place as a result of some experience involving the learning process. Both the behavior and the transfer may be positive or negative, largely depending on the interaction between the teacher and learner and/or the way the learning environment (for example, classroom, school, or home) is organized. Ideally, the teaching-learning environment in school should be positive, especially since negative experiences tend to have more powerful and lasting effects on learning.

Since no curriculum, no matter how well planned, can teach everything, the task of the teacher is to exhibit effective behaviors and make effective use of time to produce a maximum amount of trans-fer. The teacher must learn, through training and experience, to stress the content, skills, and experiences that promote maximum transfer, or what are sometimes referred to as learning outcomes.

In Chapter 6, Lyn Corno examines "The Principles of Adaptive Teaching." The concept suggests a twofold process: where teachers adapt the instruction to the needs of the learners, and learners adapt the tasks to accommodate their own goals, interests, and learning styles. Teachers are required, according to Corno, to help students to learn how to learn, or more precisely to adapt their thinking to the instructional situation. To use adaptive strategies in the teaching-learning process, the author maintains that two major student patterns or characteristics must be considered—motivation and competence. These two patterns yield four different hypothetical classrooms (high motivation/high competence; high motivation/low competence; low motivation/high competence; and low motivation/low competence), each of which presents different adaptive procedures for teachers to use in their classroom practices.

Chapter 7, "Classroom Management in the Learning-centered Classroom," is written by Carolyn Evertson and Catherine Randolph. The authors critique the relationship between classroom management, which is perhaps the number-one concern for beginning teachers, and the instructional process. Evertson and Randolph note how classrooms are organized and how classroom activities evolve as teachers make managerial decisions. They pay close attention to two types of classrooms: one characterized by a "workplace" and the other by a "learning place." They attempt to refocus the teachers' thinking from the needs of management (where control and smooth functioning are evidenced and there is high productivity in terms of output) to the needs of the learner (where there are fewer rules and routines and the emphasis is on discussion and reflection).

The next chapter, "Scaffolds for Teaching Higher-Order Cognitive Strategies," is written by Barak Rosenshine and Carla Meister, who describe seven major instructional procedures that can be used to teach cognitive strategies to improve comprehension, writing, and problem solving: (1) presenting concrete prompts that guide students' processing, (2) demonstrating the use of the prompts through modeling and talking aloud, (3) providing guided practice that reduces the difficulty of the task, (4) providing a variety of contexts for student practice, (5) providing feedback, (6) increasing student responsibility as they master the strategy, and (7) providing for independent practice. The goal of this instruction is to blend the seven strategies into a single unified whole process that can be applied easily and unconsciously to various teaching and learning situations.

Chapter 9 is written by Simon Hooper and Lloyd Rieber and examines the practice of "Teaching with Technology." The authors first outline five developmental stages of technology use: familiarization, utilization, integration, reorientation, and evaluation. The first three stages represent traditional modes of using technology, and the latter two connote the recent and full potential of educational technology. Hooper and Rieber discuss how the traditional role of technology in education, dealing with "product" technology or hardware, can be combined with new "idea" technologies that are found in printed materials and computer software. They describe three principles of learning that help make full use of technology: Learning should be an active process, learning should be based on multiple and interconnected sources, and learning should integrate prior and past knowledge. Finally, the authors outline various instructional packages that exemplify contemporary notions of using technology effectively in classrooms.

Considering that we live in a highly technocratic and scientific society, one in which knowledge has great impact on our standard of living, and in a world in which a push of a button can have an enormous impact on our lives, the extent of the scientific literacy of our citizenry has serious implications for the future of our country.

Noting that extensive literature on science literacy provides nothing but vague definitions or suggestions, Chapter 10, entitled "Teaching for Science Literacy," by John Penick, provides an operational definition of science literacy. Penick describes the classroom environment and the role and behaviors of the teacher most likely to facilitate the development of science literacy. At each step in this description, the author provides a research-supported rationale for his suggestions.

In the final chapter of Part II, Edward Wynne considers "The Moral Dimension of Teaching." After synthesizing the historical perspective of morality and teaching, the author examines two major approaches regarding teacher morality: traditional moral teaching and prophetic moral teaching. The first approach is characterized by the teacher's deep obligation to help students learn, and the need for dedication. With the second approach, the teacher is more concerned with the social order and the need to make students aware of the abuses and injustices of the world. Throughout the chapter, the relationships between moral teaching, classroom practices, and community settings are discussed.

Lyn Corno

Lyn Corno did her masters and Ph.D. work in educational psychology at Stanford University, where she worked as a graduate student with Richard Snow and N. L. Gage. She is currently professor of education and psychology at Columbia University's Teachers College, where she has been on the faculty since 1982. In addition to her faculty work, Corno chairs an advisory panel for research at the Educational Testing Service in Princeton, New Jersey, and consults with schools on teaching for self-regulated learning and the hidden curriculum in Connecticut and New York.

Lyn is a Fellow of the American Psychological Society, the American Psychological Association, and the American Association for the Advancement of Science. She has published numerous articles and chapters in educational research journals and books, is a member of the New York Academy of Science, and is presently an editor of the *American Educational Research Journal.*

Lyn is serious about education, and this is reflected in her favorite book, which is Cronbach's *Designing Evaluations of Educational and Social Programs.* Although she favors an Eastern accent and talks rather rapidly, after a while she slows down and talks more about her two children than educational psychology, and admits in her own words to being "high as a kite" about them.

Beyond the campus life at T.C., Lyn enjoys inviting friends over to her house in Darien, Connecticut, to cook fine cuisine and to talk about the local schools and community. She frequently gets to travel with her husband, Bill, and children to her parents' home in Arizona and to South Carolina to visit his parents. "Pawley's Island is our favorite spot in the Carolinas," where the family enjoys the beach and the children build sandcastles.

6 ❧

The Principles of Adaptive Teaching

Lyn Corno

Few principles of teaching have withstood the dual tests of time and directed research. One exception is the idea that "The success of education depends on adapting teaching to the needs of individual students." This principle can be found expressed in the writings of Quintilian in first century Rome, as well as in much educational theory and research during subsequent years up to the present (see Snow, 1982).

But what does this mean for the practicing teacher, and how, realistically, is adaptive teaching done? Does it, for example, result in treatment for some students that is different but unequal? Or does differentiated instruction help to ensure an excellent education for all?

TWO FORMS OF ADAPTIVE TEACHING

Modern writing defines *adaptive teaching* as teaching that attempts to **accommodate** or better **match** the needs or characteristics of students in pursuit of common or individual goals (Corno & Snow, 1986). Students differ in many interrelated qualities that influence learning from teaching. Skills and abilities, habits, and sociocultural backgrounds and values represent just a few. By addressing rather than ignoring some of the most relevant student characteristics as they plan and present instruction, teachers can increase the likelihood of helping more of their students to do well in school.

Theory suggests two aspects of adaptation should be addressed concurrently. First, teachers will need to find ways to adapt their teaching to benefit the range of students they confront (that is, to "adapt the instruction to the students" or try to see through the eyes of students). Second, teachers will need to help students learn how to adapt school tasks for themselves—to better accommodate their own personal goals, interests, and work styles (Rohrkemper & Corno, 1988).

One way teachers can help students to become adaptive learners is by cultivating attitudes and skills that students can use to learn from almost any instructional situation, including ineffective teachers they might one day encounter. It has long been recognized that students need "learning to learn" or "self-regulated learning" skills to do well academically (Novak & Gowin, 1984; Zimmerman & Schunk, 1989). In addition, the commitment and follow-through (or "will") that accompanies knowing how to learn is now understood to be critical to academic success, and teachers can effectively promote this as well (Corno, 1992).

In their concurrent efforts to "adapt instruction to students," teachers can find ways to circumvent or compensate for weak areas in students' knowledge, skills, or will. They can use techniques and procedures that reduce the mental (or "information processing") burden on students, and they can do this just long enough for further instruction to proceed. When students are not yet "self-regulating," for example, teachers can use available resources to leverage the individual attention they provide, and to supplement or structure instruction in ways that avoid demanding skills or capabilities from students that are not yet fully developed. Teachers can also shift their demands toward students' strengths, enduring interests, and related background experiences to capitalize on existing opportunities for student learning to occur.

These two aspects of adaptive teaching—(1) developing general academic learning skills and attitudes directly, and (2) compensating for weaknesses in knowledge, skills, or will by capitalizing on strengths—together play a prominent role in successful classroom teaching (see Presidential Task Force on Psychology in Education, 1993). Particularly important is the point that adaptive teaching is of most benefit when students' background experiences, existing skills, and/or motivation are either (1) "heterogeneous" or diverse, or (2) "homogeneous," but different from what historically have been defined as academic or social "norms" (Cronbach & Snow, 1977).

ADAPTATION AND DIVERSITY

Many sources have documented the increasing sociocultural diversity in American education. Most experts agree that this increasing diversity urges practitioners to rethink traditional methods based on the assumption that a given group of students is more alike than different in predictable responses to schooling (Carter & Goodwin, 1993). Of course, students have always differed on some indicators that forecast academic success. The narrow gauge of intellectual abilities, measured by standardized tests, for example, has long been described as a "normal distribution" (a bell curve) within the general population. But diversity exists in some classrooms and schools more than in others, and the more kinds of diversity with which teachers are confronted, the more important is an understanding of the nature and utility of adaptive teaching. Adaptive teaching then becomes an important addition to the knowledge base for any beginning teacher heading into the twenty-first century.

An extended discussion of the details of adaptive teaching, and the theory and research underlying it, is beyond the scope of this chapter (see instead Corno & Snow, 1986; Glaser, 1977). But an introduction to the central principles and features of adaptive teaching can be provided here—for use by beginning, as well as more experienced, teachers. The chapter will also illustrate in concrete ways how teachers might teach adaptively within today's changing schools.

THE CASE FOR ADAPTIVE TEACHING

To understand adaptive teaching, its logic must be given some attention, and so must selected evidence supporting its utility. Two growing bodies of research are particularly useful for this purpose: research on teacher expertise, and research on teacher implementation of innovations.

Teacher Expertise and Adaptive Teaching

Teachers make on-the-spot decisions to adapt to the needs of different students, but they also plan larger units or courses of instruction with adaptive goals in mind. Recent theory and research on expert teaching has included a tendency to be adaptive in teaching among the important qualities of teachers that predict expertise. Some teachers view their work as a negotiated, constructive process in which lessons are modified as they are taught according to the conditions of the classroom at the time—student interests, background experiences, and responses, for example. These teachers are often more successful than others in meeting their instructional goals. They also tend to have more extensive preparation to teach, and are more frequently regarded by co-workers as expert practitioners (Berliner, 1986; Snyder, Bolin, & Zumwalt, 1992).

Despite this evidence supporting the importance of teacher adaptations, many formal educational programs (and the legislated policies that accompany them) are disseminated to practitioners with quite the opposite guidelines and expectations.

Teacher Adaptation or Implementation of Innovations

Legislative mandates are issued for education at local, state, and national levels, and teachers are expected to comply with the recommended details of such initiatives. They are asked to "implement" programs with "fidelity"; that is, to teach in the way that program developers prescribe. Although much valuable professional experience with mandated initiatives has gone undocumented, existing evidence makes it clear that, rather than maintain fidelity to prescribed new programs, teachers instead find numerous ways to compromise developers' best-laid plans (McLaughlin, 1987).

Some teachers quietly carry out their own agendas behind closed classroom doors (Sarason, 1971). Others become "agents for change" in teaching, preferring to take innovation into their own hands. Still others become frustrated and withdraw from teaching (or "burn-out") over time (Fullan, 1982). Good teachers do not mindlessly implement the programs handed down to them. They mindfully adapt new material and ideas to suit their own teaching routines and interests, and to better support their beliefs about the learning needs of their students. Thus, research supports both the pervasiveness and the value of adaptive teaching, in principle. Theory provides the logic, and also exposes assumptions that need to be examined if the promise of adaptive teaching is ever to be achieved in practice.

THE LOGIC OF ADAPTIVE TEACHING

The logic of adaptive teaching can be illustrated by considering how classroom teachers gather information on students and use it to guide their teaching. There are two forms of raw data that teachers often work with: close observation of students, and the continuous school record.

Information for Making Instructional Adaptations

Close observation by teachers of the course *of* events in their classrooms provides data for adaptations "in-flight" as teaching proceeds. The moment-to-moment activity of classrooms has been characterized as a recurring sequence of active teacher "moves" that coordinate with "responses" generated by students (Bellack et al., 1966).

During class time, teachers (1) present organized information to which students are expected to respond, (2) monitor and evaluate student responses to this material, and (3) give appropriate feedback based on these student responses. Classroom assessments are typically rooted in questions or "solicitations"; that is, in the activities that teachers provide to solicit student responses of various levels and forms. Solicitations may be informal, as in questions asked in class, or they may be formal, as in quizzes or other assignments that encourage students to express themselves (offer thoughts for inspection) and/or to perform (Dillon, 1988).

In adaptive teaching, this classroom activity sequence departs from conventional practice to either (1) accommodate or (2) better match, individual differences in students. *Accommodating* is a useful strategy when students display diversity in "characteristics related to achievement." These are generally believed to include a variety of academic skills or cognitive abilities related to learning, and a motivation to learn or to accomplish school-related goals. Put simply, the key characteristics related to achievement may be designated "skill" and "will" (Presidential Task Force on Psychology in Education, 1993).

In contrast, *matching* is a useful strategy when a class or group of students *shares* background experiences or emotional, physical, or intellectual needs that are not well-addressed by conventional teaching (see below). If the organizational structures of school systems have previously limited these students' access to a rich or elaborated curriculum (for example, have taken them out of the regular classroom, or resulted in suboptimal classroom placements or placements in impoverished schools), then a matching approach to adaptive teaching can re-establish inclusion without demanding a "fit" into conventional teaching. So-called "conventional" teaching—consisting of mandated textbooks that students do not own, didactic or teacher-directed instruction grounded in traditional curricular disciplines and self-contained organizational settings, tracking students by ability, and a focus on completing worksheets and performing on standardized tests (Cuban, 1984; Goodlad, 1984; Kozol, 1991)—will best serve students who represent the social or academic mainstream on which these conventions have been based. Learning opportunities have been different historically for students outside that mainstream, whether they come from different cultural backgrounds or bring to school some diagnosis of a "special" academic need (Carter & Goodwin, 1994; Darling-Hammond, 1991; McCaslin & Good, 1994).

In addition to their own close observations of students, teachers also use continuous school records to make judgments about academic skills and other educational aptitudes, including previous achievements, grades, and other teachers' and parents' comments. Together, this combination of data from personal experiences and school records provides most teachers with a range of evidence for making sensible instructional adaptations. As can be imagined, however, much depends on how these data are interpreted and used. We can now consider examples of both **accommodating** and **matching** strategies in pursuit of a better understanding of the principles of adaptive teaching.

Accommodating Strategy

To accommodate diversity among students, evidence supports the utility of referencing a small number of highly relevant classes of student characteristics. Research on teacher decision making has shown that, like all people, teachers tend to make decisions based on limited amounts of familiar information, rather than undertaking an exhaustive analysis of options (see, for example, Clark & Peterson, 1986). They use *heuristics*—rules of thumb—to guide their teaching, rather than "optimizing" the choice and delivery of methods.

Studies of the factors most frequently taken into account in teacher decisions about instruction have placed two student characteristics at the top of the list. These may be referred to generally as *academic skills* and *motivation* (Clark & Peterson, 1986). Although there is great variety in the combinations of close observation and school record data teachers use as a basis for their judgments, reviews of this research have concluded that teachers are reasonably accurate in their assessments of these two general student characteristics using the data they have (see Hoge & Coladarci, 1989).

Examining Classes of Students   Imagine, then, examining a given class of students on the basis of these two student characteristics, as an initial procedure for determining the nature of adaptive accommodation. With respect to interpretation of these data, no assumption should be made that these student characteristics are fixed for any individual student over the course of instruction provided. Indeed, adaptive teaching assumes that *both* academic ability and motivation will be developed at the same time that subject matter learning takes place. Also, the moment-to-moment adaptations made on the basis of student response imply that changes in these characteristics will occur at different times and in different ways for different students. How might teachers examine their classes according to these qualities at the beginning of the year?

Figure 6.1 presents four patterns of data from four different hypothetical classrooms. The figure assumes that the teacher has used some method or procedure to quantify a judgment for each student on the two characteristics shown on the axes of the bivariate scatterplot. For example, the teacher may have used available school records, and her own assessments of verbal and other skills, to rate students on academic skill or competence. And the teacher may have made early observations of students in orientation interviews and in early class sessions, and taken anecdotes from the students' files to rate each student on motivation to learn and to do well in school.

In general, the more carefully the teacher works to compile a profile of data for each student in each of the two aptitude domains, the more valid the resulting quantified judgments are likely to be (Cronbach, 1989). It should not be assumed that these quantified judgments represent all there is to know about individuals with respect to these two characteristics. Reducing the variety of available data to numbers is but one way a teacher might examine and define the particular combination of students that constitutes a given class group.

In the case of Figure 6.1(a), the class may be characterized roughly as consisting of two different, but rather homogeneous, subgroups of students. One subgroup appears generally lower on both skill and will; the other gives evidence of being generally higher on each of these scales. Again, with respect to proper interpretation, this characterization refers to the class as a whole; the scatterplot makes it obvious that several individual students do not fit this average class profile. Although adaptive teaching assumes that treating students as individuals is optimal, practical circumstances rarely permit completely individualized instruction in classes of twenty-five or more students. Thus, this hypothetical class can be said to represent two subgroups of students—one that appears quite able academically, and one that seems to display a number of current difficulties related to school.

A different pattern is presented for the class in Figure 6.1(b), which can be characterized as generally lower in academic skill and higher in academic motivation. This class of less academically skilled students seems to be eager to do well in school; prior frustrations may not have dampened their collective interest in learning or in getting the most from their school-related experiences. This group of students displays some clear strengths a teacher can work with, and may be easier to teach than the group in Figure 6.1(a).

Figure 6.1(c) represents still another, opposite, pattern that a teacher might confront. These students appear generally lower in motivation and higher in competence. Such a group may be viewed as academically gifted but underchallenged by conventional teaching. And finally, Figure 6.1(d) illustrates a class in which there is no apparent pattern of relationship between these two

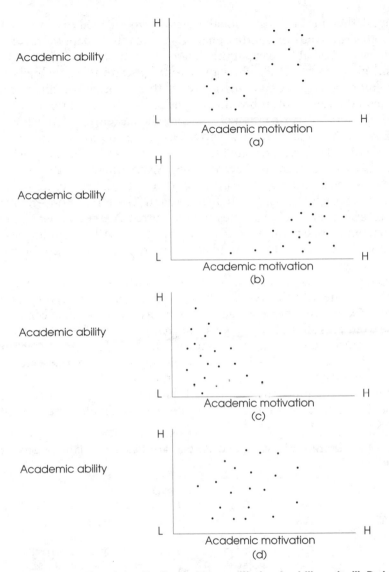

Figure 6.1 Four hypothetical classes differing in skill and will. Dots represent students within classes. L represents low and H represents high.

characteristics at all. This group of students appears to be all over the academic map.

To use adaptive accommodation, a teacher would approach each of these hypothetical classes differently. In each case, the teaching would be adapted to the differing needs of the combinations of students involved, at least for initial instruction. Importantly, however, as ongoing assessments begin to demonstrate that individual students are developing in these areas (and the overall scatterplot changes), then initial instructional decisions would need to be revised. Table 1 illustrates the kinds of instructional procedures that adaptive theory suggests would be beneficial for each of the subgroups or classes in Figures 6.1(a), 6.1(b), and 6.1(c). In Figure 6.1(d), where there is no apparent relationship between the characteristics, creative combinations of all these procedures might be profitably used; and the rule of thumb would be, the more varied the modes and avenues for teaching this diverse group of students, the better (see also below).

Each of these examples of adaptive instructional procedures has found support in either historical or emerging lines of research (Corno, 1992; Corno & Snow, 1986; Rosenshine & Stevens, 1986). Again, the idea is that these different procedures are, in theory, more likely to (1) develop the academic skills and motivation that each class or subgroup needs, and (2) capitalize on strengths judged to be present at the time that assessment occurred. Again, it must be emphasized that ongoing assessment in both areas of skill and will should be routine. Periodically, these scatterplots should be reconstructed as changes in the data are obtained.

There is no assumption in the theory of adaptive teaching that either the diagnosis or the resulting tailored instruction is static; rather, the wise adaptive teacher assumes that proper diagnosis and intervention demand constant review. These examples should also make clear that managing heterogeneity in classrooms requires refined diagnostic ability, a broad repertoire of teaching strategies, approaches, and activities, and knowledge of which of these are best paired with different student characteristics or profiles.

To frame the procedures listed in Table 6.1, we can consider three aspects of teaching that teachers most commonly adapt to individual student differences.

Table 6.1   Examples of Instructional Procedures Useful for Different Groups of Students

Will	Skill	
	Low	**High**
Low	Guided modeling of learning strategies	Challenging assignments that activate skills
	Encouragement and corrective feedback	Encouragement to adapt tasks creatively
	Seductive curricular topics and materials	Instruction tied to student interests
High	Guided modeling of learning strategies	Challenging assignments and independent work
	Actively engaging students in tasks	Interest-driven instruction
	Curricular and media options for learning the same material	Group projects

The Big Three: Grouping, Mode of Presentation, and Learning Guidance

Some aspects of teaching cannot be adapted readily by teachers—schools generally require the use of curricular materials such as textbooks that students usually do not own (and therefore cannot write upon). There are also established practices unique to particular schools (a school-wide philosophy of education, for example), and routines that departments or grade level teachers decide will best suit their own collective preferences and goals.

In contrast, it has been assumed that one aspect of teaching that teachers can readily adapt is the pace of instruction (or learning time) they provide for individual students. The notion of individualized instruction is based upon this premise, and several previous models of adaptive teaching have emphasized this "learning time" variable (Carroll, 1963; Bloom, 1981; Ornstein, 1990). But teaching usually proceeds during the calendar academic year, and teachers are under pressure to meet local objectives within prescribed time periods for most if not all of their students. When individual students fall behind or outpace the others, it has become common to refer them to specialist teachers for more individualized work (reading specialists, math tutors, resident scientists, and so on). It is impractical for many classroom teachers to alter the pace of instruction dramatically to accommodate individual students, particularly when the class size is large. And, further, when this does occur, such adaptations are not without other consequences.

When students are encouraged to work at their own pace, those who work slower often receive more attention from the teacher, while students who work faster may be overloaded with "busywork" or worksheets (McCaslin & Good, 1994). Thus, although self-pacing has a long history as a point of departure for adaptive teaching, other aspects of teaching may be more profitable for teachers to adapt when working with heterogeneous classes. Almost every teacher has some control over *grouping* students for instruction, the methods or modes in which material is *presented*, and the ways in which learning is monitored and supported or *guided*.

Grouping The longstanding practice of grouping large classes of students into smaller units for instruction has been viewed as one technique for managing individual student differences. In this case, however, diversity is considered something to be reduced rather than celebrated. The idea is the same as that discussed earlier with respect to Figure 6.1: Form small groups of students who are more alike than different and teach the groups differently (Cronbach & Snow, 1977). Unfortunately, however, research on ability and other forms of homogeneous grouping (including tracking) has again uncovered often unintended but nonetheless negative consequences. For example, there is a tendency for groups of more able students to be challenged by higher teacher and peer expectations, while students placed in lower ability groups tend to experience the reverse (McCaslin & Good, 1994). Students who speak out easily or boldly also receive more attention from teachers and from other students; attention may then be distributed along gender/racial/ethnic lines. In many cases, students placed in lower skilled groups actually receive a "watered-down," rather than a rich or elaborated, curriculum as well (Oakes, 1985).

Partly as a result of these sorts of research findings, modifications of traditional ability grouping, such as "cooperative learning," have evolved. In cooperative learning, small groups are formed to reflect the same diversity that exists in the whole class setting, and students are rewarded for completing tasks by working together rather than alone (Slavin, Karweit, & Madden, 1989). These cooperative small groups permit teachers to leverage their own time and attention, because more able students tend to teach the others while the teacher monitors the groups (Webb, 1982).

Comparative studies consistently show that students with different levels of ability (ranging from above average to learning disabled) and different sociocultural backgrounds can be more successful when working in cooperative small groups than when working in traditional ability groups (Slavin, 1987). When students are taught how to cooperate and to substitute themselves for teachers, in particular, their explanations are often good ones, and students can demonstrate improved social as well as academic skills. Individuals in the group should be offered incentives to help the students who stand to benefit most in these situations, and group rewards should be based in part on individual performance.

Thus, cooperative learning, too, is a form of adaptive teaching; but unlike ability grouping, cooperative learning helps teachers to accommodate diversity within a context of inclusion. And group size is reduced without the negative consequences that traditional ability grouping can incur (cf. Mason & Good, 1993).

Mode of Presentation Another manifestation of adaptive teaching can be seen when teachers vary their materials, media, and objectives to reach their students in multiple ways. Students differ in exposures to (and hence comfort levels with) different modes of presentation—verbal instructions, manipulatives, visual representations, and models (Salomon, 1981). When teachers vary the modalities in which their material is delivered, they are more likely to cover topics in ways that all students can readily comprehend. There are multiple channels—auditory, visual, and kinesthetic—made available for different students to access; and individual students can tune into the same material in different ways. The more ways material is accessed, and the more frequently it is reconsidered, the more memory traces that aid retention and transfer (Gardner, 1983).

Different exposures also extend to students' work styles and subject matter interests. Just as fluency with a work style reinforces its recurrence, so will enduring and current interests augment the efforts students put forth to acquire new skills (Schiefele, 1991). Adaptive teaching involves tapping into the interests and work styles of students—again, capitalizing on strengths as a way of building up weak areas.

Learning Guidance Finally, when models or examples are provided for students to observe as they grapple with the workings of complex systems and processes, and when students are urged to demonstrate both cognitive and other skills to one another, the burden of information processing for individual students is reduced, and more students can learn the same material during the same period of time (Brown, Collins, & Diguid, 1989). A display or model supplants the need for students to create internal displays on their own (Salomon, 1981).

Vicarious learning is learning by example or from observing the actions of others and their consequences. This is a powerful form of learning (Bandura, 1993). In a similar way, students' work samples and performances may become the basis for guided feedback from teachers—feedback that prompts students to take second tries. Teachers can also provide feedback that identifies the likely sources of errors and recognizes successes at the same time. Even reluctant students may then be encouraged to follow through on academic work and to try things again in the future (Bandura, 1993; Elawar & Corno, 1985).

This analysis of the accommodation strategy of adaptive teaching suggests that accommodation will be most useful when teachers confront a diverse range of students. When teachers face groups of students who have more qualities in common, the matching strategy of adaptive teaching provides another alternative. Matching is particularly useful when the qualities students have in common make them atypical, exceptional, or otherwise different from average. It is clear in much modern thinking about education that "different" should not be construed as "deficient" (Carter & Goodwin, 1994).

Matching Strategy

Matching teaching to individual student differences also means teaching to strengths. In this other side of strategic adaptive teaching, strengths are celebrated. Because conventional instruction favors students whose backgrounds are congruent with established sociocultural traditions of given communities, adaptive teaching assumes that students from (historically) minority subcultures (for example, "visible racial/ethnic groups," Carter & Goodwin, 1993) will often benefit from a different approach. Adaptive theory assumes that these students will benefit from an approach that is "culturally responsive" or culturally appropriate (Irvine, 1991).

Similarly, students who differ from the norm on factors directly related to school performance, such as verbal-intellectual ability, present another situation in which strengths might profitably be celebrated through better instructional matching. Students designated as "special" are, by definition, different from the norm. Thus, students whose first language is not English; students with established developmental delays, emotional, learning, or physical disabilities that have impeded verbal progress; as well as students who display exceptional talents or general intellectual "gifts" also stand to benefit less from conventional than from adaptive teaching. Differences such as these do not have to result in academic deficiencies or boredom if atypical students can be taught in ways that push hard on their strengths.

Two examples can be used to illustrate the matching strategy of adaptive teaching: teaching for cultural congruence or culturally responsive teaching, and teaching learning skills to learning disabled students.

Teaching for Cultural Congruence   In what has now become a classic example of "culturally responsive teaching," Au (1980) turned around the performance of students in one school in Hawaii. On school-administered standardized tests over an extended period of time, the native Hawaiian students in particular were failing to do well in reading. Possible reasons for this problem were explored by anthropologists and educational researchers.

The collected evidence showed that teachers in the school conducted reading instruction consistent with certain aspects of conventional American practice—that is, students took turns reading out loud from textbooks while other students and the teacher listened and the teacher offered corrections. Anthropologists noted inconsistencies between this way of teaching reading and the literacy event of storytelling in the native Hawaiian culture.

In the Hawaiian culture, it was common for children and adults to jointly participate in the telling of stories. As they "talked stories," both adults and peers were allowed to interrupt one another as a means for constructing a better and more interesting story. When Au asked teachers in the target school to change their reading instruction to better match this "talk story" pattern, student per-formance on reading tasks immediately began to improve. One year later, these students' reading achievement exceeded national norms.

One interpretation of what Au did for this school was help teachers see how to make their instruction resonate with an important aspect of emerging literacy indigenous to the native Hawaiian culture. Other examples of culturally respon-sive teaching show similarly positive results. Williams (1994) used matching to help a community of native Americans tailor the principles of "developmentally appropriate practice for early childhood education" (Bredekamp, 1987) to their own school settings. And Boykin (1986) found that the classroom performance of African-American children improved when teachers were assisted in providing activities that encouraged (rather than prohibited) movement and understand-ing through all five senses. It should be noted that matching does not assume there is one best way to teach *all* students from a given cultural background—clearly, there is substantial within-culture variation—but rather that delivering instruction in a way that is culturally more familiar can often produce dramati-cally positive modal results.

Teaching Learning Skills to Students with Learning Problems   Another view of matching can be found in an approach developed by Harris and Graham (1992) for teaching students with diagnosed learning disabilities. These researchers sought a better way to teach writing to groups of students with learning disabili-ties that were contributing to problems in school. A considerable amount of prior research has demonstrated that many learning disabled students do not acquire various self-regulatory strategies necessary for high-quality writing unless they are provided with explicit or direct instruction in this area; and yet, the motiva-tion or "will" of these students to succeed is often quite strong (see Brown & Campione, 1990).

Accordingly, Harris and Graham's approach emphasized the active role these students might play in their own learning. Special education teachers taught students to use self-statements, goal setting, self-assessments, self-recording, and self-reinforcement as means for monitoring and evaluating progress on their written assignments in school. The teachers modeled and reinforced these self-regulatory strategies in regular writing workshops and lessons on story structure. As students worked in small groups and individually, they were gradually led toward fluent use of the strategies on their own. By capitalizing on these students' basic eagerness to learn, this approach directly developed some skills that had been previously preventing success. Increases were observed following this instruction in many different class groups on both the quality and quantity of writing for both learning disabled and other children with special needs. And, like Au's research, these effects were found to be resilient over time.

As with culturally responsive teaching, teaching matched specifically to the strengths of students with common problems can produce strong and important improvements in educational outcomes. More research on the applications of matching strategies is needed. Only recently have researchers come to witness the positive effects on learning that can occur for previously marginalized students when teachers attend closely to the qualities that characterize particular classroom groups.

THEORY INTO PRACTICE

We can review the features of adaptive teaching as summarized by Glaser (1977; quoted in Ornstein, 1990, pp. 438–439):

1. Time, materials, and resources are flexible.

2. The curriculum provides sequence, structure, and multiple options for learning.

3. There is open display of and access to a rich variety of instructional materials and media equipment.

4. Tests provide information for teachers to make decisions.

5. Teaching students how to learn is emphasized.

6. The roles of both students and teacher are expanded.

As we have seen in this chapter, point 6 is critical in both theory and practice. Students are active participants in their own learning and have both individual and collective needs; but adaptive teaching expects them to learn ways to adapt the tasks of schooling for themselves. Adaptive teachers, in turn, are guiding and encouraging *all* students in appropriate ways. And they are constantly updating the information on which they base these critical instructional decisions.

By considering issues of adaptive teaching prior to planning instruction, teachers can determine its appropriateness for their current instructional situations. They can also be directed to the forms of adaptive teaching most suitable for their particular students. It takes little time to consider alternatives in this way, and doing so may well result in something of great benefit for many individuals who have been ill-served by other methods and approaches.

Teachers can use adaptive teaching at any grade level and in any subject area; they can use it in museums and in churches as well as in schools. Again, adaptive teaching is most relevant for situations in which students display diversity in the characteristics that predict learning from teaching, or when students as a group have been marginalized in the past. However, the principles of adaptive teaching can be applied in other situations as well, and there is evidence (mentioned earlier) that good teachers teach adaptively much of the time.

It should also be noted that there are other approaches to adaptive teaching not described here: For example, individual tutoring is, by definition, adaptive. *Mainstreaming*, a procedure for retaining special students for instruction within regular classrooms (rather than "pulling them out"), was also designed to help teachers to be adaptive with a designated few students who present special needs. Finally, in a new approach within multicultural education called *racial inclusion*, both teachers and students confront their racial identities as a way of fostering communication and promoting supportive curricular shifts that broaden rather than reduce the range of learning opportunities (Carter, 1991). Each of these approaches offers different challenges and possibilities for practicing teachers who confront the diversity of modern schooling today (see also Slavin, Karweit, & Madden, 1989).

SUMMARY

This chapter has examined some of the assumptions and research principles underlying adaptive teaching. It has attempted to illustrate how teachers might engage in adaptive teaching using two alternative strategies, called accommodating and matching. Each of these strategies capitalizes on strengths to help develop weaknesses. They differ in that accommodating helps teachers to manage classroom heterogeneity. Subgroups of students with different patterns of strengths and weakness are defined, and activities are differentiated according to the subgroups. Instruction is then tailored to benefit each subgroup's particular strengths and weaknesses. Matching, in contrast, helps teachers to emphasize the strengths of students who display similarity in qualities that may have functioned to marginalize them under conventional teaching or other unsupportive circumstances. In matching, the curriculum is purposefully enriched to resonate with interests and attitudes common to the group, and to help provide insights into unexamined assumptions regarding previous (suboptimal) teaching arrangements.

As was said at the outset of this chapter, the idea that it is profitable to adapt teaching to the needs of individual students pervades *every* arena of education and has throughout time. Isn't it about time teachers learned what this means, and how adaptive teaching might best be practiced in schools?

References

Au, K. (1980). "Participation Structures in a Reading Lesson with Hawaiian Children." *Anthropology and Education Quarterly* 11: 91–115.

Bandura, A. (1993). "Perceived Self-efficacy in Cognitive Development and Functioning." *Educational Psychologist* 28: 117–148.

Bellack, A., H. Kliebard, R. Hyman, and F. Smith (1966). *The Language of the Classroom.* New York: Teachers College Press, Columbia University.

Berliner, D. (1986). "In Pursuit of the Expert Pedagogue." *Educational Researcher* 15: 5–13.

Bloom, B. (1981). *All Our Children Learning.* New York: McGraw-Hill.

Boykin, A. W. (1986). "The Triple Quandary and the Schooling of Afro-American Children," in U. Neisser, ed., *The School Achievement of Minority Children.* Hillsdale, NJ: Lawrence Erlbaum, pp. 351–376.

Bredekamp, S., ed. (1987). *Developmentally Appropriate Practice in Early Childhood Programs Serving Children from Birth through Age 8.* Washington, D.C.: National Association for the Education of Young Children.

Brown, A., and J. Campione (1990). "Interactive Learning Environments and the Teaching of Science and Mathematics," in M. Gardner, J. Greens, F. Reif, A. Schoenfeld, A. diSessa, and E. Stage, eds., *Toward a Scientific Practice of Science Education.* Hillsdale, NJ: Lawrence Erlbaum, pp. 111–139.

Brown, J. S., A. Collins, and P. Diguid (1989). "Situated Cognition and the Culture of Learning." *Educational Researcher* 18: 32–42.

Carroll, J. (1963). "A Model of School Learning." *Teachers College Record* (May): 722–733.

Carter, R. (1991). "Racial Identity Attitudes and Psychological Functioning." *Journal of Multicultural Counseling and Development* 19: 105–114.

Carter, R., and L. Goodwin (1994). "Racial Identity and Education," in L. Darling-Hammond, ed., *Review of Research in Education*, vol. 20. Washington, D.C.: American Educational Research Association.

Clark, C., and P. Peterson (1986). "Teachers' Thought Processes," in M. C. Wittrock, ed., *Third Handbook of Research on Teaching.* New York: Macmillan, pp. 255–296.

Corno, L. (1992). "Encouraging Students to Take Responsibility for Learning and Performance." *Elementary School Journal* 93: 69–84.

Corno, L., and R. Snow (1986). "Adapting Teaching to Individual Differences among Learners," in M. C. Wittrock, ed., *Third Handbook of Research on Teaching.* New York: Macmillan, pp. 605–629.

Cronbach, L. (1989). "Construct Validation after Thirty Years," in R. Linn, ed., *Intelligence: Measurement, Theory, and Public Policy.* Urbana, IL: University of Illinois Press, pp. 147–172.

Cronbach, L., and R. Snow (1977). *Aptitudes and Instructional Methods.* New York: Irvington/Naiburg.

Cuban, L. (1984). *How Teachers Taught: Constancy and Change in American Classrooms: 1890–1980.* New York: Longman.

Darling-Hammond, L. (1991). "The Implications of Testing Policy for Quality and Equality." *Phi Delta Kappan* 73: 220–225.

Dillon, J. (1988). *Questioning and Teaching.* New York: Teachers College Press, Columbia University.

Elawar, M., and L. Corno (1985). "A Factorial Experiment in Teachers' Written Feedback on Student Homework: Changing Teacher Behavior a Little Rather than a Lot." *Journal of Educational Psychology* 77: 162–173.

Fullan, M. (1982). *The Meaning of Educational Change.* New York: Teachers College Press, Columbia University.

Gardner, H. (1983). *Frames of Mind.* New York: Basic Books.

Glaser, R. (1977). *Adaptive Education: Individual Diversity and Learning.* New York: Holt, Rinehart and Winston.

Goodlad, J. (1984). *A Place Called School.* New York: McGraw-Hill.

Graham, S., and K. Harris (1989). "Improving Learning Disabled Students' Skills at Composing Essays: Self-instructional Strategy Training." *Exceptional Children* 56: 201–214.

Harris, K., and S. Graham (1992). "Self-regulated Strategy Development: A Part of the Writing Process," in M. Pressley, K. R. Harris, and J. Guthrie, eds., *Promoting Academic Competence and Literacy in School.* New York: Academic Press, pp. 277–309.

Hoge, R., and T. Coladarci (1989). "Teacher-based Judgments of Academic Achievement: A Review of Literature." *Review of Educational Research* 59: 297–314.

Irvine, J. (1991). *Black Students and School Failure*. New York: Praeger.

Kozol, J. (1991). *Savage Inequalities*. New York: Crown Publishing.

Mason, D., and T. Good (1993). "Effects of Two-group and Whole-class Teaching on Regrouped Elementary Students' Mathematics Achievement." *American Educational Research Journal* 30: 328–360.

McCaslin, M., and T. Good (1994). "The Informal Curriculum," in D. C. Berliner and R. C. Calfee, eds., *Handbook of Educational Psychology*. New York: Macmillan.

McLaughlin, M. (1987). "Learning from Experience: Lessons from Policy Implementation." *Educational Evaluation and Policy Analysis* 9 (2): 171–178.

Novak, J., and D. B. Gowin (1984). *Learning How to Learn*. Cambridge, England: Cambridge University Press.

Oakes, J. (1985). *Keeping Track: How Schools Structure Inequality*. New Haven: Yale University Press.

Ornstein, A. (1990). *Strategies for Effective Teaching*. New York: HarperCollins.

Presidential Task Force on Psychology in Education, American Psychological Association (1993). *Learner-centered Psychological Principles: Guidelines for School Redesign and Reform*. Washington, D.C.: American Psychological Association.

Rohrkemper, M., and L. Corno (1988). "Success and Failure on Classroom Tasks: Adaptive Learning and Classroom Teaching." *Elementary School Journal* 88: 299–312.

Rosenshine, B., and R. Stevens (1986). "Teaching Functions," in M. C. Wittrock, ed., *Third Handbook of Research on Teaching*. New York: Macmillan, pp. 376–391.

Salomon, G. (1981). *Communication and Education: Social and Psychological Interactions*. Beverly Hills, CA: Sage.

Sarason, S. (1971). *The Culture of the School and the Problem of Change*, 2nd ed. Boston: Allyn and Bacon.

Schiefele, U. (1991). "Interest, Learning, and Motivation." *Educational Psychologist* 26: 299–324.

Slavin, R. (1987). "Ability Grouping and Student Achievement in Elementary Schools: A Best-evidence Synthesis." *Review of Educational Research* 57: 293–336.

Slavin, R., N. Karweit, and N. Madden, eds. (1989). *Effective Programs for Students at Risk*. Boston: Allyn and Bacon.

Snow, R. (1982). "Education and Intelligence," in R. J. Sternberg, ed., *Handbook of Human Intelligence*. Cambridge, England: Cambridge University Press, pp. 493–585.

Snyder, J., F. Bolin, and K. Zumwalt (1992). "Curriculum Implementation," in P. Jackson, ed., *Handbook of Research on Curriculum*. New York: Macmillan, pp. 402–435.

Webb, N. (1982). "Student Interaction and Learning in Small Groups." *Review of Educational Research* 52: 421–446.

Williams, L. (1994). "Developmentally Appropriate Practice and Cultural Values: A Case in Point," in B. L. Mallory and R. S. New, eds., *Diversity and Developmentally Appropriate Practice*. New York: Teachers College Press, Columbia University.

Zimmerman, B., and D. Schunk (1989). *Self-regulated Learning and Academic Achievement: Theory, Research, and Practice*. New York: Springer-Verlag.

Discussion Questions

1. Distinguish adaptive and conventional teaching.

2. Which of the two adaptive teaching strategies discussed might be described as concerned with "individual differences within a group"? Explain. Distinguish this from the strategy that might be described as concerned with "different groups of similar individuals." Explain.

3. Select a topic for instruction at a grade level of your choice, and discuss how you would teach it in a way that is culturally responsive for children from inner-city homes.

4. What kinds of instruction might be most appropriate for teaching a group of students who are both intellectually gifted and highly motivated to do well in school?

5. What are some of the potential dangers (ethical, social, political) inherent in any form of adaptive teaching, and how might thoughtful teachers counteract such dangers in their interpretations and use of these principles and strategies?

Carolyn M. Evertson and Catherine H. Randolph

Carolyn M. Evertson

Catherine H. Randolph

Carolyn M. Evertson is professor of education and is chair of the Department of Teaching and Learning, Peabody College, Vanderbilt University. In 1992 she was named Harvie Branscomb Distinguished Professor for Vanderbilt. Carolyn recalls: "My early interest in education probably started when, as a child, I received a small blackboard for Christmas. This became an important prop for playing school, and my dolls made willing and attentive pupils."

After graduating from Raymondville, (Texas,) High School, a small school in a small town in the lower Rio Grande Valley, Carolyn went to the University of Texas, Austin, where she received a bachelors degree in elementary education. Carolyn married and, when her two sons started school, education again became a keen interest. "This motivated me to earn a doctorate in educational psychology specializing in cognition and learning at the University of Texas."

After completing her doctorate, Evertson began work at the Research and Development Center for Teacher Education, University of Texas, with Jere Brophy on a project studying classroom practices employed by teachers whose students gained in achievement in reading and mathematics. The project rekindled her interest in the teaching side of the teaching/learning process.

"Our findings showed among other things that effective teachers were also good classroom managers. Findings from this project led to a large-scale study of how teachers manage and organize their classrooms that I directed with my colleagues." This work led to two texts on classroom management; *Classroom Management for Elementary Teachers* and *Classroom Management for Secondary Teachers* (Allyn and Bacon). Evertson has written a number of other books, chapters, articles, and monographs (many for beginning teachers) on teaching and classroom processes.

When asked about advice to new teachers, she points out that "teaching is something that all of us do in every aspect of our lives. We know more about good teaching than we did when I was instructing my dolls. Still, teaching well means recognizing that it is a lifelong endeavor requiring reflection, a desire to make a difference, and the courage to try."

Catherine Randolph grew up in Seattle, went to college in Vermont (Middlebury College, 1984), earned her masters degree at Stanford University (1986), and began teaching in Tennessee, where she later earned her doctorate at Vanderbilt University (1993) and is now a research assistant

116

professor. "The Pacific Northwest is still my favorite part of the country," she says, "although the Tennessee woods are a close second." Partially for this reason, Catherine lives outside Nashville in a cabin in the woods with her husband and cat, Foster.

Before returning to graduate school for her doctorate, Randolph taught high school English in a Nashville public school for three years. One lesson she learned during her first years, which she passes along as a suggestion for new teachers, is, "Make use of the knowledge and experience of your colleagues. Locate the 'expert' teachers in your school building, and don't be afraid to admit you have things to learn." For Randolph, even the best teacher preparation programs represent only the beginning stage of learning to teach. The best teachers continue to learn on the job—to reflect and think about what is happening in the classroom and how their teaching can be improved.

Randolph's most satisfying teaching experience, she recalls, was working with students on the school yearbook as the coordinating teacher. "It gave me a full picture of my students. I learned to appreciate and respect them as individuals. We worked as a team and had a tangible product at the end of the year. The students knew at least as much about producing a yearbook as I did, so we all learned together." It is this attitude of mutual respect and learning that she thinks is vital for effective teaching and should be carried over to all classrooms.

Today, when Catherine has free time she curls up in front of the fireplace listening to some soothing music or reading a good book.

7 ❧

Classroom Management in the Learning-centered Classroom

Carolyn M. Evertson and Catherine H. Randolph

Classroom management and discipline is the number-one concern of practitioners, particularly new teachers (Veenman, 1984). Classroom management studies of the past ten years have extended our knowledge of what effective classroom managers do and how they do it. The studies have helped to broaden the definition of classroom management from a focus on controlling misbehavior (Johnson & Brooks, 1979) to one that refers to the actions teachers take to create, implement, and maintain a classroom environment that supports learning.

Most studies of classroom management, however, have looked at classrooms where academic tasks and activities were fairly routinized and predictable. Relatively little research has examined different instructional contexts (for example, whole language settings, math problem solving, and so on) and what kinds of managerial decisions and teacher actions are required to enact academic tasks in these settings (Edelsky, Draper, & Smith, 1983). The questions remaining to be asked involve how management and organization support students' substantive learning and the nature and quality of the learning that is supported.

In the current climate of school reform there are clear calls for teaching problem-solving and higher-order thinking skills, integrating learning experiences within and across subject areas, and implementing multiple tasks (Resnick, 1987). The Council of Chief State School Officers (CCSSO) (1990) describes the movement: "Schools, previously asked to ensure the development of basic skills, are now required to teach all students a new, broad range of cognitive skills. . . . This new demand on schools is nothing less than a call for the democratization of thinking" (p. 2). Classrooms in which such transformations of learning are taking place will look different, just as their goals will be different. Higher-order learning "is complex; yields multiple criteria; involves uncertainty and finding structure in apparent disorder; demands self-regulation of thinking processes; and requires considerable mental effort . . ." (p. 3). Enacting these changes will require new ways of thinking about the organization and management of classrooms (see, for example, Cohen & Lotan, 1990; Marshall, 1992).

Furthermore, there is a false dichotomy that has emerged in the ways we view relationships between classroom management and instructional processes (Weade & Evertson, 1988). Effective management is typically regarded as a necessary precondition, after which effective instruction follows (Evertson, Emmer, Sanford, & Clements, 1983; Emmer, Sanford, Clements, & Martin, 1983). This conception implies that management and instruction are somehow separate processes, which can be thought of in isolation from each other. Evidence from classrooms indicates that this is not the case. Observers note, for instance, that when they watch the ongoing stream of talk and interactions in the real world and space of a classroom, distinctions between management and instruction become blurred. As these processes evolve, they are intertwined, intermingled, and in continual dynamic relation (Erickson, 1986; Green, Weade, & Graham, 1989; Weade, 1987).

The purpose of this chapter is to present and argue for the need for a conception of classroom management that encompasses a more complex view of learning, rather than reviewing exhaustively the research on classroom management that has been done to date. The chapter will attempt to focus on the existing gap between conceptions of curriculum and conceptions of pedagogy. We intend to (1) establish a definition/conceptualization of management, (2) provide examples intended to illustrate the relationship between management and instruction, and (3) propose questions to guide practice and further inquiry into classroom management.

WHAT IS A CLASSROOM?

Our first task in developing a conception of classroom management is to develop a conception of classrooms themselves. One area of research that has made important contributions to our understanding of how classroom processes function is research on classroom communication. This work focuses on both the student and the teacher as active mediators and constructors of the learning environment, identifying what students need to understand to participate in class lessons, how teachers orchestrate that participation, and how norms, rules, and expectations are signaled and resignaled across time. The teacher's management of how students may gain an opportunity to participate (for example, the student gets a reading turn, explains a concept) is communicated both verbally and nonverbally along with academic instruction. This research allows us a close look at how class activities evolve within and across settings and among students and teacher. It has implications for classroom management in that it shows how the system must be made visible, established, monitored, modified, refined, and reestablished.

Studies that have examined how classroom talk functions in educational settings suggest that different rules, norms, and expectations govern different class activities and lesson tasks. Classroom tasks have both social and academic di-

space, and materials are used efficiently maximize the opportunities students have to engage material in a meaningful way. The difference can be identified by defining terms such as *efficient* and *well-running* in classrooms where "engaging material in a meaningful way" is also defined differently. Table 7.1 illustrates some possible differences between management in work-oriented classrooms and in learning-oriented classrooms. As the table illustrates, as conceptions of learning and desired learning outcomes change, management must also change in order to be compatible with the new model.

Table 7.1 lists management concepts that recur in the literature on classroom management (task, on-task, and so on), along with possible definitions in work-oriented versus learning-oriented classrooms. The table shows management demands in a learning-oriented classroom are significantly different from those in a work-oriented classroom. As long as curriculum is conceived of as something that is delivered from teacher to students, management must be conceived of as a tool for student control; a way of getting students quiet, in their seats, and ready to receive information. If, however, we believe curriculum is actively constructed by all the participants in a setting, then the purpose of management is to facilitate active inquiry and collaboration among students. In a learning setting, the well-managed classroom will not necessarily be the quiet classroom, and on-task behavior is likely to look quite different than it does in a work setting. "Good" managers in both settings will be reflective. However, their reflections are likely to focus on different issues, about which they will come to different conclusions.

Thus far, we have argued that models of learning define models of management in a given classroom. The converse is also true: A teacher's management decisions contribute to the definition of learning that is constructed in a particular classroom over time. Management behaviors carry messages about what "counts" as knowledge in this setting, about whose ideas are of worth, and about where knowledge comes from.

The Santa Barbara Classroom Discourse Group, SBCDG (1992), argues that students' models of literacy are built across time, constructed as students learn what it means to be literate in a particular classroom setting. These models are based on information gathered from the talk and activities in which students engage, the texts they share, and how those texts are treated by teachers. SBCDG describes a particular discussion in which the notion of "character" is defined by a group of high school students working in a seminar setting with two teachers. In the process, students must define both academic content, in developing the concept of character, and social content, in negotiating how a class discussion will operate in this classroom. The teachers' management of the discussion communicates information about what counts as knowledge in this classroom, what kind of participation is acceptable, and how to handle disagreements. Each of these issues can be described as both social and academic: Characteristics of what counts as knowledge, for example, may include both the content and the form of a contribution to the discussion.

As discussion patterns are defined, they in turn define knowledge in the classroom. Consider, for example, typical discourse patterns in a traditional classroom (Mehan, 1979). The teacher initiates an interaction by asking a question

Table 7.1 Possible Definitions of Management Terms in Different Classroom Settings

Management Concept	Work-oriented Classroom	Learning-oriented Classroom
Task	Listen, follow directions, generate correct responses, answer questions	Listen, follow directions, modify directions, explore, challenge answers, generate directions, generate questions, formulate correct responses
On-task	During a listening task: sit quietly, ask questions During seatwork: write independently (usually silently), remain in seat	During a listening task: sit quietly, ask questions, propose alternatives During seatwork: discuss with peers, share ideas, move to most appropriate location for gaining needed information (library, resource materials area, and so on)
Achievement	Emphasis on accurately repeating/reconstructing information given by the teacher and/or text; standardized (mostly objective) tests	Emphasis on using information from the teacher, text, personal experience, research to generate creative or novel approaches, information, products. Individual (mostly subjective) measures
A "well-managed" class	Quiet, cooperative, smoothly functioning, little ambiguity about tasks or expectations, little conflict, "a well-oiled machine"	Noisy, cooperative, smoothly functioning, more ambiguous tasks and expectations, higher potential for conflict or disagreement, "a bee-hive of activity"
A "good" manager	Explicit, aware, reflective, directive, minimizes divergence from plan	Explicit, aware, reflective, less directive, recognizes/encourages divergence from plan

(usually a question to which he or she already knows the answer) and nominating a student to respond. Following the student response, the teacher evaluates it as correct/acceptable or incorrect/unacceptable, either directly ("Yes, good answer") or indirectly (moving on to the next question or asking the class, "Is that right?").

The pattern is an efficient discussion management technique for the teacher, allowing her or him to control pace and student involvement. As a management technique, however, it is not devoid of content. A particular view of knowledge and of the classroom is built through such interactions when they are repeated over time. In these interactions, knowledge (including knowledge of the right answer) is something the teacher has, and to which the teacher controls access. The emphasis in such interactions is on "right" answers, or the answers for which the teacher is looking, regardless of whether they seem "right" to students.

Randolph (1993) has documented how management and instruction informed each other in the discourse of a single English class that operated under a writers' workshop model. In this classroom, consistent patterns of management and instruction contributed to a particular definition of what it means to be a writer. In general, a writers' workshop involves students working at their own pace, generating their own topics, sharing writing with each other at various stages of drafting and revision, and providing feedback to their peers.

This approach claims to empower students by giving them ownership of their own work. Paralleling this claim of student power and ownership is a charge to teachers to redefine their roles in the classroom. Teachers are advised to "adopt more the role of a learner and less the role of a teacher" (Elbow, 1973, p. ix), and to function more as a "member or chair than as the sole source of knowledge and power" (Fulwiler, 1987, p. 143). These charges echo the characteristics of Marshall's metaphor of classrooms as "learning settings."

The implications of such changes for classroom management, as we have already argued, are great. When the teacher becomes co-learner, how can necessary teacher functions (organization of units, orchestration of classroom events, evaluation of student work) be accomplished? If the teacher is no longer the "sole source of knowledge and power," what kind of authority, if any, does she have in her interactions with students? The challenge for Ms. Cooper,* the teacher in the writers' workshop documented by Randolph (1993), was how to manage this highly student-centered pedagogy. Her management decisions, as expressed through her classroom talk, had the potential to support or to hinder the construction of a definition of writing as a process, and of the writing class as a student-centered learning environment. The academic and social demands of two activities, Generating Characteristics and Sharing Drafts, illustrate how management and curriculum intersect in the real world of the classroom, and how together they help to define the classroom as a learning community. While these examples alone do not provide a complete picture of this writing class, they are used here as illustrations of how the meaning-making process was influenced by the teacher's management decisions.

Generating Characteristics

This activity took place during the first week to two weeks of every unit. The teacher announced a genre that would be the topic of study for the unit; for example, the first unit was Children's Story. Students' first task in the unit was to

---

*Names used in this section are pseudonyms.

bring in a favorite children's story to share with the class. As stories were shared, the teacher led the group in generalizing from each story characteristics that were representative of all children's stories. In the children's story, characteristics included "words are simple," "not too long," "predictable," and "not a lot of print on a page." Students then used the characteristics derived from the models to begin writing their own children's stories.

The following example is taken from a Generating Characteristics discussion in the third unit, Myths and Fables. (In the example, "T" indicates the teacher; student names are pseudonyms.)

T:	What can we say about the characteristics of the morals?
Paula:	It's like something my mom always says.
Tim:	They're hard to explain.
Hillary:	It teaches a lesson.
T:	Maybe we need to explain what a lesson or moral is—how to be a better person. I'm going to put that up [on the board], unless you all have objections.

An interesting aspect of the discussion was the way teacher and student roles in generating content and managing the discussion were defined. In the excerpt above, the discussion begins with students suggesting possible answers to the teacher's question. The answers the teacher receives do not give her the information she wants (Hillary is really just restating the characteristic that is already on the chalkboard, that a fable teaches a lesson), so the teacher supplies her own answer: A moral teaches how to be a better person. In stating her answer, the teacher simultaneously clarifies her question and implicitly evaluates as inadequate the answers she has received thus far. With this new information, the discussion continues.

Laurie:	They're trying to prevent you from making mistakes.
T:	writes on the chalkboard: STORIES ARE USED TO HELP YOU BECOME A BETTER PERSON AND NOT MAKE MISTAKES.
Tim:	I disagree; sometimes some of the things are wrong.
Hillary:	Can be [wrong].
T:	Yes.
	She changes "ARE" to "CAN BE" in the sentence on the board; it now reads, STORIES CAN BE USED TO HELP YOU BECOME A BETTER PERSON AND NOT MAKE MISTAKES.

Laurie is able to supply an appropriate response, which Ms. Cooper incorporates into the characteristics she is already in the process of writing on the chalkboard.

So far, the discussion has followed a fairly straightforward initiation-response-evaluation (I-R-E) sequence (Mehan, 1979). The teacher, in the position of authority in the classroom, initiates a topic; students respond with possible answers; and Ms. Cooper evaluates them, rejecting all responses until Laurie supplies an answer that fits the teacher's expectations.

The nature of the interaction changes, however, as Tim questions the characteristic that is the joint construction of the teacher and Laurie. In effect, Tim takes on the evaluation of the response, moving the teacher into the role of co-collaborator with Laurie. Tim uses as evidence for his position the shared models that have been provided and shared by his peers. The acceptance of his evaluation supports the validity of students' earlier contributions to the class's shared knowledge base, and indicates that the teacher's response is as open to evaluation as any other participant's.

The pattern of talk described here illustrates both management and instruction. The academic content of the task, defining morals, is presented within a particular set of understandings about the roles teacher and student may take as they participate in class discussion. While the teacher appears at first to be acting in the traditional teacher role at the center of the interaction, initiating and evaluating student contributions, Tim's comment contributes to a different understanding of typical interaction patterns in this classroom. His evaluative contribution, and the class's acceptance of it, indicates that in this classroom, disagreement is acceptable, including disagreement with the teacher, and that the teacher's contributions to discussion are no more valuable than those of any other participant.

The academic demands of the task drew on students' present and prior experiences with writing to develop concrete definitions for abstract terms such as *moral*. Together, the academic and social demands of the Generating Characteristics activity contribute to a definition of writing class as a place where students and teacher learn together, rather than a place where students memorize what the teacher tells them. What counts as knowledge in writing class is thus defined as what is jointly created there through class discussion rather than as something the teacher brings in with her to give to students. Because of the close match in messages between the academic and social demands of the Generating Characteristics activity, both contributed to a definition of writing as student- (or reader-) centered.

Sharing Drafts

The Generating Characteristics activity did not occur in isolation in writing class. Instead, it was part of a process of learning about and creating writing that included a series of tasks which were academically and socially compatible with the meanings established through sharing and discussing models. For example, during each unit, students shared complete or in-progress drafts of their writing with their peers. While this sharing sometimes took place in pairs or in small groups, much more often it took place as a whole-class discussion. The interesting aspect of this activity for our purposes here was the social task structure. When a student author read his or her writing aloud to the class, that student was also delegated the responsibility of conducting the discussion about the writing. The teacher encouraged this practice by nudging students into discussions with statements like, "Jackson, you have a question." Students responded to this cue by taking on the management task of calling on their peers and responding to their questions, as in the following example.

> Jimmy reads aloud the rough draft of a myth he has been working on.

T:	Comments or suggestions? [Several hands go up.] Jimmy, some people have comments.
Jimmy:	[Looking at the raised hands.] Doris.
Doris:	That's a good idea. Is it from yesterday, when you said, "OH!"?
Jimmy:	Yes. Anyone else? [Looks around the room for raised hands.]

When Jimmy calls on Doris, he takes on the task of controlling talk. He is empowered to do so by the fact that he is the author of the writing under discussion. Students in this class took on a teacher-like role that reinforced the academic message given by the teacher, that writers "own" their work and make their own decisions on any matter which concerns that work. As this message was consistently repeated throughout the year in writing class through the teacher's management practices, students came to view each other as knowledge experts, and to see knowledge as something they shared and generated, rather than as something owned and mastered only by the teacher.

A final example from Ms. Cooper's writing class begins to provide an answer to the question that guides this discussion: What will management look like in a classroom with a learning orientation?

> It is early June, and students are sharing the products of the last writing unit, Speechwriting.

> Jackson presents his speech on the Kennedy assassination, arguing that the assassin could not possibly have been working alone. At the end of the speech, Ms. Cooper contributes an opinion. Renee turns to Jackson to get confirmation: Does Ms. Cooper's opinion agree with Jackson's research?

> The discussion between Ms. Cooper and Jackson continues, with each contributing and modifying hypotheses about what really happened to JFK.

> Ms. Cooper asks the class for comments and questions. Students respond, again directing their statements to Jackson. He leads the discussion, calling on students and processing the conversation.

> Jackson moves from the construction-paper map he has been using to illustrate his points to the chalkboard, where he diagrams JFK's parade route, the lay of the land, and the path of the shots fired.

> Ms. Cooper gets up and leaves the room to run an errand. There is no reaction from students, as Jackson's discussion continues.

In this scene from the last day of writing class, students naturally turn to Jackson with their questions about the Kennedy assassination, just as he naturally acts as the knowledge expert. Jackson takes on such typical teacher functions as managing the discussion by calling on the next speaker and answering behavior is an important issue in the classroom, it is only one aspect of classroom management. "[M]isbehavior and teacher interventions can be understood only in terms of their relation to processes of orchestrating order in classrooms. . . . [T]hey are part of the fabric of the ecological system that defines and sustains order" (Doyle, 1986, p. 418). It is this whole "fabric" that we have attempted to consider in this discussion of management. Our goal has been to address the intersection of management and disciplinary content, and how together they influence learning and definitions of learning.

Current models of classroom management must reflect current models of learning, and the ways teachers are being asked to engage students. Classroom management can support instruction, but it is an error to focus solely on management rather than considering the kinds of teaching and learning it supports or eliminates. Recent research has shown that the appearance of engagement can be deceiving unless teachers are aware of and can make visible what students are actually learning. Students can appear to be involved in tasks without engaging in the content. Bloome, Puro, and Theodorou (1989) use the term *procedural display* to describe situations where students and teachers engage in the form of an activity without being involved with the substance of the content.

Questions of organization and management are, ultimately, questions of what is valued in a particular setting. Ms. Cooper's management decisions defined student knowledge and opinions as both valid and valuable in the writers' workshop. Perhaps "management" is a misnomer for this kind of activity, coming as it does from a work/factory metaphor for the teaching-learning process. The term *orchestration* seems more compatible with learning-oriented conceptions of classrooms. The task for educators is to make sure that our conceptions of classroom management support our conceptions of learning.

References

Becker, H. S., B. Geer, and E. C. Hughes (1968). *Making the Grade: The Academic Side of College Life.* New York: Wiley.

Bloome, D., P. Puro, and E. Theodorou (1989). "Procedural Display and Classroom Lessons." *Curriculum Inquiry* 19: 265–291.

Cohen, E. G., and R. A. Lotan (1990). "Teacher as Supervisor of Complex Technology." *Theory into Practice* 29: 78–84.

Council of Chief State School Officers (1990). *Restructuring Learning for All Students: A Policy Statement by the Council of Chief State School Officers on Improved Teaching of Thinking.* Washington, D.C.: Author.

Doyle, W. (1986). "Classroom Organization and Management," in M. C. Wittrock, ed., *Handbook of Research on Teaching,* 3rd ed. New York: Macmillan, pp. 392–431.

Edelsky, C., K. Draper, and K. Smith (1983). "Hookin' em in at the Start of School in a 'Whole Language' Classroom." *Anthropology and Education Quarterly* 14: 257–281.

Elbow, P. (1973). *Writing without Teachers.* London: Oxford University Press.

Emmer, E. T., J. P. Sanford, B. S. Clements, and J. Martin (1983). "Improving Junior High Classroom Management." Paper presented at the annual meeting of the American Educational Research Association, Montreal.

Erickson, F. (1986). "Qualitative Methods in Research on Teaching," in M. C. Wittrock, ed., *Handbook of Research on Teaching,* 3rd ed. New York: Macmillan, pp. 119–161.

Evertson, C. M., E. T. Emmer, J. P. Sanford, and B. Clements (1983). "Improving Classroom Management: An Experiment in Elementary

School Classrooms." *The Elementary School Journal* 84: 173–188.

Fenstermacher, G. (1986). "Philosophy of Research on Teaching: Three Aspects," in M. C. Wittrock, ed., *Handbook of Research on Teaching*, 3rd ed. New York: Macmillan, pp. 37–49.

Fulwiler, T. (1987). *Teaching with Writing*, Upper Montclair, NJ: Boynton-Cook.

Green, J. L., and D. Smith (1983). "Teaching and Learning: A Linguistic Perspective." *The Elementary School Journal* 83: 353–391.

Green, J. L., R. Weade, and K. Graham (1989). "Lesson Construction and Student Participation: A Sociolinguistic Analysis," in J. L. Green and J. O. Harker, eds., *Multiple Perspective Analyses of Classroom Discourse*. Norwood, NJ: Ablex Publishing Corp., pp. 11–47.

Johnson, M., and H. Brooks (1979). "Conceptualizing Classroom Management," in D. L. Duke, ed., *Classroom Management* (Seventy-eighth Yearbook of the National Society for the Study of Education, Part II). Chicago: University of Chicago Press, pp. 1–41.

Marshall, H. H. (1988). "Work or Learning: Implications of Classroom Metaphors." *Educational Researcher* 17: 9–16.

Marshall, H. H. (1990). "Beyond the Workplace Metaphor: Toward Conceptualizing the Classroom as a Learning Setting." *Theory into Practice* 29: 94–101.

Marshall, H. H., ed. (1992). *Redefining Student Learning: Roots of Educational Change.* Norwood, NJ: Ablex Publishing Corp.

Mehan, H. (1979). *Learning Lessons: Social Organization and the Classroom.* Cambridge, MA: Harvard University Press.

Randolph, C. H. (1993). "An Ethnographic Study of Classroom Interaction and Literacy Learning in a Fifth/Sixth Grade Writing Class." Unpublished doctoral dissertation, Vanderbilt University, Nashville, TN.

Resnick, L. (1987). *Education and Learning to Think.* Washington, D.C.: National Academy Press.

Santa Barbara Classroom Discourse Group (1992). "Constructing Literacy in Classrooms: Literate Action as Social Accomplishment," in H. H. Marshall, ed., *Redefining Student Learning: Roots of Educational Change.* Norwood, NJ: Ablex Publishing Corp.

Veenman, S. (1984). "Perceived Needs of Beginning Teachers." *Review of Educational Research* 54: 143–178.

Weade, R. (1987). "Curriculum'n'Instruction: The Construction of Meaning." *Theory into Practice* 26: 15–25.

Weade, R., and C. M. Evertson (1988). "The Construction of Lessons in Effective and Less Effective Classrooms." *Teaching and Teacher Education* 4: 189–213.

Discussion Questions

1. Think of a lesson you have observed or participated in, or design one of your own. Analyze this lesson for social and academic task demands. In each case, how are students expected to participate, and what are they expected to know?

2. Contrast the work metaphor for classrooms with the learning metaphor. Give examples of a classroom operating under each.

3. Describe what *on-task* means in a work-oriented and in a learning-oriented classroom. As an observer, how would you identify on-task behavior in each setting?

4. What kinds of things should teachers consider when managing a learning-oriented classroom?

5. We have suggested that an alternative metaphor for classroom management is classroom "orchestration." Can you think of others? Explain.

8 ❧

Scaffolds for Teaching Higher-order Cognitive Strategies

Barak V. Rosenshine and Carla Meister

It is possible to place academic tasks (Doyle, 1984) on a continuum from well-structured to less-structured tasks. Well-structured tasks, such as mathematical computation or concrete skills (for example, using a word processor) are tasks that can be broken down into a fixed sequence of subtasks that consistently lead to the same goal. Long division computation is an example of a well-structured task. The steps are concrete and visible. There is a specific, predictable algorithm that can be followed, one that enables students to obtain the same results each time they perform the algorithmic operations. These well-structured tasks are taught by teaching each step of the algorithm to students. The research on effective teaching (Brophy & Good, 1986; Rosenshine & Stevens, 1986) is best seen as research that has helped us learn how to teach well-structured tasks.

Reading comprehension, writing, and study skills are examples of less-structured tasks—tasks that cannot be broken down into a fixed sequence of subtasks. These types of tasks are called less-structured tasks, and sometimes higher-order tasks, precisely because they do not have the fixed sequence that is part of well-structured tasks. One cannot develop algorithms for teaching less-structured tasks. This chapter is about the instructional procedures that have been developed since 1980 for teaching less-structured tasks. The new instructional developments have consisted of teaching students *cognitive strategies* that they can use to aid their completion of higher-order cognitive tasks. Cognitive strategies are *heuristics*, that is, prompts, supports, hints, and guides that a student can use. A cognitive strategy is not a direct procedure; it is not an algorithm to be precisely followed. Rather, a strategy is a heuristic that serves to support or facilitate learners as they develop internal procedures that enable them to perform the higher-level operations. Teaching students to generate questions about their reading is an example of a cognitive strategy. Generating questions does not directly lead, in a step-by-step manner, to comprehension. Rather, in the process of generating questions, students need to search the text and combine information, and these processes serve to help students comprehend what they read.

Cognitive strategies have been developed and taught in a number of subject areas. Students have been taught specific cognitive strategies to assist them in reading (Paris, Cross, & Lipson, 1984; Pearson & Dole, 1987; Perkins, Simmons, & Tishman, 1989; Pressley et al., 1990), in mathematics problem solving (Schoenfeld, 1985), in physics problem solving (Larkin & Reif, 1976), in writing (Englert & Raphael, 1989; Scardamalia, Bereiter, & Steinbach, 1984; Scardamalia & Bereiter, 1985), and in study skills (Alvermann, 1987; Armbruster, Anderson, & Meyer, 1991).

TEACHING COGNITIVE STRATEGIES

How does one teach cognitive strategies? One cannot develop an algorithm to teach cognitive strategies. Rather, cognitive strategies have been taught by providing students with *scaffolds* to help them learn the strategies. Scaffolds are forms of support provided by the teacher (or another student) to help students bridge the gap between their current abilities and the intended goal (Palincsar & Brown, 1984; Paris, Wikkon, & Palincsar, 1986; Tobias, 1982; Wood, Bruner, & Ross, 1976). "The metaphor of a scaffold captures the idea of an adjustable and temporary support that can be removed when no longer necessary" (Brown & Palincsar, 1989, p. 411).

A scaffold allows learners "to participate at an ever increasing level of competence" (Palincsar & Brown, 1984, p. 122). Scaffolding procedures operate to reduce the complexities of problems and break them down into manageable chunks that the child has a real chance of solving (Bickhard, 1992). Examples of scaffolds include providing simplified problems, modeling of the procedures by the teacher, and thinking aloud by the teacher as he or she solves the problem. Scaffolds may also be tools, such as cue cards or checklists. Scaffolds are gradually withdrawn or faded as learners become more independent, although students may continue to rely on scaffolds when they encounter particularly difficult problems.

Although scaffolds can be applied to the teaching of all skills, they are particularly useful, and often indispensable, for teaching higher-level cognitive strategies, where many of the steps or procedures necessary to carry out these strategies cannot be specified. Instead of providing explicit steps, one supports, or scaffolds, the students as they learn the skill.

What follows are ideas for teaching less-structured, higher-level tasks. There were four steps in developing these ideas. First, we located studies that had taught cognitive strategies in reading and writing. Next, we evaluated their effectiveness and learned that these studies have been successful in improving student comprehension and writing. Then we looked at the instructional procedures that were used in these studies and found a number of common procedures. We abstracted and grouped those procedures and present them in this chapter. We found that those procedures fit into seven categories, as shown in Table 8.1. Those pro-

Table 8.1   Components for Teaching Higher-order Cognitive Strategies

1. Locate or develop a concrete prompt that can guide students' processing.
2. Demonstrate use of the prompt through modeling and thinking aloud.
   a. Model the process of using the concrete prompt.
   b. Think aloud as choices are made.

3. Guide initial practice through techniques that reduce the difficulty of the task.
   a. Start with simplified material.
   b. Complete part of the task for the student, when appropriate.
   c. Provide cue cards to help them use the concrete prompt.
   d. Present the new material in small steps.
   e. Anticipate student errors.

4. Provide a variety of contexts for student practice.
   a. Provide teacher-led practice.
   b. Collaborative social dialogue.

5. Provide feedback and self-checking procedures for the student.
   a. Offer teacher-led feedback.
   b. Provide checklists.
   c. Provide models of expert work.
   d. Suggest fix-up strategies.

6. Increase student responsibility as they master the strategy.
   a. Diminish prompts and models.
   b. Gradually increase the complexity and difficulty of the material.
   c. Diminish student support.
   d. Practice putting all the steps together (consolidation).
   e. Check for student mastery.

7. Provide independent practice.
   a. Provide extensive practice.
   b. Facilitate application to new examples.

Caution: This list offers only suggestions for consideration when teaching cognitive strategies. It is not intended to be used as a tool for evaluation.

cedures are presented in this chapter as an aid to help you teach less-structured tasks to your students.

1. Locate or Develop a Concrete Prompt That Can Guide the Student's Processing

In the studies we reviewed, the first step in teaching a cognitive strategy was the development of a scaffold called a *concrete prompt*. These prompts are concrete references on which students can rely for support as they learn to apply the cognitive strategy. The prompt can be a guide for proceeding or an analogy. The purpose of this section is to illustrate the concept of concrete prompts by giving examples of those that have been developed and used successfully in intervention studies. A good deal of space here is spent on concrete prompts because this topic is so important for the teaching of cognitive strategies.

Concrete prompts are a key element in teaching higher-level cognitive strategies. In your own teaching, you will need to apply concrete prompts that have been developed, and you will also need to develop your own concrete prompts to help your students. To help you in both tasks, we provide a number of examples of concrete prompts. All these prompts come from studies where students who were taught to use these prompts had significantly higher achievement than control students who were not so taught.

For example, in some studies, students were taught to develop the cognitive strategy of generating questions. This strategy was taught as a way to improve reading comprehension. In some studies, the investigators gave the students "question words"—who, what, when, where, why, how—and taught them to use these words as prompts. These six simple question words were the concrete prompts.

Another set of concrete prompts to facilitate questioning comes from a study by King (1990), where students were provided with and taught to use a list of *question stems* that served to help the students form questions about a particular passage:

How are _____ and _____ alike?
What is the main idea of _____?
What do you think would happen if _____?
What are the strengths and weaknesses of _____?
In what way is __ _ related to _____?
How does _____ affect _____?
Compare _____ and _____ with regard to _____.
What do you think causes _____?
How does _____ tie in with what we have learned before?
Which one is the best _____ and why?
What are some possible solutions for the problem of _____?
Do you agree or disagree with this statement: _____? Support your answer.
What do I (you) still not understand about _____?

To help teach students the cognitive strategy of *summarizing,* Baumann (1984) and Taylor (1985) used the following prompts:

1. Identify the topic.

2. Write two or three words that reflect the topic.

3. Use these words as a prompt to help figure out the main idea of the paragraph.

4. Select two details that elaborate on the main idea and are important to remember.

5. Write two or three sentences that best incorporate these important ideas.

Other investigators developed specific concrete prompts to help students improve their writing. For example, Englert, Raphael, Anderson, Anthony, and Stevens (1991) provided Plan Sheets that cued students to consider their audience ("Who am I writing for?" "Why am I writing this?"), and Organize Sheets that helped students sort their ideas into categories ("How can I group these ideas?" "What is being explained?" "What are the steps?").

Other concrete prompts were developed by Scardamalia, Bereiter, and Steinbach (1984) to assist students during the writing process by stimulating their thinking about the planning of compositions. These prompts or cues took the form of introductory phrases and were grouped according to the function that they served: planning a new idea, improving, elaborating, goal setting, and putting it all together. Students first determined the type of cue needed, then chose a particular cue to incorporate into the silent planning monologue. Some of these cues are given below:

Planning Cues Used for Opinion Essays

New Idea

Elaborate

An even better idea is . . .
An example of this . . .
An important point I haven't considered yet is . . .
This is true, but it's not sufficient so . . .
My own feelings about this are . . .
A better argument would be . . .
I'll change this a little by . . .
A different aspect would be . . .
The reason I think so . . .
A whole new way to think of this topic is . . .
Another reason that's good . . .
I could develop this idea by adding . . .
No one will have thought of . . .
Another way to put it would be . . .

Improve

A good point on the other side of the argument is . . .

I'm not being very clear about what I just said so . . .

Goals

I could make my main point clearer . . .
A goal I think I could write is . . .

A criticism I should deal with in my paper is . . .
My purpose . . .

I really think this isn't necessary because . . .

Putting It Together

I'm getting off topic so . . .
If I want to start off with my strongest idea, I'll . . .
I can tie this together by . . .
My main point is . . .

a. Prompts for Organizing Expository Material   There are prompts that have been used to help students *organize* expository material. Applying these prompts enables readers to organize the larger material into smaller and more meaningful parts, and such organization can facilitate both comprehension and recall. The best known organizing prompt is an outline. Another organizing prompt is a thematic map in which the elements are organized around a single theme. Berkowitz (1986) recommends that one apply the following steps when using this prompt:

Draw a central box with five or six boxes around it.

Write the title of the article in the central box.

Skim the article to find four to six main ideas.

Write these ideas in each of the boxes and underline them.

Find two to four important details to list under each main idea.

Draw lines connecting each box to the main idea.

b. Prompts for Processing Expository Material   Study skills or learning strategies involve both organizing and processing new material. The purpose of processing is to increase the number and strength of connections in the long-term memory so that the material is more easily recalled. Asking students to use and apply the previously mentioned prompts for generating questions and/or summarizing material aids processing and helps develop learning strategies, because these procedures require students to do more than simply read the material. They require students to focus on the central ideas and restate them in their own words.

Summary   A number of concrete prompts for helping students develop cognitive strategies are presented above. The prompts used in these studies were derived from two sources: Some were derived from studying the strategies used by experts, and other prompts were simply invented by the investigators. In your teaching, one tactic will be to locate or invent cognitive strategies that you can use in your teaching.

2. Demonstrate the Use of the Prompt through Modeling and Thinking Aloud

After finding or developing a concrete prompt, the next step is to help students learn to use the prompt. Two overlapping procedures have been used in intervention studies to help teach students to use and apply the concrete prompts: modeling and thinking aloud.

a. Model the Process of Using the Concrete Prompt   In these studies, the instruction began with introducing, explaining, and demonstrating the utility of the concrete prompt. Then the teacher modeled its application as the students observed. Thus, when students were taught to generate questions, the teacher modeled how to use the cues to think of questions related to a particular passage. When teaching students to write a summary, the teacher modeled the process of identifying the details of a paragraph or passage, using the details to form a main idea, and stating the details in the summary. In writing an explanation paper, the teacher used the planning cues in a self-talk or inner dialogue style. The teacher modeled how to use the Plan-Think sheet as a way to record ideas and thoughts about the topic.

Modeling of the process by the teacher gradually diminished as students began to take on more of the responsibility for completing the task. The teacher continued to model only the part(s) of the process that students were unable to complete at that particular time. Often during the transitional stage, when students were ready to take on another part of the task, the teacher continued to model, but requested hints or suggestions from the students regarding how to complete the next step in the task. Several studies also relied on more capable students to provide the modeling.

b. Think Aloud as Choices Are Being Made   Another scaffold is "thinking aloud," where the teacher verbalizes his or her thought processes as the concrete prompt is being used. For example, when teaching students to generate questions, the teacher describes the thought processes that occur as a question word is selected and integrated with text information to form a question. A teacher might think aloud while summarizing a paragraph, illustrating the thought processes that occur as the topic of the passage is determined and then used to generate a summary sentence.

Anderson (1991) provides illustrations of a teacher using think-alouds to illustrate how he might use one of the following cognitive strategies in reading:

For clarifying difficult statements or concepts:
   I don't get this. It says that things that are dark look smaller. I know that a white dog looks smaller than a black elephant, so this rule must only work for things that are about the same size. Maybe black shoes would make your feet look smaller than white ones would.

For summarizing important information:
   I'll summarize this part of the article. So far, it tells where the Spanish started in North America and what parts they explored. Since the title is "The Spanish in

California," the part about California must be important. I'd sum up by saying that Spanish explorers from Mexico discovered California. They didn't stay in California, but lived in other parts of America. These are the most important ideas so far.

For thinking ahead:
So far this has told me that Columbus is poor, the trip will be expensive, and everyone's laughing at his plan. I'd predict that Columbus will have trouble getting the money he needs for his exploration.

As individual students accepted more responsibility in the completion of a task, they often modeled and thought aloud for their less capable classmates. Not only did student modeling and think-alouds actively involve the students in the process, but it allowed the teacher to better assess student progress in the use of the strategy. Thinking aloud by the teacher and more capable students provided novice learners with a way to observe "expert thinking" usually hidden from the student. Indeed, identifying the hidden strategies of experts so that these can become available to learners has become a useful area of research (Collins et al., 1989).

3. Guide Students through Initial Practice Using Techniques that Reduce the Difficulty of the Task

In the studies that taught cognitive strategies, a number of scaffolds were used to regulate the difficulty of the task and guide student practice. These scaffolds are described as follows.

a. Start with Simplified Material   In order to help the learner, many investigators began with simpler exercises and then gradually increased the difficulty of the task. This allowed the learner to begin participating very early in the process. For example, in a study by Palincsar (1987), the task of generating questions was first simplified to that of practicing how to generate questions about a *single sentence.* The teacher first modeled how to generate questions, and this was followed by student practice. Then the complexity was increased to generating questions after reading a *paragraph,* followed by student practice. Finally, the teacher modeled and the class practiced generating questions after reading an entire *passage.*

When learning the strategy of summarizing, students in the study by Dermody (1988) first learned how to write summary statements of single paragraphs. After students received guided practice on this task, teachers showed them how to combine several summary statements to produce a single summary for a longer passage, and had them practice this more difficult task. Thus, in the study by Palincsar (1987) the task of processing a paragraph was reduced to first processing a sentence; in the study by Dermody (1988) the task of processing a passage was reduced to first processing a paragraph.

Another form of regulating difficulty is to begin with simpler materials that do not cause as much cognitive strain. Such simplification occurred when teaching summarization, where the investigator located materials that were one or two years below the students' reading level and used these materials during initial instruction (Lonberger, 1988). As the students became more proficient, the level of the materials was increased.

b. Complete Part of the Task for the Student   In many of the studies, instruction on the cognitive strategy began with the teacher completing most or all of the task through modeling and thinking aloud. The teacher continued to carry out the parts of the task not yet introduced to the students or those parts students were unable to complete at the time. Sometimes, the students' participation began at a very simple level. For example, as the teacher modeled the strategy, the students were asked to provide the label. Or students were requested to state the next step in the process the teacher needed to model. As student involvement increased, teacher involvement was withdrawn. Teachers provided hints, prompts, suggestions, and feedback when students encountered difficulties in their attempts to complete part of the task. Sometimes these difficulties required a temporary increase in teacher involvement until students were able to overcome the difficulty.

c. Provide Cue Cards to Help Students Use the Concrete Prompt   In some of these studies, students received cue cards containing the concrete prompts they had been taught. Having a cue card relieves the strain on the limited working memory by "downloading" the task from the working memory to the card (Perkins, Simmons, & Tishman, 1989). A student can look at the cue card to recall the concrete prompt instead of having to hold the prompt in one's limited working memory. This allows the student to expend more effort and thought on the actual application of the prompt. For example, in the study by Billingsley and Wildman (1984), the teacher gave students a card containing the list of question words (for example, who, what, why . . .) they could use to generate questions. Singer and Donlan (1982) taught students to use the elements of story grammar (for example, leading character, goal, obstacles, outcomes, and theme) as prompts to generate questions, and gave them lists of these story elements for reference.

Wong and Jones (1982) provided each student with cue cards printed with the following concrete prompts to use as they generated questions on the main idea of the passage:

1. Why are you studying this passage? (So you can answer some questions you will be given later.)

2. Find the main idea/ideas in the paragraph and underline it/them.

3. Think of a question about the main idea you have underlined. Remember what a good question should be like.

4. Learn the answer to your question.

5. Always look back at the questions and answers to see how each successive question and answer provides you with more information.

Eventually the cue cards were removed and students were asked to formulate questions or write summaries without them. Cue cards were used in studies at all levels, from third grade through college.

d. Present the New Material in Small Steps   When presenting a concrete prompt with several steps or component parts, the difficulty can be regulated by "teaching in small steps," that is, by first teaching one step or part and providing for student practice before teaching the next part. In this way, students deal with manageable, yet meaningful, bits. In a study (Blaha, 1979) in which students were taught a strategy for summarizing paragraphs, the teacher explained and modeled the first step, identifying the topic of a paragraph, and the students then practiced this skill. Then she taught the second step, the concept of main idea, and students practiced finding the topic and locating the main idea together. Following this, she taught students the third step, identifying the supporting details, and the students practiced that part of the task. Finally, the students practiced doing all three steps of the strategy.

e. Anticipate Student Errors   Another way to regulate the difficulty of learning a new cognitive strategy is to anticipate and discuss potential student errors. When teaching students the cognitive strategy of summarization, one teacher anticipated errors in summarizing by presenting a summary with a poorly written topic sentence and asking students to state the problem. In another study (Brady, 1990), the investigator noticed that students had a tendency to produce summary statements that were too broad, often providing only the general topic of the passage (for example, "This paragraph was about toads."). To help students avoid this error, Brady developed a simple yet successful concrete prompt: He suggested students begin their summary statements with the phrase "This paragraph tells us that _____." This prompt significantly improved the quality of summary statements.

When teaching students to generate questions, the teacher showed questions that were inappropriate because they were about a minor detail and then asked students to state why they were inappropriate. Or, the teacher showed questions that were too broad to be answered from the text and asked students to explain why the questions were inappropriate. The students then used these hints and suggestions as they generated their questions.

One characteristic of expert teachers is their ability to anticipate student errors prior to instruction. One teacher stated, "With experience, you can pinpoint mistakes students make ahead of time. The more you teach, the more you realize where the pitfalls are" (Borko & Livingston, 1990, p. 490).

4. Provide a Variety of Contexts for Student Practice

Two contexts were used to provide for supervised student practice: teacher-guided practice and collaborative social dialogue.

1. Reread the difficult portion of the text.

2. Read ahead to see if the problems clear up.

3. Consult an expert source such as a teacher or parent.

4. Ask a friend for help.

Bereiter and Bird (1985) analyzed protocols of adult expert readers thinking aloud while reading difficult text and identified on-line fix-up strategies used by skilled readers when they encountered difficulty in comprehension of text during initial reading. From these identified strategies used by expert readers, Bereiter and Bird selected the four main comprehension fix-up strategies used by those readers. The strategies included the following:

1. Restating confusing text in simpler or more familiar terms

2. Backtracking or rereading

3. Demanding relationships between sections of the text

4. Formulating the difficulty as a problem

Students who received instruction in these strategies—instruction that identified, modeled, and explained the strategies and provided students with practice in identifying and applying the strategies—significantly increased their use of these strategies and made significant gains in reading comprehension.

6. Increase Students' Responsibility as They Master the Strategy

Just as it is important to simplify material and provide support for students in the initial stages of learning a cognitive strategy, it is also important to diminish the number of prompts and provide students with practice using more complex material. Thus, responsibility for learning shifts from the teacher to the student. This gradual decrease in prompts and supports and gradual increase in student responsibility has been described as a shift in the teacher's role from that of coach to that of supportive and sympathetic audience (Palincsar & Brown, 1984).

a. Diminish Prompts and Models

After the students in the study by Wong and Jones (1982) had used cue cards to develop fluency in performing the task, the cue cards were removed and students were asked to write summaries without these prompts. In the study by King (1990), in which students used half-completed sentences as references when generating questions, the teacher withdrew the supports after the guided practice, and students were left to generate questions on their own.

As students used cue cards during guided practice, they gradually internalized the prompts on the concrete prompt or the process that accompanied their use. Once the cue cards were removed, students were able to rely on the internalized structure of the prompt.

b. Gradually Increase the Complexity of the Material Increasing the complexity of the material was evident in the study by Palincsar (1987) in which students learning to generate questions began by working on a single sentence, then a paragraph, and finally an entire passage. Schoenfeld (1985) sequenced the problems he presented to his students when teaching mathematical problem solving. He first gave students problems they were incapable of solving on their own. This step provided the motivation for learning the problem-solving strategy he planned to introduce. After presenting the strategy, he provided problems that were easily solved when the strategy was applied. As students became skilled at applying the strategy, a new strategy was introduced. Interspersed among these new problems were several problems requiring the application of previously taught problem-solving strategies, forcing students to discriminately apply the strategies learned to the types of problems encountered. As the course progressed, students were expected to combine strategies to solve complex problems.

c. Diminish Support Provided Students In some studies, the support that students received from other students was also diminished as work progressed. For example, in the study by Nolte and Singer (1985), students first spent three days working in groups of five or six and then three days working in pairs before working alone on the task.

In the Englert et al. (1991) study, in which students were taught cognitive strategies in writing, students first participated in a collaborative dialogue that centered on the application of the newly learned strategies to a whole-class writing project. Students were then allowed to choose their own topic, applying the same strategies used in group writing. Students were encouraged to collaborate with peers by sharing ideas, discussing each other's writing, asking questions, getting feedback, reporting progress, or asking advice. The teacher provided additional support by finding examples of strategy use or problems found in the students' writing, displaying them on the overhead. The teacher initiated a class dialogue on the student examples, focusing the discussion on the strategies used, the problems encountered by the students, and possible solutions. After the students completed this piece of writing, the teacher asked them to independently write another paper for publication in a class book.

d. Provide for Consolidation Activities When a series of steps has been taught and practiced separately, as in some summarizing and writing strategies, one of the final tasks during guided practice is having students practice putting the component parts of the strategy together. A teacher can then assess student implementation of the complete strategy, correct errors, and determine whether additional teaching or practice is necessary. Such assessment is important before students begin independent practice.

e. Check for Student Mastery Before independent practice, it is important to check students to see if the tasks have been learned and to provide additional instruction and practice where necessary. Thus, when students are taught to generate questions, there is a need to test them on their mastery of this task. To some extent, a teacher is receiving feedback from students as they practice the task, but there also may be an advantage to more systematic feedback, such as when all students are given the same passage or paragraph and are asked to generate questions. In this systematic way, all students, even the quiet ones, can be checked and additional instruction can be provided for those who need it.

7. Provide Independent Practice with New Examples

The goal of independent practice is to develop "unitization" of the strategy, that is, the blending of elements of the strategy into a unified whole. The extensive practice, and practice with a *variety* of materials—alone, in groups, or in pairs— also *decontextualizes* the learning. That is, the strategies become free of their original "bindings" and can now be applied, easily and unconsciously, to various situations (Collins et al., 1989). More accurately, the variety of materials serves to link the strategy to a richer set of contexts, and all of these contexts now suggest the strategy.

Cognitive Strategy Instruction in Writing, the program implemented in the Englert et al. (1991) study, provided students with several opportunities to apply the strategies they had been taught, first in a whole-group setting, then individually with peer and teacher assistance, and then a third time independently. As students worked in class on the second writing assignment, intermittent class discussions focused on examples of student work placed on the overhead projector. These examples illustrated the flexibility of the strategies when applied to a number of different topics and in a number of different ways. The students then independently applied the strategies to a third and final writing assignment on a topic of their choice.

Teaching without Concrete Prompts

There are some tasks that are so difficult that concrete prompts have not been developed, and other tasks in which the concrete prompts can only serve to scaffold a part of the task. What does one do then? In such cases, the teacher spends more time modeling and thinking aloud, more time discussing the models, and more time providing checklists and expert models for comparison.

THEORY INTO PRACTICE

The first step in using this research in practice is to locate or develop concrete prompts that can be taught to your students. These prompts can be found in journals such as *Educational Leadership* and *The Reading Teacher*, as well as in publications on learning strategies. An excellent compilation of prompts is available in the book *Strategic Learning in Content Areas*, published by The Wisconsin Department of Public Education. Prompts can also be located by asking your fellow teachers for the prompts that were most successful for them.

When demonstrating to students how to use these prompts, it is useful to start by modeling your use of the prompt. After that, you might think aloud when using the prompt. You might do this by discussing the choices you are making, the reasons for the choices, the places where you are uncertain, and the procedures you use to get through the uncertainty. Thinking aloud is useful because it can reveal to the students the strategies that they might use.

During the initial practice, many researchers have found it useful to start with simplified material and then gradually increase the difficulty of the task. Other researchers start with regular material but complete part of the task for the students. When a strategy has a number of steps, then there is practice after each step. All these procedures can serve to reduce the difficulty of the task for the students and increase the chances for success.

It is useful to be able to anticipate the errors that students make and the parts that will be most difficult for them. Then you can discuss these problems with the students and suggest ways in which they can recognize these problems and handle them. If you are teaching a subject for the first time, then (1) you might ask other teachers to identify the most common problems that students have, or (2) you might work the problems yourself, paying attention to the parts that you find the hardest to do.

After the initial instruction, when students are applying a strategy and working problems, it is useful to have students working in groups of two or three. In that setting, one student can help and explain to the other. Having to explain something not only benefits the recipient, but the process often helps the explainer organize and clarify his or her own thinking. Sometimes one student can explain, another can listen, and a third can check and comment on the quality of the explanation.

During initial practice, it is also useful to supply students with cue cards that contain the prompts so that they can refer to them as they work. It is also helpful to suggest and model the use of "fix-up" strategies; strategies that students might consider applying when they are stuck or when the process isn't working smoothly.

Feedback is important. After students have received feedback from the teacher on their work, other procedures can be used to help the students check their work. As discussed previously, one procedure is providing students with a model of the completed task (such as a summary or an essay) against which students can check their work. Another feedback procedure is a checklist.

Just as the initial work was made simpler for the student, later work can consist of increasing student responsibility by decreasing the prompts and increasing the complexity of the material.

Finally, there is a need for extensive practice and application to new examples so that students will be able to use the new strategies flexibly and independently.

SUMMARY

This review of the methods used in studies about the teaching of cognitive strategies in language arts has yielded a number of new instructional procedures that might be added to the teacher's armamentarium. These elements enlarge our technical vocabulary and repertoire of instructional practices useful in the teaching of both well-structured skills and cognitive strategies in the classroom.

One advancement in this research is the introduction of the concept of scaffolds (Palincsar & Brown, 1984; Wood, Bruner, & Ross, 1976). The procedures for instruction in the use of these scaffolds provide us with suggestions for thinking about how to help students learn a variety of cognitive strategies.

An important new concept is that of providing students with concrete prompts. These prompts are a special type of scaffold, one that is specific to the cognitive strategy being taught, yet the general idea can be applied to a variety of different contexts. Examples include the different prompts that help students generate questions, the prompts that suggest procedures for summarizing, and the questions to consider when planning an essay.

In summary, because higher-level cognitive strategies cannot be taught as a series of explicit steps, there is a need for a great deal of student practice to help overcome this problem. This practice can take a variety of forms, yet all of them apply the notion of scaffolding and fading. As guided practice begins, the majority of the task is completed by the teacher through modeling and thinking aloud. As practice progresses, students take on more responsibility in completing the task and teacher support is gradually withdrawn. As guided practice nears completion, students complete all of the task independently, with little or no support from the teacher. Previously withdrawn scaffolds can be temporarily reintroduced into the instruction as students encounter difficulties.

References

Alvermann, D. (1994). "Secondary School Reading," in P. D. Pearson, ed., *Handbook of Reading Research*, vol. 2. New York: Longman.

Anderson, V. (1991, April). "Training Teachers to Foster Active Reading Strategies in Reading-disabled Adolescents." Paper presented at the annual meeting of the American Educational Research Association, Chicago.

Armbruster, B., T. H. Anderson, and J. L. Meyer (1991). "Improving Content Area Reading Using Instructional Graphics." *Reading Research Quarterly* 25: 140–157.

Baumann, J. F. (1984). "The Effectiveness of a Direct Instruction Paradigm for Teaching Main Idea Comprehension." *Reading Resarch Quarterly* 20: 93–115.

Bereiter, C., and M. Bird (1985). "Use of Thinking Aloud in Identification and Teaching of Reading Comprehension Strategies." *Cognition and Instruction* 2: 131–156.

Berkowitz, S. (1986). "Effects of Instruction in Text Organization on Sixth-grade Students' Memory for Expository Reading." *Reading Research Quarterly* 21: 161–178.

Bickhard, M. H. (1992). "Scaffolding and Self-scaffolding: Central Aspects of Development," in L. T. Winegar and J. Valsiner, eds., *Children's Development within Social Context*, vol. 2. Hillsdale, NJ: Lawrence Erlbaum.

Billingsley, B. S., and T. M. Wildman (1984). "Question Generation and Reading Comprehension." *Learning Disability Research* 4: 36–44.

Blaha, B. A. (1979). "The Effects of Answering Self-generated Questions on Reading." Unpublished doctoral dissertation, Boston University School of Education.

Borko, H., and C. Livingston (1989). "Cognition

and Improvisation: Differences in Mathematics Instruction by Expert and Novice Teachers." *American Educational Research Journal* 26: 473–499.

Brady, P. L. (1990). "Improving the Reading Comprehension of Middle School Students through Reciprocal Teaching and Semantic Mapping Strategies." Unpublished doctoral dissertation, University of Oregon.

Brophy, J. E., and T. L. Good (1986). "Teaching Behavior and Student Achievement," in M. C. Wittrock, ed., *Handbook of Research on Teaching*, 3rd ed. New York: Macmillan.

Brown, A. L., and A. S. Palincsar (1989). "Guided, Cooperative Learning and Individual Knowledge Acquistion," in L. B. Resnick, ed., *Knowing, Learning, and Instruction: Essays in Honor of Robert Glaser*. Hillsdale, NJ: Lawrence Erlbaum.

Brown, A. L., and J. C. Campione (1986). "Psychological Theory and the Study of Learning Disabilities." *American Psychologist* 41: 1059–1068.

Collins, A., J. S. Brown, and S. E. Newman (1989). "Cognitive Apprenticeship: Teaching the Crafts of Reading, Writing, and Mathematics," in L. Resnick, ed., *Knowing, Learning, and Instruction: Essays in Honor of Robert Glaser*. Hillsdale, NJ: Lawrence Erlbaum.

Davey, B., and S. McBride (1986). "Effects of Question-generation on Reading Comprehension." *Journal of Educational Psychology* 78: 256–262.

Dermody, M. M. (1988). "Effects of Metacognitive Strategy Training on Fourth Graders' Reading Comprehension." Unpublished doctoral dissertation, University of New Orleans.

Englert, C. S., and T. Raphael (1989). "Developing Successful Writers through Cognitive Strategy Instruction," in J. Brophy, ed., *Advances in Research on Teaching*, vol. I. Newark, NJ: JAI Press.

Englert, C. S., T. E. Raphael, L. M. Anderson, H. M. Anthony, and D. D. Stevens (1991). "Making Strategies and Self-talk Visible: Writing Instruction in Regular and Special Education Classrooms." *American Educational Research Journal* 28: 337–372.

King, A. (1990). "Enhancing Peer Interaction and Learning in the Classroom through Reciprocal Peer Questioning." *American Educational Research Journal* 27: 664–687.

Larkin, J. H., and F. Reif (1976). "Analysis and Teaching of a General Skill for Studying Scientific Text." *Journal of Educational Psychology* 72: 348–350.

Leinhardt, G. (1986). "The Development of Expert Explanation: An Analysis of a Sequence of Subtraction Lessons." Unpublished manuscript, University of Pittsburgh, Learning Research and Development Center.

Lonberger, R. B. (1988). "The Effects of Training in a Self-generated Learning Strategy on the Prose Processing Abilities of Fourth and Sixth Graders." Doctoral dissertation, State University of New York at Buffalo.

Manning, B. H. (1988). "Application of Cognitive Behavior Modification: First and Third Graders' Self-management of Classroom Behaviors." *American Educational Research Journal* 25: 193–212.

Meichenbaum, D., and J. Goodman (1971). "Training Impulsive Children to Talk to Themselves: A Means of Developing Self-control." *Journal of Abnormal Psychology* 77: 115–126.

Nolte, R. Y., and H. Singer (1985). "Active Comprehension: Teaching a Process of Reading Comprehension and Its Effects on Reading Achievement." *The Reading Teacher* 39: 24–31.

Palincsar, A. S. (1986). "The Role of Dialogue in Providing Scaffolded Instruction." *Educational Psychologist* 21: 73–98.

Palincsar, A. S. (1987). "Collaborating for Collaborative Learning of Text Comprehension." Paper presented at the annual conference of the American Educational Research Association, April, Washington, D.C.

Palincsar, A. S., and A. L. Brown (1984). "Reciprocal Teaching of Comprehension-fostering and Comprehension-monitoring Activities." *Cognition and Instruction* 2: 117–175.

Paris, S. G., K. K. Wikkon, and A. S. Palincsar (1986). "Instructional Approaches to Reading Comprehension," in E. Z. Rothkof, ed., *Review of Research in Education* 13. Washington, D.C.: American Educational Research Association.

Pearson, P. D., and J. A. Dole (1987). "Explicit

Comprehension Instruction: A Review of Research and a New Conceptualization of Instruction." *Elementary School Journal* 88: 151–165.

Perkins, D. N., R. Simmons, and S. Tishman (1989, March). "Teaching Cognitive and Metacognitive Strategies." Paper presented to the annual meeting of the American Educational Research Association, San Francisco.

Pressley, M., J. Burkell, T. Cariglia-Bull, L. Lysynchuk, J. McGoldrick, B. Schneider, S. Symons, and V. E. Woloshyn (1990). *Cognitive Strategy Instruction.* Cambridge, MA: Brookline Books.

Raphael, T. E., and P. D. Pearson (1985). "Increasing Student Awareness of Sources of Information for Answering Questions." *American Educational Research Journal* 22: 217–237.

Rinehart, S. D., S. A. Stahl, and L. G. Erickson (1986). "Some Effects of Summarization Training on Reading and Studying." *Reading Research Quarterly* 21: 422–437.

Rosenshine, B., and R. Stevens (1986). "Teaching Functions," in M. C. Wittrock, ed., *Handbook of Research on Teaching*, 3rd ed. New York: Macmillan.

Scardamalia, M., and C. Bereiter (1985). "Fostering the Development of Self-regulation in Children's Knowledge Processing," in S. F. Chipman, J. W. Segal, and R. Glaser, eds., *Thinking and Learning Skills: Research and Open Questions.* Hillsdale, NJ: Lawrence Erlbaum.

Scardamalia, M., C. Bereiter, and R. Steinbach (1984). "Teachability of Reflective Processes in Written Composition." *Cognitive Science* 8: 173–190.

Schoenfeld, A. H. (1985). *Mathematical Problem Solving.* New York: Academic Press.

Singer, H., and D. Donlan (1982). "Active Comprehension: Problem-solving Schema with Question Generation of Complex Short Stories." *Reading Research Quarterly* 17: 166–186.

Taylor, B. M. (1985). "Improving Middle-grade Students' Reading and Writing of Expository Text." *Journal of Educational Research* 79: 119–125.

Tobias, S. (1982). "When Do Instructional Methods Make a Difference?" *Educational Research* 11: 4–10.

Vygotsky, L. S. (1978). *Mind in Society: The Development of Higher Psychological Processes* (M. Cole, V. Steiner, S. Schribner, and E. Souberman, eds. and trans.). Cambridge, MA: Harvard University Press.

Wong, Y. L. and W. Jones (1982). "Increasing Metacomprehension in Learning Disabled and Normally Achieving Students through Self-questioning Training." *Learning Disability Quarterly* 5: 228–239.

Wood, D. J., J. S. Bruner, and G. Ross (1976). "The Role of Tutoring in Problem Solving." *Journal of Child Psychology and Psychiatry* 17: 89–100.

Discussion Questions

1. Take a less-structured task in your teaching field. Develop a concrete prompt to help teach that task.

2. Give an example of the following for teaching the less-structured task you chose for Question 1.

   a. Modeling and thinking aloud as you use that prompt to solve a specific problem

   b. Starting with simplified material and gradually increasing the complexity of the task

   c. Completing part of the task for the student

3. Give an example of the following for teaching the less-structured task you chose for Question 1.

   a. Anticipating errors and difficult areas

    b. Providing cue cards

    c. Providing a checklist

    d. Suggesting fix-up strategies

4. Give an example of the following for teaching the less-structured task you chose for Question 1.

    a. Checking for student mastery

    b. Providing for extensive practice

    c. Facilitating application of new examples

5. There are many academic tasks that are considered difficult to teach because they do not follow simple algorithms, and because teaching them requires the use of scaffolds. Some of these are listed below. Select one of these (or select one of your own) and suggest how some of the scaffolds described in the article can be used to help teach this task.

    a. Finding the least common denominator for fractions

    b. Identifying participles

    c. Using who and whom

    d. Writing a research report that doesn't sound like a copy from the *World Book*

    e. Tolerating ambiguity when reading literature

    f. Writing good thesis statements

    g. The concept of "theme" in high school literature

    h. Teaching mitosis in biology

Simon Hooper and Lloyd P. Rieber

Simon Hooper

Lloyd P. Rieber

Simon Hooper is of British stock—born, bred, and schooled in England. After completing a teacher education program in 1978 at the University of Durham, he taught secondary math until 1982 in Croydon. He shipped ahoy in 1982 and completed his doctorate at Penn State in 1989 under the tutelage of Professor Michael Hannafin, who he claims "challenged and stimulated his mind."

An assistant professor of education at the University of Minnesota, Simon has published some thirty chapters and articles in prestigious journals including the *Journal of Education Research* and *Educational Psychologist.* His favorite education book, during the last five years, is Jonathan Kozol's *Savage Inequalities* because, as he says, "it addresses many of the issues and concerns that initially attracted me to teaching." He recommends that young teachers read *Phi Delta Kappan* and *Educational Leadership* to keep up with the professional literature, and he describes the best teachers as having four traits: "organization, enthusiasm, genuine interest in students, and a love for learning." His advice to teachers is "don't be afraid of failure. Effective teachers make mistakes from which they learn to be better teachers."

Simon's research interests are with computers and instructional systems. But for fun, he plays squash regularly and sails during holidays along the southwest coast of England with his four children and wife, Kate.

Lloyd Rieber was born in Pittsburgh and went to South High School. After receiving his B.S. in elementary education from the University of Pittsburgh in 1979, he taught elementary school in New Mexico until 1984. Three years later, he received his Ph.D. in curriculum and instruction from Pennsylvania State University with an emphasis on instructional technology, and where he also met Simon Hooper.

Lloyd is currently an associate professor at the University of Georgia and has written some thirty articles on cognitive psychology, instructional design, and computer animation. He wrote his first book recently about learning in the computer age, and he is past president of the Association for the Development of Computer-Based Instructional Systems (ADCIS).

According to Rieber, the best teachers "recognize and celebrate the diversity of their students." He maintains that teachers need "to nurture the inventor, explorer, and researcher in both themselves and their students." They also need to reduce their talking in class and let their students do more talking. For professional reading, he recommends that teachers "keep current by reading *Teaching Magazine* and *The Computing Teacher.*"

9

Teaching with
Technology

Simon Hooper and Lloyd P. Rieber

Classroom teaching is a demanding job. Most people outside education probably think teachers spend most of their time teaching, but teachers are responsible for many tasks that have little to do with classroom instruction. Beyond planning and implementing instruction, teachers are also expected to be managers, psychologists, counselors, custodians, and community "ambassadors," not to mention entertainers. If teaching sounds like an unreasonable, almost impossible, job, perhaps it is.

It is easy to understand how a teacher might become frustrated and disillusioned. Most teachers enter the profession expecting to spark the joy of learning in their students. Unfortunately, the other demands of the classroom are very distracting and consuming. We envision technology as a teacher's liberator to help reestablish the role and value of the individual classroom teacher. To do so, two things must happen. First, the perspective of the classroom must change to become learner-centered. Second, students and teachers must enter into a collaboration or partnership with technology in order to create a "community" that nurtures, encourages, and supports the learning process (Cognition and Technology Group at Vanderbilt, 1992).

It is important to note that the focus of this chapter is on educational technology as compared to technology in education. There is a difference. *Technology in education* is often perceived in terms of how many computers or videocassette recorders are in a classroom and how they might be used to support traditional classroom activities, but this is a misleading and potentially dangerous interpretation. It not only places an inappropriate focus on hardware, but fails to consider other potentially useful "idea" technologies resulting from the application of one or more knowledge bases, such as learning theory. *Educational technology* involves applying ideas from various sources to create the best learning environments possible for students. Educational technologists also ask questions such as how a classroom might change or adapt when a computer

Utilization

The utilization phase, in contrast, occurs when the teacher tries out the technology or innovation in the classroom. An example is a social studies teacher who uses role-playing simulations learned in a workshop or graduate course. Obviously, teachers who reach this phase have progressed further than familiarization, but there is the inherent danger that a teacher will become prematurely satisfied with his or her limited use of the technology. The attitude of "At least I gave it a try" will likely interfere with any enduring and long-term adoption of the technology. Teachers who progress only to this phase will probably discard the technology at the first sign of trouble because they have made no commitment to it. This is probably the highest phase of adoption reached by most teachers who use contemporary educational media, including the computer. If the technology were taken away on Monday, hardly anyone would notice on Tuesday.

Integration

Integration represents the "break-through" phase. This occurs when a teacher consciously decides to designate certain tasks and responsibilities to the technology, so that if the technology is suddenly removed or is unavailable, the teacher cannot proceed with the instruction as planned. The most obvious technology that has reached this phase of adoption in education is the book and its derivatives, such as worksheets and other handouts. Most teachers could not function without the support of such print-based technologies. Another example, though perhaps amusing to some, is the chalkboard. Most teachers would find it extremely difficult to teach without it. Hence, the "expendability" of the technology is the most critical attribute or characteristic of this phase (Marcinkiewicz, 1991, 1993). Although integration is the end of the adoption model for many, it really only represents the beginning of understanding educational technology. For some teachers, the integration phase marks the beginning of a professional "metamorphosis," but only if they progress even further in their adoption pattern.

Reorientation

The reorientation phase requires that educators reconsider and reconceptualize the purpose and function of the classroom. It is marked by many characteristics, probably the most important of which is that the focus of the classroom is now centered on a student's learning, as opposed to the teacher's instruction. A teacher who has reached the reorientation phase does not view good teaching as the delivery of content (that is, the teaching "acts" of explaining, managing, or motivating). Instead, the teacher's role is to establish a learning environment that supports and facilitates students as they construct and shape their own knowledge. In this phase, the learner becomes the *subject* rather than the *object* of education.

Teachers in the reorientation phase are open to technologies that enable this knowledge construction process and are not threatened by being "replaced" by technology. In fact, these teachers will probably include technology in their class-rooms without necessarily feeling the need to be "experts" themselves. Their interest is in how technology allows their students to engage the subject matter. It would not be unusual for students to be more competent than their teachers with the technology. For example, consider a history teacher who discovers that students prefer to create HyperCard stacks that replace a traditional term paper assignment (Hoffmeister, 1990). If the teacher has a reoriented view of education that is student-centered, the teacher will focus on how intensely the student has engaged the content, not on how well the stack is "programmed." The teacher will emphasize (and evaluate) how well the student has become both a researcher and an explorer due to the availability of the computing tool. Whether the teacher possesses more or less technical skill with HyperCard than the student is inconsequential. In addition, the teacher learns about history and HyperCard along with the student. Of course, the teacher's greater experience is an indispensable resource and guide to the student. Rather than viewing a technology as something that must be mastered beforehand and presented to students in a controlled and systematic way, a teacher in the reorientation phase would encourage and expect students to appropriate the technology in ways that could not be anticipated.

Evolution

The final phase, evolution, serves as a reminder that the educational system must continue to evolve and adapt to remain effective. There will never be a final solution or conclusion, and to be searching for one means that one is missing the point. The classroom learning environment should constantly change to meet the challenge and potential provided by new understandings of how people learn. As previously discussed, this appropriate application of basic knowledge for some useful purpose is what defines educational technology, and living up to this definition is the hallmark of the evolution phase.

TRADITIONAL ROLE OF TECHNOLOGY IN EDUCATION

There have been two main types of technology in education that we choose to label as "product technologies" and "idea technologies." Product technologies include (1) hardware, or machine-oriented, technologies that people most often associate with educational technology, such as the range of audio-visual equipment, both traditional (that is, film strips, movies, audiocassette players/recorders) and contemporary (that is, videocassette players/recorders, laserdiscs, computers, CD-ROM); and (2) software technologies, such as print-based material (that is, books, worksheets, overhead transparencies) and computer software (that is, computer-assisted instruction). In contrast, idea technologies do not have such tangible forms.

Of course, idea technologies are usually represented in or through some product technology. For example, simulations are, by and large, idea technologies. Simulations try to give people experiences with events and concepts not generally possible (for example, travel back in time), probable (for example, ride aboard the space shuttle), or desirable (for example, the greenhouse effect) under normal conditions. The idea of a simulation must be realized through some product, such as computer software. In this way, the idea is supported or made possible by the product. A classic example of the distinction between product and idea technologies is Henry Ford's assembly line. The concept of the assembly line is an idea technology that transformed industry in the United States. However, the conveyor belts, workstations, and factories that one sees in old photographs show the product technologies that were used to support the original idea.

The distinction between product technologies and idea technologies is important because most of the historical attempts to use technology in education have focused on product technologies, such as teaching machines, educational television and films, and, most currently, computers (Reiser, 1987). Consequently, the role and value of these product technologies were how they supported the established beliefs and practices of classroom teachers. These established practices were largely based on behavioral models that emphasized the transmission and delivery of predetermined content. These approaches exemplify the "student as bucket" metaphor, where the emphasis is on "pouring knowledge" into students' minds by designing and delivering well-planned and controlled instruction. Learning is viewed as a consequence of receiving the information. We believe that contemporary notions of educational technology must go well beyond this philosophy of learning and education. Teachers who adopt technologies without considering the belief structure into which these products and ideas are introduced are necessarily limited to the third phase of integration, though, as previously mentioned, few progress that far.

Consider an example of a product technology reaching the integration phase —the hand-held graphing calculator. Many high school math teachers use graphing calculators in their teaching. In fact, there are several brands on the market that use a transparent liquid crystal display (LCD) so that the calculator can be placed on an overhead projector. The use of these calculators easily passes the expendability test for many teachers: Their teaching would be seriously disrupted if the calculators were removed. They would be unable to convey the same information given a quick and sudden return to the static medium of the overhead or chalkboard.

However, the degree to which the teacher's instruction has been altered because of the graphing calculator is critical in determining if the teacher is on the verge of entering the reorientation phase. If the calculator allows the teacher to focus on students' conceptual understanding of the mathematical function, perhaps because of the calculator's ability to draw a graph using real-time animation, then the teacher has begun to rethink and reflect on the partnership between how product and idea technologies can help students' learning. The teacher will derive satisfaction from how the technology was harnessed to enable and empower students to understand and apply the mathematical ideas. This teacher is on the brink of entering into the reorientation phase. Such a teacher will probably seek to turn the technology (that is, the calculator) over to the students for them to begin constructing mathematics.

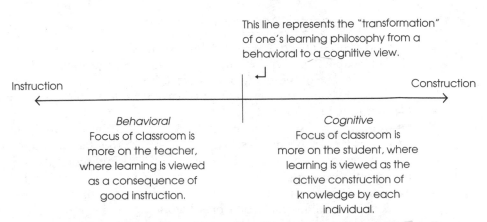

Figure 9.2 **Philosophies of learning and teaching can be viewed as a continuum with extreme educational interpretations of behaviorism (for example, instruction) and cognitivism (for example, construction) at either end. Any one educator's philosophy resides somewhere on this line. The threshold between the two views marks a critical point of "transformation" for an educator.**

On the other hand, if the instructional strategies employed by the teacher are virtually the same as those used before the graphing calculator was introduced, then it is very likely that the teacher's adoption of the technology will end with integration, since nothing has changed or improved other than the mode of delivery. In this case, although the product technology of the calculator has been integrated, the underlying idea technology of "present, practice, and test" remains unchanged and unchallenged.

The distinction between educators who enter and stall at the integration phase versus those who are "transformed" and enter the reorientation phase is best characterized as a magical line on an "instruction/construction" continuum, as illustrated in Figure 9.2. The utilization and integration of any one technology can be defined by this continuum. The technology of a computer spreadsheet, for example, when used only by a teacher for grade management or as part of an instructional presentation of, say, the principle of averages in a math class, is integrating only the product technology without changing the underlying philosophical base in which it is applied. The philosophical base, in this example, would be an instruction-centered classroom where a teacher manages the presentation and practice of predetermined and preselected content.

Consider instead a teacher who uses the same spreadsheet to have students build and construct the knowledge themselves, whether it be the principle of mathematical averages or a range of "what if" relationships in economics or history. In this case, the product technology of the spreadsheet is directly supporting the idea technology of a "microworld" where students live and experience the content rather than just study it (Dede, 1987; Papert, 1981; Rieber, 1992).

What are the most fundamental principles of learning that underlie the most contemporary views of idea technologies that will help all educators enter into the reorientation phase of adoption? This is the goal of the next section.

CONTEMPORARY ROLE OF TECHNOLOGY IN EDUCATION

Among many educational goals, three cognitive outcomes are that students should be able to remember, understand, and use information (Perkins, 1992). Apparently, one of these outcomes is very difficult to achieve. After more than a decade of schooling, many students leave school unable to use much of the content they have learned.

Students' inability to apply their learning is attributable to the shallow processing that often occurs in school. Schoolwork often focuses on remembering and organizing lesson content, but rarely on making information meaningful. Meaningful learning is the product of building external connections between existing and new information. Mayer (1984) identified three learning stages that affect meaningfulness: selection, organization, and integration. Information must initially be selected. Selected information must be organized in working memory if it is to be transferred to long-term memory. Information that is not organized is meaningless. The nature of the organization determines the degree of meaningfulness. Information that is integrated within familiar knowledge or experiences is more durable than information that is not associated to prior knowledge. In school, students select information that they memorize and organize sufficiently to enable satisfactory performance on tests, but they often fail to integrate the information by relating it to previous experiences or knowledge stored in long-term memory. Consequently, one outcome of education, it seems, is a large reserve of inert information that is eventually forgotten (Cognition and Technology Group at Vanderbilt, 1992). For example, how many of us can remember how to compute the sine of a triangle?

How can teaching with technology facilitate deeper, more meaningful cognitive processing? Moreover, what framework should be used to inform such decisions? In a sense, teaching with technology is unlikely to differ greatly from teaching in general. Effective technology-based teaching is more likely the result of teachers' abilities to design lessons based upon robust instructional principles than of the technology per se (Savenye, Davidson, & Smith, 1991). Consequently, guidance for designing effective technology-based classrooms should be grounded in the literature on effective pedagogy in general.

Recently, researchers have identified several principles to guide effective teaching (Koschman, Myers, Feltovich, & Barrows, in press). Although designed primarily for instruction in complex and ill-structured domains, the principles are relevant for many instructional tasks. Most real-world tasks are ill structured. Problems that are "well structured" generally occur only in classroom settings. In the following section we will examine three principles and consider the implications of each for using technology in the classroom.

Principle 1: Effective Learners Actively Process Lesson Content

During the past thirty years the shift from behaviorism to cognitivism has modified our conceptions of effective learning and instruction. One of the most consistent themes to emerge from the transition is that learning is an active process.

This means that effective learning requires students to do more than simply respond to stimuli. Instead, learners must actively seek and generate relationships between lesson content and prior knowledge.

One common myth is that product technologies increase interactivity and thereby improve learning. The source of this perception is not difficult to trace. The results of research on students' attitudes toward working with product technologies, especially computers, are generally positive (Martin, Heller, & Mahmoud, 1991). Furthermore, research appears to support the belief that product technologies improve learning (Kulik, Bangert, & Williams, 1983). Yet, product technologies alone do not ensure learning (Clark, 1983). Indeed, in some cases they may detract from learning by diminishing the amount of effort a student invests.

In general, learning requires students to invest considerable mental effort in the task. However, students appear to vary the effort they invest during learning according to their self-perceptions and their beliefs about the difficulty of learning from different media. Salomon (1984) found that children who believed themselves to be effective learners invested greater effort when a learning task was perceived to be challenging than when it was perceived to be easy. However, children with low self-efficacy invested greater effort when learning was perceived to be more attainable than challenging. In other words, high-ability learners may invest more mental effort in a challenging task, such as reading a book, than in a task perceived to be easy, such as learning from TV. Low-ability students may invest more effort in a task they believe to be attainable than one they perceive to be challenging.

We are by no means opponents of product technologies in education. However, we recognize the importance of blending product and idea technologies into "technological partnerships." An example of an effective technological marriage is that of a musical symphony. A good symphony combines an ideal blend of musical instruments (product technologies) and musical compositions (idea technologies). Misusing the capabilities of the instruments or underemphasizing the composition of the musical score will detract from the final production of the symphony. Similarly, effective uses of technology in education require a blend of product and idea technologies. Together, they form environments that unite technological capability with pedagogical necessity—combining what can be done with what should be done.

Too often in education we have failed to find the right blend of technologies. In particular, the capabilities of product technologies are overemphasized. For example, product technologies are often used to increase cost efficiency by replacing the classroom teacher or by transmitting lessons to larger audiences via satellites and telephone lines. Such approaches are often misdirected. Although the importance of increasing access to education should not be devalued, reproducing existing materials is unlikely to improve educational quality. Rather, using technology as delivery media may perpetuate or even exacerbate existing problems. The benefit of technology is not simply its potential to replicate existing educational practice, but its ability to combine idea and product technologies to encourage students to engage in deeper cognitive activity.

Principle 2: Presenting Information from Multiple Perspectives Increases the Durability of Instruction

Although instruction has traditionally focused on learning specific content, much of contemporary curriculum development focuses on solving problems that require learners to develop ever-evolving networks of facts, principles, and procedures. The National Council of Teachers of Mathematics (1989), for example, suggested that greater emphasis be placed on solving open-ended "real world" problems in small groups, connecting mathematics with other content areas, and using computer-based tools to allow students to speculate and explore interrelationships among concepts rather than spending time on time-consuming calculations. To achieve such goals, learning should take place in environments that emphasize the interconnectedness of ideas across content domains and help learners to develop flexible networks of propositions and productions (Gagné, 1985). Presenting content from a single perspective is unlikely to reflect the complexity inherent in many concepts. In contrast, repeated exposure to information from varying perspectives helps learners to establish the interrelationships necessary to mediate deep processing and effective retrieval of lesson concepts.

Cooperative learning and hypermedia represent technologies with significant potential for developing multiple perspectives. Cooperative learning is an idea technology that stimulates the development of alternative perspectives through exposure to multiple viewpoints. Two important differences exist between cooperative learning and traditional instruction. First, information to be learned by the students is not transmitted by the teacher. Instead, students teach each other in small groups of between two and five students. Second, students are made responsible for each other's learning. Students must ensure that every member of their group achieves the lesson's objectives. These experiences appear to benefit students of all abilities. More able students gain from the cognitive restructuring associated with teaching, and less able students benefit from the personalized attention available from group members. Moreover, groups appear to create environments in which all members benefit from exposure to diverse attitudes and opinions that are often unavailable in the traditional classroom.

Hypermedia is a product technology that represents a shift in beliefs about how information should be presented to and accessed by students. Hypermedia refers to computer programs that organize information nonsequentially. Information is structured around series of nodes that are connected through associative links. *Node* is the term used to describe an information chunk that is stored in the hypermedia program. Information in a node may be represented through text, illustrations, or sounds. Associative links, which allow users to navigate among nodes, represent the main difference between traditional ways of presenting information on the computer and hypermedia (Jonassen, 1991).

Whereas traditional instruction often presents information sequentially to make the content easier to comprehend, hypermedia allows users to browse through an information base and to construct relationships between personal experience and the lesson. In doing so, it is often claimed, learning becomes more meaningful as students generate webs of semantically and logically related information that accommodate the learners' knowledge structure rather than that of the teacher or designer. Although hypermedia environments can be used to present information sequentially to students, when carefully designed, users can create different diverse pathways through a lesson resulting in multiple cognitive representations of the content. By allowing exploration, students are encouraged to discover interrelationships that are often missed in traditional presentations of lesson content and to search for information that meets individual needs. Hypermedia is especially effective when users are encouraged to explore a database, to create links among information nodes, and even to modify a knowledge base based on new insight into content structure (Nelson & Palumbo, 1992).

Hypermedia and cooperative learning represent technologies that can make learning more meaningful. However, both must be managed carefully to achieve the intended outcomes. In cooperative learning, potentially damaging social effects often occur when individual accountability is not maintained. Similarly, hypermedia projects often focus on presenting information and rarely fulfill their promise as knowledge construction kits. Furthermore, although each can be used independently, the learning benefits may be magnified when they are combined. Although many computer lessons are designed for single users, the benefits appear to multiply when used collaboratively (Hooper, 1992).

Principle 3: Effective Instruction Should Build upon Students' Knowledge and Experiences and Be Grounded in Meaningful Contexts

Philosophical beliefs about how educational goals can best be achieved have shifted from emphasizing curriculum content to focusing on learners' knowledge and experiences (Pea & Gomez, 1992; Tobin & Dawson, 1992). During the 1960s and 1970s considerable emphasis was placed on curriculum projects that focused on the structural analysis of content. These projects produced curriculum materials that emphasized helping learners better understand lesson content. For many years, education followed a correspondingly curriculum-centered approach. Teaching focused on analyzing learning tasks and identifying strategies to achieve specific learning outcomes.

Recently, research emphasis has shifted from examining the structure of curriculum materials to determining the cognitive state of the learner. Education is presently concerned less with transmitting the "optimal" structure of lesson content than with building onto the current knowledge level of the student. This perspective has implications for teaching with technology. First, instruction should attempt to build upon each student's experiential base. What a student learns from education is, to a large extent, a function of prior knowledge. One role of technology, therefore, is to bridge personal experiences and formal instruction. Technology should also be sufficiently flexible to adapt to students' on-going instructional needs. One of the hallmarks of a master teacher is the ability to recognize and repair students' misunderstandings and misconceptions. When learning difficulties arise, therefore, technology-based instruction should be sufficiently flexible to adapt to students' experiences.

Closely related to building upon students' knowledge and experiences is the belief that instruction should be grounded in familiar contexts. Teachers often decontextualize instruction to stimulate transfer and improve instructional efficiency (Merrill, 1991). Recently, however, researchers have argued that such practices actually hinder transfer. Instead, they claim, instruction should be rooted in real-life problem-solving contexts. One such approach, known as situated cognition (Brown, Collins, & Duguid, 1989), involves teaching across multiple contexts before generating rules. Grounding instruction in meaningful contexts appears to have both cognitive and affective benefits. One of the axioms of cognitive psychology is that learning occurs by building upon previously learned experiences. Teaching in familiar contexts appears to help learners to relate new information to those experiences. Contextualization also appears to have a strong motivational component. Learning in a familiar context may make learning more personally relevant than decontextualized learning (Keller & Suzuki, 1988).

Microworlds illustrate how technology can improve meaningfulness by building upon students' experiences and providing a relevant learning environment. A microworld is a special learning environment that accurately models a phenomenon and adapts the complexity of instruction to match the learner's level of understanding. Rieber (1992) designed Space Shuttle Commander, a computer microworld to teach Newton's Laws of Motion. By exploring the microworld, students generate a visceral understanding of the interrelationships that exist among lesson concepts. Microworlds offer opportunities for students to transfer understanding to the real world and to examine and manipulate concepts in a manner that would otherwise be impossible. The microworld contains several difficulty levels to accommodate varying levels of user expertise and introduces an element of fantasy to motivate learners by using the scenario of traveling through frictionless space in a space shuttle.

THEORY INTO PRACTICE

In this section we present three examples of educational products that incorporate many of the principles outlined earlier in the chapter. None of these products ensures that learning will take place. The key ingredient in each case is the idea technology employed by the teacher.

The Jasper Woodbury Problem Solving Series

The Adventures of Jasper Woodbury (Cognition and Technology Group at Vanderbilt, 1992) is a video package that reflects contemporary beliefs about learning and instruction. Important differences exist between the Jasper series and traditional educational TV. Each episode of the Jasper videos presents instruction in a motivating and realistic environment that encourages students to explore, and to identify and solve real problems. Furthermore, teachers are encouraged to blend idea technologies such as cooperative grouping and problem-based learning with the videos to make learning active, meaningful, and motivating. Perhaps the most striking difference between the Jasper materials and traditional educational TV concerns the role played by the students. Educational TV often transmits information to students who may or may not participate in the learning experience. In contrast, the Jasper series requires students to be actively engaged. While watching the video, students must collect information. Following each episode, a problem is presented. The problem challenges the students to use the information collected during the lesson to identify and solve subproblems en route to solving the larger problem.

The Voyage of the Mimi

The Voyage of the Mimi is a multimedia curriculum package developed at the Bank Street College of Education that integrates print, video, and computer materials in learning about science and mathematics. Video is used to present the package's context for learning: a realistic, fictional account of the adventures of the crew of the Mimi, a boat hired by a team of scientists to study humpback whales (a second Mimi series has also been produced using the context of Mayan archaeology). The context was chosen based on research conducted at Bank Street that indicated that people, and especially children, share a general fascination with whales. Mathematics and science become the crew's most important tools as they conduct their whale research or engage in many other problem-solving activities. Video is also used to present a series of documentaries showing real scientists at work using many of the principles introduced in the dramatic episodes. The computer materials provide students with interactive activities, usually simulations and games, that closely mirror the adventures of the Mimi's crew in the video. The print-based materials include a text version of the video and consumable workbooks for the students to complete. The Mimi materials were developed to be sufficiently flexible to provide teachers with multiple entry levels to the materials (Martin, 1987). Teachers can choose to use the materials to augment or to replace all or part of their curriculum. The materials provide for a range of learning outcomes from initial concept information to problem solving. The materials can also be used individually by students or cooperatively in groups.

The Geometric Supposer

The Geometric Supposer (Schwartz & Yerushalmy, 1985a) is a computer-based geometry tool that teaches deductive reasoning by providing students with opportunities to experiment with geometry. Traditionally, geometry teaching has employed passive instructional strategies by focusing on teaching definitions, theorems, and proofs. In contrast, the Geometric Supposer stimulates active learning by encouraging learners to discover geometric properties (Schwartz, 1993).

The program allows students to perform two functions that are difficult to achieve in noncomputer-based environments. First, it allows students to construct electronically any geometric shape that can be made with a straight edge and a compass. Moreover, the program "remembers" the construction and will repeat the procedure on similar shapes when instructed to do so. Second, the program can automatically measure and report any element of a construction, thus allowing users to instantaneously observe the outcomes of any manipulations of the geometric figures. Together, these features allow students to create constructions, hypothesize about geometric relationships, and test and observe the validity of their conjectures. For example, students studying relationships among the medians of a triangle may attempt to identify and test principles by examining results across several different cases (Schwartz & Yerushalmy, 1985b).

Putting It Together

It is important to recognize that the learning outcomes achieved using any of the materials outlined above will reflect the idea technology employed. The idea technology will also indicate the level of technology adoption to which the teacher has risen. Three idea technologies have been outlined by the Cognition and Technology Group at Vanderbilt (1992).

1. *Basics First* advocates mastering basic skills before attempting similar problems embedded in the video. Teachers who use this approach may have entered the utilization phase, but have not entered the integration phase. Few instructional differences would result if the videos were removed from the classroom. Similar problems could easily be generated from other sources.

2. *Structured Problem Solving* involves capitalizing on the design features inherent in the videos, but restricting students' progress to prevent errors and disorientation. For example, teachers might use structured worksheets to guide students' progress. Teachers who focus on rigid lesson structuring may have reached the integration phase, but probably have not entered into reorientation.

3. *Guided Generation* involves using activities that reflect many of the principles outlined earlier in the chapter. That is, activities that help students to generate meaningful relationships. The teacher focuses on guiding students and exploring issues that may be novel or unfamiliar to both teacher and student. Teachers who use Guided Generation would probably have entered the reorientation or evolution adoption phases.

SUMMARY

In this chapter we have examined why technology has failed to impact education in the past and outlined the conditions necessary for technology to be used effectively in the future. To be used effectively, idea and product technologies must be united and teachers must venture beyond familiarization and utilization and into the integration, reorientation, and evolution phases of technology use. Teachers who learn to integrate technology may go on to reconceptualize their roles in the classroom. Guided by research findings from cognitive psychology and other related areas, teachers can create environments in which students actively engage in cognitive partnerships with technology.

References

Brown, J., A. Collins, and P. Duguid (1989). "Situated Cognition and the Culture of Learning." *Educational Researcher* 18 (1): 32–42.

Clark, R. (1983). "Reconsidering Research on Learning from Media." *Review of Educational Research* 53: 445–459.

Cognition and Technology Group at Vanderbilt (1992). "The Jasper Experiment: An Exploration of Issues in Learning and Instructional Design." *Educational Technology Research and Development* 40 (1): 65–80.

Dalton, D. (1989). "Computers in the Schools: A Diffusion/Adoption Perspective." *Educational Technology* 29 (11): 20–27.

Dede, C. (1987). "Empowering Environments, Hypermedia and Microworlds." *The Computing Teacher* 15 (3): 20–24, 61.

Dwyer, D., C. Ringstaff, and J. Sandholtz (1991). "Changes in Teachers' Beliefs and Practices in Technology-rich Classrooms." *Educational Leadership* 48 (8): 45–52.

Gagné, E. (1985). *The Cognitive Psychology of School Learning*. Boston: Little, Brown and Co.

Hoffmeister, J. (1990). "The Birth of Hyper-School," in S. Ambron and K. Hooper, eds., *Learning with Interactive Multimedia: Developing and Using Multimedia Tools in Education*. Redmond, WA: Microsoft Press, pp. 199–221.

Hooper, S. (1992). "Cooperative Learning and Computer-based Instruction." *Educational Technology Research and Development* 40 (3): 21–38.

Jonassen, D. (1991). "Hypertext as Instruction Design." *Educational Technology Research and Development* 39 (1): 83–92.

Keller, J., and K. Suzuki (1988). "Using the ARCS Motivation Model in Courseware Design," in D. Jonassen, ed., *Instructional Designs for Microcomputer Courseware*. Hillsdale, NJ: Lawrence Erlbaum, pp. 401–434.

Koschman, T., A. Myers, P. Feltovich, and H. Barrows (in press). "Using Technology to Assist in Realizing Effective Learning and Instruction: A Principled Approach to the Use of Computers in Collaborative Learning." *Journal of the Learning Sciences*.

Kulik, J., R. Bangert, and G. Williams (1983). "Effects of Computer-based Teaching on Secondary School Students." *Journal of Educational Psychology* 75: 19–26.

Marcinkiewicz, H. (1991). "The Relationships of Selected Personological Variables to the Use of Available Microcomputers by Elementary School Teachers." Doctoral dissertation, The Pennsylvania State University.

Marcinkiewicz, H. (1993). "Computers and Teachers: Factors Influencing Computer Use in the Classroom." *Journal of Research on Computing in Education*, in press.

Martin, C. D., R. Heller, and E. Mahmoud (1991). "American and Soviet Children's Attitudes toward Computers." *Journal of Educational Computing Research* 8 (2): 155–185.

Martin, L. (1987). "Teachers' Adoption of Multimedia Technologies for Science and Mathematics Instruction," in R. D. Pea and K. Sheingold, eds., *Mirrors of Minds: Patterns of Experience in Educational Computing*. Norwood, NJ: Ablex Publishing Corp., pp. 35–56.

Mayer, R. (1984). "Aids to Text Comprehension." *Educational Psychologist* 19: 30–42.

Merrill, M. D. (1991). "Constructivism and Instructional Design." *Educational Technology* 31 (5): 45–53.

National Council of Teachers of Mathematics

(1989). *Curriculum and Evaluation Standards for School Mathematics.* Reston, VA: Author.

Nelson, W., and D. Palumbo (1992). "Learning, Instruction, and Hypermedia." *Journal of Educational Multimedia and Hypermedia* 1: 287–299.

Osman, M., and M. Hannafin (1992). "Metacognition Research and Theory: Analysis and Implications for Instructional Design." *Educational Technology Research and Development* 40 (2): 83–99.

Papert, S. (1981). "Computer-based Microworlds as Incubators for Powerful Ideas," in R. Taylor, ed., *The Computer in the School: Tutor, Tool, Tutee.* New York: Teachers College Press, Columbia University, pp. 203–210.

Pea, R., and L. Gomez (1992). "Distributed Multimedia Learning Environments: Why and How?" *Interactive Learning Environments* 2 (2): 73–109.

Perkins, D. (1992). "Technology Meets Constructivism: Do They Make a Marriage?" *Educational Technology* 31 (5): 18–23.

Reiser, R. (1987). "Instructional Technology: A History," in R. Gagne, ed., *Instructional Technology: Foundations.* Hillsdale, NJ: Lawrence Erlbaum, pp. 11–48.

Rieber, L. (1992). "Computer-based Microworlds: A Bridge between Constructivism and Direct Instruction." 40 (1): 93–106.

Rieber, L., and P. Welliver (1989). "Infusing Educational Technology into Mainstream Educational Computing." *International Journal of Instructional Media* 16 (1): 21–32.

Rogers, E. (1983). *Diffusion of Innovations*, 3rd ed. New York: The Free Press of Glencoe.

Saettler, P. (1990). *The Evolution of American Educational Technology.* Denver, CO: Libraries Unlimited.

Salomon, G. (1984). "Television Is Easy and Print Is Tough: The Differential Investment of Mental Effort in Learning as a Function of Perceptions and Attributions." *Journal of Educational Psychology* 76: 647–658.

Savenye, W., G. Davidson, and P. Smith (1991). "Teaching Instructional Design in a Computer Literacy Course." *Educational Technology Research and Development* 39 (3): 49–58.

Schwartz, J., and M. Yerushalmy (1985a). *The Geometric Supposer.* Pleasantville, NY: Sunburst Communications.

Schwartz, J., and M. Yerushalmy (1985b). 'The Geometric Supposer: An Intellectual Prosthesis for Making Conjectures." *The College Mathematics Journal* 18: 58–65.

Schwartz, J., ed. (1993). *The Geometric Supposer: What Is It a Case Of?* Hillsdale, NJ: Lawrence Erlbaum.

Tobin, K., and G. Dawson (1992). "Constraints to Curriculum Reform." *Educational Technology Research and Development* 40 (1): 81–92.

Discussion Questions

1. How did the high school you attended use technology in the classroom?

2. Describe the characteristics of teachers at each level of technology adoption.

3. Compare and contrast "product" and "idea" technologies. How would you use technology in the classroom?

4. Why has technology consistently failed to impact education?

5. Can technology improve the quality of education? What can be done to help teachers to use technology effectively in the classroom?

6. Describe the teaching traits of a teacher whom you believe to be effective. Where would you place that teacher on the continuum of technology adoption? Explain you decision.

John E. Penick

John E. Penick, professor of science education at the University of Iowa, completed an undergraduate degree in biology and chemistry at the University of Miami in 1966. Following graduate work in biology, he began his educational career as a teacher of biology and chemistry at Jackson High School in Miami, Florida. After earning a Ph.D. in science education at Florida State University, he taught at Loyola University of Chicago for several years before moving to Iowa.

Penick has spent most of his postsecondary professional career identifying outstanding science teachers and designing teacher education programs to help all teachers optimize their potential. He is well known for supporting a more active learning role for students, a role often described as the STS approach to science learning. He has presented his ideas at conferences and to government agencies in more than twenty countries in Europe, Southeast Asia, the Middle East, and the Caribbean, and in all parts of the United States. In doing so, he claims to have collected "more than one million miles with United's Frequent Flyer Program."

His publications, more than 300, are often directed at describing and promoting outstanding teachers and teaching. His most significant work is a series of seventeen monographs, *Focus on Excellence*, published by the National Science Teachers Association, and dedicated to recognizing individual science teachers and the exemplary science programs they had developed. From this seven-year project, Penick developed many strong notions about the characteristics of exemplary teachers. Currently he is funded by the National Science Foundation to spend the next four years developing an innovative high school biology curriculum, *BioCom*.

Not one to just spend his time in classrooms, reading, or writing, John plays a serious game of racquetball with his much younger graduate students, declaring them eligible to graduate only after they win two out of three games. He also enjoys downhill skiing with his family (usually in Colorado), reading for fun, and eating fine cuisine. He adds, "I like to cook and favor an old manicotti recipe provided by my mother-in-law and a delicate crepes florentine. Both have home-made noodles to add to their delicacy." An instrument-rated pilot with a commercial license, he often does his own flying to workshops and conferences, making use of the technology he writes about.

His advice to the beginning teacher is to join several professional organizations related to your teaching discipline, read the journals they publish, and attend as many conferences and workshops as you can, all the while reflecting on your teaching. Then, continually monitor your teaching, comparing what you are doing with what you know you should be doing. "Develop your own research-based rationale, discuss it with compatible colleagues, and reread and revise it regularly."

John's favorite education book is *The Saber Tooth Curriculum* because "it still makes sense today." He has been married to Nell, a Ph.D. family therapist, for thirty years, who says, "he can't get away with anything at home." Not only does he cook, but he also cleans and shops.

10 🦃

Teaching for Science Literacy

John E. Penick

In 1620 Francis Bacon declared that scientific effort had as a goal human service and enhancing intellectual reason for the general welfare. While the rhetoric of today is different, the message continues in the same vein. According to Bowyer (1990), science and technology literacy are essential for economic development, now and in the future, and must be given priority in our schools. Our lack of science literacy has been established most consistently by Miller (1983), beginning with his studies of levels of science literacy in the early 1980s. His approach tested the ability of individuals to recognize terms, processes, and concepts in science. He reported that only 5 percent of students understand the scientific approach to problem solving and development of knowledge. Miller's later work (1989) indicated that only 6 percent of adults in the United States and 7 percent of adults in the United Kingdom can be considered science literate. Further, he found that age and number of high school science courses completed are not predictive of literacy level.

Baker (1991), in a similar line of research, demonstrated that males are more science literate than females, possibly because of how science is taught and the reward mechanisms that may favor masculine approaches to science learning. Hirsch (1987), noting that most Americans know little science, includes science as a specific component of cultural literacy, part of the knowledge base needed to thrive in the modern world. Many of the issues related to science literacy revolve around whether such literacy is more a function of knowledge, skill, or attitude. And all agree that we need citizens who understand and appreciate science (Gatewood, 1968).

SCIENCE LITERACY: SOME DEFINITIONS AND SUGGESTIONS

Some describe the science literate as knowing concepts or principles of science (Demastes & Wandersee, 1992; Hirsch, 1987), while others speak of attitude and action components. Shamos (1990) proposed that an educated man should feel comfortable when reading or talking about science in a nontechnical way, and summarized well the thinking of many individuals who focus on "science appreciation." Hurd (1958), apparently the first to use the term *science literacy*, included appreciation of science, the nature of science, science knowledge, and how all of these combine to resolve problems in the real world. Regardless of definition, even a cursory reading of the literature reveals that most everyone still uses science literacy as a rationale for whatever they are doing in the science classroom, and all have an opinion about the nature and need for science and technology literacy for all, regardless of age or educational attainment.

The American Association for the Advancement of Science (AAAS) (1989, 1992) ascribes to the science literate "habits of mind to be inquisitive, critical participants in the affairs of the world." Agreeing with a multidimensional focus and noting that a person may be literate in one aspect but not another, the Biological Sciences Curriculum Study (1993) identifies four hierarchical levels of biological literacy: nominal, functional, structural, and multidimensional.

Since biological literacy is a hierarchy, individuals must possess a lower type of biological literacy before achieving a higher order form. A nominally literate person, for example, can identify terms and concepts as biological in nature but possesses misconceptions and has naive explanations of science concepts. The functionally literate person uses a science vocabulary and defines terms correctly, but often has only memorized them without understanding. At the level of structural biological literacy, individuals understand "conceptual schemes of biology, understand procedural knowledge and skills, and can explain biological concepts in their own words." The multidimensional science literate "knows the place of biology among the other sciences, knows the history and nature of biology, and understands the interactions between biology and society." Unfortunately, most science classrooms teach for nominal literacy at best.

Some go so far as to say that science literacy is either unnecessary or impossible. Cohen (1987) indicates that most workers of the near future in developed countries will be in the service sector, where there may be less need for the intellectual knowledge or the habits of scientists. Shamos (1994) has long advocated that true science literacy for most people is probably unrealistic because even many scientists might be considered science illiterates. He adds that scientific literacy is not essential to prepare people for an increasingly technological society. But, again, all indicate that our students should leave school appreciating and understanding the nature of science and the role of science in society. Yet, rare is the classroom where these are the avowed goals.

Science/Technology/Society

Exceptions are those classrooms in which teachers consciously attempt to teach science and technology by focusing on societal issues, most of which have a science or technology aspect. Called the STS (science/technology/society) approach, in these situations students as well as teachers begin by identifying issues and related problems of personal interest. In the true STS classroom, students always move beyond mere learning and take action on their ideas and findings. In the process, STS students use a variety of resources, especially adults in their communities, and usually decide for themselves how the investigation shall take place. STS classes approach learning from a very multidisciplinary and student-centered perspective, as students use analytical, communication, and investigative skills.

Several major goal clusters characterize the STS classroom, regardless of the central subject matter under discussion:

1. *Knowledge for meeting personal needs.* Education should prepare individuals to use knowledge for improving lives and for coping with an increasingly technological world.

2. *Knowledge for resolving current social issues.* Education should produce informed citizens prepared to deal responsibly with science-related social issues.

3. *Knowledge for assisting with career choices.* Education should give all students an awareness of the nature and wide variety of subject-related careers open to citizens of varying aptitudes and interests. (Harms & Yager, 1981)

STS means focusing on the personal needs of students, weaving concepts, skills, and processes into their daily lives. Experienced teachers have found that beginning with issues allows students a chance to start with broad perspectives and narrow their focus as they become more adept and knowledgeable. For instance, one teacher in a difficult class in Davenport, Iowa, during a lesson on plate tectonics, found his students arguing about the value of some very expensive basketball shoes. Some students felt strongly that they were overpriced and no different than less costly types. Others, equally strong in their perspective, declared that the more expensive models were, in fact, better. Since the students were quite engaged, the teacher helped them focus their attention on identifying the issues and problems inherent in the issues.

One thing led to another and soon the students were calling major shoe manufacturers (using the toll-free numbers they all have) to find out about shoes. They learned of the use of specialized polymers (and had to do more study to find out what those were) and found that shoes involved far more science and technology than any would have imagined. During their three weeks of study they even spoke to a sports physicist, who described the way shoes and polymers are tested before the final design is set.

While these students probably never got back to plate tectonics, they did learn that they, themselves, could identify problems and how to resolve them. They discovered that there is not a single, exact answer to most of their questions but that, by asking enough of the right questions, they could get closer to satisfaction. This realization is what STS teachers seek. They know that knowledge of plate tectonics does not differentiate between successful and less successful people. However, they will tell you they think that successful people are able to delve into an issue, seek information and consensus, and use their knowledge much in the same ways as those students in Davenport.

Interestingly, evidence is mounting rapidly that concentrating on the three STS goals above allows one to virtually ignore the usual major goal of teachers: *Prepare students for additional learning in the discipline.* Study after study (Yager, 1993b) indicates that when students are personally involved in their learning they learn and retain knowledge and skills far better. And, through doing so, they become better able to work with others, learn to make reasonable decisions, and find that the boundaries between school and community become more transparent.

STS classes also reflect the best of what we know about how students learn. Since STS classes are taught within the individual student's frame of reference, students are expected to construct their own meaning, identify their own way of learning, and pursue their own interests. Students also come to realize that they are learning science or social studies or mathematics, not merely how scientists or mathematicians use the skills, knowledge, and processes of their discipline.

Science and Other Disciplines

Edward Teller (1957), father of the hydrogen bomb, looked at the need for a science education from a different perspective. He spoke convincingly of the universality of drama and theater in all cultures for thousands of years. In his analysis, no one would deny the value of drama or the need for actors to carry it out, and the strong support that drama should receive from citizens and nations. In the same way, we should be preparing citizens to be a most appreciative and understanding scientific audience. From this he reasoned that science education should prepare students to appreciate science, much as music, art, or drama appreciation classes prepare students to understand and enjoy these aspects of their culture.

Making the same connection, Shamos (1994) describes how a curriculum designed to teach science appreciation would be amusing, interesting, motivating, enjoyable, and only incidentally career-oriented or even useful to the individual. Similarly, Trefil (Hirsch, 1987) said that, "the purely instrumental utility of scientific knowledge may be less important than the wider value to be gained from being acquainted with science as one of the great expressions of the human spirit. . . . From a humanistic point of view, its attainments are on a par with great achievements in art, literature, and political institutions, and in this perspective, science should come to be known for the same reasons as these other subjects." Interestingly enough, primary school classrooms are far more likely to reflect the desired climate for creating science literate students, intrinsically motivated to study and enjoy learning about science, than are secondary classrooms.

If our students left a K–12 education feeling that they understood how science and scientists generate knowledge, the role of science in society, that science classes had been enjoyable and worthwhile, and that they could continue to learn, we might find them more accepting of the potentially esoteric nature of basic science research, more skeptical of both scientific and nonscientific claims, and feeling more self-efficacious in regard to science.

Although the exact nature of science literacy or even a need for science education is not clear from the writings of most who call for science literacy, we need students who are knowledgeable and confident in science and who appreciate science, scientists, and the scientific establishment. So, regardless of the issues involved or the rationale for teaching for science literacy, it is worth pursuing how such literacy might be attained. Here, the research is far more clear if we consider science literacy as defined by the National Science Teachers Associa-

Table 10.1   Qualities of Scientifically and Technologically Literate Persons (NSTA Task Force, 1990)

- Uses concepts of science and of technology and ethical values in solving everyday problems and making responsible decisions in everyday life, including work and leisure.

- Engages in responsible personal and civic actions after weighing the possible consequences of alternative options.

- Defends decisions and actions using rational arguments based on evidence.

- Engages in science and technology for the excitement and the explanations they provide.

- Displays curiosity about and appreciation of the natural and human-made world.

- Applies skepticism, careful methods, logical reasoning, and creativity in investigating the observable universe.

- Values scientific research and technological problem solving.

- Locates, collects, analyzes, and evaluates sources of scientific and technological information and uses these sources in solving problems, making decisions, and taking actions.

- Distinguishes between scientific/technological evidence and personal opinion and between reliable and unreliable information.

- Remains open to new evidence and the tentativeness of scientific/technological knowledge.

- Recognizes that science and technology are human endeavors.

- Weighs benefits and burdens of scientific and technological development.

- Recognizes the strengths and limitations of science and technology for advancing human welfare.

- Analyzes interactions among science, technology, and society.

- Connects science and technology to other human endeavors (for example, history, mathematics, the arts, and the humanities).

- Considers the political, economic, moral, and ethical aspects of science and technology as they relate to personal and global issues.

- Offers explanations of natural phenomena that may be tested for their validity.

tion (NSTA) in 1990 or by the American Association for the Advancement of Science (AAAS) in 1989 (see Tables 10.1 and 10.2).

Worth noting at this point are the clear omissions from these two lists: specific knowledge of science concepts, skills, and facts. Almost all of the items focus on personal characteristics and thinking patterns, generic attributes that cut across disciplines and grade levels. From the slighting of content knowledge comes another issue-laden suggestion for improving science learning: *Less is more.*

At the heart of this issue resides the notion that by teaching less content while simultaneously providing more opportunities for thought, decision making, and application of knowledge, we will place students in positions where they develop true meaning and understanding of whatever they are studying, much like the lists call for. At the same time, "less is more" advocates emphasize teaching science (or anything else, for that matter) for the here-and-now rather than as preparation for the next level of schooling. In essence, they say, quit practicing for some future event and make school meaningful, useful, and important

Table 10.2   Capabilities of the Scientifically Literate High School Graduate (AAAS, 1989)

- Poses a question that can be addressed by the scientific method (for example, states a hypothesis).
- Provides a scientific explanation for a natural process (for example, photosynthesis, digestion, combustion).
- Assesses the appropriateness of the methodology of an experiment.
- Reads and understands articles on science in the newspaper.
- Reads and interprets graphs displaying scientific information.
- Believes that scientific knowledge is worth pursuing even if it never yields practical benefits.
- Defines basic scientific terms (for example, DNA, molecule, electricity).
- Designs an experiment that is a valid test of a hypothesis.
- Engages in a scientifically informed discussion of a contemporary issue (for example, should a child with AIDS be allowed to attend public school?).
- Assesses the accuracy of scientific statements (for example, the seasons change with the distance of the earth from the sun).
- Gives an instance of how a scientific discovery or idea has affected society (for example, the term theory of disease).
- Is inclined to challenge authority on evidence that supports scientific statements.
- Describes natural phenomena (for example, the phases of the moon).
- Applies scientific information in personal decision making (for example, ozone depletion and the use of aerosols).
- Locates valid scientific information when needed.

now. Such a focus on the present and a significant reduction in content coverage does not preclude someone going on to become a scientist. But it does help ensure that all citizens have a more positive outlook on science.

SUGGESTIONS FOR IMPROVEMENT

Even though definitions of science literacy are far from definitive or consistent, suggestions for how to improve abound. And, much like the definitions, the suggestions vary widely in their concepts, meaning, insight, and usefulness. Most are somewhat vague and would be of little use to an unenlightened teacher. They range from Ali's (1974) less than useful suggestion that we "provide learners with scientific knowledge" or Zeidler and Lederman's (1989) "change the language of teachers," to Penick and Bonnstetter's (1993) contention that teachers, by playing specific facilitative roles, can create classrooms where students learn science in an atmosphere of innovation. In the same vein, the AAAS, which has advocated developing students' "habits of mind," promotes teaching "consistent with the spirit of inquiry."

Focusing on the teacher, Hamm (1992) suggests we improve teaching by becoming more innovative, involving teachers in all aspects of curriculum development and teacher enhancement, and developing new curriculum models that pay more attention to students. Also looking at the role of the teacher, Penick and Bonnstetter (1993) list a series of student goals they find commonly associated with science literacy as an expectation. Beginning with these goals (such as communication skills, creativity, and application of knowledge), they describe relationships among goals and the roles of teacher and students, always attempting to describe observable behaviors and roles of the teacher.

With the exception of Ali's emphasis on science content, the advocates of improving science teaching for science literacy tend to advocate ideas that are applicable to nearly all concept-oriented subject areas. They refer to many teaching and learning processes that are general, not specific to a particular discipline.

ENHANCING SCIENCE LITERACY

While the definitions of science literacy are somewhat vague and the need for such literacy is often couched in broad general terms, a number of common elements of both definition and need remain. Most science experts seem to agree that the science literate person has the following characteristics:

1. Has a demonstrated interest in science and technology

2. Has an understanding of some basic science concepts

3. Has the ability and desire to learn more, expanding interest and understanding on one's own

4. Takes action, seeks out, and applies knowledge in ways that demonstrate these interests

5. Appreciates science and feels that knowledge is useful in resolving every-day problems and issues

6. Understands the nature and history of science in relation to present-day efforts, ideas, and practices

7. Effectively communicates science ideas to others

8. Creatively seeks alternative solutions and problems

9. Shows self-confidence and comfort in dealing with science

These characteristics imply considerable student activity and initiative. Clearly, they are not characteristics best developed in the traditional passive classroom described by Goodlad (1983), where knowledge presumably flows from the text and teacher into the student. For students to attain the nine qualities attributed to the science literate requires that they actively do aspects of each, systematically and personally. Thus, the science classroom would be a place where you would see students showing interest and understanding, expressing a desire to learn more, and taking action to learn and apply knowledge.

Science literacy is not something that can be given to an individual; rather, the roles of both student and teacher and the ensuing classroom climate must be conducive to developing such characteristics. We have learned much of how students learn; that they construct knowledge based on their own ideas and experience (Driver et al., 1985). For students to construct meaningful knowledge is the challenge facing teachers and curriculum developers. Equally important in the education of children is that all classrooms in every school subject should reflect the same goals and teaching strategies. Looking at the science literacy goals above reveals, again, that these are the same characteristics desired in most classrooms. To have them become a reality, they must be nurtured in all other classrooms as well.

Looking at each of the nine characteristics leads easily to a vision of what students might be doing if they were, in fact, developing that particular quality. While we would not expect to see all qualities as an overt focus of a single student, we know that the conditions conducive to developing each must be pervasive, continuous, and occur over a significant period of time if the person is to change in the desired direction. And one discipline-centered class alone can do little more than begin to develop these. To be truly successful, all classes and all subjects in a school must be involved in a coordinated fashion.

For instance, if we truly want the individual to apply knowledge in ways that demonstrate personal interests, we would expect to see each student in math, science, and other classes raising his or her own (and thus numerous) solutions to problems and trying a variety of approaches and techniques. Multiple solutions imply that different students are working in different ways and at different times. Thus, a classroom where all students are working on the same problem in the same way at the same time is probably a classroom where science literacy has a rather narrow definition rather than the multitude of characteristics listed previously.

At the same time, in a classroom where students are learning to apply knowledge, we would expect to see considerable student activity as students would be at different points in their development, with some working mentally or physically, alone or in groups. Since the students themselves apply the knowledge, we would find the teacher working with students not as the source of all knowledge but as a resource to be taken advantage of. Demonstrations would be out and student project work would be in. Students would be doing most of the work of the classroom and the teacher's role would be quite nontraditional.

Looking at the characteristics described in Tables 10.1 and 10.2, we could proceed to list qualities and actions in the classroom where each is being fostered. And, at the same time, we note that in most instances the desired actions of the students are very similar. Typically, they are working together in some way, communicating, making decisions, and drawing their own conclusions. Interestingly enough, neither the NSTA nor the AAAS list includes specific content knowledge, only examples.

At issue in all of this are the specific goals we have set for our students. Is our highest priority to be quick computational accuracy and knowledge of thousands of terms, formulas, and concepts, or is it to be the characteristics described by NSTA and AAAS? Can we really teach for such personal attributes, and are they transferable to nonschool settings? Some would even contend that there is nothing new here; the teacher described as seeking science literacy is nothing more than the "good" teacher often described in the literature of all disciplines. Regardless, there are too few teachers of this caliber in our schools and classrooms today.

THEORY INTO PRACTICE

The teacher working toward creating a science literate class, striving to attain the student characteristics listed, must avoid those teacher behaviors and roles that squelch desired student behaviors and systematically enhance those that are needed. Of course, this means that teachers must be clearly and consciously aware of their own behaviors, something Good and Brophy (1991) have pointed out is rare.

But, being specifically aware of one's own behavior and role, while necessary, is not sufficient. The effective teacher of science literacy must have a clear and well-justified rationale for teaching and the classroom skills to implement it (Penick & Bonnstetter, 1993). Such a rationale includes clearly articulated overall goals for students, a plan for achieving these goals (including a well-defined role for the teacher and evaluations consistent with student goals). Regardless of the subject matter being taught, tying together the rationale and classroom skills requires that the teacher have adequate knowledge of his or her discipline and pedagogical content knowledge, allowing the teacher to create a classroom climate where desired learning takes place.

In creating the classroom climate, the teacher's role assumes a paramount position. Many of the characteristics of science literacy require considerable intellectual freedom if they are to be achieved. Such intellectual freedom does not imply social freedom but focuses, instead, on providing opportunity for raising issues and questions, trying out solutions, and communicating with others. Intellectual freedom requires a safe environment where one feels comfortable suggesting possibilities, asking questions without fear of humiliation, and initiating action to test personal ideas. An intellectually safe classroom also provides multiple opportunities to interact with others. This is the same classroom climate advocated by most current leading educational thinkers, even when they speak of the arts, social sciences, or humanities. In all instances, they speak of the humanity of the students and the need to develop self-respect as well as a respect for the subject being taught.

In this classroom, we would expect to see the teacher purposefully and systematically creating an intellectually safe environment by reducing unnecessarily explicit directions (Flanders, 1951) (part of science is figuring out *how* to do something, not just having it happen after following a recipe), avoiding teacher generated evaluation (Trefinger, 1978) (in science, evaluation is contingent on causes and consequences; evaluation arises out of testing ideas), and by asking each student to create explanations for phenomena. In doing so, students must consider what they have done, the evidence and data collected, and how these can be fitted together into a rational explanation. In addition, forming an explanation leads naturally to ideas for testing the explanation in ways that are not arbitrary.

The instructional strategy of the teacher seeking science literacy usually begins by providing a strong student stimulus in the form of an activity or issue. Initially, students are expected to explore, seeking ideas, raising questions, and finding out what is known, both by themselves and by other students. This is not a time for the teacher to provide all the knowledge. At this time, the teacher provides resources as needed, asking questions that probe and seek clarification, using extensive and purposeful wait time (Rowe, 1986), and avoids evaluation. The focus will be on getting students to delve deeper into the activity, to find some aspect of personal interest to pursue. Such action takes time and this teacher is patient, knowing that not all students move at the same rate. While in many ways this strategy is not unlike that of early educators such as Dewey, Taba, and Sternberg, it is far more specific than they described, more research-based, and aimed at all students, not just the intellectually gifted. In addition, recent research on student misconceptions (Driver et al., 1985; Yager, 1991) has demonstrated clearly that we must systematically interact with students to determine their ideas and seek ways to intervene as they construct new meaning.

As students work, the teacher observes, watching for clues to student understanding or teachable moments where provided information or material might spur students on or allow new insights into the problem being investigated. At the same time, this teacher is carefully listening to students and asking open questions with the same goal in mind. In both cases, the teacher is trying to take actions that reveal the teacher's logic, a most critical step in communicating science and teaching students how to solve science problems. This is what good, progressive teachers have always done but is rarely what teachers have been taught to do. And, since it is a model rarely used, most of us have not experienced it in ways that allow us to imitate it in our own classrooms.

When experts (teachers, for instance) solve a problem, they make a number of small, discrete steps in logic. When communicating how to solve a problem, however, they often skip steps that seem obvious to them but which are unseen by the novice. Most of us have watched as the teacher solved a math problem on the chalkboard, swiftly and surely moving parts of the equation around, dividing by various units, and miraculously coming to a solution. Unfortunately, while we are enjoying the beautiful show of force, we often have no idea *how* they decided to divide as they did or chose the other actions they took. These small, logical decisions on how to solve the problems are exactly what our students need to learn, but they will not if we do it for them and never reveal the process clearly.

We also know quite well that individuals construct their own meaning out of the information they have gathered and been exposed to (Yager, 1993). This idea, referred to as constructivism, plays a key role in the classroom where science literacy is a goal. A constructivist teacher recognizes that we cannot impart meaning, only information. Unfortunately, much of the time the information is tangential, extraneous, or even irrelevant. Regardless, students try their best to rearrange it into patterns that make sense to themselves (Kagan, 1971). The end result is often information and patterns of meaning that have no real meaning to the students.

A similar situation exists in English, history, or mathematics classes: Students develop their own meaning, often contrary to what is desired by the teacher. In all instances, teachers must converse with students, taking them deeper and deeper into the concepts, before we reach a point where the knowledge is weak and fabricated into flimsy conceptual structures. Often teachers find that these structures crumble easily under the slightest stress of scrutiny and question.

We have considerable evidence that a student who is helped systematically to build meaning around each of the nine characteristics of the science literate will, in fact, develop most of those same characteristics. We know that interest often comes from success, and this is a success-oriented classroom, free of arbitrary evaluation and praise. And with success comes self-confidence, comfort, and opportunities to risk and become more creative. At the same time, risk and creativity enhance understanding of concepts that come from both mental and physical manipulation of ideas and objects (Piaget, 1964). Manipulations that are imitative are far less likely to lead to insight than are actions designed and evaluated by the learner. Learning to learn should be developed as the teacher models learning and reveals logic in any subject (Anderson & Brewer, 1946).

With the focus of the class on doing science, students will learn that action and applying knowledge is the normal course of events in the science classroom. And, the National Assessment of Educational Progress (Mullis and Jenkins, 1988) indicates a strong positive correlation between high cognitive scores and students reporting that in their classroom the teacher stressed applications of knowledge. These same students are more likely to find science useful in everyday life. While this was a report of science learning, it seems rather obvious that the same ideas and classroom descriptions could apply equally well to a variety of classrooms.

The child-centered class, where students are busily engaged in doing in order to learn, continues to be well supported in the literature.

The end result is a teacher who is conscious of the powerful, pervasive role of the teacher and who carefully orchestrates a variety of teacher actions. The most prevalent sequence of behaviors in this strategy would be to

1. Provide stimulating materials, issues, or ideas

2. Ask thoughtful, open-ended questions

3. Wait for student responses

4. Acknowledge, without evaluation, what students say

5. Wait for and encourage, verbally and nonverbally, responses

6. Ask students for clarifications and explanations

7. Use student ideas in posing new questions

Several aspects are key to achieving success with this model. First, the teacher must provide something stimulating for students, finding a way to present it in ways where the students can make decisions and choices (Kohn, 1993). Students must see the teacher as a caring helper working with individuals, not a judge dealing with the masses; they need to feel safe, to have success if they are to develop science literacy (Fisher et al., 1980; Marlave & Filby, 1985). Teacher questions must be of the sort that cannot be answered by a simple "yes" or "no," and are best if the teacher is truly seeking information rather than testing to see what the student knows. The best classroom dialogue is similar to adult conversation. Adults rarely ask each other test questions (What is Avogadro's number?); instead, they ask each other questions to ascertain feelings, ideas, or to gain information not previously held or forgotten. No one likes being tested. Plus, students soon forget what they memorized for the test, regardless of the subject being learned.

Wait time (or lack of it) is also a key behavior. Without wait time students quickly learn that the teacher does not really want much of a response. Plus, with short wait times only the brightest and quickest students respond (Rowe, 1986). Wait time II, waiting *after* a student has responded, also leads to much more cross-talk where students are challenging each other, offering additional ideas, and truly getting involved in the discussion. It appears that if a teacher could merely learn to ask good questions and then wait, classroom teaching of all subjects and student science literacy would improve measurably.

Watching a classroom in which the teacher explicitly seeks science literate students, we would expect to see a classroom rich in materials, ideas, and action. Students at every grade level would be visually stimulated and the focus would not be on the teacher as sole dispenser of knowledge. Rather, students of all ages would see that real knowledge is generated within themselves as they explore, analyze, and explain the activities in which they are engaged (Penick & Bonnstetter, 1993). The teacher must be prepared to create a classroom that organizes, stimulates, and makes readily available a wide range of resources and ideas and actions that encourage students to achieve the desired roles and goals. What we know of how children learn leads us to suggest a more problem- and issue-centered laboratory approach where students use materials in a hands-on and minds-on fashion.

Key to effective teaching is allowing students numerous opportunities to make significant decisions about both what they investigate (the problem) and how they approach it (the process). Evidence from the 1986 National Assessment of Educational Progress indicates that students prefer and have the highest achievement scores in classes that are innovative (Mullis & Jenkins, 1988). If we assume that innovative teachers are those who do something different, we have good evidence that a strikingly visible alternative to traditional teachers and teaching is valued and welcomed by students.

Teacher Education

To enhance teaching in context with science literacy, teacher education should be viewed as having as much status as any other educational program. To do this, we must take teacher education programs as seriously and spend as much as we do on other university programs such as science and engineering. This would probably require that teacher education programs be viewed as serious and re-spected parts of the most prestigious universities, not isolated in what are often perceived as second-class programs.

Becoming a teacher, like almost all professions, requires that a person change certain behaviors. Such changes require time, intensity, thought, and practice. As a result, teacher education programs should provide time for extensive and intensive intellectual and skill work in education. Teachers need time for clinical experience in schools and time to reflect systematically on their actions.

Equally dated, perhaps, is the notion of a "methods" class. Rather than a methods class, prospective teachers need a full-scale immersion into their pro-fession from both a content and a pedagogical point of view. Who can take se-riously a profession where someone studies chemistry (or history or literature) for four years, takes one, three-hour methods course, and is then considered a qualified teacher? No other field has such a limited repertoire of professional courses focusing on the actualities (not just theory) of the work to be done.

To break the current cycle of many teachers being less than adequately pre-pared to teach, universities must change their curriculum and instruction to reflect the needs of prospective and inservice teachers. These needs include pro-grams of study that contain science courses appropriate for teachers at a given level. Primary teachers, for example, need activity-centered science courses, not lectures on thermodynamics. Even secondary teachers, who may reasonably teach considerable content, need laboratory-centered science courses if they are to truly learn to teach in a hands-on fashion. Yet, the trend in the United States is to eliminate undergraduate science labs, as they are viewed as inefficient and wasteful of effort. And, even though such university courses might be relatively basic, content-wise, for a graduate student in that field, they should provide gradu-ate credit for those post-graduates who are just beginning the study of that discipline. Finally, courses must be offered at times conducive to attract inservice teachers and to mingle pre- and inservice teachers while both are learning. Many of these could combine pedagogical content knowledge with the subject matter being taught. Should not prospective teachers focus on *how* as well as *what* is taught?

Curriculum

Curriculum in a reformed educational system would allow for teacher and student decision and interest. Materials would include much that is teacher-developed, and we must enhance the availability of local language and context in all teaching materials. Curriculum would cease to be solely the textbook (Brandwein, 1981) and would come to be viewed as a flexible, ever-changing field within which students and teachers plan and conduct an optimal educational experience.

Equally important, curriculum would begin with relevant issues. As students work to resolve them they would encounter specific details, facts, and skills in context. This is in sharp contrast to the current norm, where students are taught skills and knowledge directly and out of context and are then expected to apply them at some later date. Most of our adult and useful knowledge comes from within a meaningful context and a need to know. In the real world of science, the laboratory represents the beginning of knowledge generation rather than the end where students merely confirm what they have been told, as it is in much of school science. The same applies in most other school subjects. The knowledge we integrate and learn most readily is that in which we found meaning and substance; knowledge generated from problems we identified and solved. Often, this is knowledge we can see around us in our homes, neighborhoods, and communities.

Evaluation

Evaluation of students should be conducted as an integral part of the teaching and learning process. In this sense, evaluation allows the student and teacher to know where they are and, perhaps, how and when to move on. Evaluation of students would allow for and encourage self-evaluation, often with evaluation imbedded in the curriculum. In essence, evaluation would be an essential part of the learning process, not the end of it. Evaluation would include all the goals for students, not just the discipline-centered ones. Students would see evaluation as useful and desirable, not threatening.

Evaluation of teachers would be consistent with the stated roles of teachers, not directly based on student outcomes. Teachers would be expected to self-evaluate prior to any evaluation by others. And, all evaluation would be consistent with an established rationale for teaching. Much as with students, evaluation would be continuous and ongoing; an essential and integral component of the teaching process. Teachers of all subjects must evaluate and change as they teach rather than wait until the students are long gone to initiate changes.

SUMMARY

While science literacy is not clearly defined in a sentence or two, we do have considerable consistency in descriptions of the characteristics of science literate persons. These descriptions assume a person who appreciates science and the scientific endeavor, who uses science daily, and who feels empowered to learn science as needed.

While little formal evidence exists to show the economic value of science literacy, most agree that the characteristics described are those which we want of ourselves and others. No one would be against having the personal attributes listed by AAAS or NSTA. The larger issue is, perhaps, not including content-specific knowledge as part of the goal structure. Yet, groups (such as NSTA and AAAS) that have tried to specify the knowledge to be known have not gained widespread support for those lists.

Much of the evidence supports that we can enhance science literacy (as defined by AAAS and NSTA), and the best procedures for doing so are relatively clear and probably equally relevant to a variety of school subject areas. Teachers must promote science literacy openly and directly, but through teaching strategies that are considerably different than the norm. Teachers (and their classroom climates) must be intellectually open, with systematic opportunity for student decision making and action. Students will construct their own meanings; our task is to help ensure that those meanings are congruent with the desired reality while helping them learn how to use what they have built.

As we have known for years, all of this requires a well-educated and professional teacher; a teacher who learns with students, who provides stimulation, and who, above all, fosters a safe environment where ideas and issues flourish. The teacher, like the gardener, cannot make the seeds grow. But, both can prepare the environment, strive to eliminate interferences, and nurture desired growth. And, both require skill, education, and considerable thought and foresight.

References

Ali, M. (1974). *Secondary Science Education in Bangladesh.* Report from the National Secondary Education and Science Development Center, Dhaka.

American Association for the Advancement of Science (1989). "Capabilities of the Scientifically Literate High School Graduate." Unpublished paper.

American Association for the Advancement of Science (1992). *Project 2061—An American Reform Initiative for Science Literacy.* Washington, D. C.: American Association for the Advancement of Science. The Author.

Anderson, H. H., and J. E. Brewer (1946). "Studies of Classroom Personalities II: Effects of Teacher's Dominative and Integrative Contacts on Children's Classroom Behavior." *Applied Psychology Monographs,* 8.

Baker, D. R. (1991). "A Summary of Research in Science Education." *Science Education* (June): 330–333.

Biological Sciences Curriculum Study (1993). *Developing Biological Literacy.* Colorado Springs, CO: The Author.

Bowyer, J. (1990). *Scientific and Technological Literacy: Education for Change.* United Nations Educational, Scientific and Cultural

Organization. World Conference on Education for All. Thailand, March 5–9, 1990.

Brandwein, P. F. (1981). *Memorandum on Renewing Schooling and Education.* New York: Harcourt Brace Jovanovich.

Branscomb, A. W. (1981). "Knowing How to Know." *Science, Technology, and Human Values* (January): 5–9.

Champagne, A. B., and L. E. Hornig (1987). "Critical Questions and Tentative Answers for the School Science Curriculum," in A. B. Champagne and L. E. Hornig, eds., *This Year in School Science 1986: The Science Curriculum.* Washington, D.C.: American Association for the Advancement of Science, pp. 1–12.

Cohen, R. A. (1987). "A Match or Not a Match: A Study of Intermediate Science Teaching Materials," in A. B. Champagne and L.E. Hornig, eds., *This Year in School Science 1986: The Science Curriculum.* Washington, D.C.: American Association for the Advancement of Science, pp. 1–12.

Demastes, S., and J. H. Wandersee (1992). "Biological Literacy in a College Biology Classroom." *BioScience* (January): 63–65.

Driver, R., E. Guesne, and A. Tiberghien (1985). *Children's Ideas in Science.* Amsterdam: Milton Keynes–Open University Press.

Fisher, C. W., D. C. Berliner, D. D Filby, N. S. Marlave, L. S. Cahen, and M. M. Dishaw (1980). "Teaching Behaviors, Academic Learning Time, and Student Achievement: An Overview," in C. Denham and A. Lieberman, eds., *Time to Learn.* Washington, D. C.: U.S. Department of Education, pp. 28–53.

Flanders, N. A. (1951). "Personal-social Anxieties as a Factor in Experimental Learning Situations." *Journal of Educational Research* (March): 113–124.

Gatewood, C. (1968). "The Science Curriculum Viewed Nationally." *The Science Teacher* (April): 20.

Good, J. E., and T. L. Brophy (1991). *Looking in Classrooms,* 5th ed. New York: Harper-Collins.

Goodlad, J. (1983). A *Place Called School.* New York: McGraw-Hill.

Hamm, M. (1992). "Achieving Scientific Literacy through a Curriculum Connected with Mathematics and Teaching." *School Science and Mathematics* (January): 6–9.

Harms, N. C., and R. E. Yager, eds. (1981). *What Research Says to the Science Teacher,* vol. 3. Washington, D.C.: National Science Teachers Association.

Hirsch, E. D. (1987). *Cultural Literacy.* Boston: Houghton Mifflin.

Hurd, P. D. (1958). "Science Literacy: Its Meaning for American Schools." *Educational Leadership* (January): 13–16.

Kagan, J. (1971). *Understanding Children.* New York: Harcourt Brace Jovanovich.

Kohn, A. (1993). "Choices for Children: Why and How to Let Students Decide." *Phi Delta Kappan* (September): 8–20.

Marlave, N. S., and N. N. Filby (1985). "Success Rate: A Measure of Task Appropriateness," in C. W. Fisher and D. C. Berliner, eds., *Perspectives on Instructional Time.* New York: Longman.

Miller, J. D. (1983). "Scientific Literacy: A Conceptual and Empirical Review." *Daedalus* (January): 29–48.

Miller, J. D. (1989). "Scientific Literacy." Paper presented at the 1989 Annual Meeting of the American Association for the Advancement of Science, San Francisco.

Miller, J. D., R. W. Suchner, and A. Voelker (1980). *Citizenship in an Age of Science: Changing Attitudes Among Young Adults.* New York: Pergamon.

Mullis, I. V., and L. B. Jenkins, eds. (1988). *The Science Report Card: Elements of Risk and Recovery.* Princeton, NJ: Educational Testing Service.

National Science Teachers Association (1990). NSTA Position Paper, "Qualities of a Scientifically and Technologically Literate Person." Washington D.C.: The Author.

Penick, J. E., and R. J. Bonnstetter (1993). "Classroom Climate and Instruction: New Goals Demand New Approaches." *Journal of Science Education and Technology* (January): 389–395.

Piaget, J. (1964). "Development and Learning, Part 1 of Cognitive Development in Children." *Journal of Research in Science Teaching* (January): 74–85.

Rowe, M. B. (1986). "Wait Time: Slowing Down May Be Speeding Up!" *Journal of Teacher Education* (January–February): 43–50.

Shamos, M. (1990). "Scientific Literacy Where It Counts?" *Journal of College Science Teaching* (February): 196–197.

Shamos, M. (1994). *The Myth of Scientific Literacy.* Unpublished book manuscript.

Teller, E. (1957). Testimony Before the U.S. Senate Armed Services Committee, November 27.

Treffinger, D. (1978). "Guidelines for Encouraging Independence and Self-Direction among Gifted Students." *Journal of Creative Behavior* (January): 14–20.

Yager, R. E. (1991). "The Constructivist Learning Model." *The Science Teacher* (September): 52–57.

Yager, R. E., ed. (1993). *What Research Says to the Science Teacher*, vol. 7. Washington, D.C.: National Science Teachers Association.

Zeidler, D. L., and N. G. Lederman (1989). "The Effect of Teachers' Language on Students' Conceptions of the Nature of Science." *Journal of Research in Science Teaching* (December): 771–783.

Discussion Questions

1. What characterizes a "safe" environment for students?

2. How would you explain how wait time causes student to
   a. respond more often?
   b. provide more evidence for their statements?
   c. give longer answers?
   d. speculate more on ideas presented by the teacher and others?

3. Following Morris Shamos' ideas, how would you design the curriculum if "science appreciation" is the primary goal?

4. Many of the ideas presented in this chapter are not unique to science. Looking at the ideas presented in Tables 10.1 and 10.2, see how many could easily be modified to fit a discipline other than science.

5. A student teacher asks, "How do you conduct a successful discussion?" Based on this chapter, what specific advice would you give this person?

6. What would the ideal teacher education program look like?

Edward A. Wynne

An ex-labor lawyer who practiced for ten years in New York City and Washington, D.C., Ed Wynne went back to school in his mid-thirties to get a doctorate in education and sociology at Berkeley. His academic role model was the famous James Coleman. Since graduating, some twenty-five years ago, Wynne has been teaching at the University of Illinois at Chicago and is professor of education.

Those early days of cross-examining opponents and questioning clients carries over today with Wynne's teaching technique. In action, he purposely instills a certain amount of stress in his classrooms to encourage his students to think and defend their reasoning. He recommends teachers be familiar with their professional literature, but he has no favorite education books or journals. Rather, he urges "teachers to become grounded in the basic intellectual literature about human values," regardless of their subject or grade level, and "to guard against fads and frills which afflict education." His concept of good literature includes Dostoyevsky, Austen, Melville, Thoreau, Hawthorne, Freud, and *The Federalist Papers.*

That's heavy, but he wants to stretch our minds and make us think—what good teaching and learning should be about.

It is Wynne's legal background and interest in human valuing that has led him to publish some one hundred articles and ten books—all which in his view have "moral, ethical, and social overtones." His two most recent books, *Reclaiming Our Schools* and *A Year in the Life of an Excellent Elementary School,* are, for Ed, his most significant books.

And, although he is sixty-five years old, and at an age where many of his colleagues are talking about retirement, Wynne has no such plans. "I've been getting up at 6:30 AM for the last twenty years, and doing my Canadian exercise drills. Retirement is a modern artifact, an industrial invention," he says. From the looks of his cluttered desk and floor-to-ceiling papers, you get the idea he is serious when he says "I prefer to visit schools, observe teachers, teach, and write for the next twenty years." One has to wonder if he has some secret about life.

11 ❦

The Moral Dimension of Teaching

Edward A. Wynne

It is often uncertain what is meant by remarks about the "moral dimension of teaching." Despite such ambiguity, many people recognize that teaching, in many ways, is clearly a moral activity. The problem arises when one tries to precisely define that noble proposition. What does "moral teaching" mean in concrete terms? And what implications does this meaning have for present and potential teachers? Whatever the final answers to these ambitious questions, it seems that, in our era, there is an increasing concern with such issues (see, for example, Greene, 1973; Noddings, 1992; Sockett, 1993; Strike & Soltis, 1985). Indeed, educators are displaying growing interest in the moral roots of their craft.

We all realize that the moral concerns prevailing in our era are relatively diffuse: Many people seem to have conflicting values about important public and personal issues. However, one widely shared understanding does underlie the word *moral*: Moral questions, in the end, are not determined by consensus. True, a consensus is often desirable in such matters. But, in issues of importance, the moral man or woman may properly feel compelled—after humble reflection, and counseling with others—to act in the face of general opposition. This urgency which sometimes applies in moral issues injects a special dimension into discussions about teaching and morality.

Incongruously, despite the confusion surrounding the concept of moral teaching in our era, it is hard to identify a clear statement on behalf of amoral teaching—teaching removed from all moral concerns. Many writings about teaching say little or nothing about its moral component. However, a careful reader senses that if the charge of "amorality" was laid against any such composition, the author would typically contend he or she still favors moral teaching; that topic should simply be addressed elsewhere. In any event, this chapter will assume that everyone favors "moral teaching," whatever the term means to different people. The problem for each teacher is to determine what definition of morality should apply to his or her work.

The audience for this chapter is adults; students in college or graduate school. By this time in their lives, much of their basic moral identities have been formed. Such formation largely comes from their family and religious experiences, and their lives as children and adolescents. As teachers, their challenge will be to adapt such basic values to a new and different role—instructing the children of other adults. This chapter will strive to help readers manage this adaptation.

To facilitate this process of adaptation, the chapter will

1. Examine the relevant history about morality and teaching, and show its connection to our contemporary education scene

2. Identify and contrast the two main approaches regarding teacher morality: traditional moral teaching and "prophetic" moral teaching

3. Discuss the relationship between classroom (or schoolwide) community and moral teaching and

4. Integrate these topics into a brief summation

HISTORICAL PERSPECTIVES

The work of the historian Arnold Toynbee (1934–1959) is a good starting point for our search. Toynbee identified twenty-one "civilizations," most of them now expired, existing on the five inhabited continents. He concluded that these civilizations encompassed all the major social systems in human history. The civilizations existed between 4000 BC (in Egypt) up to Western civilization beginning before AD 700 and continuing into our era. Meyers (1968) examined thirteen of these civilizations, where enough information was available to describe each civilization's form of education. He concluded that, despite their dispersion in time and space, the scattered "education systems" displayed many common themes.

For instance, all of the systems stressed intimate tutor/learner relationships as basic to education—not formal institutions, like schools, but person-to-person contacts. The prime goal for these educational arrangements was transmitting moral knowledge to learners—an understanding of what conduct was right or wrong, and why. In this regard, Meyers' statement about education in the early Chinese, Hindu, and Grecian civilizations is typical:

> The prime aim . . . was the development of the character of the student; the training was fundamentally moral . . . the relationship that existed between the tutor and the pupil was one of friendship and love, close and intimate . . . the pupil associated constantly with his tutor and observed his speech, his manners, his social and moral attitudes.

The moral emphasis pervading traditional education had important implications for teachers. If teachers were to transmit morality, they were simultaneously obligated to practice morality in dealing with pupils. No one imagined that evidently immoral teachers could teach morality to pupils. Such traditional moral instructors apparently operated on their own, almost as free agents. But their instructional freedom was really constrained by important principles. Typically, such principles were founded on religious and social frameworks. As it were, the prevailing religion, or system of popular moral beliefs in their civilization, supplied the moral framework for each teaching situation.

Meyers found that moral transmission was coupled with the teaching of social or mechanical skills, for example, a foreign language, writing, or teaching about myths, poetry, or rhetoric. But even such skills were embedded in a body of human and moral relationships. The teachers transmitting such knowledge were concerned with their students growing into morally sound adults. The intimate nature of such teaching situations naturally facilitated moral transmission.

It was understood by all that "poor teaching" would have grave moral ramifications for the developing student in particular, and the society in general. Thus, poor teaching would breach a teacher's religious or moral obligations. Concomitantly, insufficient application by a student might also have moral ramifications.

Meyers also found that, sometimes, in the later stages of particular civilizations, teaching became less morally focused—more stress was laid on forms, rituals, and technical knowledge. He felt such shifts were generally associated with the spread of decadence throughout each society.

These traditional and pervasive concerns with moral instruction by teachers extended into our own Western civilization. For instance, in early American colonies, such moral emphases in teaching were common (Bailyn, 1960). Indeed, teaching morality represented the foundation of mainstream American public education—in both the instructions to teachers and the curriculum presented to pupils—until about 1930 (Tyack & Hansot, 1982).

The curriculum during these years, and the instructional training provided for teachers, consistently stressed themes such as moral conduct by pupils, character formation, the centrality of diligence, respect for elders, and equivalent virtues. Sometimes such presentations were explicitly religious, based on Christian foundations. On later occasions, the presentations took a more secular form. But, in either case, pedagogical norms saw teacher/pupil relationships in largely moral terms. And this moral concern still continues in some American public schools and individual classrooms in our era.

The vocabulary applied in our era to describe teachers' moral roles has been notably tempered. The tempering has occurred in deference to the prevailing secular—and even antireligious—intellectual climate. Often, the assumption seems to be that the teacher is merely a highly skilled technician, delivering some package to his clients.

MORAL TEACHING: THE TRADITIONAL PERSPECTIVE

However, the idea that teaching can be divorced from its moral foundations can be described as an historical anomaly: a brief divergence from an enormously long-term pattern. Still, contemporary Western civilization has moved an enormous distance from the other civilizations described by Toynbee and Meyers.

How does one translate the universal educational principles such authors identify into policies for our own particular era and place?

A contemporary teacher's first moral obligation is to provide his or her students with the best possible instruction in the subject matter assigned. The unique morality of contemporary teaching consists of the teacher's deep obligation to help the student learn. In a sense, the principle seems to be like that which applies to all persons who sell certain goods or services; give the customer his money's worth. But the matter of "money's worth" has a special meaning for teachers and students.

Teachers should be uniquely dedicated because they control the vulnerable and exposed children of other adults. Children are often incapable of defending themselves from exploitation by negligent or selfish teachers. Children are also in the process of growth and development; therefore, irresponsible or careless teaching may have profound effects on their life opportunities. Furthermore, typical school and classroom activities are often comparatively isolated from the observation of other adults. Due to such seclusion, teachers are less subject to adult monitoring than most persons providing customers with goods or services. Teachers have more freedom to engage in exploitation than most suppliers of services. Because of such opportunities for abuse, the teacher's fidelity to the best of his or her craft is critical. It is a moral obligation.

Assume that this traditional sense of a deep moral obligation to committed teaching is recognized. Then, it is easy to identify the major elements of moral teaching.

Traditional moral teachers work hard at teaching; they

1. Come to work regularly and on time

2. Avoid clock watching

3. Become well informed about their subject matter

4. Plan and conduct their classes with care

5. Grade and return students' papers promptly

6. Strive to have pupils display age appropriate, responsible conduct

7. Regularly review and update their instructional practices

8. Willingly cooperate with or, if necessary, confront, parents of under-achieving pupils

9. Are strongly disposed to cooperate with their colleagues and observe school policies, so the whole institution works effectively

10. Avoid defensiveness about supervisory oversight

11. Tactfully but firmly criticize existing unsatisfactory school policies, and propose constructive improvement

12. Pursue employment in more wholesome schools if current unsatisfactory policies cannot be improved

The general basis for the preceding catalogue is evident: Most pupils lack the authority or sophistication to protect themselves against individual time-serving teachers; however, traditional moral teachers, despite their students' vulnerability, still do the right thing. Moral teachers strive to make their classrooms and their whole school work well. They observe school rules and policies. If a "moral" teacher has doubts about a particular school policy, he or she is obligated to thoughtfully discuss such differences with colleagues and/or administrators. Oftentimes, there is more good sense underlying existing schoolwide policies than individual teachers recognize.

However, assume the teacher—after deliberation—finally believes the particular policies are basically unwise. If so, a moral teacher's responsibility is to work with other colleagues to improve such policies. Assume such responsible efforts at improvement fail. Even assume that a teacher's own in-class morality (or commitment to teaching) is handicapped by the prevalence of unwise schoolwide policies. Then, traditional moral teachers recognize their responsibility to try to work in moral environments—environments where teachers are supported and encouraged to practice moral instruction. And so such moral teachers begin to look around for truly moral schools in which to practice their craft. After all, American teachers are not indentured. They are employees in a comparatively free job market. Over a number of years, most teachers who seriously pursue other teaching alternatives can find sites more congenial for moral instruction.

The concept of striving to cause appropriate learning ties moral teaching to traditional themes such as duty, obligation, loyalty, sacrifice, and obedience to legitimate authority. All of such themes are part of an ancient tradition of connecting moral conduct to visible behavior (Durkheim, 1961; LeVine & White, 1986; MacIntyre, 1982). Another way of explaining the tradition is by relating it to the theme of "character" (Wynne & Ryan, 1993).

Character is derived from the Greek root word, *to mark*. The term signifies persisting, visible acts. The idea is that moral persons have good character. We can examine their morality, which is often related to an internal state of mind, by observing the elements of their visible conduct. Teachers who display good or bad character through acts or words provide students with examples of human virtues or flaws. The basic test of whether a teacher is moral is whether he or she displays good character.

AN ALTERNATIVE PERSPECTIVE: THE TEACHER AS PROPHET

The traditional concept of moral teaching—just explicated—can be contrasted with another contemporary theme: the teacher as a "prophet."

The theme of the prophetic teacher was perhaps first expressed by John Dewey's colleague, George Counts (1932). He recited his views in a provocatively titled booklet, *Dare the Teachers of America Build a New Social Order?*

The prophetic teacher does not stress the direct, immediate obligations of pupils and teachers. Instead, he or she is more concerned with provoking pupils to act against perceived general injustices in the external world, for example, pollution, war, racism, and sexism. The emphasis is not so much on the teacher as a diligent craftsmen; instead, the approach focuses on teaching students to strive for a notably better world (Freedman, 1990; Kohl, 1968; Kozol, 1967; Postman & Weingartner, 1969). Such prophetic teaching can occur either via innovative classroom practices and/or consciousness-raising instruction.

Readers may recall that, in the Judeo-Christian tradition, prophets were courageous, far-sighted persons who called on "the people" to adopt certain important values and moral practices which had fallen into disregard. (Of course, there is also the concurrent tradition of "false prophets.") How do such prophetic moral concerns relate to a teacher displaying a character approach? To teachers practicing traits such as duty and commitment?

There is some divergence between the approaches of teacher as moral craftsman versus teacher as prophet. This divergence needs explication.

The traditional "moral craftsman" approach has a basic philosophical premise. The approach assumes that most of the correctable evils that affect our lives spring from the acts of individual human beings. Those acts are rooted in the practice of traits such as selfishness, laziness, intolerance, and the like. It is essential that teachers who are moral craftsmen work hard at suppressing such traits in their own conduct, and displaying countervailing traits, such as generosity, diligence, and tolerance. Furthermore, pupils should be encouraged to immediately display equivalent virtues in their day-to-day life. The approach recognizes that some persons can apply attractive virtues to bad ends: A thief may be brave, a diligent person may be greedy, and so on. Despite such deficiencies, the traditional assumption is that it is generally wise teaching strategy to stress that teachers and pupils practice such virtues.

The "prophetic" approach to moral teaching has a different emphasis. The approach stresses particular programmatic goals for which pupils and teachers should strive. Certain evils and deficiencies are identified in the world and the teacher tries to encourage pupils to mobilize and correct such evils. Or, at least, pupils are taught to recognize such evils—even if the evils are not widely perceived elsewhere in the society.

It is rare for either of the two approaches to be applied exclusively. Few teachers who are moral craftsmen propose teaching students good traits so they can be loyal members of the Mafia; nor do proponents of the prophetic approach disparage diligence. Still, there is an undeniable tension between the two. The craftsman, as it were, stresses "process." It is not so important what subject matter is taught. Instead, the first emphasis is on how it is taught (and learned)—with diligence, planning, some sensitivity to existing precedents and values, and so on. Presumably, if pupils and teachers apply (and learn) such morally sound approaches, the short- and long-range decisions they make now or later about private and public issues will tend to be wise.

Conversely, the prophetic approach assumes that certain traits can be deemphasized—like foresight, compared to spontaneity and immediate relevance—in the pursuit of desirable policy goals, such as mobilizing students against pollution. As it were, it is more important that pupils feel and act strongly and dramatically against pollution than that they pursue some remote and technically ideal solution. And, if responsible adults are uncertain of what to do about pollution, it is still important that pupils be stimulated to do something apparently constructive.

CONTRASTING TRADITIONAL AND PROPHETIC MORAL TEACHING

There are bodies of contemporary literature describing the in-classroom or in-school operation of both the traditional and prophetic approaches to moral teaching. It will be constructive to consider two contrasting examples.

From a character perspective, the traditionalist moral teaching of Jamie Escalante is especially illustrative (Matthews, 1988). (Escalante's conduct is also portrayed in the relatively accurate and vivid commercial film, "Stand and Deliver.")

Escalante was a Bolivian schoolteacher. He emigrated to America in the 1970s, became a citizen, and chose to earn a California state teaching certificate in the face of many handicaps—even though he could make more money more easily working as a computer technician. He was driven to teach.

After teaching math for several years in Garfield Public High School, a Latino ghetto school in Los Angeles, Escalante evolved a novel approach to instruction. His ideas were conspicuously successful. Due to his approach, he was able to teach a number of Garfield students the skills needed to pass the national advanced placement exam in calculus. Those students then went on to successful college attendance. Before Escalante's program, no Garfield student had ever passed the calculus AP exam. Several years after the initiation of his program, fifty students in Garfield were passing the calculus exam each year, and other advanced placement courses were successfully underway in the school.

The details of Escalante's instructional approach are significant. But, for the purposes of this chapter, it is more important to stress that his approach was (1) highly moral, and (2) essentially character-oriented. To be specific, the approach stressed:

1. Escalante's moralistic approach to the subject of calculus instruction (and learning). Morality, to him, meant diligence, honesty, commitment, and deep caring. Both Escalante and his students were equally subject to such moral obligations, though the responsibilities of each of the two entities took separate forms.

2. Escalante's willingness to work very hard to help his pupils.

3. Each individual pupil's voluntary decision to sign (or to choose not to sign) a contract to enlist in the program, and carry out the foreseeable arduous assignments (personal commitment and responsibility are key elements of character development).

4. Escalante's determination to hold each pupil to his or her contract—and provide all conceivable forms of support. He walked the last mile, and made similar demands on his pupils.

5. Escalante's acquiescence to an external criteria—the advanced placement exam—as a test of successful learning. Despite his independence and

imagination, he believed in his accountability to external legitimate authority.

The assumptions underlying Escalante's process are relatively traditional: The world will be a morally better place if his students succeed in "learning" how to work very hard, make and keep difficult but wise commitments, accept the instruction of dedicated and able teachers, and so on. It is even possible that his subject matter—instead of calculus—could just as well have been Latin, chemistry, or astronomy.

Imagine that Escalante's successful pupils, as mature adults, have to make and act on decisions about public or private issues with moral content. Presumably, the mature pupils' decisions and conduct will be more moral for their having learned calculus in his class. After all, it was the same passion for doing things "right"—to serve others—that drove Escalante into teaching instead of working with computers, and which stimulated him to create and operate his successful program.

Several educators and administrators in Garfield sympathized with Escalante and supported him in his efforts (while other Garfield faculty were indifferent, or opposed Escalante). Such evidence indicates that a character approach to moral teaching is still alive in our time. Such an approach has generally prevailed since 4000 BC. Any teaching approach that has persisted as an ideal for almost sixty centuries undoubtedly has many "natural" forces working on its behalf.

As for the prophetic perspective, the contemporary literature on this approach is far more voluminous than that describing the character approach (Freedman, 1990; Kohl, 1968; Kozol, 1967; Postman & Weingartner, 1969). Thus, it is more appropriate to offer a composite image of the teacher as a semiprophet, rather than focusing on one practitioner. In drawing his composite, we must recognize that much of this literature is semiautobiographical, and may often lack an objective perspective; thus, the composite sketch may include some qualifications about what "really" happened. The descriptive literature portrays the prophetic teacher as

1. Usually surrounded by mediocrity, as was Escalante (a character-oriented teacher). But the prophetic teacher typically appears even more alone than Escalante.

2. Far less patient with the school environment than Escalante—who essentially made public school teaching his lifelong career, and did not resign after a year or two and write a book about his efforts.

3. Strongly opposed to the traditional curriculum. Escalante only wanted his students supplied with top-of-the-line standard texts, and admired calculus partly because it was a traditional subject.

4. Sympathetic to students' personal opinions about class subject matter and the teaching and grading process.

5. Unconcerned whether all students in his class worked hard at studying or learning.

6. Enormously confident about his or her ability to master and accurately teach classes covering a variety of the complex subject matters.

7. Optimistic about almost all students' abilities to master demanding topics and analyze public issues with appropriate maturity.

8. Concerned with maintaining students' spontaneity and enthusiasm.

9. Dedicated to assign imaginative activities in the teaching and learning process.

10. Uncomfortable—or hostile—at the idea of subjecting pupils' learning to external examination.

Both the character-oriented teacher and the prophetic teacher often question the status quo. But the character-oriented teacher wants to improve the status quo; the prophetic teachers wants to dramatically transform it. The character-oriented teacher takes only moderate risks with other peoples' children; the prophetic teacher takes somewhat greater risks, in the hope of attaining greater gains.

MORALITY AND GROUP LIFE

There are two areas of overlap in the concerns of character-oriented and prophetic teachers. One area has already been noted: Members of each group believe teaching is largely a moral activity. They only differ in defining what morality consists of.

Another important overlapping concern between the approaches also needs consideration: Members of both groups share a belief in the importance of the classroom as a community. Neither group believes a classroom is merely composed of twenty to thirty pupils, each of whom should be encouraged to address solely his or her personal concerns. Classrooms should be small communities—groups of persons who share certain common concerns and goals, beyond the immediate and desperate self-interest of each pupil-citizen (Wynne & Ryan, 1993). This stress on the importance of community life means that community members, including pupils and teachers, share many moral concerns with each other. Thus, classroom communities are necessary to teach pupils moral conduct and, indeed, cannot even persist unless such moral principles prevail among group members.

However, there are significant distinctions between the community emphases favored by the two groups of educators. Such differences and similarities can be identified—and their operational implications for teacher recognized—by returning to our preceding Escalante/prophet contrast. Traditional and prophetic moral teachers both try to create communal classrooms where

1. Students are expected and encouraged to help and care for each other in many ways—both academically and nonacademically.

2. Nonacademic collective activities are used to enhance group solidarity (for example, parties, fundraising).

3. Symbols are identified to enhance group identity (for example, slogans, class jackets, or "T" shirts).

4. Teachers express a sense of identity with the class as a group.

5. The teacher tries to arrange class scheduling so students and teachers spend significant lengths of time—even successive years—with each other. (Escalante even arranged for all his classes to meet in one special room—their turf.)

6. The teacher tries to stimulate a strong sense of moral concern throughout the class (for example, honesty, kindness, and diligence).

7. The teacher tries to undertake school duties that permit his participation in pro-community activities (for example, managing student athletic teams or clubs).

Despite the preceding instances of parallel concerns, there are also issues where the pro-community priorities of traditional and prophetic teachers often clash.

1. Traditional teachers, as far as possible—and allowing for pupils' age capabilities—try to make community involvement deliberate, voluntary, and informed. Not every pupil can or will become involved in the community; indeed, maturing children cannot be drafted into morality. Encouragement is fine; however, compulsion is out. Prophetic teachers display less concern than traditional teachers about including potentially unsympathetic members. They are more inclusive or optimistic about holding diverse groups together.

2. Traditional teachers identify classroom community aims congruent with the goals of the external society. Prophetic teachers may be more inclined to stress class action against supposedly abusive external institutions.

3. Traditional teachers comfortably stress both group goals—all class members pass the exam—and individual goals—each class member also hoped, personally, to pass the same exam. Prophetic teachers may choose to solely emphasize collective success. They often see individual goals as encouraging undesirable competition.

THEORY INTO PRACTICE

Assume that a potential teacher wants to be a moral teacher and is willing to accept the traditional definition of the moral teacher as his or her starting point. In other words, our beginner realizes his or her first aim is to work hard to cause pupils to learn the desired material. Then, how should he or she conduct his professional life?

First, the actual or potential teacher must recognize the demands underlying such moral commitment. He must know or learn the subject matter he is responsible for; identify the curriculum he is assigned to teach; plan a series of thoughtful lessons to present; teach the material; design and put into effect homework, tests, and other measures to assess and motivate pupil learning; construct and apply a discipline plan appropriate to the class level and pupils involved; solicit the counsel of peers and supervisors in constructing and carrying out his plans; identify, learn, and observe the policies of the school relevant to his work; maintain a friendly but business-like demeanor with his pupils and their parents; provide pupils (and families) with accurate, prompt praise or constructive criticism; become informed about the problems and strengths of particular pupils and their families; be prepared to put in extra time to get important things done; participate in school activities in addition to teaching, so the whole institution works better; constantly assess the practices and plans he is now applying, so they may be improved in the near or intermediate future; stay informed about important ideas and improvements affecting his field; and be available to students who need extra help.

Obviously, no beginning teacher can do all of these things well the first time, and no reasonable supervisor will expect a beginner to display such perfection. Furthermore, the targets indicated by the list inevitably imply some degree of compromise: For example, all-out striving to be deeply informed about pupils' and families' private lives may take too much time away from class preparations or grading papers.

However, the list is a target for teachers to aim towards. And it also implies some of the reasons why extraordinary teacher morality is rare. For example, the list makes no reference to the honorable private aspirations relating to courtship, family obligations, supplementing professional income through one or another means, or engaging in reasonable recreation.

But the matter of teacher morality should not be painted too bleakly. Striving to be a moral teacher is a high demand/high payoff activity. The moral practices sketched above often have a benign and important impact on pupils and professional peers. The moral teacher can frequently see how his or her wholesome efforts positively affect the pupils and families they work with. This does not mean that everything, all of the time, will work out well for a teacher. No school or classroom can be a utopia. But the moral teacher can still expect to see a plausible connection between his or her moral professional conduct and the benefits they provide for students. Such perceptions are a powerful form of encouragement.

SUMMARY

It is impossible for schools and teachers to avoid morally affecting pupils, when they have them under their control for twelve years or more. All adults in such prolonged relationships with children inevitably have a moral impact on their formation—for better or for worse. Thus, teachers must be concerned about the morality they transmit to students.

In all other previous cultures, and through much of Western and American history, educators explicitly recognized their roles as moral instructors. "Recognized" means such teachers consciously strove to increase their pupils' morality, and discussed, with other adults, ways to increase their skills in moral transmission.

Comparatively recently, the formal dedication of American educators to teaching morality has somewhat moderated. This change is a notable shift in educational priorities. It has been accompanied by notable long-term increases in disorder among young Americans from many social classes. No one suggests that such patterns of increasing disorder are largely due to changes in teaching policies about moral instruction. However, it does seem safe to predict that we are now seeing a revitalization of the previous long-term educational concern over teaching morality. Since we know that moral concerns are an important part of adults' motivations to work in teaching, this shift in priorities should be pleasing to many teachers. But the shift does mean that teachers must now give more explicit concern to topics such as how to transmit morality, and what moral priorities should be applied.

References

Bailyn, B. (1960). *Education and the Forming of American Society*. Chapel Hill, NC: University of North Carolina Press.

Counts, G. (1932). *Dare the Teachers of America Build New Social Order?* New York: John Day.

Durkheim, E. (1961). *Moral Education*. New York: The Free Press.

Freedman, S. (1990). *Small Victories*. New York: Harper & Row.

Greene, M. (1973). *Teacher as Stranger*. Belmont, CA: Wadsworth.

Kohl, H. (1968). *Thirty Six Children*. New York: New American.

Kozol, J. (1967). *Death at an Early Age*. Boston: Houghton Mifflin.

LeVine, R., and M. White (1986). *Human Conditions*. New York: Routledge & Kegan Paul.

MacIntyre, A. (1982). *After Virtue*. South Bend, IN: University of Notre Dame Press.

Matthews, J. (1988). *Escalante. the Best Teacher in America*. New York: Holt.

Meyers, E. A. (1968). *Education in the Perspective of History*. New York: Harper Brothers.

Noddings, N. (1992). *Challenge to Care in Schools*. New York: Teachers College Press, Columbia University.

Postman, N., and C. Weingartner (1969). *Teaching as a Subversive Activity*. New York: Delacorte.

Sockett, H. (1993). *The Moral Basis for Teacher Professionalism*. New York: Teachers College Press, Columbia University.

Strike, K. A., and J. F. Soltis (1985). *The Ethics of Teaching*. New York: Teachers College Press, Columbia University.

Toynbee, A. J. (1934–1939). *A Study of History* (10 vols.). New York: Oxford University Press.

Tyack, D., and E. Hansot (1982). *Guardians of Virtue: Public School Leadership in America. 1820–1980*. New York: Basic Books.

Wynne, E. A., and K. Ryan (1993). *Reclaiming Our Schools*. New York: Macmillan/Merrill.

Discussion Questions

1. What do you believe is the most important trait a teacher should possess? What behaviors—acts or words—let us know if a teacher has, or lacks, such a trait? Explain your conclusions.

2. From your experience as a pupil or teacher, give an example of a teacher you see as extremely dedicated to doing his or her job well. Give an example of a teacher who did not try hard enough. Explain your conclusions.

3. What are the most important barriers you see (or anticipate) will stand in the way of your becoming an excellent teacher? Why are they important and/or difficult?

4. Since moving into, or towards, education as a career, has there been any change in your perspective about what makes a good teacher? What has that change been, if it has occurred? Why do you think it occurred?

5. Can you think of an example(s) of a teacher giving you—or some other pupil(s)—advice or criticism about a moral issue, for example, lying, kindness, unkindness, criminal activities, sexual relations, observing lawful rules? What were the incidents? What principles, if any, about teacher conduct can you derive from the incidents?

Part III ❧

The Culture, Language, and Cognition of Teaching

The notion of "effective teaching" has produced an idealized model of the teacher, one who is businesslike and structured, capable of managing classroom activities and organizing the physical and social setting of the classroom, clear about instructional goals, knowledgeable about content and ways of teaching it, and capable of using a variety of methods and materials. The recommended teaching behaviors that have evolved have been generic, and have not always been applicable to specific students or subjects. We continue to make these recommendations because the behaviors are observable, and we can easily isolate and define them.

However, researchers are learning that teaching is more complex, and defining what effective (or ineffective) teachers do or think is more messy and less precise than we might want to admit. A number of researchers are moving beyond the science and products of teaching and turning to the cultural, linguistic, and thinking processes involved in teaching—what some educators might call the context of teaching, and still others might call the nonbehavioral aspects of teaching. Hence, researchers are trying to explain and interpret how these contextual factors (culture, language, and cognition) help us understand teacher and student behavior—and how these contextual factors illustrate forms of communication and relationships that take place in the classroom and form the classroom setting (or ecology). The field is also becoming more accepting and appreciative of ethnographic methods of research, qualitative phenomena, and reflective thinking in describing the teaching act.

In the first chapter of this part, Philip Cusick examines "The Culture of Students, Teachers, and Reformers." The author points out that students represent a variety of ethnic groups, classes, and cultures, and the school is charged with the task of inculcating this diverse group into the prevailing norms and values of the larger society. A long history of student opposition toward schools has evolved, largely based on a clash of cultures. Teachers, as agents of schools, develop a culture of control that becomes embedded in their pedagogy to deal with this opposition—in turn, which critics and reformers oppose and view as a major problem of schooling that needs to be changed. For Cusick, student resistance in classrooms and schools will not go away, and so the cultural conflict between students and teachers will endure. He feels that the best way to resolve the conflict between teachers and critics of teachers is to have critics teach so they experience student resistance firsthand.

In Chapter 13, Dona Kagan explains the "Research on Teacher Cognition," that is, aspects of teacher beliefs and thinking about students, subject matter, and classroom events. She analyzes the self-images of teachers and the decisions they make while teaching. The analysis moves us away from behavioral and observable research on teaching, the kind of theories that have dominated past research on teaching, to new qualitative methods and teacher assessment procedures. She believes that education students graduate from teacher education programs without changing their original beliefs or attitudes about teaching; thus, there is a need to restructure teacher edu-cation around the theme of "self-reflection."

Next, "Learning from Teachers' Perspectives," by Marilyn Cochran-Smith and Susan Lytle, emphasizes the need to learn about teaching from teachers—from the basis of practice, not theory. The questions and issues raised by teachers at school meetings and university-based classrooms, as well as their insights, viewpoints, and strategies, represent the "inside" view of teaching. The study of teachers by researchers, which has dominated the professional literature for decades, represents the "outside" view of teaching. In order to improve the connection between theory and practice, the authors maintain there is a need to stress the inside view of teaching—to make the teachers' perspectives more public and to encourage research by teachers.

Chapter 15 is written by Kathy Carter, Walter Doyle, and Mark Riney: They synthesize the research that has utilized the framework of "Expert-Novice Differences in Teaching." The novice is usually considered a beginning teacher, whereas the expert is experienced and often considered effective or exemplary by his or her supervisors or administrators. The differences between the novice and expert teacher with regard to thinking and behaving, their methods for planning and organizing classrooms, teaching subject matter, and reacting to students are explored by the authors. The authors rely on investigative studies based on observations and interpretations, analysis of video tapes, and interviews whereby teachers have been asked to recall classroom events and their reactions to these events.

In Chapter 16, Allan Ornstein reports on various ways in which narrative inquiry and storytelling are shaping research on teaching. In his chapter, "Beyond Effective Teaching," he describes how process-product research has been criticized and replaced by qualitative concepts and methods: a new paradigm involving metaphors, stories, personal biographies, the notion of expert and exemplary teachers, reflection, interviews, case studies, and voice. The author raises some questions about these qualitative approaches—to what extent the messages may reflect personal, moral, and/or political agendas.

In Chapter 17, Robert Stake and Linda Mabry examine one of the new qualitative methods for evaluating what teachers think and how they come to know and improve their own teaching practices. In "Case Study for a Deep Understanding of Teaching," the authors argue that good teaching is not based on reading or understanding research or theories of teaching, but rather on studying and analyzing what teachers do, how they feel, and what they think when they are teaching. This is best achieved through case studies—and by integrating the themes and messages of the studies with our own philosophies and experiences.

In the final chapter of Part III, Thomas Lasley and Thomas Matczynski detail the nature and need for "Reflective Teaching." Although there is no evidence to suggest a direct correlation between teacher reflection and student achievement, the authors contend that reflection enables the teacher to explore in depth various dimensions of teaching and classroom practices. Through reflection, teachers examine the consequences of their actions and explore philosophical and ethical issues related to teaching. Various school organizational factors, administrative behaviors, and teacher evaluation instruments are discussed as potential barriers that hinder reflection. The need is for teachers and administrators to implement a collaborative school culture that fosters reflective practices.

Philip A. Cusick

Philip A. Cusick has been hiking, biking, and camping to relax and escape on weekends and holidays ever since his teenage days in rural upper New York. Actually he hasn't done the best job of escaping since coming to Michigan State in 1970. Phil is the author of more than thirty research articles and some important books including *Inside High School* (Holt, Rinehart, 1973), *The Educational Ideal* and *The American High School* (Longman, 1983), and *The Educational System* (McGraw-Hill, 1992). He is co-author of *Selling Students Short* (1986), and is presently writing another book on social class and culture.

Cusick is professor of educational administration. He did his bachelors work at Elmira College, New York (1965) and his doctorate at Syracuse University (1970). He spent six years as a high school English teacher in the Elmira school district, served as a school administrator, and also taught at Colgate University. Phil claims he is winding down a little, and gets to enjoy the woods a little more often and experience the change of seasons in Michigan.

As you might guess, Phil is not much of a conversationalist. His motto is "just do it and have some fun while doing it."

12 ❧

The Culture of Students, Teachers, and Reformers

Philip A. Cusick

Erickson (1987) argues that for modern organizations, an appropriate definition of culture is "the relationship between the content of cultural knowledge and the specific life situation of the persons and groups in which the knowledge is held" (p. 14). To understand culture, the central question becomes "given certain kinds of daily experience, what kind of sense do people make of it and how does their sense-making influence their . . . actions?" (p. 14). Following this notion and focusing on teachers as a set of place holders with their own situation and knowledge, we will consider the culture of teachers relative to two other cultures, students on one side, classroom critics on the other. The notion of a group's culture arising from competition with other groups is also taken from Erickson, who thinks of schools as settings where "cultural differences are drawn along the lines of status, power and political interest" (p. 13). The sense that teachers make of their situation and the behavioral patterns that they develop and adhere to is their culture. One can understand that culture as one understands what goes on between teachers maintaining their place in the system and those with whom they compete for control of that place.

Schools have two mandates: first that they be universal, and second that they be egalitarian. Universalism means that schools take everyone. Egalitarianism is more complicated. It demands not only that schools treat students equally, but that they increase the sum of equality among them. Following the two mandates, schools are both large and specialized, and for all overt friendliness and talk of community, family, and small town values, they operate as modern organizations. They are monopolistic and serve a mass market; they are vertically integrated, practice economies of scope and scale, and expand by creating new services. And like modern organizations, schools are internally flexible, assigning

---

*Portions of this argument are taken from Cusick (1992).

people and resources at lower levels to solve problems. Defining and solving problems by individuals at lower levels is noteworthy in this discussion of culture, because it extends the image of teachers as problem solvers. In sum, we conceive of the school as a modern organization where teachers compete for place. We will argue that the behaviors teachers demonstrate most consistently and hang onto most strongly are the ones they develop in response to problems presented by their students. These are also the behaviors that attract the most attention of critic/reformers.

THE STUDENTS PRESENT THE PROBLEM

Schools take everyone and assume that everyone can and wants to learn what they have to teach. Following this mandate, schools present fairly uniform and distinct notions about learning, about verbal and intellectual patterns, social mobility, status, competition, role, and one's place in society.

> Classroom sociocultural systems exhibit a core norm and value orientation . . . [which includes] . . . emphasis on temporal and spatial coordination, routine housekeeping tasks, ranking, the reinforcement of student self-control, compliance and obedience, regimentation, coming to attention and waiting. (Johnson, 1985, p. 51)

Juxtaposed to the standard classroom culture is the variety of classes and cultures presented by the students who come to school from as broad an array as exists in our society, each with different ideas about the elements Johnson lists. The school is charged with making some unity of this diversity. As Cuban (1984) explains:

> The overriding purposes of the school, not always apparent but nonetheless evident, are to inculcate in children the prevailing social norms, values and behaviors that will prepare them for participation in the larger culture. The structure of school life, what knowledge is highly valued and what pedagogical practices occur, mirror the norms of the larger class and economic system. (p. 240)

In effect, schools ask students to do what in many cases they would not do naturally and to do it in a highly stylized environment. As Tracy Kidder (1989) notes concerning the school environment:

> The problem is fundamental. Put twenty or more children of roughly the same age in a little room, confine them to desks, make them wait in lines, make them behave. It is as if a secret committee, now lost to history, had made a study of children and having figured out what the greatest number were least disposed to do, declared that all of them should do it. (p. 115)

Furthermore, the teacher is not faced with fifteen or twenty or thirty-five individuals, each with his or her own little tabula rasa, but with a set of young citizens who have already-formed and often-opposing notions about things schools teach. Moreover, the school environment, with its habit of massing students in the same place, is such that a single student's class- and culture-based predilections are often matched and reinforced by fellow students with similar notions. These friendship groups are often more strongly normed than the classrooms in which they operate. And their notions of appropriate behavior and the place of schooling in life may or may not fit the school's notions. The scene is rife with potential opposition. Opposition may be exhibited by a single child or by groups coming from classes and cultures that do not believe what the school presents is worth knowing. The argument is not that opposition is all that goes on or that classrooms are out of control or that the incidents described are common. The argument is that opposition is always present, always problematic, and always the teacher's first consideration. Several classroom researchers have described how students join with others wherever they are in the school to exhibit behaviors different from and in opposition to those promulgated by staff.

Noting first that most teachers described in such studies are among their school's best (which is why they and the school authorities allowed them to be observed), we will describe some of the problems. Chris Zajac, as described by Kidder (1989), had every day to deal with Clarence, who in a single day:

> . . . got angry at Alice over a classroom game; kicked Alice in the back of the legs on the way to reading; was rude to Pam, who scolded him; got even by punching Arabella during indoor recess; hit Arabella again right in front of Chris, which was unusual, and when Chris got him in the hall, called her a bitch. (p. 99)

Chris had more than Clarence to contend with. The previous year she had a gang of five who "whenever she turned her back, threw snots and erasers and made armpit farts at the children who were trying to work" (p. 35). Mr. Geoffrey, described by Smith and Geoffrey (1968), had to contend with Pete:

> . . . a very short boy, the smallest in the class . . . he does literally no schoolwork or homework. The kind of truce that Geoffrey seems to have made is, "if you sit there and keep your mouth shut and don't bother anyone, I won't bother you either.". . . [E]ven though he is the oldest child in the classroom, or at least one of the oldest, he has one of the lowest achievement records in the class. He can't do much above third or fourth grade level. Third, his general attitude is, "I can't, I won't and you can't make me." (pp. 58–59)

Or Miss Jorden (Moore, 1967), who had to deal with Pamela, who:

> . . . starts looking on a desk for her nickel. She moves over and talks to another girl toward the front of the room. Miss Jorden puts an arm around her and tries to get her back into the seat in a friendly fashion.
>
> "Miss Jorden, somebody took my nickel" she repeats about six times in a loud voice. She then tells Miss Jorden, "Alvin has my nickel."
>
> Miss Jorden asks Alvin, "Do you have the nickel?"
>
> He says, "I do not."
>
> "He got my nickel," Pamela insists. She now has a red, white and blue scarf in her hand and is playing with it by putting it over her head, bringing it down over her face and wrapping it around her neck.
>
> Miss Jorden takes hold of her and asks Alvin again, "Do you have the nickel?" He says no and Miss Jorden says to Pamela, "OK honey, we'll look for it later."
>
> Pamela goes over to the closet, puts the scarf away and returns to her chair. But rather than sit down, she stands in front of her desk, going through papers, probably looking for the nickel. (pp. 28–30)

Several minutes later, Pamela is still proclaiming "I lost my nickel," and Miss Jorden is still trying to get Pamela to sit and get the rest of the class on track.

Incidents like these occur all the time in classrooms. They are what teachers face and what they have to overcome to get on with the work of the school. Officially, such behaviors are treated as random. But the frequency of occurrence belies terming these behaviors random. Students—just as teachers—are experiencing school, making some sense of the experience given their own backgrounds and inclinations, and constructing actions according to their sense making. And enough of them construe behaviors that are so unlike those promulgated by the school that the possibility for opposition exists in every classroom; opposition that must be controlled by the teacher if orderly discourse is to proceed. Such is the view of Johnson (1985), an anthropologist, who described purposeful opposition to the school's majority culture.

> Black males continually attempt(ing) to dominate the classroom. These students, however, are not merely being rambunctious; they are rebelling and attacking the value system of the classroom culture. They attack books, literacy, and work and they consciously interrupt the activities of other students. They attack the social system of the classroom. Autonomy, for example, is a core classroom social norm, attacked by those Black males whose orientation and interactional frame of reference are toward their own peer group rather than toward the teacher. (pp. 206–207)

Unlike the situations with Clarence, Pete, and Pamela, the referent for Johnson's students is not the teacher espousing the school's way; it is students with others like themselves asserting their own way. Willis (1977) described the same phenomenon among working-class students in England who recreated in school the factory culture to which they aspired. They were great admirers of their factory-working fathers and resented the teachers' implication that someone who worked in or planned to work in a factory was deficient. In school, they used their group not merely for friendship and diversion, but as a refuge, as a bastion of factory culture that they thrust in front of them in opposition to the school culture. Willis's lads, too, attacked books, literacy, teachers, and students who complied with the teachers' demands. The group defined the limits of acceptable school behavior, limits that did not include academic learning.

> *Willis:* What's the last time you've done some writing?
>
> *Fuzz:* Oh are, last time was in careers, 'cos I wrote "yes" on a piece of paper, that broke me heart.
>
> *Willie:* Why did it break your heart?
>
> *Fuzz:* . . . 'cos I was trying to go through the term without writing anything. 'Cos since we've come back I ain't done nothing. (p. 27)

Like Johnson's Black males, Willis's students put great emphasis on group loyalty, fun, and ridiculing the teacher and the school's admonitions that they should improve themselves through education. They did not want to improve themselves; they were content with their lives and their futures.

Everhart (1983), in his study of junior high schools, also showed how students use groups to protect one another; to stand between the teacher and one of their own. The group behaves in such a way as to subvert instruction, to turn the lesson into entertainment with other students as the audience, and to make the teacher and his efforts the butt of the joke. Mr. Von Hoffman was trying to elicit some oral reports and John was unprepared but was going to report anyway:

> "Come on John, give your report or sit down." John started but began laughing again.
>
> "Great report, Mr. Von Hoffman," said Mike clapping, "give him an A."
>
> "Outstanding," Chris said, "best report of the year."
>
> "OK John, sit down please."
>
> "No no, I'll give it. Tell Chris to stop laughing."
>
> Mr. Von Hoffman then walked to the back of the room, stood next to Chris's seat and said to John, "Begin."
>
> "I have some pet rabbits at home and I'd like to tell you about raising them. First you have to feed them and I feed them food that rabbits eat."
>
> Chris raised his hand. "What kind of food do rabbits eat?"
>
> John replied, "They eat rabbit food which I buy at the rabbit food store." (Everyone in the class laughed.) (p. 173)

Later, and in reference to the class. Chris explained to Everhart how the group operated.

> We've got this deal. John, Mike, me and a couple of other guys, like when one says something the other guy backs him up so he doesn't get into a lot of trouble. That's why the rabbit story was so neat. I was able to help John out by asking questions so he could finish his report. He hadn't even started it until we talked about it in class. (p. 175)

The opposition can be even more strongly voiced from traditionally alienated groups such as the Sioux at Pine Ridge, where Wax, Wax, and Dumont (1964) described classes characterized by "silence and order. Hours may pass without a publicly audible word being uttered by a student. The extraordinary discipline in these upper grades is the creation of the Indian pupils who enforce it upon themselves and upon their teacher" (p. 99).

An observer described one interaction:

> *Teacher:* "What do we do while we're in line?"
> Silence.
> *Teacher:* "If you spill something, what do you do? Do you just leave it there?
> Silence.
> She now asks for a volunteer to write the rule on the board and stood there at the front of the room with chalk in hand pleading for one. Half the boys at the rear of the room raised the tops of their desks, some mak-

ing a pretense of looking for materials, others just plain hiding behind them, while other boys tried to make themselves invisible. (p. 99)

Perhaps an equally or possibly more alienated group are those students perennially at the bottom of the achievement scale and subject to separate and remedial treatments. Reba Nukom Page (1992) studied classes for such students in two high schools and found that those students do indeed cause trouble, but not because they are slow or less able. They are reasonably quick but too unpredictable for regular classes. They reject the student role. They are disrespectful, not of the teacher-as-person but of the teacher-as-expert, as possessor of information that they don't think they need. When a topic of interest hooks them, they turn it their way and conduct a lively, full, and wide-ranging discourse; they bring in personal information, opinions, and their interpersonal relations. They disagree, complete one another's sentences, and take the discourse away from teachers, treating teachers not as experts but as equals. Thus they force the teacher away from knowledge provider into caretaker, baby sitter, and police officer. In such classes, teachers are barely in control; they surf events and discourse rather than direct them.

Some students come from long lines of people opposed to majority values and the schools that promulgate them. Okey (1990) studied the families of several students who dropped out of school and found a generations-old pattern of opposition to and failure in school. Grandparents, parents, older siblings, and cousins had failed in school, socially and academically, and came to resent teachers whom they saw as prejudiced against them. Okey explained that the dropouts' families were present, not future, oriented, had little or no use for school knowledge, no middle class upward mobility, and no use for school knowledge. Their families had histories of drinking, fighting, smoking, drugs, and multiple and early sexual relationships. And they allowed their children into adult status early, which meant the children were bringing those behaviors into school. So as students they ran afoul, not only of teachers trying to teach them academic material, but of administrators trying to get them to behave. From the early years, school was a series of unhappy conflicts, and eventually they discovered what older family members already knew: School is not worth the trouble. Dropping out makes sense.

Students can not only oppose the teacher, they can also oppose other students. A central tenet of school is that we should and can all get along under the same roof at the same time. But we don't all get along, and when we become adults and are free to make choices, we do not associate with those whom we dislike. Students are not allowed that adult freedom and are frequently placed in classes with others whom they do not get along with. And not getting along, if made manifest, can ruin a class. Cusick (1983) described how in biracial urban schools, where the issue of race dominated everything, a teacher could not bring up the matter and keep peace between Black and white students. And if the matter came up, even inadvertently, the Blacks and whites would be out of their seats and threatening one another with guns and older brothers. In another study, Cusick (1985) recounted how among students in an urban Catholic school who were both rightist Poles and leftist Hispanics, a speech by a teacher-invited leftist Guatemalan almost lead to a riot, with the Poles calling the Hispanics "communists" and the Hispanics calling the Poles "fascists."

In the classroom, social ideals run into social reality: What we would like to be runs into what we are. What we are is represented by the students with all the social, cultural, class, and caste differences coming in and measuring who they are and what they know against what school says is, should, and could be. What we would like to be is represented by the teacher espousing an ecumenical, cheerful, and tolerant view of the world and of what is plausible and what is possible. The situation is rife with potential conflict, and the conflict is most often between the teacher trying to enforce institutional ends and the students "striving to realize themselves in their own manner" (Waller, 1932, p. 196). The opposition may take the form of rebellion, but more often it appears more subtly—calculated resistance, diversion, recalcitrance, fun—what Waller describes as "laughing off the teacher . . . taking refuge in self-initiated activities that are always just beyond the teachers' reach" (p. 196).

The argument is not that classrooms are out of control or that a majority of students or even many students cause trouble. The argument is that classroom control is always problematic. It always has to be attended to, even in classes with a majority of students in sympathy with the school's endeavors. Further, the argument is that asserting and maintaining the primacy of the school-espoused values and behaviors, and the primacy of instructional goals in the face of student opposition, are the elements upon which teacher culture is based. For teachers, control is the major issue. The way they handle it is both the basis of their culture and the subject of the next section.

TEACHERS RESPOND TO THE PROBLEM

The argument in the remaining sections is twofold. First, by countering student opposition—real and potential—teachers develop a culture of control. Second, it is that teacher-control culture that critic/reformers see as education's basic problem and toward which reformers direct their efforts. To critic/reformers, control is a nonissue, or at most one that schools fabricate in pursuit of bureaucratic ends.

It is certainly true that schools are bureaucracies and that they solve problems bureaucratically. Imposing coherence on a diverse populace is a school problem, and schools solve it by dividing students into groups according to age, interest, and ability. Schools differentiate vertically and sequentially, segmenting students into progressively more specialized subsets, and give broad latitude to teachers to define and solve problems. This arrangement allows schools to teach Spanish, remedial reading, chemistry, music and art, and special education in the same building. Segmenting serves several functions, among them that it turns the students over to teachers to deal with behind closed doors and in their own ways. With messy situations such as those described in the first section all but invisible, the control problem is out of sight and understated. So the organization goes on smoothly and public confidence is maintained.

Consider the situation. Students enter schools from as broad an array of classes and cultures as exist in society, many with their own ideas about what schools call "education," ideas which may or may not match the schools' or the teachers' ideas. Then they have to both learn the things schools consider important and learn them in the company of others quite different from themselves. Consider what would happen if adults were placed in a situation where they had to undertake complex tasks in the company of and in cooperation with those different from themselves. Rules of social engagement would always be under negotiation and no one would relax until some central authority imposed some structure and rules.

Such is the case in schools. Rather than allowing or asking students to work out their own terms of accommodation, teachers take center stage and, in the interest of getting on with the endeavor, do it for them. Teachers maintain the central position in the class, and articulate the desired experience. They play down interruptions, ignore side comments, and get on with instruction by breaking knowledge into discrete pieces, pacing instruction, and suppressing students' oppositional tendencies. The result is teacher-centered classrooms, where as Goodlad (1984) says, "teachers talk and lecture while students listen and write." But Goodlad admits that teacher tactics are reasonable given students' propensity to drift into activities that for instructional purposes are unproductive:

> The organization and conduct of the classroom so that individuals work alone may not be conducive to productive team effort and the learning of collaborative values and skills, but at least it can prevent, to a considerable degree, the spillover of group allegiances and rivalries from outside the classroom and the emergence within of cliques and intergroup confrontations. (pp. 110–111)

McNeil (1986) was most analytical about the ways teachers control students. She said that teachers, regardless of their differences in personality and ideology, used four instructional techniques. The first, which was prevalent across differences in teacher ideology, is fragmentation: for example, the "reduction of any topic to fragmented or disjointed pieces of information" (p. 167). The second is mystification, which involved the surrounding of "a controversial topic with mystery in order to close off discussion" (p. 169); and the third tactic is omission of topics considered important by students. McNeil described how, when the students got too excited about the topic, their natural divisions and their varied enthusiasms took over the discussion, to the detriment of teacher control. The fourth is defensive simplification, "winning the students' compliance by promising that the topic will not go to any great depth" (p. 174). While the sum of these tactics, distilled from classrooms in four schools, would appear to make teaching or attending to teachers a deadening experience, McNeil's teachers were knowledgeable, excited, and interesting. That they used such tactics for control did not make them bad teachers. Nor could one criticize Kidder's (1989) favorite, Chris Zajac, who

> . . . turned her eyes to the children solving problems on the board. "Very good, Margaret. Do you understand it now?" There was more whisper-

ing behind her. Again, her left hand shot back. "Horace, do your own work." Another flash card for Felipe while she called over her other shoulder. "Henrietta, come on up here." Then she turned her head all the way around, toward the low math scholars at their desks behind her. "Horace, are you all done?"

"No."

"Then why are you talking to Jorge?"

She turned back around and said to Felipe and Jimmy: "What's the matter with you two? The minute I turn my back you have to talk. What number do you carry Jimmy?"

"The four."

"Very good. Got it now? Okay Jimmy, you can go back to your desk." (pp. 36–37)

Ms. Zajac demonstrates control at its best. She has to attend to Felipe and Jimmy's propensity to pursue their own agendas rather than the instructional agenda. She also has to instruct at the same time.

Some teachers all of the time and maybe all teachers some of the time lapse into boring off-the-point lectures. But just as often, teacher-centeredness is carried on in a skilled and sensitive manner, with the details and the overall plan going on simultaneously. Smith and Geoffrey, in their *Complexities of an Urban Classroom* (1968), illustrate how the teacher managed his classroom as a "complex pattern of activities, interactions and sentiments" (p. 49). He "grooves" his class into "a kind of interaction in which the teacher issues a series of minor directives and obtains a series of minor complying responses from the children" (p. 265), molding the class into a coherent social system. He wants the students to understand that (1) learning should be going on all the time, and (2) learning is work.

Geoffrey takes center stage and manipulates his role to assure his own primacy. He expands it or contracts it in order to keep the class moving, in order to both press for and embody the norms of work. He paces lessons. He assigns students roles and plays alternate to each one assigned. The class is a social system, and half the roles belong to him. As described by Moore (1967), Ms. Caplan does the same thing in her fourth grade class.

"What number would you try for the problem 5 into 185?" "Suppose there are 96 children and you want to divide them into 4 equal teams?" "Will 4 go into 16 again?" "What is a shorter method of adding?" "How many of you feel this is right?" To the students' correct answers, she gives a steady stream of affirmative and complimentary responses. "Some of you are getting very good." "Yes, it (a whole number) can be anything. Can it also be money?" To a student with an almost-correct answer, "Think a moment George. Is this correct?" The students are quiet, orderly, wait anxiously to participate. And it is not that she has the best students. Juan was a problem child in earlier years but presents no problem of discipline to Ms. Caplan. (pp. 100–101)

Sometimes such teacher-centered and control-oriented instruction is better. Sometimes—depending on the teacher—it is worse, but it is always teacher-centered and most teacher-centered in more problematic situations. In classes for what Powell, Farrar, and Cohen (1985) call the "unspecial students":

> . . . passivity rather than intensity predominates. The lecture method is popular in classes for the unspecial. One teacher said the middle kids were "desirous to have me lead"; they like to "just sit there and listen and take notes." They also like to stay with facts and details. "They'll get edgy when you start in," says one English teacher who encountered resistance to probing questions. "They say that you're destroying the story." They often preferred "busy work" such as worksheets because it's "controlled and structured, and they can get immediate feedback and build up marks." (p. 186)

Sometimes, as Reba Nukom Page (1992) describes, in the interest of eliminating problems of group discourse, teachers will attend to each student singly. Such instruction keeps the teacher in the center, gives her primacy over the student being attended to, isolates students from one another and prevents them from coalescing into opposition groups. It is a tenuous undertaking.

> [I]f Sue needs help on question 5 of the worksheet, she blurts out a demand for assistance, even when discussion on another question is in progress. If her demand is not acknowledged, it is repeated, usually more loudly: "I can't find this word!— Ellison. I CAN'T FIND THIS WORD I SAID I'm gettin MAA-AD." (p. 89)

Mr. Ellison does what he can, giving fifteen to thirty seconds to each student, but competitiveness for the floor feeds the distance of students from one another and from him.

Cusick and Wheeler (1987) described several classrooms with quite able students, but teachers stayed in the center and articulated the experience, selecting students to contribute pieces to the dialogue. In the honors classes there was no opposition. Students wanted to go to competitive colleges so they needed high grades so they paid attention. The teacher knew the material; the students did not. But they knew you don't go to Yale with C's. So they paid attention. In less academic classes, where the material was more arbitrary and the students less interested, teachers were more heavy handed, allowing less time for students' individual responses and interspersing the lecture with constant admonitions to "listen up" and "pay attention." Otherwise students would drift away. In less academic classes, teacher-centeredness is the rule.

Erickson (1987) advises those who wish to understand culture to ask, "given certain kinds of daily experience, what kind of sense do people make of it and how does their sense making influence their . . . actions?" (p.14). Consider teachers' daily experience. The organization gives each a group of students as diverse as our society has to offer, students who may not buy into the culture that school promulgates or who may be open to conflict with the school or with each other. The teacher has to turn that aggregate into a collective with discernible procedures. If he or she cannot, the class will lapse into anarchy. Instruction will fail. The teacher will be fired and another brought in and told to "Get the class under control." To avoid anarchy, get on with the business, and keep their jobs, teachers keep themselves central in the classroom, control the dialogue, manage interactions, and articulate the instructional experience. They stay center stage.

A criticism of the argument is that control is overemphasized. But the issue emerged without prompting from observational studies that show it to be the overwhelming issue, even in the best teachers' classrooms. Control is always integrated into their instruction. Their relative isolation gives teachers freedom to work out this problem individually and quietly. The responsibility and the accompanying autonomy give them a respected niche in the organization, a place where they are in charge, entrusted with important matters, and free to be themselves. Ms. Zajac, Mr. Baxter, Mr. Geoffrey, and Ms. Jorden are all "teachers" in a bureaucratic sense. But each operates autonomously and individually. Teacher individuality and teacher autonomy are corollaries of classroom control. In the next section, we will move to those standing outside of classrooms—critics and reformers—and see what they say about the teachers' culture.

CRITIC/REFORMERS VIEW THE PROBLEM

A synthesis of reformist writings will show that what was asserted in the previous section about teacher behavior is also what critic/reformers assert about teacher behavior. But while the author of this chapter argues that teachers behave reasonably given student opposition, critic/reformers see teacher control as a major reason for reforms being "blunted at the classroom door" (Goodlad, 1984). Critic/reformers assume that control will flow naturally from the students' interest in content, not artificially from teacher primacy. They argue that the problem is not student opposition or resistance; it is the bureaucracy that forces teachers into controlling behaviors. The students are not the problem; the school is the problem. Subsequently, they want to restructure schools and change teacher behavior.

Critic/reformers decry the fact that more than a decade after *Nation at Risk* (1983) and after "virtually every state had acted to impose the higher standards called for by the commission . . . but all of these efforts, however well intentioned, have scarcely touched the classroom. . . . Our schools seem firmly anchored in the old" (*Education Week*, 1993, p. 3). The old, as that writer explains, is a teacher-centered classroom that critic/reformers do not like and on which they blame education's problems. To the authors of the *Education Week* article quoted above, "a good school is a child-centered school where students take more responsibility for their own learning, where teachers lecture less and coach more . . ." (p. 4), and where, according to Magdalene Lampert, "understanding and intellect are more highly valued than they typically have been" (Rothman, 1993, p. 10).

No one synthesizes the vision better than Theodore Sizer (1984) who, operating from his Coalition of Essential Schools, wants schools that focus on academic learning, not bureaucratic processing. Sizer wants structure flexible enough to allow for intellectual exploration so that teachers can coach inquiring students who will seize on intellectual currents. In his Essential Schools, students would be engaged with teachers in the common tasks of learning. Natural discipline would emerge from cooperative involvement. Sizer does not blame control on teachers but on the bureaucracy that forces teachers into controlling behaviors and away from teaching. The teachers' obsession with order is a byproduct of the schools' out-of-control bureaucracy.

Similar in thinking is the Holmes Group (1986), which in its major publication, *Tomorrow's Teachers*, argues the importance of "teaching and learning for understanding," which the authors define as situations that encourage "lasting learning—the kind that allows students to go on 'learning for a lifetime'" (p. 8). "Teaching for understanding won't happen in classrooms where students sit silent and passive" (p. 11). Holmes' authors admit that higher standards may trouble some students who will have to work harder, but even these students will persevere if the schools are communities wherein academic efforts are meshed with good citizenship. In such settings, students will explore, take part in conversations about what they are exploring, and take active roles in the community. Holmes' authors concede that while there is nothing wrong with a good lecture, classrooms should be "communities of learning" (p. 8). *Conversation, experience, interpretation, criticism, engagement, voice, participation,* and *purpose* are some of the words Holmes' authors link with teaching for understanding (p. 12). In Holmes' classrooms, students will become "complex meaning makers . . . who learn the deepest kind of literacy" (p. 14). Teachers will "observe their students, follow them closely, find out what excites them and help them do that" (p. 16). Schools will not be "the grim places that too many are," but communities where skill building is accompanied by understanding, where "students' main work (is) to tackle and explain complexity rather than to complete simple assigned tasks," and where "every child makes a contribution to the classroom using his or her own experience" (p. 19).

Holmes' authors have read studies describing student opposition, but they discount the notion that students bring opposition into school. It is not learning that students resist; it is teacher-controlled classes. Students would like to learn but are prevented from doing so by the oppressive structure. If they behave badly it is because the school denies them reasons to behave better. Holmes' authors make no mention of conflicts between what the school promulgates and what the students bring, save to admit that not all students are alike and that the school should accommodate student diversity. They assume that most students come to school if not already socialized, at least open to the school's version of the majority culture. Student differences are not a problem but an opportunity, and schools "should build on the linguistic and cultural capital students bring with them so that . . . students can possess both mainstream meanings and the culture of their own community" (p. 22). Critic/reformers want schools to be more child-centered. They believe that schools have misplaced educational goals; have become too bureaucratic, too taken up with their processes, their specialties, their tests and requirements; and too dominated by the necessity of moving masses of students around on schedule.

Tomorrow's Schools (Holmes Group, 1990), a later report, says that the limited and traditional view of teaching is presenting information and keeping order. The authors want students to "achieve mastery of content and the complex social relations of the classroom in a way that fosters student learning as well as an attachment to learning" (Holmes Group, 1990, p. 29). Holmes' authors envision collaborative classrooms where students with less information drive students with more. They also want better educated teachers who will "lead a life of the mind . . . be reflective and thoughtful . . . seek to understand so they may clarify for others, persons who can go to the heart of the matter." Additional preparation in the humanities will help them "reformulate content so as to engage a variety of pupils" (p. 53) and . . . [provide them] "with opportunities to contribute to the development of knowledge in their profession, to form collegial relationships beyond their immediate working environment, and to grow intellectually as they mature professionally" (p. 56). The authors also want to diminish the power of the organization relative to teachers. Well-prepared teachers will not just follow guidelines. They will examine and critically interpret materials in terms of their own understanding of the subject matter, and scrutinize the content in light of their own comprehension. Preparing to teach will include (1) detecting and correcting errors in texts, and (2) structuring and segmenting the material into forms better adapted to the teachers' understanding and in prospect more suitable for teaching. Holmes' authors want teachers to be able to advocate, "comprehend, reason, transform and reflect" (Holmes Group, 1990, p. 1).

Better than anyone, Gerald Grant (1988) described the problems occasioned by bringing together and trying to accommodate different students in the same school and in the same classes. But he too saw bureaucratic processes as alienating because the resulting fragmentation prevented the emergence of a common ethos that might serve as an incentive to learn. For Grant, too, diversity is a problem not because it is the source of opposition but because of schools' attempts to stifle it:

> When you take a bureaucratic mode of organization and put on top of it a legalistic mode of accountability, what it does is standardize further, which reduces the professional discretion to personalize for children, which then creates more kids who don't fit. In all our good intentions, we have made matters worse. (p. 35)

The argument in previous sections suggested that student diversity, if unchecked, would prevent the class and individual students from attaining the school's and their own goals. In the interest of preventing that destruction, teachers take control, suppress diversity, and thus get on with the endeavor in an orderly way. Grant believes that "schooling's traditional competitive ethos tends to reduce teachers to merely coping with cultural diversity," and he advocates cooperative classrooms that will be "learning communities . . . and will embrace rather than smother cultural diversity." Teachers will "draw upon students' diversity to make learning dynamic and interesting" (p. 35). For Grant the problem is not student diversity; the problem is that schools suppress student diversity.

Other critic/reformers call for "systemic reform" of education's fragmented governance system. Representing this collectivist lobby are Smith and O'Day (1990), who note that there have been "only minor changes . . . in the nature of classroom practices" (p. 233), and who advocate a system wherein "teaching and learning rather than control and discipline" (p. 235) are paramount. They reason that change is frustrated by "the fragmented educational governance system" that encourages short-term and often conflicting goals and policies. The fragmented nature of the system, the obscurity of classrooms, and the distance of classrooms from policy makers combine into "a chaotic, multilayered, and fragmented . . . system (which) has spawned mediocre and conservative curricula and instruction in our school" (p. 261). These authors propose a revised system wherein the state would design and orchestrate the implementation of a "coherent instructional guidance system [consisting of] challenging and progressive curriculum frameworks, a supportive organizational environment and instructional content directed toward complex thinking and problem solving." In a more coherent and managed system, a system with more "system" to it, national groups could set standards that would be implemented and tested in classrooms.

Those authors would no doubt support The National Board for Professional Teaching Standards (NBPTS), that wants schools wherein "student initiative and inventiveness are both stimulated and applauded and expectations are high for all students" (NBPTS, 1989, p. 5). National Board advocates would like to break the one teacher/one classroom syndrome and build a system of teachers with broader responsibilities, but a more narrow focus; teachers who elevate specialization to a higher level. "Teachers who [are] adept at diagnosing a student misunderstanding in mathematics . . . could review students' work from throughout the school . . . [and] . . . work with fellow teachers in formulating a solution to each case" (NBPTS, 1989, p. 11).

The argument of the chapter is that students, either because of their opposition to school or because they need the knowledge students have, encourage teachers into a culture of control. Critic/reformers agree. However, they do not attribute the culture to students. They attribute it to the schools' misplaced obsession with order and believe that teacher control is education's biggest problem. Unwilling to blame students for fomenting the problem or teachers for fitting in a bad situation, critic/reformers blame the structure that places teachers in situations where they have to resort to control.

Critic/reformers want classrooms to be communities centered around subject matter. In communal classrooms with teachers better trained in disciplines and pedagogy, control will flow naturally from the common ethos. A large part of the problem is the single teacher-single classroom arrangement, so the critic/reformers suggest team teaching and cooperative learning, techniques that will take the articulating-directing burden off one teacher and place it onto a group of teachers or a group of teachers and students. And most of all, since they blame the differentiated and bureaucratized structure, critic/reformers direct their efforts toward making a more enlightened structure: less bureaucratic and less specialized, less busy, and hence less demanding of teachers' time and attention. Furthermore, to reformers, student differences are not a problem. The problem is that the school does not know how to manage the differences and diversity and so resorts to control. Change the context of control, or, one might say, the culture of control, and teachers will behave differently. But will they? Are teachers who stay in the center of the class being irrational? Are they misinformed? Are they oppressed by the bureaucracy? Or do they know just what they are doing and doing what they want to do? Is teacher centrality just an irrational obsession? Let us examine this triple-sided issue as it goes on among students, teachers, and critics.

THEORY INTO PRACTICE

The descriptive studies are consistent. The majority of students, and not just lower-class students, do not take to academic learning naturally. If given the opportunity, they drift off into informal interactions around their youthful interests. The teacher has no choice but to take the center and control the class. If he or she does not, there is no class, only individuals, dyads, and groups, each following a different agenda. And high-powered honors students who want the knowledge, grades, and acceptance into good colleges, also encourage teachers to maintain centrality. The teachers "know" the calculus, physics, or poetry. The students want to know it, perhaps not for love of learning, but to rise to the top of the majority culture. They want to know what the teacher knows and they ask the teacher to tell them.

It is not so complicated except for critic/reformers who see teacher centrality as a barrier to improved education. They argue that teacher control stifles the students' natural inclination to learn. Their's is a Rousseauian argument. Children are naturally inclined toward the good; the state corrupts children by turning them away from their natural inclinations. In this case, the state is the school, which with its oppressive structure turns children away from their natural inclination to learn. Critic/reformers do not consider either that academic learning is of limited interest or that by the time students enter school, they are already socialized into diverse cultures, some of which value academic learning, some of which do not. There is a natural conflict between the school and students. Teachers have to solve that conflict and they do so by carrying the class. It is their natural reaction. Were they not to do it, the class would fall apart. Or in the case of the eager students, they (the students) would go home and tell their parents that the teacher was not instructing them in the content they need to compete with other eager students. The parents would quickly contact the principal, and so on. Teachers who take center stage know what they are doing.

Teacher centrality has other advantages. The school structure segments students into classes with single teachers. In such schools, teachers are in charge, autonomous, responsible, and empowered. Most of us structure our jobs the way we want them to be, and teachers like to be in control of the class. They like to lead discussions; sometimes they like to lecture; they like to be in control. They like to close the door. As Lortie (1972) showed, the intrinsic reward of teaching is being alone with the class and being in charge. That is what it means to teach. But critic/reformers discount the rewards that teachers obtain from the present structure. They see their suggestions as empowering teachers, but in the schools they propose, power will be transferred from the individual teacher to a larger collective. The teacher will find him or herself less autonomous and less in charge.

At issue are the conflicts that arise between the school, speaking for the majority, and students who resist the majority, and between teachers in control of their classes and reformers who want classroom control transferred to someone or something else. Students resist teachers; teachers resist reformers. Students have their cultures on their side. Teachers have their numbers and their resistance on their side. Critic/reformers have their publications, their national audience, and legislators who read or hear about their criticisms and make policies to correct alleged deficiencies. They also have a comfortable distance from students, which lures them into underestimating the resistance teachers face. It is a running conflict and, at present, a standoff.

Where is resolution? In the opinion of this author, the most stable element in the conflict is the students, who for their own and some good reasons resist academic learning. As the descriptive studies show, the students never take easily to academic instruction. Their resistance is enduring. So teachers will continue to do what they have to do to force the issue. On the other hand, classrooms can be improved and the suggestions of the critics are being taken seriously by policy makers. In practice, school reform is going to enter the classrooms, one way or the other. The point is to make it serve the interests of students and teachers. The fear is that reform will force teachers into unnatural teaching behaviors that will not work. Perhaps the best way to resolve the conflict between reformers and teachers is to bring the reformers closer to the classrooms so they can experience student resistance and reluctance first hand. If reformers and teachers came closer together at least some of the conflict might be resolved.

SUMMARY

Culture is formed from necessity. When faced with a set of problems and limited possibilities, a group does what it has to do. Classroom teachers do what they have to do. Opposition and conflict are the classroom's context. It is not that students are disorderly or mean spirited. It is that classrooms are crowded, mentally and physically restricting, verbose, and contrived. It is not easy for students or for teachers outnumbered by students twenty or thirty to one. Teachers have to overcome student opposition, reduce conflict, and teach the curriculum. From necessity comes their culture.

It is a culture of control. Teachers keep center stage, dominate the dialogue, establish a personal relationship with each student, and attend swiftly to aberrations. With the teacher in control, conflict is neutralized, curriculum is moving, and goals are being met. If the teacher is not in control, conflict will erupt, the curriculum will be lost, and the goals will not be met. Teacher centrality and teacher control are facts of classroom life, as well as teachers' preferred mode of instruction. When in charge, they are autonomous and responsible. They are doing what they want to do.

Teacher centrality is the target of reformers who believe that students would take naturally both to the content and to one another if the teacher would get out of the way. Reformers don't blame teachers nor certainly students. They blame the structure that forces teachers into control. "Change the structure, then get the teachers out of the way," say the reformers, and "reform can begin." But can it? Teachers are suspicious, unwilling to give up their preferred mode, and doubtful that students would take naturally to academic material, whatever the structure. Their experience tells them otherwise. "You don't know the kids," say the teachers. Reformers may not "know the kids," but they are not powerless. They control education's communication exchange and their ideas find their way into policy. Conflict between teachers and reformers will continue.

References

Cuban, L. (1984). *How Teachers Taught: Constancy and Change in American Classrooms, 1890–1980.* New York: Longman.

Cusick, P. (1985). "Finding Meaning in Teaching." *Education and Urban Society* 17: 355–364.

Cusick, P. (1992). *The Educational System: Its Nature and Logic.* New York: McGraw-Hill.

Cusick, P. A., and C. Wheeler (1987). *Improving Education through Organizational Change* (Report no. 400-83-0052). Washington, D.C.: National Institute of Education.

Education Week. (1993, Feb. 10). "Charting a Course for Reform: The Next 10 Years." *Education Week* (Special Report): 3–4.

Erickson, F. (1987). "Conceptions of School Culture." *Educational Administration Quarterly* 23 (4): 1–14.

Everhart, R. (1983). *Reading, Writing and Resistance: Adolescence and Labor in a Junior High School.* Boston: Routledge & Kegan Paul.

Goodlad, J. (1984). A *Place Called School: Prospects for the Future.* New York: McGraw-Hill.

Grant, G. (1988). *The World We Created at Hamilton High.* Cambridge, MA: Harvard University Press.

The Holmes Group (1986). *Tomorrow's Teachers: A Report of the Holmes Group.* East Lansing, MI: Author.

The Holmes Group (1990). *Tomorrow's Schools: Principles for the Design of Professional Development Schools.* East Lansing, MI: Author.

Johnson, N. (1985). *Westhaven: Classroom Culture and Society in a Rural Elementary School.* Chapel Hill, NC: The University of North Carolina Press.

Kidder, T. (1989). *Among Schoolchildren.* Boston: Houghton Mifflin.

Lightfoot, S. (1983). *The Good High School.* New York: Basic Books.

Lortie, D. (1972) *Schoolteacher.* Chicago: University of Chicago Press.

McNeil, L. (1986). *Contradictions of Control: School Structure and School Knowledge.* New York: Routledge & Kegan Paul.

Moore, G., Jr. (1967). *Realities of the Urban Classroom.* Garden City, NY: Anchor Books.

National Board for Professional Teaching Standards (1989). *Toward High and Rigorous Standards for the Teaching Profession: Initial Policies and Perspectives of the National Board for Professional Teaching Standards.* Washington, D.C.: Author.

The National Commission on Excellence in Education (1983). *A Nation at Risk: The Imperative for Educational Reform.* Washington, D.C.: U.S. Department of Education.

Okey, T. (1990). "The Family's Perspective on the Individual's Decision to Drop Out of High School." Unpublished doctoral dissertation, Michigan State University.

Page, R. N. (1992). *Lower Track Classrooms: A Curricular and Cultural Perspective.* New York: Teachers' College Press, Columbia University.

Powell, A., E. Farrar, and D. Cohen (1985). *The Shopping Mall High School: Winners and Losers in the Educational Marketplace.* Boston: Houghton Mifflin.

Rothman, R. (1993, Feb 10). "Obstacle Course:

Barriers to Change Thwart Reformers at Every Twist and Turn." *Education Week* (Special Report): 9–13.

Sizer, T. (1984). *Horace's Compromise.* New York: Houghton Mifflin.

Smith, L., and W. Geoffrey (1968). *Complexities of an Urban Classroom.* New York: Holt, Rinehart and Winston.

Smith, M., and J. O'Day (1990). "Systemic School Reform." *Politics of Education Association Yearbook,* pp. 233–266.

Waller, W. (1932). *Sociology of Teaching.* New York: Russell & Russell.

Wax, M., R. H. Wax, and R. Dumont, Jr. (1964). "Formal Education in an American Indian Community." *Social Problems* 11: 1–126.

Willis P. (1977). *Learning to Labor: How Working Class Kids Get Working Class Jobs.* Hampshire, England: Gower Publishing House.

Discussion Questions

1. Is teacher centrality necessary to instruction? to order?

2. Suppose teachers did not maintain centrality. What would they do?

3. Why do reformers criticize teachers?

4. What do reformers criticize most?

5. If the reformers' suggestions were taken seriously, what would teachers do?

6. Add up all the reform suggestions you can think of. Whose interests do they serve?

Dona M. Kagan

Patt Kagan (1905–1990)

*This chapter
is dedicated
to my mother
and my best friend,
Patt Kagan*

As a youngster, Dona M. Kagan wanted to be a writer and majored in English at Vassar College and Barnard College, where in 1968 she received a B.A. She earned an M.A. from Teachers College, Columbia University, in 1969 and then taught English in junior and senior high schools in New York and Arizona. In 1978 she completed a Ph.D. in educational psychology at Arizona State University.

Kagan is now a professor of education and is affiliated with the University of Alabama in Tuscaloosa. Her specializations include teacher cognition, teacher education, and school-university partnerships. She is the author of more than eighty-five articles published in such influential journals as the *American Education Research Journal*, *Review of Educational Research*, *Elementary School Journal*, and *Phi Delta Kappan*. In 1993 the State University of New York Press published her first book, *Laura and Jim and What They Taught Me About the Gap Between Educational Theory and Practice*. It is an entertaining study of two outstanding high school teachers in Tuscaloosa and how their views of teaching differ from those of two education professors at the University of Alabama.

Dona's greatest professional satisfaction has always come from working with public school teachers: helping them evaluate instruction or study aspects of their own practices. She claims to be "strongly committed to moving the professional literature of education to more entertaining and narrative genres that capture the dramatic texture of classroom life and the personalities of students and teachers."

Dona believes in reincarnation and hopes that she is burning off a lot of bad karma that she has accumulated. She loves antique roses and animals and lives with four cats "who are trying to teach (her) how to be a human being."

13 ☙

Research on Teacher Cognition

Dona M. Kagan

About ten years ago a significant change occurred in the research on classroom teaching. Scholars began to shift their focus to the decisions and beliefs that underlie teachers' classroom behaviors. Instead of concentrating solely on the visible aspects of teaching, investigators began to consider aspects of teaching that are nonobservable. These include teachers' beliefs about classrooms, children, schools, and learning; the decisions that go into planning, delivering, and reflecting upon a lesson; beliefs about the subject matter to be learned; perceptions of classroom events; and beliefs about the role of teachers and their self-images.

In ten years this has grown rapidly into a discrete subfield of inquiry that is generally referred to as the study of teacher cognition. In pursuit of this kind of research, scholars from around the world have united in an International Study Association on Teacher Thinking (ISATT). Members share findings through publications and annual meetings.

It may seem strange that such an obvious topic could ever be a "new" focus of research. However, until the notion of teacher cognition emerged formally in the early 1980s, virtually all classroom research was behavioral (observational). That is, investigators labored to reduce "effective" teaching to a list of discrete behavioral acts, like the number of questions or utterances of praise that a teacher employed during a lesson. Behaviors that were shown to be statistically related to student achievement (their scores on standardized tests) were labeled "effective teaching."

These behavioral studies were statistical in method and usually involved large numbers of subjects. Called *process-product* research, it burgeoned during the 1970s and spawned teacher evaluation scales that were based on the assumption that classroom teaching was amenable to precise calibration. It also promoted programs of preservice teacher education that were based on a scientific, technical view of classroom teaching. The wave of cognitive research that began in the 1980s would change the landscape of research and teacher education in fundamental ways.

By the early 1990s, research on teacher cognition has splintered into many subfields, and no single review could possibly do justice to the entire body of literature. This chapter is meant to be an introduction only. It is not comprehensive, and if you want to really learn about this area of inquiry you will need to follow up on some of the references that are listed at the end of the chapter. Articles that you may find particularly helpful include Clark and Peterson's (1986) chapter on teacher cognition in the *Handbook of Research on Teaching;* Kennedy's (1987) chapter in the *Review of Research in Education;* and several of my own literature reviews (Kagan, 1988, 1989, 1990, 1992).

ORIGINS

Research on teacher cognition can be traced back to 1975, when Panel 6 of the National Institute of Education (NIE) issued a report entitled "Teaching as Clinical Information Processing." Although teacher cognition was not a completely new concept at the time, this report launched it as a formal area of investigation. The report described teachers as clinical problem solvers analogous to physicians, in that they are responsible for aggregating and interpreting information about clients (students), combining this information with their own beliefs, and making judgments based on these data.

In effect, the NIE panel proposed a marriage between the field of cognitive psychology, especially research on problem solving, and the study of classroom teaching. A decade earlier, cognitive psychology had been applied to the study of problem solving in the field of medicine, yielding a standard model of diagnostic decision making: a description of the decisions that most experienced physicians use when attempting to diagnose a patient's ailment (Elstein, Shulman, & Sprafka, 1978). With this productive agenda of cognitive research in mind, the NIE report called for a comparable agenda of research focusing on the problem solving of classroom teachers.

Much of the early research on teacher cognition reflects the influence of the diagnostic/treatment model that emerged from studies of physicians. That is, at first educational researchers looked for standard linear sequences of decision making among expert or experienced teachers (Clark & Peterson, 1986; Peterson & Clark, 1978; Shavelson & Stern, 1981). However, researchers soon discovered that problem solving in the classroom looked quite different. There appeared to be no standard model that was employed by most experienced teachers, and teachers' decision making was far from linear (Kagan, 1988).

THE FIRST WAVE OF STUDIES

One of the most unexpected and fruitful findings that emerged from early studies was the discovery that experienced teachers made relatively few conscious decisions while performing. Instead, they appeared to operate on automatic pilot, following well-established routines and resorting to conscious decisions only when routines were disrupted (Shavelson & Stern, 1981). This introduced the notion of automaticity, a characteristic of experienced classroom teaching that has been confirmed by many studies (Calderhead, 1983, 1987; Housner & Griffey, 1983).

Researchers began to refer to automatic routines as "schemas"; patterns of thought and action that could be recalled unconsciously by experienced teachers to help interpret and respond to complex classroom stimuli. In accordance with cognitive theory, researchers speculated that well-formed schemas allowed experienced teachers to screen out irrelevant information and reduce the cognitive work load, leaving working memory free to monitor ongoing classroom activity.

Here it is helpful to know that cognitive psychologists had already demonstrated that schemas are an effective way for human beings to store together three different types of knowledge relevant to problem solving: *declarative* (definitions, facts), *procedural* (how to use facts), and *metacognitive* (insights about thinking and problem solving). Cognitive psychologists had studied the problem solving of experts and novices in a variety of knowledge domains (for example, engineering, physics, chess, computer programming, and so on) and discovered that novices tended to use declarative knowledge, whereas experts had access to procedural and metacognitive knowledge. This means that experts tend to transform declarative information into procedures and action sequences that can be applied directly to a problem at hand (Anderson, 1983; Chi, Feltovich, & Glaser, 1981; Glaser, 1985).

Berliner (1986, 1987) was among the first scholars in education to tie these findings explicitly to teachers' classroom problem solving. He and his colleagues demonstrated that the schemas possessed by novice and experienced teachers appeared to be qualitatively different. Experienced teachers were able to identify and interpret patterns in classroom events, to analyze them using procedural rather than declarative knowledge, and to infer from them to help solve problems. In contrast, novice teachers tended to process more information, be unaware of meaningful patterns, and rely on declarative rather than procedural knowledge.

In studying problem solving across various knowledge domains, cognitive psychologists had also proven that the task environment usually affects the way problems are solved. Using this insight, educational researchers began to take closer looks at classroom ecology (the task environment confronted by teachers) and tried to classify systematically the different kinds of instructional tasks manifested in classrooms. Studies of the classroom environment lead to two important conclusions.

The first was that teachers' professional knowledge could be described in terms of three broad categories: content knowledge, pedagogical knowledge, and pedagogical content knowledge (Wilson, Shulman, & Richert, 1987). *Content knowledge* refers to a teacher's understanding of the academic material to be learned. For example, a social studies teacher could perceive history in a number of alternative ways: as the study of leadership, human nature, or warring economic systems. *Pedagogical knowledge* refers to the teacher's repertoire of generic teaching techniques, like cooperative learning, role playing, or group work—techniques that are equally relevant to all academic content domains. *Pedagogical content knowledge* refers to the teacher's repertoire of techniques that are specifically designed to make a particular academic subject accessible to students. For example, a social studies teacher might use primary reference materials (letters, diaries), maps, or the art (paintings, music) of a particular historical period to facilitate students' learning.

One could construe this tripartite scheme as the knowledge bases that underlie skill in classroom teaching, because an experienced teacher must draw upon each in order to construct a lesson. Accordingly, many colleges of education have begun to describe their programs of preservice teacher education in terms of "knowledge bases," and "knowledge base" has begun to appear frequently in the titles of handbooks and textbooks on teaching. In addition, the Educational Testing Service in Princeton has developed a standardized test for teacher candidates that is based on this tripartite view of teachers' professional knowledge.

The second conclusion inferred from studies of the classroom environment is that it is extremely complex, varied, and fast paced. This implies that a functional model of cognitive processing for teachers would have to be extremely flexible and largely automatic. Leinhardt and Greeno (1986) were among the first to propose a generalized model of classroom problem solving which they inferred from mathematics lessons presented by expert elementary teachers.

The model, or "planning net," that Leinhardt and Greeno inferred for a particular lesson resembled a flowchart—decision paths that converged at primary activity structures. Surrounding each activity structure (of the lesson) were alternative consequences, goals, corequisite and prerequisite conditions—each in turn leading to alternative paths of action that the teacher could take. Leinhardt and Greeno suggested that part of the skill of teaching involves deciding which decision paths to pursue and whether to insert unplanned activity structures spontaneously. The model they proposed was modular and hierarchical, allowing a teacher to access an enormous body of information with amazing speed. Unlike the model that researchers had discovered for physicians' diagnostic problem solving, Leinhardt and Greeno's planning net differed in form and content for different lessons and different teachers.

The hierarchical shape of the model suggested by Leinhardt and Greeno was consistent with a general principle that had been discovered by cognitive psychologists a decade earlier: As the complexity of the task environment increases, problem solving strategy tends to become hierarchical. This allows a complex problem to be decomposed into a collection of modules and subproblems that are more solvable (Anderson, 1983; Simon, 1973). A skilled teacher orchestrates and rearranges modules (standardized routines and activity structures) in response to classroom cues.

THE SECOND WAVE OF STUDIES

From decision-making models researchers turned to the study of teachers' pedagogical beliefs: the assumptions about pupils, schools, learning, and the role of the teacher that they bring with them to the classroom. Some of the most provocative findings came from investigations of the origins of teacher belief.

For example, studies showed consistently that preservice candidates came to university programs with extensive (albeit sometimes unconscious) assumptions about teachers, students, and learning. Scholars speculated that many of these assumptions were drawn from candidates' own experiences as students in classrooms. Unfortunately, candidates appeared to graduate from programs with their beliefs unchanged, suggesting that university influence on professional practice may be negligible at best (Kagan, 1992; Weinstein, 1990).

Moreover, surveys of experienced teachers found that after leaving their university programs, most acquire new ideas from fellow teachers and their own experiences (Rosenholtz, 1989; Smylie, 1988; Zahorik, 1987). Researchers began to speculate that for a university program to influence the classroom practices of novice or experienced teachers, it must effect true conceptual change.

Thanks to research on learning and teaching science, we know something about the process of changing people's beliefs. It tends to be revolutionary rather than evolutionary; the result of a dramatic confrontation between existing beliefs and data (often called a *discrepant event*) that cannot be explained by existing beliefs. Learners must then be given extended opportunities to examine their existing beliefs in light of the new data and to modify their beliefs accordingly. This is an active process that does not occur automatically when instruction conforms to the traditional information-giving (lecture) format.

Extrapolating from this, some researchers of teacher cognition suggested that an effective program of teacher education—one that changes students' beliefs about classrooms and learning—must expose and challenge teachers' preexisting beliefs. Even after entering practice, the pedagogical beliefs of most teachers remain remarkably persistent and stable. We still know very little about why and how teachers' beliefs and practices evolve over time (Kagan, 1989), but some important clues have emerged from empirical studies. For example, researchers who examined the effectiveness of state or school initiatives mandating curricular change found that changes in teachers' practices are always associated with changes in their beliefs. When practice does change, it represents a mixture of the old and the new; teachers integrate new methods into their highly personalized perspectives (see, for example, Cohen, 1990). Thus, promoting professional growth and change among teachers requires more than the introduction of new information and materials. It requires extended opportunities for teachers to examine their preexisting beliefs and to adapt and integrate the new. If they are not assisted in this process, teachers are likely to misinterpret and distort new mandated curricula.

Beneath every experienced teacher's practice lies a complex, coherent pedagogy that enables the teacher to function in the highly uncertain environment of the classroom, where the "correct" solution to problems is never apparent or indisputable. The subjective and context-dependent nature of "correct" solutions makes classroom teaching a somewhat unique kind of problem solving. The most cursory examination of textbooks on teaching reveals that there are no simple laws or models—only alternative ways to explain the phenomena encountered in classrooms. Thus, in order to function, a teacher must render highly subjective value judgments.

The specific nature of those judgments appears to be strongly influenced by a teacher's biography and personality, particularly the teacher's own classroom experiences as a student and the teacher's interactions with figures of authority (Bullough, Knowles, & Crow, 1992; Goodson, 1992). One of the most significant kinds of beliefs a teacher holds concerns his or her sense of self-efficacy.

Self-efficacy refers to a teacher's generalized expectancy concerning the ability of teachers to influence students, as well as the teacher's beliefs concerning his or her ability to perform certain professional tasks. A teacher's sense of self-efficacy has been positively related to a number of specific classroom behaviors, including the tendency to use praise rather than criticism; to persevere with low achievers; to be task oriented, enthusiastic, and accepting of students' opinions; and to raise students' levels of achievement in reading and mathematics. Teachers who believe that they can make a difference in students' performance appear to accept responsibility for student failure as well as success.

Another discrete research agenda has emerged around content-specific beliefs—a teacher's orientation to specific academic content. This includes the teacher's epistemological conceptions of the field as well as judgments about appropriate instructional activities, goals, and forms of evaluation. Content-specific beliefs have been found to correlate with a variety of instructional variables. For example, researchers found that math and science teachers who have conceptual understandings of their fields tend to emphasize conceptual explanations and to modify textbooks, whereas teachers with superficial understandings tend to lean heavily on prepared texts, rarely modifying them.

Similarly, a teacher's orientation to literature (reader, text, or context oriented) appears to determine the nature of instructional activities used in English classes. Similar results were found in regard to history teachers. Finally, elementary teachers with more (rather than less) cognitively based views of mathematics were found to make more extensive use of word problems during instruction, display greater knowledge of their students' problem-solving strategies, and produce students who excelled on measures of mathematical problem solving (for specific empirical studies related to the above findings, see Kagan, 1992).

In sum, researchers have found that a teacher's beliefs usually reflect the actual nature of instruction that the teacher provides to students. This does not preclude the possibility that a teacher's beliefs might vary when teaching different academic content. That is, teacher belief may be mediated by epistemological differences inherent in respective content areas or by the kinds of instructional materials that happen to be available.

ACCESSING AND EVALUATING TEACHER COGNITION

The tasks of eliciting and evaluating a teacher's thoughts and beliefs are not as straightforward as they seem, for researchers have encountered several problems as they studied teacher cognition. Thoughts and beliefs cannot usually be accessed directly by simply asking a teacher to explain why and how he or she went about planning a lesson or dealing with a particular classroom problem. There are several reasons for this.

First, teachers are often unaware of their thoughts and beliefs, because they are held and applied unconsciously. Second, teachers do not normally verbalize their thoughts aloud and thus may not possess language with which to describe them. Teachers may also be reluctant to admit beliefs that are unpopular or that have negative connotations. Finally, one cannot simply infer beliefs and cognitions from actions, because teachers can employ the same classroom practices for very different reasons.

Moreover, much of the cognition that underlies classroom teaching appears to be context specific; that is, it is embedded in teachers' recollections of particular classroom events and particular students. In fact, researchers found that one of the most productive ways to uncover a teacher's beliefs can be through narrative, by asking a teacher to recall particularly memorable examples of classroom interaction. In recent years this has led to a new interest in the "stories" teachers tell and the ways they make sense of their lives, an avenue of inquiry that we will return to later in this chapter.

By the late 1980s researchers had invented a variety of tools and tasks for eliciting and evaluating teacher cognition. One could find Likert-type self-report scales of cognition, like "tests" of teachers' self-confidence and self-efficacy (Bunting, 1985; Dembo & Gibson, 1985). Although short answer tests are the quickest way to measure cognition, they have serious limitations. They are easy to fake, and teachers may not relate to the language used in standardized questions. Thus, standardized scales may mask or misrepresent a teacher's highly personalized definitions and beliefs.

One can also find interview questions and think-aloud tasks in the literature. In think-aloud tasks, researchers ask teachers to verbalize aloud what they are or were thinking during a performance. For example, a researcher might provide a teacher a written description of a particular classroom problem and ask the teacher to explain how he or she would go about solving it. When trying to capture the cognition underlying actual classroom performance, researchers might use a videotape of the teacher's lesson to help the teacher recall what he or she was thinking.

Teachers' responses to such tasks or to interview questions are usually audiotaped, transcribed, and then coded for various categories of cognition. Many different systems have been used to derive categories. One of the most widely used is van Manen's (1977) three levels of teacher reflection: *Technical Rationality* (the lowest level that focuses on the efficient application of knowledge to attain educational goals, as given), *Practical Action* (clarifying pedagogical goals and consequences), and *Critical Reflection* (the highest level that considers the moral and ethical implications associated with educational goals). Coding systems based on van Manen's hierarchy were used by researchers, in some cases to evaluate the effects of preservice programs that tried to promote self-reflection (Zeichner & Liston, 1985).

Concept mapping has also been used to evaluate teacher cognition. Teachers are given (or asked to generate) key words and are then asked to arrange them in a "map." For example, key words pertaining to "reading instruction" might be used to elicit teachers' beliefs about this topic. The spatial arrangement, or map, that a teacher creates with the key words can then be evaluated quantitatively or qualitatively, often for the purpose of measuring complexity of thought (see, for example, Morine-Dershimer, 1989).

Unfortunately, all of these methods of assessing teacher cognition suffer from two common failings. With the exception of short-answer scales, each is time consuming: Teachers must be evaluated individually, and audiotapes must often be transcribed verbatim. In addition, there is no evidence that any of these methods has ecological validity (Kagan, 1990). This term refers to the relevance of a method or measurement to actual classroom practice. In other words, researchers have yet to prove that relationships exist between any measures of teacher cognition and teachers' actual classroom behaviors or valued student outcomes. Thus the value of teachers' self-reflection remains debatable: Are some kinds better than others? Are better teachers more self-reflective? Do their students learn more?

THEORY INTO PRACTICE

As Calderhead (1993) has suggested, the insights provided by research on teacher cognition can be used in a variety of ways. Theoreticians (educational researchers and teacher educators) are just beginning to explore some of them.

Teacher Education

In light of what we now know about conceptual change and the persistence of novices' pedagogical beliefs, some colleges of education have begun to make dramatic changes in their programs of preservice teacher education. Reforms have generally focused on making course work more self-reflective, requiring candidates to expose and examine their preconceptions about classrooms, students, teachers, and learning. Toward that end, candidates may be asked to keep reflective journals, interview experienced teachers about their thinking, or conduct intensive case studies of particular pupils.

Case-based instruction, common in legal and medical education, has also been suggested as a way to help preservice candidates begin to think like teachers (Merseth, 1991). Casebooks of classroom problems have begun to appear along with suggestions about how to discuss them with preservice candidates. The *writing* (as opposed to the reading) of classroom cases by teachers may also be a fruitful way to promote self-reflection (Shulman, 1992). However, it is interesting to note that there is as yet no empirical research documenting the value of case-based instruction over more traditional instruction or the processes by which novices learn from cases.

Teacher Evaluation Systems

Almost all existing systems used by school districts or universities to evaluate teachers' classroom performances are purely behavioral in nature. They focus exclusively on teachers' actions and ignore the decision making and beliefs that underlie actions. A clear implication of research on teacher cognition is that exclusively behavioral evaluation scales provide a distorted and inaccurate picture of teaching skill. As mentioned earlier, publishing houses, like the Educational Testing Service in Princeton, are in the process of developing and piloting a new generation of teacher tests that consider cognition as well as behavior. Hopefully state and district evaluation systems will undergo similar changes in years to come.

Teacher Research

One of the best ways to promote growth and change in teachers' beliefs and practices may be by effecting conceptual change through self-reflection: helping teachers see their own practices in new lights. This supposition has led to renewed interest in "action" or "teacher research." A group of teachers (often with the assistance of an educational researcher) works collaboratively, selecting some aspect of their classrooms to study intensely. They then collect and analyze a variety of qualitative data (their own daily journals, interviews with students, observations or videos of classroom lessons, and so on) and often present findings to fellow teachers (Lytle & Cochran-Smith, 1990). Researchers have yet to document the professional growth that can be attributed to participation in teacher research, but teachers' own evaluations are very positive.

New Kinds of Research

Earlier in this chapter I mentioned that researchers of teacher cognition discovered that much of what a teacher knows about his or her craft is highly contextualized, embedded in specific recollections of classes and pupils. One of the best ways to elicit this sort of knowledge is to ask a teacher to narrate personal stories. This insight has lead to a new interest in narratives that retain teachers' voices. Close analysis of the language teachers use, particularly the images and metaphors they employ to describe their work, can reflect implicit beliefs and assumptions about classrooms and students (Connelly & Clandinin, 1988; Elbaz, 1991). Scholars are beginning to infer common themes and characteristics about teachers' narratives, particularly in terms of their sense of caring (Elbaz, 1992; Kagan & Tippins, 1991).

As contemporary classroom research becomes more qualitative in nature, narrative is beginning to acquire credibility as a tool and format for research. Case studies of particular teachers and schools are appearing in greater frequency in almost every subspecialization of educational research. Biography is also emerging as a research method, largely due to the insight that biography profoundly affects teachers' beliefs and practices (Bullough, Knowles, & Crow, 1992; Kompf, 1993).

Thus the scholarly literature on teaching and teacher education is beginning to assume radically new shapes. Instead of striving for scientific objectivity, as did the process-product research of the 1970s, much of contemporary research attempts to capture subjective perceptions of teachers, truly inside views of classroom life. Scholars are just beginning to grapple with some of the more profound implications of the move to subjective viewpoints: for example, the issue of validity, how generalizable and representative findings from a single inquiry may be in regard to other teachers and classrooms (Eisner, 1991).

SUMMARY

Research on teacher cognition represents an attempt to marry cognitive psychology and research on problem solving to the study of classroom teaching. One cannot help but wonder whether the NIE panelists who called for this agenda of research in 1974 could have imagined some of the directions studies would take or the sweeping effects they would have on educational research and teacher education.

As research on teacher cognition has evolved over the past decade, it includes a methodologically varied body of literature focused on teachers' pedagogical beliefs; the decisions involved in planning for, delivering, and reflecting upon performance; teachers' perceptions of classroom events and their own images as teachers; and the influence biography may have on teachers' beliefs and practices. This literature has firmly established that teaching is far more than meets the eye.

Beneath the classroom practice of every experienced teacher one finds an elaborate and coherent set of beliefs about schools, students, and learning. Change in classroom practice requires change in deep-seated beliefs. This usually requires extended opportunities for teachers to examine their preexisting beliefs and to incorporate new methods, materials, or insights into their highly personalized perspectives. This insight has already caused teacher educators to question the utility of traditional programs of teacher education. In some cases, colleges of education have restructured programs so they will promote self-reflection among novices.

Similarly, instructional materials used in teacher education have begun to reflect the insights derived from research on teacher cognition. Casebooks of real or realistic classroom dilemmas have appeared and may be one way to help novice teachers reflect on their own beliefs and begin to think like teachers. Standardized tests and evaluation systems of teaching skill are also beginning to change, now that researchers have demonstrated that much of teaching competence is unobservable.

Researchers of teacher cognition began by looking for a standard, linear model of decision making analogous to the model of diagnostic problem solving that was found among experienced physicians. Instead, educational researchers found that problem solving among teachers was highly idiosyncratic, flexible, and dependent upon teacher and classroom context. Much of teachers' decision making appears to be automatic, facilitated by schemas and routines that can be accessed and manipulated unconsciously. This probably allows a teacher to navigate the highly complex, unpredictable, and fast-paced environment of the classroom.

New forms of educational research have begun to appear in the wake of this literature. Narrative and biography are gaining credibility as methods that capture subjective views of the classroom. Scholars are just beginning to debate the reliability and validity of these new genres.

It is difficult to predict what the future holds for research on teacher cognition or which of its effects will be lasting. The fields of teacher education and educational research have proven to be fickle in the past, leaping from one fad to another. In recent years research on teacher cognition has grown rather amorphous (less concentrated on a few identifiable topics), suggesting that it may be destined to retain significance as a research methodology rather than a substantive topic of inquiry. It is ironic and perhaps telling that one can find almost no trace of this research agenda in the daily working life of schools. Most teacher evaluation systems remain strictly behavioral—checklists derived from the process-product studies of the 1970s—and the term *teacher cognition* is unfamiliar to most teachers.

It is probably safe to assume that at least one fundamental insight is here to stay: Classroom teaching cannot be reduced to a quantifiable science. It appears to be a highly personal form of self-expression that is inextricably connected to a teacher's biography and sense of self. There is far more to good teaching than meets the eye.

References

Anderson, J. R. (1983). *The Architecture of Cognition.* Cambridge, MA: Harvard University Press.

Berliner, D. C. (1986). "In Pursuit of the Expert Pedagogue." *Educational Researcher* 15 (7): 5–13.

Berliner, D. C. (1987). "Ways of Thinking About Students and Classrooms by More and Less Experienced Teachers," in J. Calderhead, ed., *Exploring Teachers' Thinking.* London: Cassell, pp. 60–83.

Bullough, R. V., J. G. Knowles, and N. A. Crow (1992). *Emerging as a Teacher.* New York: Routledge & Kegan Paul.

Bunting, C. E. (1985). "Dimensionality of Teacher Education Beliefs: An Exploratory Study." *Journal of Experimental Education* 53: 182–192.

Calderhead, J. (1983, April). "Research into Teachers' and Student Teachers' Cognitions: Exploring the Nature of Classroom Practice." Paper presented at the annual meeting of the American Educational Research Association, Montreal.

Calderhead, J. (1987). "Introduction," in J. Calderhead, ed., *Exploring Teachers' Thinking.* London: Cassell, pp. 1–19.

Calderhead, J. (1993). "The Contribution of Research on Teachers' Thinking to the Professional Development of Teachers," in C. Day, J. Calderhead, and P. Denicolo, eds., *Research on Teacher Thinking: Understanding Professional Development.* London: Falmer Press, pp. 11–18.

Chi, M. T., P. Feltovich, and R. Glaser (1981). "Categorization and Representation of Physics Problems by Experts and Novices." *Cognitive Science* 5: 121–152.

Clark, C. M., and P. L. Peterson (1986). "Teachers' Thought Processes," in M. C. Wittrock, ed., *Handbook of Research on Teaching*, 3rd ed. New York: Macmillan, pp. 255–296.

Cohen, D. K. (1990). "A Revolution in One Classroom: The Case of Mrs. Oublier." *Educa-*

tional Evaluation and Policy Analysis 12: 311–330.

Connelly, M., and J. Clandinin (1988). *Teachers as Curriculum Planners: Narratives of Experience.* New York: Teachers College Press, Columbia University.

Dembo, M. H., and S. Gibson (1985). "Teachers' Sense of Efficacy: An Important Factor in School Improvement." *Elementary School Journal* 2: 173–184.

Eisner, E. W. (1991). *The Enlightened Eye: Qualitative Inquiry and the Enhancement of Educational Practice.* New York: Macmillan.

Elbaz, F. (1991). "Research on Teachers' Knowledge: The Evolution of a Discourse." *Journal of Curriculum Studies* 23: 1–19.

Elbaz, F. (1992). "Hope, Attentiveness, and Caring for Difference: The Moral Voice in Teaching." *Teaching and Teacher Education* 8: 421–432.

Elstein, A. S., L. S. Shulman, and S. S. Sprafka (1978). *Medical Problem Solving: An Analysis of Clinical Reasoning.* Cambridge, MA: Harvard University Press.

Glaser, R. (1985). "The Nature of Expertise" (Occasional paper no. 107). Columbus, OH: National Center for Research in Vocational Education, Ohio State University.

Goodson, I. F., ed. (1992). *Studying Teachers' Lives.* New York: Teachers College Press, Columbia University.

Housner, L. D., and D. C. Griffey (1983, April). "Teacher Cognition: Differences in Planning and Interactive Decision Making Between Experienced and Inexperienced Teachers." Paper presented at the annual meeting of the American Educational Research Association, Montreal.

Kagan, D. M. (1988). "Teaching as Clinical Problem Solving: A Critical Examination of the Analogy and Its Implications." *Review of Educational Research* 58: 482–505.

Kagan, D. M. (1989). "Research on Computer Programming as a Cognitive Activity: Implications for the Study of Classroom Teaching." *Journal of Education for Teaching* 15: 177–189.

Kagan, D. M. (1990). "Ways of Evaluating Teacher Cognition: Inferences Concerning

the Goldilocks Principle." *Review of Educational Research* 60: 419–469.

Kagan, D. M. (1992). "Implications of Research on Teacher Belief." *Educational Psychologist* 27: 65–90.

Kagan, D. M., and D. J. Tippins (1991). "How Teachers' Classroom Cases Express Their Pedagogical Beliefs." *Journal of Teacher Education* 42: 281–291.

Kennedy, M. (1987). "Inexact Sciences: Professional Education and the Development of Expertise." *Review of Research in Education* 14: 133–167.

Kompf, M. (1993). "Construing Teachers' Personal Development: Reflections on Landmark Events through Career Mapping," in C. Day, J. Calderhead, and P. Denicolo, eds., *Research on Teacher Thinking: Understanding Professional Developing.* London: Falmer Press, pp. 167–176.

Leinhardt, G., and J. G. Greeno (1986). "The Cognitive Skill of Teaching." *Journal of Educational Psychology* 78: 75–95.

Lytle, S. L., and M. Cochran Smith (1990). "Learning from Teacher Research: A Working Typology." *Teachers College Record* 92: 83–103.

Merseth, K. K. (1991). *The Case for Cases in Teacher Education.* Washington, D.C.: American Association for Higher Education and American Association of Colleges for Teacher Education.

Morine-Dershimer, G. (1989). "Preservice Teachers' Conceptions of Content and Pedagogy: Measuring Growth in Reflective Pedagogical Decision-making." *Journal of Teacher Education* 40: 46–52.

Peterson, P. L., and C. M. Clark (1978). "Teachers' Reports of Their Cognitive Processes during Teaching." *American Educational Research Journal* 15: 555–565.

Rosenholtz, S. J. (1989). *Teachers' Workplace: The Social Organization of Schools.* New York: Longman.

Shavelson, R. J., and P. Stern (1981). "Research on Teachers' Pedagogical Thoughts, Judgments, Decisions, and Behavior." *Review of Educational Research* 51: 455–498.

Shulman, J. H., ed. (1992). *Case Methods in*

gram *Evaluation and Learner Assessment* (ERIC, 1989) and *The Pennsylvania Framework: Reading, Writing, and Talking Across the Curriculum* (Pennsylvania Department of Education, 1988), as well as many articles on literacy, teaching, and professional development.

Cochran-Smith and Lytle are friends and colleagues who go back professionally to the time they were enrolled in the same doctoral program. Both have worked closely with student teachers and experienced teachers for years in communities of learners.

14 🕿

Learning from Teachers' Perspectives

Marilyn Cochran-Smith and Susan L. Lytle

INTRODUCTION

For much of the fifty-year history of research on teaching, teachers and their work have been the topics of other people's research and study. Despite the usual relegation of teachers to the receiving end of theory and knowledge about practice, however, teachers themselves have also written about their work over the last several decades. It is teachers' unique perspectives on classrooms and schools that make it possible for us to learn about teaching and learning from the inside. From teachers' perspectives, we can learn how teachers negotiate the terrain between following and leading the learner, how they integrate knowledge from a variety of sources, how they come to understand individual learners' constructions of knowledge, how they question the assumptions underlying curriculum and schooling, how they make decisions to alter and evaluate routines and practices, and how they invent frameworks to understand their current work and also ask new questions about it.

Teachers' Questions

It may appear to be self-evident that the questions teachers ask emanate from their day-to-day work in classrooms and schools, but this is not a trivial issue. In traditional university-based classroom research, researchers' questions reflect careful study of the existing theoretical and empirical literature and, sometimes, negotiation with the teachers in whose classrooms they collect data. Teachers' questions, on the other hand, often emerge from discrepancies between what is intended and what occurs. Initially these may be experienced as concern about a student's progress, a classroom routine that is floundering, conflict or tension among students, or a desire to try out some new approach. This questioning process is highly reflexive, immediate, and referenced to particular children and classroom contexts.

Although teachers' questions are not necessarily framed in the language of educational theory, they are indeed about discrepancies between theory and practice. Although they are not always motivated by a need to generalize beyond the immediate case, they are often relevant to a wide variety of contexts. The questions of teachers are, at once, more general than those that concentrate on the effectiveness of specific techniques, materials, or instructional methods and more specific than interpretive questions that explore the meanings of customary school and classroom events. Teachers' questions emerge from neither theory nor practice, but from their critical intersections. They reflect teachers' inescapable responsibility to the here and now of school life as well as their ongoing need to construct intellectual perspectives for understanding their work. A major way we can learn from teachers' perspectives, then, is by paying close attention to the problems of practice that they identify and investigate, problems that outside researchers may never address simply because they do not stand in the same relationship to the practice of teaching.

Teachers' Writing

In our own work on teacher research, we have proposed four categories that acknowledge a wide range of teachers' writing: teachers' journals, published and unpublished; essays in which teachers analyze classrooms, learners, curricula, and school organizations; teachers' oral inquiries convened specifically for reflection and questioning; and teachers' classroom studies. This kind of research is deeply contextualized in the everyday events of schools and classrooms and in the lived experiences of teachers and their students. Although many teachers work in schools that have not institutionalized inquiry, most teacher-writers are members of cross-school, school-university, or unaffiliated communities wherein inquiry is regarded as a central task of learning from teaching across the professional lifespan.

In this chapter, we draw on teachers' texts to reveal what we can learn from teachers' perspectives in three broad domains: the interrelationships of language, literacy, and learning; the cultures of teaching and schools; and teachers' learning and professional development. We explore teachers' writing in these three domains to elaborate the theory-practice relationships that are central, quoting at some length from teachers' work in order to provide direct access to their ways of explaining and representing relationships rather than filtering teachers' perspectives and interpretations through our own. Although we are drawing heavily on teachers' texts, we do not presume to speak for teachers. Rather, this chapter represents our efforts to understand and present publicly what we are learning from teachers' perspectives from our own positions as university-based teacher educators and researchers. Most of the teachers' texts used in this chapter are taken from our recent book *Inside/Outside: Teacher Research and Knowledge* (Cochran-Smith & Lytle, 1993), a collection of five of our own conceptual essays about teacher research followed by twenty-one pieces written by beginning and experienced teachers in the Philadelphia area. We use these texts as exemplars partly because they are the texts we know most intimately and partly because they stand as rich and evocative examples of what we can learn from teachers' perspectives.

DOMAIN I: LANGUAGE, LEARNING, AND LITERACY

The first domain includes teachers' explorations of the experiences of individual students, classroom interactions, and home-school connections in language, learning, and literacy—how teachers, students, and even parents jointly construct the language and literacy curriculum as they learn from and with each other.

Exploring the Domain

Language is the central medium through which we teach and expect our students to demonstrate their learning. Teachers' work in this domain often describes and analyzes the interplay of children's and teachers' questions and observations, drawing on students' work over time to construct case studies of individual learners (Buchanan, 1993). Other teachers take the classroom as the unit of analysis by examining group talk or uses of print (Feldgus, 1993); the interpretive norms of readers and writers within the social contexts of classrooms, family, and community values (Johnston, 1993); ethnicity and language differences and how these may create barriers between students and teachers and/or between students and their own aspirations (Farmbry, 1993; Joe, 1993); problems of practice associated with textbook-centered instruction, ability grouping, and standardized testing (Black et al., 1993; Cone cited in Cochran-Smith & Lytle, 1993); and how the curriculum emerges from ongoing language interactions as teachers and students jointly construct content, language, and social life (Strieb, 1993; Howard cited in Cochran-Smith & Lytle, 1993). Writing in this domain often traces teachers' deepening understanding of the issues by drawing on early experiences as well as the framing and reframing of dilemmas over time. One of the most important insights we get from teachers' perspectives on language, learning, and literacy is that varying notions of literacy out of school, particularly those of parents and other community members, play a significant role in the construction of literacy learning in school (Belzer, 1993; Headman, 1993).

Domain I, Elementary School Example:
A Deaf Writer's Journey

In a study of language, learning, and literacy at the elementary school level, Penny Starr (1993) looked at the language development of one child—a ten-year-old boy profoundly deaf since birth. Analyzing his writing strategies over time, she proposed that writing development was a process of negotiating between the worlds of American Sign Language (ASL), his primary communicative language, and the English he encountered in print and books. The following excerpt shows how her questions developed over time.

I am a teacher at the Pennsylvania School for the Deaf (PSD) in Philadelphia. . . . [My school] is a private, state-chartered city school that serves approximately 170 deaf students aged 2 through 15. At PSD, ASL is used when teaching in the classroom and is an essential part of the school's education and communication philosophy. One of our key goals is to encompass all cultures and languages to enhance learning. The teachers at PSD immerse children in a language-filled environment, and ASL is recognized and supported throughout the school. Everyone at PSD can sign, with varying degrees of ASL fluency.

For two years, our classroom community has been reading, writing, talking, and learning. We are nearing the end of our two years together. Are the children really that different from hearing writers? How? Have they adapted different processes, changed them, perhaps revised a little to better suit their needs as deaf writers? Does their lack of fluency in English impede their progress as writers? How do they compensate, and how do they overcome? Most of all, how are they faring right now? If together we are builders of knowledge and makers of meaning . . . how can I continue to encourage them to build bridges? . . .

These questions have been with me since I began teaching at PSD. [But] it was not until these two years that I began to search deeper for some answers. . . . I began to look closely at one student's strategies, process, and progress in our community of writers. I chose to look closely at one writer's progress over two years with me, in the hopes that understanding one child more fully would increase my understanding of them all.

Starr's writing, like the writing of other teachers, is unique in what it can tell us about theory-practice connections in teaching. Her rich observations of day-to-day events show us from the inside how questions mediate the worlds of theory and practice as she plans for, implements, and assesses various interventions.

Hearing people compose and prewrite before the pen is to the paper. We listen to our own words in our head, our own inner speech, to hear how the words sound together. . . . When the deaf compose, is this inner speech an outer visible sign? Do they invent, compose and build meaning in the primary language of ASL? Michael sits, signs to himself, writes some, and then goes back to sign and revise what he has written. As he signs to himself, he does not really watch his hands but rather gets a feeling for the signs flowing together. For Michael, the writing and constant rewriting that we as hearing people do in our heads, seems to be done by the visible rehearsal of signs in his inner speech of ASL. In observing Michael compose and write, I believe this is what he is doing. I also have many questions. Is his whole inner speech an outer visible speech or does he have both an inner speech *and* an outer visible speech? Have they been blended into one or are they two distinct processes for Michael? . . . If the practice for hearing people is the sound, then is the practice for deaf people the visual? Had Michael adapted the sound of words to the look of his signs? Was he checking how his writing "sounded" by signing it?

Starr's musings capture the complex interplay of a teacher's implicit theory of language learning, her experiences as a language learner herself, and close observations of Michael's writing processes. Often this interplay means struggling to reconcile observations and beliefs that appear to be conflicting. The insights that result from struggling with seemingly discrepant information lead not just to strategies for teaching one child but, as Starr suggests above, for understanding more generally the ways that children grapple with language and learning tasks in school.

Domain I, Secondary School Example: Becoming Mean and Sensitive

Teachers' writing about language, learning, and literacy shows us how teachers and students together negotiate what counts as knowledge in the classroom, who can have knowledge, and how knowledge can be generated, challenged, and evaluated. In the secondary school example that follows, Robert Fecho (1987, 1989, 1993) was prompted by the realization that there was a discrepancy between his intentions and what was going on in the classroom. He began a study of teacher-student writing conferences after viewing videotapes of his classroom and feeling dissatisfied with what he saw.

> While some students were able to advance their own agendas and seek answers to their own questions, far too many students sat and waited for me to question, to figure out, and to change their writing. Although conferencing was successful in altering my relationships with the students, what occurred between us was still much too close to a teacher-centered classroom. . . . I resolved to take a more systematic look at my conferencing. Aside from the generic ethnographic question of, "What happens?" specifically, I was interested in what occurred in the conferences over the course of one school year—did the structure and work change . . . ? Did similarities and differences exist across conferences? Did the passing of time allow students to develop as conference participants?

Fecho set out to understand how face-to-face talk about writing functioned and varied over time when a white teacher worked with more than thirty African-American adolescents in an urban comprehensive high school. He concluded a report of his research with these words.

> In one of our interviews, Geeman [one of Fecho's students] mentioned that our conferencing experience had led him to take second looks at the writing he did for other classes. He liked the idea that he could be his own critic, that he could [in his words] be "mean and sensitive" to himself. I understood exactly what he meant. For myself, in the conference I had to be "mean" in order to resist my student's reliance on my expertise, but also "sensitive" to their needs and opinions. But looking at the phrase again, I realized that it also comments on my teacher research. As I find myself getting woozy watching tapes and reading transcripts, I know that I must continue looking for what the tapes may reveal, must continue to separate the real from the imagined, must continue seeing my practice with mean and sensitive eyes. For if I don't, who will?

Although Fecho initiated and conducted the research, his students' inquiries brought unexpected insights into his own work. As Fecho wrestled with the implications of sharing power, both he and his students came to view knowledge differently. Fecho's work is especially instructive because of his long tenure as a teacher and because he has written about his efforts to co-investigate issues of power and language with his students over a number of years. In a recent essay, for example, Fecho explored the theoretical bases of his practice and the linguistic and cultural resources of his students through the lenses of race, culture, and difference by making knowledge of language the subject as well as the medium of instruction. Read as a portrait of one teacher's evolving critical pedagogy, Fecho's essays and studies weave together his classroom experiences with his collaborations with colleagues in his school and school district, where reform and school restructuring have been major efforts over a five-year period.

DOMAIN II: THE CULTURES OF TEACHING AND SCHOOLING

In the second domain, teachers' writing investigates the cultures of teaching and schooling, particularly professional socialization, teacher-to-teacher collaboration, and the changing nature of the teacher's workplace.

Exploring the Domain

In this domain, some teachers reconsider what they read and were taught about issues during preservice teacher education programs on the one hand, and their actual experiences as student teachers and new teachers on the other hand (Joe, 1993). Others study how school administrators construct the professional socialization of teachers new to the system (Wunner, 1993). Teachers' writing in this area also explores the intellectual lives of teachers, raising questions about teachers as readers and members of interpretive communities with distinct perspectives on research and practice (Brody et al., 1993; Fecho, 1993). These describe the link between teachers' emerging intellectual interests and the transformations that occur in classroom curriculum and instruction. The writing of teachers from different worlds—grade levels, races, professional experiences, and points in time—enriches our frames of reference for understanding teacher culture and how teachers themselves see relationships among teaching, learning, and schooling (Harris, 1993; Wiggington cited in Cochran-Smith & Lytle, 1993).

Domain II, Elementary School Example:
In Response to Community Needs

In an essay on the culture of teaching during the beginning years, Jennifer Eastman (Cochran-Smith & Lytle, 1993) analyzed her efforts to meet the social, emotional, and academic needs of culturally diverse groups of students by making problematic, rather than accepting, common assumptions. These included beliefs about student motivation and potential for achievement, families' capacities for supporting children's learning, the appropriateness of the curriculum, and the efficacy of teachers in ameliorating what often appear to be insurmountable problems.

Eastman wrote this essay at the end of her first year for an audience of current student teachers considering urban teaching. It reveals what happens when new teachers begin with the assumption that the school success of urban children depends on changing the status quo and that individual teachers play a part in that success, either by design or by default.

> This essay is based on my own experiences as a new teacher in a public school in a very poor section of Philadelphia, where I do not feel defeated and do not see the staff or the school or the children as defeated.... As a new teacher in a new system, new school, new neighborhood, I believed that caring about these children, and getting through the first year without quitting or leaving them was one success. And even this was not easy. The first year, many days I felt incompetent, silly, not in control, unable to figure out simple lesson plans, afraid of any kind of change, nervous about trips, worried about parent meetings and conferences . . . [I] discovered that I need to operate on several different levels of involvement: in my classroom, with other teachers on joint projects, on school-wide projects, and on community/ political issues. These different involvements keep me from feeling too much despair at any one problem by seeing hope for change in all these areas. . . .

In the essay, Eastman described her responses to particular problems and even tragedies that had occurred in her school during the first year. Her writing reveals how individual teachers with an activist's stance can contribute concretely to social change even when problems appear overwhelming.

> In response to [a teaching] assistant's shooting death, I wrote and received a grant for a school-wide study of Puerto Rican culture, with a library corner of books and materials on Puerto Rico in [the assistant's] name . . .
>
> In response to the family problems encountered by some of the children, I invited four children to participate in an origami club on Mondays, which gives me the opportunity to show some special attention to children who lack it at home.
>
> In response to the needs of families, I helped to write a grant . . . to provide family-oriented services after school . . .
>
> In response to a need to form connections with other teachers, I am currently writing another grant with the other kindergarten teacher on a circus theme, culminating in taking our children and their parents to the circus . . .
>
> In response to the difficulty communicating with parents, I initiated monthly parent meetings . . . We write a monthly newsletter and calendar . . . and in our meetings we have [Spanish-English] translators as we go over the monthly schedule and school-related information.

Learning from this teacher's perspective, we see that there are many ways even for beginning teachers to take a proactive stance on reforming the school environment for culturally diverse populations. What is most striking about this excerpt is that Eastman entered the teaching force as a learner, not expecting to apply ready-made answers to complex problems but expecting to observe, talk to other teachers and parents, get to know the community, and build her own networks of resources, projects, and services. Teachers' writing about the cultures of schools and teaching demonstrates how teachers at varying points across the professional lifespan construct their own agendas for reform within their own classrooms and school communities.

Domain II, Secondary School Example:
Looking Back Over Twenty Years of Teaching

Mickey Harris (1993) examined her work life over a twenty-year period by using a personal journal to document her experiences in one urban high school that changed dramatically in its demographics, school climate, and programs during her tenure there. Harris' work also provides a rich portrait of the teacher as writer—as one who both interprets and shapes the culture of teaching and also uses writing as a way to negotiate new understandings. In the introduction to selected excerpts from the journal, Harris wrote:

> In an earnest effort to sort out my thoughts and to dialogue with self about my profession, I began a diary on my first day of teaching in 1969. . . . Just as Strieb [a Philadelphia teacher colleague] used her journal to mirror her life and the lives of her community of students and parents within and beyond the boundaries of the schoolyard, my teacher's tabloid has graphically revealed to me how my life and world affect my practice. Subsequently, I can trace with each reviewing of my "professional journal" how my journey of inquiry in the classroom has transacted with and shaped my life. My commentaries may change from time to time but the vignettes of students' lives continue to inform and reform my vocation. Flannery O'Connor has wisely judged a story to be good when "you can continue to see more and more in it, and when it continues to escape you."

Each of Harris' entries depicts a specific moment in a teacher's experience—the intertwining of her personal, professional, and political lives. The following excerpts, selected from entries over a twenty-year period, capture the rich texture of urban teaching from the perspective of a teacher who is deeply invested in both her students' life chances and her own use of writing to know her own knowledge.

Day 8: September 29, 1969

Well, they said I wouldn't last and here I am. I've been here one full week and I've been called "Yo, teach!" more times than I can count. I've had my hall pass stolen, my coat locker broken into, and my class lists keep changing from day to day. As soon as I memorize a name and connect that name with a face, both disappear. Where are all of these people coming from and where do they go when they leave me? . . . My students range from sweet to silent, somnolent to sarcastic. They don't seem to be sure of the fact that I'm going to stay. Although I arrived here on September 22nd, I was their fourth teacher. The guy who lasted for one looong day said that he'd rather flee to Canada than to get a deferment this way . . .

March 17, 1979

Happy Saint Patrick's Day! Today was indeed a great day for the Irish. My fifth period seniors turned in their final papers on *Tess of the D'Urbervilles*. I have thirty-one students and thirty-one papers. This is success! . . . At noon, we had early dismissal and took the bus to the Ritz Theatre to view Polanski's version of *Tess* . . .

After the show . . . a debate spontaneously erupted between David and Lisa on the subtle and not so subtle differences between rape and seduction with a wonderful comparison between the film and novel. When the manager of this "artsy" movie house joined us on the sidewalk, I was afraid that he would ask us to disperse immediately. Instead the man, a great judge of scholars, reported that the other theatre-goers . . . were delighted to hear the animated reactions of young people to a classic. Sure and begorrah, I'm so proud.

September 28, 1981

This is my seventh strike since 1969. Each one seems to get more bitter, more frustrating. . . .While we carry our signs, Ramona, Ed, Rosemarie, and I plan the year, schedule class trips, and watch substitute teachers go into a virtually empty building. I have spoken to most of the seniors who will be in my advisory. William and Denise meet me outside of school on Mondays and Fridays. They collect work and college applications from their fellow classmates. I write my comments, questions, and suggestions; then my super helpers distribute our bizarre communiqué. This class of seniors is concerned about a shortened year, college rejections, postponed graduation. Some have secured jobs that may lure them out of the classroom. Others are feeling as if no one really cares about them.

I worry about teacher morale too. Two of the finest teachers in the district are gone. They told me in June that one more strike would end their careers. Many parents arc putting their children into private or parochial schools. The ultimate sorrow occurred when I finished picketing and returned home. The editorial in the *Inquirer* let me know that we are incompetent, greedy, overpaid drones who want to drain the coffers of a bankrupt city . . .

In rare instances like this one, teachers' writing in the second domain gives us an intimate understanding of a single teacher's work life over a long period of time. Harris' explicitly autobiographical work provides evocative detail about the changing nature of the school as workplace. Writing like this offers richly contextualized pictures of teaching as part of the complex landscape of school cultures and communities, their histories, and the political and social climate of the times.

DOMAIN III: PROFESSIONAL DEVELOPMENT ACROSS THE LIFESPAN

The third domain of teacher writing focuses on the ways that teachers learn about and from teaching across the professional lifespan. In particular, it raises questions about the functions and strategies of inquiry in professional development and in knowledge generation and reform in both local and public contexts.

Exploring the Domain

Writing in this domain, teachers explore their own learning, particularly the role of inquiry in professional development. Teachers describe, for example, group uses of structured oral inquiries as ways of knowing about individual children, learning diversity, and curriculum construction for particular local communities. This work often provides thick descriptions of classroom events and participants, drawing on the language of classroom interactions, students' work, and teachers' retrospective analyses of learning processes as well as their underlying assumptions and values (Colgan-Davis, 1993; Kanevsky, 1993). Using as data their journals, interviews with students, and colleagues' questions and recommendations, teachers show us that teaching and inquiry into teaching are social, messy, and distinctly nonlinear processes. Some teachers reveal the ways they use inquiry to build understanding of teaching and learning and raise questions about the relationship of the educational literature and their ongoing teaching experiences in the classroom, juxtaposing questions, theories, and practices (Brody et al., 1993). Other teachers analyze the logic of their own evolution as teachers and teacher-researchers by examining questions and writing over time and for a variety of audiences and contexts. In this work, teachers reinterpret their teaching practices and explore personal change and its relationship to changes that occur as schools and curricula undergo restructuring (Pincus, 1993; Sims, 1993).

Domain III, Elementary School Example: White Privilege and the Culture of Power

Teachers often describe professional development by reconsidering assumptions about the histories and cultural and linguistic backgrounds of others, about the motivations and behaviors of children, parents, and other teachers, and about the most appropriate pedagogies for particular groups of learners. In an essay about her own learning, for example, Dionne Enea (Cochran-Smith & Lytle, 1993), a white student teacher in the first few months of her preservice teacher education program, drew on her experiences of race, class, and gender as well as her experiences in a student teaching classroom. Part of what we can learn from this is how beginning teachers pose questions as they begin to learn about teaching and the ways they use other people's research to uncover interpretive frameworks and explore in ways that are tentative, evolutionary, and personal.

> I found Lisa Delpit's article, "The Silenced Dialogue: Power and Pedagogy in Educating Other People's Children" (1988), to be very disturbing, and I've linked this to the way that I felt when we read in class Peggy McIntosh's "White Privilege: Unpacking the Invisible Knapsack" (1989). The fact that something called "White privilege" exists in our society is easy for someone who is White to ignore, and I think that it made me uncomfortable to have to face up to these truths that I otherwise never consider in my everyday experiences. . . .
>
> It is easy for me to simply say that I do not judge individuals in terms of race, but after thinking about the validity of Lisa Delpit's (1988) and Bernardo Ferdman's (1990) articles, I realize that this is nowhere near enough. If cultural identity does indeed play a role in how a child learns, as Ferdman claims in "Literacy and Cultural Identity," then as a teacher my responsibility goes far beyond treating people as equals. Am I one of those White liberals whom Delpit believes ignores the fact that a culture of power and its rules exist, and who tries in vain to address successfully issues of race in an educational system designed by White males to perpetuate a society that holds them in a dominant and advantaged position?
>
> If the bottom line is, "We teach who we are," how can I effectively teach those who are not like myself? How much will "who I am" make me blind to the needs and experiences of those who are different from me? I fear that Lisa Delpit's article,

which seems to make so much sense, is right. Does the fact that I am White leave me with my hands tied because I will never be able to escape my position in the "culture of power" to teach those who do not hold this power?

Teachers' writing in this domain provides a window into the way even the newest teachers begin to construct the dilemmas inherent in teaching. This kind of writing gives us a sense of the ways teachers struggle to formulate questions rather than to move too quickly to premature conclusions. Perhaps even more significant, however, is what it reveals about teachers' efforts to move beyond long-held beliefs to take on the responsibility for educating themselves about the cultural and linguistic resources children bring to school.

Domain III, Secondary School Level Example: Lighting Fires

In the secondary school example that follows, Shirley Brown describes the link between her emerging intellectual interest in feminist scholarship and the transformation that occurred in the texts she used in her classroom and the invitations she offered students for making sense of those texts. She argues that using the "mother tongue" was critical to her development as a teacher and feminist as well as to the inquiries of her G.E.D. classes of pregnant and parenting teens.

> About five years ago I became keenly aware of a lack of fire in my classroom. Lessons were going forward, youngsters were learning, passing tests, etc. But, where was the engagement, the sense that there was meaning in the classroom, that students could use what school had to offer in their everyday life? . . . It wasn't that there was no room for Poe's stories [and for the stories of others in "the canon"] in my classroom, but there was a need for a different kind of curriculum—one that encouraged engagement and started fires. . . .
>
> It was in [a seminar on women writers] that the world of women's studies opened up for me and made clear the importance of the personal in the classroom, the power of curriculum and language, and the gaps in my education. By the time I finished the seminar, I was transformed. I was reading through a different lens, envisioning a different classroom dynamic, and looking for nonconventional sources of information. This seminar was not an academic exercise, but a way to view the world very differently. . . .
>
> As for my own classroom, the curriculum continued to become more inclusive. . . . Students used their journals to make connections between Jamaica Kinkaid's "Girl" piece and their own mothers and/or between "Girl" and how their own children would see them as parents. They wrote about courage and determination after reading Maya Angelou's "And Still I Rise," about injustice in J. W. Houston's *A Farewell to Manzanar,* about civil disobedience in Richard Rive's "The Bench," about difficult choices in Langston Hughes' "Professor," about desperation and suicide in old age in Arna Bontemps' "A Summer Tragedy," about jealousy and mothering in Cynthia Ozick's "The Shawl," about domestic violence in Ann Petry's "The Winding Sheet," and about the will to live in Alice Walker's "To Hell with Dying." I could feel the fire in the room.

One of the most striking aspects of this domain of teacher writing is what it shows us about teaching when teachers stand in direct relationship to their own knowledge, to their students as knowers, and to knowledge generation in the field. As Freire (1971) has suggested, teachers who analyze and write about their work are "knowing subjects," constantly learning from the process of teaching. What we learn from teachers' perspectives in this domain, then, is how teachers "learn from teaching" when they regard their classrooms and schools as research sites and sources of knowledge. When learning from teaching is taken to be the primary task of teachers across the lifespan, a distinctive set of assumptions about knowledge, collaboration, and inquiry applies. Teachers are assumed to be among those who have the authority to know, that is, to construct knowledge about teaching, learning, and schooling, and their research becomes a significant part of a redefined knowledge base for teaching. Knowledge from the academy is not accepted unproblematically but rather is taken to be rich and generative, providing conceptual frameworks, detailed information from other contexts, new problems and dilemmas, confirming and disconfirming evidence, and grist for further deliberations.

THEORY INTO PRACTICE

Since John Dewey's (1904) writings at the beginning of this century, scholars and researchers have devoted considerable attention to understanding the relationships of knowledge and teaching. From various disciplinary perspectives and research paradigms, scholars have asked what it means to know about teaching— what can be known, how it can be known, who has the authority to know, and how knowledge can or should be used for theoretical and practical purposes. What is most often suggested is that the knowledge that makes teaching a profession comes from authorities outside of the profession itself, and that what makes teachers professional is using this knowledge base in their daily practice. From this perspective, teachers are knowledgeable in that they have insights as well as experience and skills, which they call upon to explain phenomena and make judgments about practice, but they do not participate in the generation of knowledge (Fenstermacher, 1986; Reynolds, 1989). We agree that there is a rich body of information generated by university researchers that ought to inform the practice of teaching and that making that knowledge accessible for teachers' critical appraisal and adaptation is an essential endeavor. But if we learn about theory-practice relationships in teaching only from outsiders' perspectives, then this knowledge is exclusionary and disenfranchising.

The examples of teachers' writing that we have included in this chapter demonstrate that we can indeed learn about teaching from teachers' perspectives, from their insiders' views that make visible the ways students and teachers together construct knowledge. When teachers act as researchers in their classrooms and write about their work, they draw on interpretive frameworks built from their own histories and intellectual interests, and, because the research process is embedded in practice, the relationship between knower and known is significantly altered. When we learn from teachers' perspectives, there is no necessity to "translate findings" or "transform theory into practice" in the conventional sense, because findings and theories are no longer regarded as things simply received by teachers who are expected to adapt or implement them in their particular situations. In the examples in this chapter, we have tried to demonstrate that teachers play a critical role as knowers. We believe that they participate in building knowledge both locally and publicly—for the individual teacher, for communities of teachers, and sometimes for the larger field of university-based researchers and teacher educators, policy makers, and school administrators. By examining cases of individual teachers in a variety of contexts, we have shown how inquiry provides teachers with a way to know their own knowledge—how they and their students negotiate what counts as knowledge in the classroom and how interpretations of classroom events are shaped.

We are proposing that connecting theory and practice should be regarded as a process that is "inside/outside" rather than simply "outside-in," a juxtaposition that calls attention to the distinctly nonlinear relationships of knowledge and teaching, as they are embedded in the contexts and the relations of power that structure the daily work of teachers and learners in both the schools and in the university. As teachers' perspectives on teaching are made more public, we believe they will present a radical challenge to current assumptions about the relationships of theory and practice, schools and universities, and inquiry and reform. Research by teachers represents a distinctive way of knowing about teaching and learning that alters, not just adds to, what we know in the field. Because we see teacher research as both interpretive and critical, however, its contribution will not be in the form of generalizations about teaching (this time from the "inside" perspective), nor will teacher research be benign and evolutionary, a process of accumulating new knowledge and gradually admitting new knowers to the fold. Rather, learning from teachers' perspectives fundamentally redefines the notion of "knowledge" for teaching, alters the locus of the knowledge base, and realigns the practitioner's stance in relation to knowledge generation in the field.

Legitimating the knowledge that comes from practitioners' research on their own practice is a critical dimension of change in both school and university cultures. In challenging the university's hegemony in the generation of expert knowledge for the field, teachers also challenge the dominant views of staff development and preservice training as transmission and implementation of knowledge from outside to inside schools. Thus it has the potential to reconstruct conceptions of the ways teachers learn across the professional lifespan so that inquiry is regarded as an integral part of the activity of teaching and a critical basis for decisions about practice. Classrooms and schools are treated as research sites and sources of knowledge most effectively accessed when teachers collaboratively interrogate and enrich their theories of practice.

When teacher development is reconfigured as inquiry and teacher research as challenge and critique, they become forms of social change wherein individuals and groups labor to understand and alter classrooms, schools, and school communities. These transformations will inevitably cause conflict, as those traditionally disenfranchised begin to play increasingly important roles in generating knowledge and in deciding how it ought to be interpreted and used. Teacher research, furthermore, makes visible the ways teachers and students negotiate power, authority, and knowledge in classrooms and schools. As a way of knowing, then, teacher research has the potential to alter profoundly the cultures of teaching—how teachers work with their students toward a more critical and democratic pedagogy, how they build intellectual communities of colleagues who are both educators and activists, and how they position themselves in relation to school administrators, policy makers, and university-based experts as agents of systemic change.

SUMMARY

Despite the fact that teachers are generally regarded as the receivers of knowledge about teaching and learning, they have also written about their work in schools and classrooms in rich and evocative detail over the last several decades. This chapter explored what we can learn about teaching when we pay close attention to teachers' perspectives in three major domains: language, learning, and literacy relationships; the cultures of teaching and schooling; and teachers' professional learning and development. We have drawn on two examplars from each of these domains, one at the elementary and one at the secondary level. Taken together, these reveal—from teachers' perspectives—how teachers negotiate the terrain between following and leading the learner, how they integrate knowledge from a variety of sources, how they come to understand individual learners' constructions of knowledge, how they question the assumptions underlying curriculum and schooling, how they make decisions to alter and evaluate routines and practices, and how they invent frameworks that allow them to understand their current work and also ask new questions about it.

References

Belzer, A. (1993). "Doing School Differently," in M. Cochran-Smith and S. L. Lytle, *Inside/Outside: Teacher Research and Knowledge.* New York: Teachers College Press, Columbia University.

Black, L., H. Bousel, L. B. Byer, L. Cimakasky, D. Coy, P. Freilich, B. Hartman, D. Hilton, S. Joe, D. Lawrence, M. M. Hanley, J. Snyder, J. Swenson, and B. Winklestein (1993). "Leaving the Script Behind," in M. Cochran-Smith and S. L. Lytle, *Inside/Outside: Teacher Research and Knowledge.* New York: Teachers College Press, Columbia University.

Brody, D., E. Cornman, M. R. Crouse, L. Greenspun, J. Klavens, T. D. Miller, K. Patton, E. Powers, M. C. Ritchie, P. Rogers, and D. M. Schefer (1993). "Faith, Love, and Polka Music," in M. Cochran-Smith and S. L. Lytle, *Inside/Outside: Teacher Research and Knowledge.* New York: Teachers College Press, Columbia University.

Brown, S. (1993). "Lighting Fires," in M. Cochran-Smith and S. L. Lytle, *Inside/Outside: Teacher Research and Knowledge.* New York: Teachers College Press, Columbia University.

Buchanan, J. (1993). "Listening to the Voices," in M. Cochran-Smith and S. L. Lytle, *Inside/Outside: Teacher Research and Knowledge.* New York: Teachers College Press, Columbia University.

Cochran-Smith, M., and S. L. Lytle (1993). *Inside/Outside: Teacher Research and Knowledge.* New York: Teachers College Press, Columbia University.

Colgan-Davis, P. (1993). "Learning About Learning Diversity," in M. Cochran-Smith and S. L. Lytle, *Inside/Outside: Teacher Research and Knowledge.* New York: Teachers College Press, Columbia University.

Delpit, L. (1988). "The Silenced Dialogue: Power

and Pedagogy in Educating Other People's Children." *Harvard Educational Review* 58: 280–298.

Dewey, J. (1904). "The Relation of Theory to Practice in Education." *The Third NSSE Yearbook, Part 1.* Chicago: University of Chicago Press.

Farmbry, D. (1993). "The Warriors, the Worrier, and the Word," in M. Cochran-Smith and S. L. Lytle, *Inside/Outside: Teacher Research and Knowledge.* New York: Teachers College Press, Columbia University.

Fecho, R. (1987). *Folding Back the Classroom Walls: Teacher Collaboration via Cross Visitation.* Philadelphia: University of Pennsylvania, Philadelphia Writing Project.

Fecho, R. (1989). *On Becoming Mean and Sensitive: Teacher to Student Writing Conferences in the Secondary Classroom.* Report prepared for the NCTE Research Foundation.

Fecho, R. (1993) "Reading as a Teacher," in M. Cochran-Smith and S. L. Lytle, *Inside/Outside: Teacher Research and Knowledge.* New York: Teachers College Press, Columbia University.

Feldgus, E. (1993). "Walking to the Words, in M. Cochran-Smith and S. L. Lytle, *Inside/Outside: Teacher Research and Knowledge.* New York: Teachers College Press, Columbia University.

Fenstermacher, G. (1986). "Philosophy of Research on Teaching: Three Aspects," in M. C. Wittrock, ed., *Handbook of Research on Reaching*, 3rd ed. New York: Macmillan.

Ferdman, B. M. (1990). "Literacy and Cultural Identity." *Harvard Educational Review* 60 (2): 182–201.

Freire, P. (1971). *Pedagogy of the Oppressed.* New York: Herder and Herder.

Harris, M. (1993). "Looking Back: 20 Years of a Teacher's Journal," in M. Cochran-Smith and S. L. Lytle, *Inside/Outside: Teacher Research and Knowledge.* New York: Teachers College Press, Columbia University.

Headman, R. (1993). "Parents and Teachers as Co-Investigators," in M. Cochran-Smith and S. L. Lytle, *Inside/Outside: Teacher Research and Knowledge.* New York: Teachers

College Press, Columbia University.

Joe, S. (1993). "Rethinking Power," in M. Cochran-Smith and S. L. Lytle, *Inside/Outside: Teacher Research and Knowledge.* New York: Teachers College Press, Columbia University.

Johnston, P. (1993). "Lessons from the Road: What I Learned through Teacher Research," in M. Cochran-Smith and S. L. Lytle, *Inside/Outside: Teacher Research and Knowledge.* New York: Teachers College Press, Columbia University.

Kanevsky, R. (1993). "Descriptive Review of a Child: A Way of Knowing About Teaching and Learning," in M. Cochran-Smith and S. L. Lytle, *Inside/Outside: Teacher Research and Knowledge.* New York: Teachers College Press, Columbia University.

McIntosh, P. (1989). "White Privilege: Unpacking the Invisible Knapsack." *Peace and Freedom* 10–12.

Pincus, M. R. (1993). "Following the Paper Trail," in M. Cochran-Smith and S. L. Lytle, *Inside/Outside: Teacher Research and Knowledge.* New York: Teachers College Press, Columbia University.

Reynolds, M. C., ed. (1989). *Knowledge Base for the Beginning Teacher.* Oxford, England: Pergamon Press.

Sims, M. (1993). "How My Question Keeps Evolving," in M. Cochran-Smith and S. L. Lytle, *Inside/Outside: Teacher Research and Knowledge.* New York: Teachers College Press, Columbia University.

Starr, P. (1993). "Finding Our Way: A Deaf Writer's Journey," in M. Cochran-Smith and S. L. Lytle, *Inside-Outside: Teacher Research and Knowledge.* New York. Teachers College Press, Columbia University.

Strieb, L. (1993). "Visiting and Revisiting the Trees," in M. Cochran-Smith and S. L. Lytle, *Inside/Outside: Teacher Research and Knowledge.* New York: Teachers College Press, Columbia University.

Wunner, K. (1993). "Great Expectations," in M. Cochran-Smith and S. L. Lytle, *Inside/Outside: Teacher Research and Knowledge.* New York: Teachers College Press, Columbia University.

Discussion Questions

1. What are the implications for K–12 teaching of "learning from teachers' perspectives" as described in this chapter?

2. What are the implications for research and policy making of "learning from teachers' perspectives" as described in this chapter?

3. What are the obstacles that constrain, and the conditions that support, the institutionalization of teacher inquiry in K–12 schools and classrooms?

4. How do/don't current school reform and restructuring efforts take these obstacles and conditions into account?

5. In addition to the three domains of teacher writing described in this chapter, what are other domains in which it is especially important to "learn from teachers' perspectives"? Why?

6. How is learning about theory-practice relationships from teachers' perspectives different from and/or similar to learning about them from university-based researchers' or policy makers' perspectives?

Kathy Carter, Walter Doyle, and Mark Riney

Kathy Carter

Walter Doyle

Mark Riney

Kathy Carter is associate professor of teaching and teacher education at the University of Arizona. Prior to joining the faculty at Arizona, she was a high school teacher for seven years in the Dallas area and worked for several years conducting research and inservice activities for state and federal education agencies. Her favorite teacher was her eleventh grade American Literature teacher. "She had an uncanny ability to make the characters in short stories and novels come alive." She was full of energy and enthusiasm, and Kathy recommends today that new teachers model this type of behavior in their own classrooms.

Carter serves on the editorial boards of the *Elementary School Journal*, *Journal of Teacher Education*, and *Teaching and Teacher Education*. From 1990 to 1992 she was vice president of Division K (Teaching and Teacher Education) of the American Educational Research Association. Her thirty publications address issues in teacher knowledge, teacher education, and classroom management.

For relaxation, Kathy jogs, hikes, and bird watches in the Arizona mountains, and she takes weekly trips to the zoo and museums with her spouse and son, Griffin.

We are now in Walter Doyle's cluttered office, where books and papers are stacked knee-high and family pictures dot the walls in all directions. Several portraits of Einstein, for some reason, hang side to side with Walt's personal photos. The connection is not easy to make, although I am told that Albert also had a cluttered office—and Walt adds that "he was a wise and gentle man."

Doyle is professor of teaching and teacher education at the University of Arizona. He received all three degrees—B.A., M.A., and Ph.D.—from the University of Notre Dame and taught several years of junior and senior high school English. Prior to Arizona, he was on the faculty of North Texas State University and the University of Texas at Austin, where he was a colleague of Carolyn Evertson and Gary Griffin, who are also contributors to this text.

Walter has co-edited one text and published some seventy-five articles in areas of classroom management, teacher effectiveness, and curriculum theory. He asserts that "expertise in teaching is grounded in a teacher's understanding of curriculum as a classroom event and ability to navigate the complex demands of classroom settings."

Walter also hikes and jogs along the mountain

257

peaks in Arizona and takes trips to the zoo and museum. But instead of bird watching, he flicks photos.

Mark Riney completed his doctoral studies in the department of teaching and teacher education at the University of Arizona in 1994. His special interests are in the areas of curriculum development and curriculum history. He is also a full-time English teacher who has taught for twelve years. His favorite education books are the *Handbook of Research on Teaching* and the *Handbook of Research on Curriculum,* because these volumes provide teachers with a comprehensive overview of pedagogy and curriculum. His primary advice for beginning teachers is threefold. First, teachers should know their content area extremely well because they can't teach what they don't understand. Second, it is important for teachers to structure their classroom management strategies carefully because teachers can't teach a class they can't manage. Third, beginning teachers ought to understand that becoming an expert teacher takes a number of years.

15 ❧

Expert–Novice Differences in Teaching

Kathy Carter, Walter Doyle, and Mark Riney

In Jack London's famous short story, "To Build a Fire," a newcomer to the Yukon travels alone when the temperature is 50 degrees below zero. Although he knows that this temperature is extreme, he disregards an oldtimer's warning not to travel because he does not understand the danger inherent in such weather. He is, the narrator tells us, "quick and alert in the things of life, but only in the things, not in the significances" (London, 1985 [1904], p. 417).

This contrast between newcomer and oldtimer, between "novice" and "expert," has slipped comfortably into the language of educational research and practice over the past decade. Not only has considerable effort been expended to study differences between teachers grouped along this continuum, but the expert-novice framework itself has also become a compelling image throughout the teaching and teacher education community. Thus, studies that do not include explicit comparisons between novices and experts are often interpreted in light of this contrast. Similarly, students in initial preparation programs are now widely referred to as novices, and models of teacher development based on this framework are beginning to emerge (Berliner, 1988).

This chapter has four main purposes: (1) to sketch the core features of expert-novice research; (2) to provide a synopsis of what has been learned about teaching from studies that have utilized this framework; (3) to examine critically the contributions and limitations of this tradition both as an approach to the study of teaching and as a conception of teachers' ability and knowledge growth; and (4) to explore the practical implications of work in this area for teachers and teacher educators.

The structure we have chosen to achieve these objectives involves answering a series of basic questions about the research foundations of the expert-novice framework and about the issues this line of thinking raises for teaching and teacher education. Our intention is to provide readers with easy and efficient access to this tradition by focusing primarily on the intrinsic character and significance of this work. Those interested in more technical aspects of this research are directed to the formal reports listed in the references at the end of the chapter.

THE RESEARCH BASE

In this section, we examine the origin and basic structure of expert–novice studies and the findings that have emerged from this research. Although a broad perspective on expert-novice research is adopted, special attention throughout the section is centered on investigations of expertise in teaching.

What Is an Expert–Novice Study?

Although there is some variation across studies, the classic design for expert–novice research involves

1. the identification of experts in a domain, usually with reference to some high-level performance criterion (for example, the achievement of "Master" status in chess, or peer nomination as an expert in medical diagnosis);

2. the selection of novices or nonexperts in that domain, typically beginning students;

3. the formulation of prototype problems or scenarios, such as identifying patterns on chess boards or interpreting an x-ray plate, to which both the experts and the novices are asked to react;

4. systematic comparisons of the performances of the experts and the novices in these problem situations.

Where Did This Framework Originate?

Much of the research on expertise in teaching was modeled after the expert–novice studies that evolved within the more general study of human information processing in cognitive psychology (see Berliner, 1987; Chi, Glaser, & Farr, 1988). The tradition began with the study of chess masters (Chase & Simon, 1973; de Groot, 1965) and was later expanded to include medical diagnosis, electronics, computer programming, mathematics, science, and related technical fields. Such studies have significance not only for basic cognitive science but also for designing expert systems that simulate human capabilities (Benfer, Brent, & Furbee-Losee, 1991).

Who Are the Experts and Novices?

In many of the domains used for expert–novice studies, indicators of expertise are fairly clearly delineated by status, tests, or other forms of distinction. One becomes a Chess Master, for example, by winning chess games. However, in less well-structured fields, such as medicine or teaching, the manifestations of expertise are more elusive. In the latter areas, investigators select experts on the grounds of years of experience, peer status or nomination, judgments based on direct observation of performance, and the like.

Swanson, O'Connor, and Cooney (1990), for instance, contrasted problem-solving abilities between twenty-four expert teachers who had an average of twenty-eight years of experience and novices who had an average of a half-year of experience. The novices in this study were enrolled in an educational psychology course; the experienced teachers were considered experts if they had ten or more years of experience, had earned a master's degree, were rated as outstanding by an administrator, and were selected to be mentor teachers. Sabers, Cushing, and Berliner (1991) began their selection of experts with a pool of fifty-five teachers nominated as exemplary by school superintendents and principals, and then selected seven as the most expert on the basis of three classroom observations.

Some investigators have made distinctions between beginners and advanced beginners (Oppewal, 1993; Sabers, Cushing, & Berliner, 1991). This differentiation is usually based on amount of formal preparation in either subject matter or pedagogy, prior teaching experience, or some combination of the two.

How Have Expert–Novice Differences in Teaching Been Studied?

As indicated above, expert–novice research typically involves constructing prototypical problems in a domain and then contrasting the performance of experts and novices on these problems. In other words, the differences between experts and novices are usually observed under standardized laboratory conditions that allow for direct comparisons.

In research on teaching, most investigators have followed this practice of using laboratory tasks to reveal expert-novice differences. Carter, Sabers, Cushing, Pinnegar, and Berliner (1987), for example, posed a planning problem in which subjects were asked to prepare to take over an investigator-defined class in mid-year to examine expert-novice differences in processing and using information about students. Similarly, Housner and Griffey (1985) asked expert and novice physical education teachers to think aloud as they planned lessons on soccer and basketball dribbling, and then to respond to simulated recall interviews using videotapes of the lessons they taught to four children.

To capture expertise at work during lessons, investigators often use written vignettes, slides, or short videotaped segments to depict classroom events. Carter, Cushing, Sabers, Stein, and Berliner (1988) asked experts and novices to respond to slides of classroom scenes. Peterson and Comeaux (1987) examined differences between experienced and novice secondary social studies teachers in their discussion of videotapes of three separate four-minute classroom scenes (Oppewal, 1993). Finally, Sabers, Cushing, and Berliner (1991) used three separate monitors simultaneously to show different views of a science lesson.

Other investigators have used more natural teaching situations to examine expert-novice contrasts. Fogarty, Wang, and Creek (1982) conducted simulated recall interviews around fifteen-minute lessons taught by experienced and novice teachers as part of the regular basic skills curriculum. Ropo (1987) used a combination of classroom observations and clinical interviews to examine the differences in conceptions of planning and teaching between expert and novice mathematics teachers. Borko and Livingston (1989) also focused on mathematics and used observations and interviews to explore differences in expert and novice teachers' planning, teaching, and postlesson reflections. Rich (1993) studied teachers who were implementing cooperative learning in their classrooms. Finally, in an impressive series of expert-novice studies, Leinhardt and her colleagues (Leinhardt & Greeno, 1986; Leinhardt & Smith, 1985) used extensive observations (twenty to thirty hours), interviews, think-alouds, and experimental tasks (for example, estimating overlap between the curriculum and standardized test items).

What Aspects of Teaching Expertise Have Been Examined?

The bulk of the studies of expert-novice differences in teaching have focused on classroom management (Sabers, Cushing, & Berliner, 1991), discipline problems (Swanson, O'Connor, & Cooney, 1990), and general instructional strategies (Rich, 1993). This emphasis often prevails even when the research is conducted with teachers in a particular curriculum specialization (Borko & Livingston, 1989, in math; Housner & Griffey, 1985, in physical education). Less frequently, investigators have focused on subject matter expertise or a combination of subject matter and classroom knowledge (Leinhardt & Greeno, 1986, on elementary school mathematics) or what Tochon and Munby (1993) call "didactics" (that is, transformations of content into a form for teaching) and "pedagogy" (that is, the actualization of teaching in classroom events). A focus on subject matter connects expert-novice research with the emerging work on pedagogical content knowledge (see Grossman & Richert, 1988; Shulman, 1986). The relative neglect of subject matter knowledge in expert-novice research is unfortunate, since such knowledge appears to play a discernible role in distinguishing between novice and expert performance (Borko & Livingston, 1989).

What Have We Learned About Teaching Expertise?

Findings from expert-novice studies are typically stated in highly abstract terms. A representative list across the various domains that have been studied would include the following assertions (Chi, Glaser, & Farr, 1988):

1. Experts, because they have richly elaborated schemata, see broad patterns in problems, tasks, and cases in their domain.

2. Experts easily think of problems and cases in terms of underlying principles, whereas novices typically focus on superficial attributes.

3. Experts are typically efficient: They complete tasks and solve problems quickly with few errors.

4. Experts initially seek to understand the basic structure of problems and situations, whereas novices rush to apply algorithms or simple interpretations.

5. Experts, in comparison to novices, have greater short- and long-term memories, in large part because of their familiarity with a domain and the automaticity of their processing rather than superior innate abilities.

6. Expertise is largely specific to a domain. Experts in one domain (for example, radiology) are likely to perform as novices in another (for example, chess).

Specifically within the area of teaching, expert–novice studies (see previous review) have suggested that expert teachers, in contrast to novices, have large stores of event knowledge of classroom situations, management routines, and instructional strategies, and they use this knowledge of patterns to interpret classroom scenes and identify areas that require immediate attention. Expert teachers also tend to focus attention on student participation and the work students are accomplishing, and they have well-formed curriculum scripts, that is, cognitive frameworks for organizing their understanding of subject matter as it plays itself out in classroom events and the sequencing of content both within and between events. Finally, this knowledge of events and curriculum enables expert teachers to scan situations efficiently, react flexibly and improvisationally to immediate circumstances and contingencies, and see large configurations of sequences and purposes.

In contrast, novices' planning is typically reported as being less efficient and less grounded in underlying conceptions of classroom events and subject matter structures. Similarly, their performance is characterized as more hesitant, less flexible in response to changing circumstances, and more easily disrupted by unexpected events than those of experts.

In a recent extension of the expert–novice tradition, Tochon and Munby (1993) focus on differences in what they call "time epistemologies" between experts and novices. These investigators found that expert teachers, in contrast to novices, have a more synchronic view of time, that is, they focus on incidents occurring simultaneously at a point in time rather than simply on the anticipated sequence of planned activities or events. Tochon and Munby argue that this synchronic sense enables experts to fuse plans with emerging circumstances and thus adapt lessons, modulate rhythms, and pursue alternative paths to their objectives.

Finally, expertise in teaching, as in other domains, is situated. Rich (1993), for example, found that expert teachers often performed in quite novice-like ways when attempting to implement an instructional scheme they had not tried before.

ISSUES AND INTERPRETATIONS

Up to this point we have concentrated on painting a fairly straightforward picture of the basic structure of expert-novice studies and the findings that have emerged from systematic efforts to compare experts' and novices' performances. We now turn to the sense that has been made of these findings and the issues that surround efforts to interpret and apply this research tradition to teaching and teacher education. Attention in this section is on the significance of the expert–novice framework for the educational community in general.

What Sense Has Been Made of Expert–Novice Findings?

In broad terms, the results from expert–novice research have been interpreted in two ways. The first involves the use of such findings as grounds for defining the content of teacher education programs and for judging the competencies of graduates of such programs. The view is, in other words, that teacher education should aim at fostering expertise in teaching and, thus, curriculum and assessment should be grounded in what we know about how experts think and act.

The second interpretive emphasis has been placed on teacher development, that is, the path from novice to expert, despite the fact that this path from novice to expert is largely uncharted. To an increasing extent, however, investigators have focused on aspects of the development of expertise (Oppewal, 1993; Tochon & Munby, 1993), and Berliner (1988) has proposed a stage model to map this journey. This model, similar in many respects to that developed by Dreyfus, Dreyfus, and Athanasiou (1986), defines movement from the learning of context-free rules that are applied often inflexibly to an increasing understanding of the episodic nature of classrooms and the acquisition of procedural knowledge. Next, the "competent performer" achieves greater flexibility and can differentiate more reliably between what is important and what is unimportant. Then a more holistic view across situations and greater pattern recognition emerge, allowing for more rapid adaptation to changing circumstances. Finally, expertise is reached as automaticity and improvisational facility unfold.

What Makes the Expert–Novice Framework So Attractive?

The above interpretative perspectives go a long way toward explaining why the expert–novice framework has so rapidly become a standard image in the education community. The framework not only connects teaching and teacher education to the knowledge explosion in cognitive science, but it also addresses the enduring questions of how to define the content of teacher education—a traditional function of research on teaching—and how to understand teacher development and the processes of learning to teach—a central preoccupation of teacher educators. It is not surprising, then, that educators would find this approach appealing.

It is important to note that these questions of curriculum and development were not a part of the original expert–novice agenda in cognitive psychology, in which the focus was on cognitive structures and information processing. The initial intent, in other words, was not to use expert–novice comparisons to improve practice in, say, chess, electronics, or medicine. However, improvement is a natural instinct in the education community. Moreover, the differences between experts and novices that have been uncovered are often so dramatic that one finds it hard to resist being curious about how these differences arise.

What Limitations Are Inherent in the Expert–Novice Design?

Strictly from the perspective of research method, there are two troublesome areas in expert–novice studies. The first area involves validity. The use of laboratory tasks to study differences between expert and novice teachers has the advantage of all experimental arrangements: By holding conditions reasonably constant, direct comparisons among individual performances are possible. At the same time, the tasks themselves are often quite artificial and decontextualized. Thus, the representativeness and validity of the performances and their comparisons are called into question. On the other hand, the use of natural teaching situations enhances validity. However, since situations can differ in a variety of uncharted ways, comparability of tasks across subjects is a serious problem in making performance comparisons.

A second problem of method centers on what might be called domain problems. In clearly structured game or technical domains, such as chess, electronics, and radiology, indicators of expertise are fairly clear and differences between experts and "just plain folk" are easily discernible. Moreover, it is likely that problems and cases in such domains have well-specified (although not necessarily easily specified) underlying structures. Finally, experts in these domains are likely to have well-structured interpretations and solution strategies, at least for the types of problems that are posed in most expert–novice studies.

In less clearly formed domains, such as teaching, hidden or perhaps invisible criteria can enter into the process of selecting experts and novices, thus distorting the results in ways that are not open to scrutiny. Similarly, the complexity of both situations, solution paths, and their match in less well-structured domains may mean that the listing of simple differences between experts and novices masks both instability within each of these categories (Oppewal, 1993; Rich, 1993) and many of the quite intricate processes of both knowledge acquisition and use (Spiro et al., 1987).

Solely from the perspective of a cognitive psychologist's interest in knowledge structures, these validity and domain problems may not be especially onerous. However, when one turns to the task of educating novices, the issues of how a domain of expertise is defined, how differences are investigated, and how one thinks about the path from novice to expert become central.

What Limitations Are Inherent in the Expert–Novice Image of Teaching Expertise?

Findings from expert–novice studies are typically formulated as highly abstract propositions about elemental processes rather than as rich representations of the complexities of episodes and situations. Such formulations are certainly consistent with the original intention of such research within cognitive psychology. Moreover, they are consistent with the long-standing effort within education to define a small number of highly general indicators of teaching effectiveness to serve as instruments for the remote control of teaching practice (Doyle, 1990).

At the same time, the image of teaching expertise that emerges from this account is sparse and reductionistic. As with past attempts to define teaching effectiveness, such an image narrows our understanding of what it means to teach and what knowledge and experiences are required to teach well. Moreover, this research framework perpetuates the dubious view that only a very few teachers ever achieve proficiency.

What Limitations Are Inherent in the Expert–Novice Perspective on Teacher Development?

Despite the best intentions of researchers, the setting up of expert–novice comparisons tends to convey two attitudes or perspectives. The first is that novices are inadequate with respect to the core tasks that need to be accomplished in a domain. Although it is clear that beginners in any area have a lot to learn, the deficit model inherent in expert–novice research can easily undervalue the role of preconceptions in the process of learning to teach. Recent studies suggest that preconceptions among novice teachers are quite robust (Calderhead & Robson, 1991; Carter, 1990; Knowles & Holt-Reynolds, 1991; Weinstein, 1988). What teacher education candidates know about teaching from their long "apprenticeship of observation" (Lortie, 1975) and the thinking they have done in deciding to become teachers shapes in powerful ways what they learn from courses and classroom experiences. Any approach to teacher development that ignores or minimizes what novices bring with them to teaching is likely to miss the mark.

A second perspective fostered, again inadvertently, by the expert-novice framework is that teacher development is largely a linear function of experience, that is, more experience leads to more expertise. Such a view is probably incomplete and does little to inform teacher education practice. Although experience certainly plays a role in development, experience alone is hardly sufficient for achieving expert proficiency. Experience can lead to misconceptions rather than insights (Feiman-Nemser & Buchman, 1986) or to problem-minimizing rather than problem-solving strategies (Scardamalia & Bereiter, 1989). There are also likely to be curves and discontinuities in the strand of development, as beginning teachers grapple with competing agendas, the demands of time, and the rhythms and changing circumstances of the classroom (Clandinin, 1988; Rich, 1993; Tochon & Munby, 1993). Finally, formal courses and opportunities to share experiences and reflect on practice are context ingredients known to have an impact on how teachers think and act (Grossman & Richert, 1988; Oppewal, 1993; Ross & Regan, 1993).

What Alternatives Exist for Understanding Teacher Expertise?

Given the popularity of the expert–novice framework, much of the thinking about teacher expertise in the education community has been cast in this mold.

But, as the previous discussion of limitations suggests, and as Carter (1993) and Doyle (1990) have argued elsewhere, there are viable alternatives to a strict expert-novice design. It is possible, in other words, to step outside the expert–novice frame to locate knowledge about teaching and teachers that informs both classroom practice and our understanding of teacher development. Indeed, such an outside perspective may well be essential: One would hardly expect to enrich the knowledge base for medical practice, for instance, by simply studying differences in cognitive structures between novice and expert physicians.

For illustrative purposes, we briefly discuss two directions of inquiry that we believe hold promise for enriching our understanding of the character of teacher expertise and its development.

The first alternative can be found in what might be called "classroom system theory" (Carter & Doyle, 1987; Doyle, 1986, 1992). This work is concentrated on unraveling the basic structure of the action systems that organize classroom life, the academic tasks that embody the curriculum in action, the strategies teachers use to set these systems and tasks in place in classroom situations, and the interpretive processes teachers and students use to navigate these complex management and curricular environments.

Propositions about these features of teaching are formulated inductively from close studies of classroom life rather than deductively from general conceptions in psychology, sociology, or philosophy. Teachers of varying levels of experience and proficiency are watched in an assortment of situations in an effort to understand the demands they face and the ways in which they address these demands. Indeed, as in the study of language structures, "mistakes" in teaching often reveal more about the basic character of classroom processes than smooth performances.

A complete rendering of classroom system theory is beyond the limits of this chapter. One example, however, will serve to illuminate its essential properties. The concept of "academic task" refers to the implicit and explicit instructions students receive that frame how they are to interact with and process subject matter in a class (Doyle, 1983). These instructions occur in the form of assignments, instructional suggestions and directives, teachers' reactions to students' performance and products, and students' prior experience with various task forms. Students may be asked to memorize terms, use reliable formulae to generate answers, express opinions, or create original products that reflect their understanding of basic principles. Tasks differ according to the degree of teacher specification (ambiguity) and the level of accountability for performance (risk).

This task framework captures the curriculum in motion in a class and provides an opportunity to explicate the various paths that can be used by teachers and students to interpret and come to terms with this curriculum. Thus it becomes possible to get behind the topic labels and surface agendas of classrooms and gain insight into the processes by which teaching and learning occur in these settings. Such a model enables teacher educators to name some of the fundamental dimensions involved in creating and orchestrating classroom events and, thus, explicate the substance of the schemata teachers use to interpret classroom scenes and act in productive ways.

A second alternative to the expert–novice framework can be found in the rich literature emerging on teachers' narratives or stories (Ben-Peretz, 1991; Carter, 1993; Connelly & Clandinin, 1990; Goodson, 1992; Schubert & Ayers, 1992). This literature includes narratives generated collaboratively by teachers and researchers as well as stories told in teachers' own voices. Moreover, the focus of these narratives ranges from specific classroom events to broad life histories.

Narrative has a number of distinct advantages as an approach to studying teaching (Carter, 1993). In the first place, stories demand characterization. Rather than the typically anonymous "stick figures" of experts or novices, stories provide personifications of real persons with intentions and feelings as well as strategies and schemata. Stories also involve plot, that is, a patterning of action around a theme with temporality and causality as central processes and issues. Thus, the richness and complexity of classroom scenes and teachers' experiences can be represented in the narrative form of explication and analysis. Finally, several scholars (for example, Bruner, 1985; Mitchell, 1981) have noted that narrative is a fundamental mode of human knowing, one that is especially suited to the knowledge that arises from action.

From these perspectives of action and personal insight, stories would seem to be particularly useful as sources for a rich understanding of the complex patterns of teacher development, patterns that are often masked in expert-novice studies. At the same time, stories would seem to be an especially powerful form of knowledge representation for teacher education, in that they bring the novice close to the details of classroom life within which management and instruction occur and to the motives and feelings that accompany action in these environments.

One final advantage of narrative inquiry needs to be underscored here. Stories provide a means for the expression of teacher voice, and especially women's voices, which have long gone unheard in educational research. In most expert–novice studies, the researchers speak for the participants and often do so in the formal language of cognitive psychology. Much can be learned by listening to the novices and experts speak for themselves.

THEORY INTO PRACTICE

We now come to the end of our brief survey of the nature of expert–novice studies and the issues these studies raise for theory and practice in the teaching and teacher education community. In this section, we reflect back on this journey and attempt to draw out some major themes or "lessons" that seemed to emerge along the way.

What Have We Learned?

There seem to be at least four major lessons that can be learned from the study of differences between novices and experts. These are:

1. *Teaching practice has strong cognitive roots.* Experts differ from novices not only in what they are able to do (behavior) but also and more funda-

mentally in what they know and how they think about what they do (cognition). Thus, efforts to prepare novices or improve teaching practice must involve more than skills or procedures. Teachers must learn to think about practices, to discern central from peripheral issues, and to embed the new into their prevailing understandings of classrooms. Along similar lines, beginning teachers must focus attention not simply on what to do but also on how to think about the circumstances they face and what actions in these circumstances are possible.

2. *Teachers know classroom forms.* That is, expert teachers understand how such things as motivation, learning, time, and curriculum manifest themselves within the complex array of classroom incidents filled as they are with competing agendas and intricate rhythms. Thus, abstract propositions from basic disciplines are of limited utility until enmeshed in classroom realities.

3. *Teachers' understandings are tied to everyday events.* In other words, experts know most about those contingencies with which they deal on a regular basis. Change, therefore, is likely to be quite difficult since new forms make classroom situations more unpredictable than they normally are and limit the utility of much that teachers have expertise in. There is an important lesson here for administrators who would have change occur swiftly.

4. *The differences between novices and experts are frequently dramatic.* The framing of what novices know is qualitatively different from that of experts. One should not expect instant experts from teacher education. It takes a long time and considerable support to learn to teach.

5. *Novices begin their journey with maps already in mind.* Although novices may appear naive on several key dimensions of expert teaching, they are not blank slates. They have robust notions of what it means to teach and how they will behave as teachers. The understandings they bring with them to teacher education cannot be ignored, although we still have much to learn about how to take them into account. Novices should work to understand their existing cognitive frames.

SUMMARY

Although we have raised fundamental questions about the expert–novice tradition, we would also underscore that much has been learned from the effort to think about expertise in teaching and how it might be achieved. The frame itself, then, has been fruitful. At the same time, we would urge that the study of expert–novice differences in teaching be seen as a starting point rather than a finished agenda. Knowing these differences is important, although not always surprising. But understanding what these differences mean is the much more arduous and important task in front of us.

References

Ben-Peretz, M. (1991). "Scenes from the Past: Retired Teachers Remember." Paper presented at the Fifth ISATT Conference, University of Surrey, Guilford.

Benfer, R. A., E. E. Brent, and L. Furbee-Losee (1991). *Expert Systems*. Newbury Park, CA: Sage Publications.

Berliner, D. C. (1986). "In Pursuit of the Expert Pedagogue." *Educational Researcher* 15: 5–13.

Berliner, D. C. (1988). *The Development of Expertise in Pedagogy*. Charles W. Hunt Memorial Lecture, New Orleans, American Association of Colleges for Teacher Education.

Borko, H., and C. Livingston (1989). "Cognition and Improvisation: Differences in Mathematics Instructed by Expert and Novice Teachers." *American Educational Research Journal* 26: 473–498.

Bruner, J. (1985). "Narrative and Paradigmatic Modes of Thought," in E. Eisner, ed., *Learning and Teaching the Ways of Knowing* (Eighty-fourth Yearbook of the National Society for the Study of Education). Chicago: University of Chicago Press, pp. 97–115.

Calderhead, J., and M. Robson (1991). "Images of Teaching: Student Teachers' Early Conceptions of Classroom Practice." *Teaching and Teacher Education* 7: 1–8.

Carter, K. (1990). "Teachers' Knowledge and Learning to Teach," in W. R. Houston, ed., *Handbook of Research on Teacher Education*. New York: Macmillan, pp. 291–310.

Carter, K. (1993). "The Place of Story in Research on Teaching and Teacher Education." *Educational Researcher* 22: 5–12.

Carter, K., K. Cushing, D. Sabers, P. Stein, and D. C. Berliner (1988). "Expert-Novice Difference in Perceiving and Processing Visual Classroom Information." *Journal of Teacher Education* 39: 25–32.

Carter, K., and W. Doyle (1987). "Teachers' Knowledge Structures and Comprehension Processes," in J. Calderhead, ed., *Exploring Teachers' Thinking*. London: Holt, Rinehart and Winston.

Carter, K., D. Sabers, K. Cushing, S. Pinnegar, and D. C. Berliner (1987). "Processing and Using Information about Students: A Study of Expert, Novice, and Postulant Teachers." *Teaching and Teacher Education* 3: 147–157.

Chase, W. G., and H. A. Simon (1973). "The Mind's Eye in Chess," in W. G. Chase, ed., *Visual Information Processing*. New York: Academic Press, pp. 215–281.

Chi, M. T. H., R. Glaser, and M. J. Farr, eds. (1988). *The Nature of Expertise*. Hillsdale, NJ: Lawrence Erlbaum.

Clandinin, D. J. (1988). "Developing Rhythm in Teaching: The Narrative Study of a Beginning Teacher's Personal Practical Knowledge of Classrooms." *Curriculum Inquiry* 19: 121–141.

Connelly, M., and D. J. Clandinin (1990). "Stories of Experience and Narrative Inquiry." *Educational Researcher* 19: 2–14.

de Groot, A. D. (1965). *Thought and Choice in Chess*. The Hague: Mouton.

Doyle, W. (1983). "Academic Work." *Review of Educational Research* 53: 159–199.

Doyle, W. (1986). "Classroom Organization and Management," in M. C. Wittrock, ed., *Handbook of Research on Teaching*, 3rd ed. New York: Macmillan, pp. 392–431.

Doyle, W. (1990). "Themes in Teacher Education," in W. R. Houston, ed., *Handbook of Research on Teacher Education*. New York: Macmillan, pp. 1–24.

Doyle, W. (1992). "Curriculum and Pedagogy," in P. W. Jackson, ed., *Handbook of Research on Curriculum*. New York: Macmillan, pp. 486–516.

Dreyfus, H. L., S. E. Dreyfus, and T. Athanasiou (1986). *Mind Over Machine*. New York: The Free Press.

Feiman-Nemser, S., and M. Buchman (1986). "Pitfalls of Experience in Teacher Preparation," in J. D. Raths and L. G. Katz, eds., *Advances in Teacher Education*, vol. 2. Norwood, NJ: Ablex Publishing Corp., pp. 61–73.

Fogarty, J., M. C. Wang, and R. Creek (1982). "An Investigation of Perceptions and Strategies of

Experienced and Novice Interactive Teachers." Paper presented at the annual meeting of the American Educational Research Association, New York.

Goodson, I. F., ed. (1992). *Studying Teachers' Lives*. New York: Teachers College Press, Columbia University.

Grossman, P. L., and A. E. Richert (1988). "Unacknowledged Knowledge Growth: A Re-examination of the Effects of Teacher Education." *Teaching and Teacher Education* 4: 53–92.

Housner, L. D., and D. C. Griffey (1985). "Teacher Cognition: Differences in Planning and Interactive Decision-Making between Experienced and Inexperienced Teachers." *Research Quarterly for Exercise and Sport* 56: 45–53.

Knowles, G., and D. Holt-Reynolds (1991). "Shaping Pedagogies through Personal Histories in Preservice Teacher Education." *Teachers College Record* 93: 87–113.

Leinhardt, G., and J. Greeno (1986). "The Cognitive Skill of Teaching." *Journal of Educational Psychology* 78: 75–95.

Leinhardt, G., and D. Smith (1985). "Expertise in Mathematics Instruction: Subject Matter Knowledge." *Journal of Educational Psychology* 77: 3, 247–271.

London, J. (1985 [1904]). "To Build a Fire," in F. Hodgins and K. Silverman, eds., *Adventures in American Literature*. New York: Harcourt Brace Jovanovich, pp. 417–428.

Lortie, D. (1975). *Schoolteacher*. Chicago: University of Chicago Press.

Mitchell, W. J. T., ed. (1981). *On Narrative*. Chicago: University of Chicago Press.

Oppewal, T. J. (1993). "Preservice Teachers' Thinking about Classroom Events." *Teaching and Teacher Education* 9: 127–136.

Peterson, P. L., and M. A. Comeaux (1987). "Teachers' Schemata for Classroom Events: The Mental Scaffolding of Teachers' Thinking during Classroom Instruction." *Teaching and Teacher Education* 3: 319–331.

Rich, Y. (1993). "Stability and Change in Teacher Expertise." *Teaching and Teacher Education* 9: 137–146.

Ropo, E. (1987). "Teachers' Conceptions of Teaching and Teaching Behavior: Some Differences between Expert and Novice Teachers." Paper presented at the annual meeting of the American Educational Research Association, Washington, D.C.

Ross, J. A., and E. M. Regan (1993). "Sharing Professional Experience: Its Impact on Professional Development." *Teaching and Teacher Education* 9: 91–106.

Sabers, D., K. Cushing, and D. Berliner (1991). "Differences among Teachers in a Task Characterized by Simultaneity, Multidimensionality, and Immediacy." *American Educational Research Journal* 28: 63–88.

Scardamalia, M., and C. Bereiter (1989). "Conceptions of Teaching and Approaches to Core Problems," in M. C. Reynolds, ed., *Knowledge Base for the Beginning Teacher*. New York: Pergamon, pp. 37–46.

Schubert, W., and W. Ayers, eds. (1992). *Teacher Lore: Learning from Our Own Experience*. New York: Longman.

Shulman, L. S. (1986). "Those Who Understand: Knowledge Growth in Teaching." *Educational Researcher* 15: 4–14.

Spiro, R. J., W. P. Vispoel, J. G. Schmitz, A. Samarapungavan, and A. E. Boerger (1987). "Knowledge Acquisition for Application: Cognitive Flexibility and Transfer in Complex Content Domains," in B. C. Britton and S. M. Glynn, eds., *Executive Control Processes in Reading*. Hillsdale, NJ: Lawrence Erlbaum, pp. 177–199.

Swanson, H. L., J. E. O'Connor, and J. B. Cooney (1990). "An Information Processing Analysis of Expert and Novice Teachers' Problem Solving." *American Educational Research Journal* 27: 533–556.

Tochon, F., and H. Munby (1993). "Novice and Expert Teachers' Time Epistemology: A Wave Function from Didactics to Pedagogy." *Teaching and Teacher Education* 9: 205–218.

Weinstein, C. (1988). "Preservice Teachers' Expectations about the First Year of Teaching." *Teaching and Teacher Education* 4: 31–40.

Discussion Questions

1. You have been appointed to a school-level committee to advise the principal about the type of inservice program that would be of greatest help to your colleagues in implementing a new cooperative learning model in your school. What insights into this inservice design can be derived from the expert-novice literature?

2. What conceptions of teaching did you bring with you into teacher education? Where did you acquire these ideas? What role did they play in your learning to teach? How have they changed with classroom experience?

3. If you were asked to address a group of beginning student teachers on the subject of classroom management, what three essential ideas would you incorporate into your remarks? Why do you consider these ideas essential? Why is it likely that beginning student teachers would need to hear these ideas?

4. If you were asked to nominate colleagues or former teachers as experts for an expert–novice study, what aspects of their professional accomplishments would you consider? Why?

5. If you could interview a truly expert teacher, what would you want to know? Why?

6. In most expert–novice studies, researchers describe the thinking of expert and novice teachers. How might the findings of these studies differ if experts and novices told their own stories?

Allan C. Ornstein

Allan Ornstein feels he is entitled to another biography since he has written two chapters for the book. As the editor, he will have it his way—and also interview himself.

Ornstein grew up on the beaches of Arverne, a tiny town of 3,000 on the Rockaway (NY) peninsula. He attended P.S. 42, Far Rockaway High School, and the City College of New York—which was then tuition-free. "I still recall when some 25,000 to 30,000 students boycotted classes for two or three days because the bursar's fees tripled from $5.00 to $15.00. We saw the beginning of the end of free higher education in New York. Eventually, many years later, we were proven right."

Between 1962 and 1970, Ornstein received two masters and a doctorate from Brooklyn College and New York University, worked five of those years as an inner-city teacher in the Bedford Stuyvesant area of Brooklyn, and then as a full-time instructor at New York University and Fordham University. "Those were the days when deans were deans: Dan Griffin was at N.Y.U. and Harry Rivlin was at Fordham. They were great education leaders."

I recall too: "I lived in a two-room flat over a butcher shop on Henry Street in Brooklyn Heights, and then in a fourth-floor walk-up on Sheridan Square, in the Village, while attending N.Y.U. Off-Broadway plays were free and Pizanno wine cost $2.50 per gallon. Wednesday nights were spent at Fridays, on the East side, and the summers were spent on the beaches of Long Island, particularly Amaganset, New York, and Nantucket, Massachusetts, or on the highways and byways of the U.S.A., the Caribbean, and Europe. Those were the days, until about 1965, when you could have lunch in a local tavern in Berlin for 50 cents—a beer with bratwurst—or a five-course dinner with a bottle of red cabernet on the side streets of Belgrade or Prague for one American dollar." To appreciate those prices, you have to remember the world when there was no plastic money.

Since 1971, Ornstein has been at Loyola University of Chicago. He is a former Fulbright Hayes Scholar, and subsequent member of the screening committee for the Fulbright Hayes Scholarship Awards. His best-known book, *Foundations of Education*, was originally published in 1976 and is about to appear in its sixth edition. He hopes to revise it until 2006, and then retire his pencil which still makes the point in an age of computers. "I guess some people would say I'm a dinosaur."

Although he no longer spends time on the local beaches, because there are no waves to surf in the midwest, he still frequents Europe and the Caribbean on a regular basis, now with his wife and three children. Although the four of them are not impressed by his surfing prowess today, and sometimes refer to him as "Al . . . Bundy," they admire his uncanny ability to navigate the winding streets of Paris, Rome, and Vienna—without maps or the ability to pronounce street names. How does he do it? He attributes it to his younger days in Manhattan and current Gingko pills. (At least two pill people—Giroux and Rosenshine—should partially know what he is talking about.)

16 ❧

Beyond Effective Teaching

Allan C. Ornstein

For more than the last fifty years, the method of conducting research on teaching involved an attempt to systematize it into discrete categories such as teacher styles, behaviors, characteristics, competencies, methods, and so on, and to measure it with teacher observations, rating scales, questionnaires, checklists, and/or personality inventories. About twenty years ago the method was slightly modified: The categories were converted into *processes*, and correlated with student performance or outcomes on standardized tests, and referred to as *products* (Ornstein, 1990, 1994). Thus evolved the notion of "process-product" research.

Although teaching was described as a complex act, influenced by subtle human conditions and swift teacher-student interactions, it was assumed that the skilled researcher could capture and analyze the teaching act, and deal with numerous variables and variations through selected sampling, large numbers of subjects, tests of statistical significance, and the power of data replication. What emerged was a professional literature that had meaning to those who had been enculturated into the community of researchers with their own discourse and methods of translating and evaluating the information. Practitioners were basically shut out of the discussion, since they lacked the specialized research skills and esoteric knowledge needed to participate in the discussion.

The results of the studies, and the discussions that followed, often focused on isolated teacher behaviors, methods, and so on, sometimes written in the form of recommendations or rules for teachers to follow. However, there was little regard to what the behaviors or methods meant in relation to the realities of the classroom or to what had transpired in the classroom prior to the observation(s) of the teacher's behaviors (processes) or to the measured results (products). Research on teaching was often atomized into tiny behaviors, methods, and so on, while ignoring the whole picture; that is, larger patterns or relationships of teaching and learning. Therefore, a teacher could be judged "good" or "effective," depending on the instrument or checklist, by "coming to class on time," "writing clear objectives on the blackboard," "monitoring seatwork," or "reviewing homework"—while not teaching students how to think or problem solve, and not being fair minded or even emotionally balanced.

A teacher adept in behaviorist tasks or comfortable teaching facts and low-level skills tended to be favored by the evaluation instruments, since the instruments usually focused on small segments of observable or measurable behaviors, and the tests that measured student outcomes were knowledge-based items. A teacher who stressed abstract or divergent thinking, humanistic or moral practices, was discriminated against (and still is) since these were hard-to-measure processes and were therefore ignored by most evaluation instruments.

A NEW PARADIGM ABOUT TEACHING

Beginning in the 1980s, and unfolding dramatically in the 1990s, the research on teaching has been moving away from the *quantitative* and empirical format, with prescriptive methods and designs and "objective" findings. No longer are we dealing with prediction and control, large samples, group-based statistical analysis, hypothesis testing, and generalizable data. We now have a new paradigm, what proponents and critics alike call *qualitative* or ethnographic research. This new research design is based on field-based methods—conversations, interviews, and case studies of one, two, or a few subjects—usually written in narrative or story form. According to Peshkin (1993), one of the proponents, the new research deals with *descriptions* of people and situations, *explanations* of knowledge and behavior, *interpretations* of theories and assumptions, and *evaluations* of practices and policies.

The new paradigm is highly descriptive and expressive in language, what ethnographers call "thick descriptions." Instead of dealing with statistically based categories, clinically based descriptions, and verifiable data, we have narratives and portrayals that are highly personal and morally persuasive. The tendency is to associate individual stories of teachers with social or educational reform, and to write with a purpose—to challenge readers to rethink their notions of teaching (and schooling). To a large extent, the new research on teaching is highly political and embedded with messages about power, justice, and inequality. A good deal of the information and results cannot be replicated because they are based on storytelling; in fact, much of the data are suspect because of the small number of subjects and the fact that there are few checks for controlling the storytellers' social lens.

In the past, there has been strong reluctance on the part of the research community to engage in this type of narrative inquiry, since this was considered unscholarly and even dysfunctional for career advancement at the university level. Telling stories about people, in our case about teachers and students, has not been the kind of research activity considered appropriate for social scientists; rather more appropriate for journalists and the lay public (Barone, 1992; Sizer, 1968). Since the rise of the American university, accompanied by social science paradigms (as illustrated in the early days by the works of Charles Darwin, G. Stanley

Hall, and William James), academia has coated its publications with professional jargon and technical meaning to separate itself from the lay public and nonacademic audience.

Storytelling, descriptive prose, and/or narrative inquiry were labeled as popular writing for a lay or mass audience—and dismissed as nonscientific and lacking in methodological rigor. Even textbook writing has been dismissed as second-rate, since it is written in the common idiom for large numbers of students to understand, and because it reports or analyzes knowledge but does not advance it.

Now, storytelling is considered an acceptable form of research, perhaps even cutting edge by advocates of the new paradigm. The traditional language for presenting findings was based on a prescriptive, nonemotional format, translated into a technical and specialized knowledge, and written for the benefit of a few other researchers; however, the language of the new paradigm is rich in the vernacular and common idiom. It is highly vicarious, in some cases packed with empathy and emotions, and is to be shared with a larger audience—including students (studying to be teachers) and practitioners (those already teaching), as well as researchers.

The new research is written at a level that empowers anyone who can read the *New York Daily News* or *Chicago Tribune*. It is not meant to scare away people who lack professional knowledge and theoretical insights; rather it is meant to describe in dramatic and convincing ways what teachers do and to permit the reader to experience events in the lives of the people (usually teachers) being described.

The new research, based on storytelling and narrative inquiry, has grown into a cottage industry, with its own premises and principles about teaching, and its own brand of "metatalk" or jargon and methodology. Today, it dominates space in the prestigious educational journals and sessions at educational research meetings. To a large extent, it has replaced traditional research on teaching, what most of us in the field refer to as process-product research, under the guise that the old methods of inquiry were too linear, restricting, and mechanistic (Cziko, 1992; Pinar, 1992); male dominated (Carter, 1993; Grumet, 1988); remote from and irrelevant for teachers (Elbaz, 1991; Kagan, 1992); and used by administrators and policy makers (largely male) to control teachers (largely female) by denying the latter the right to speak for and about themselves (Doyle, 1992; Fish, 1990).

The new paradigm, in theory, provides for collaboration between researchers and practitioners. It is considered by humanistic educators to enrich the discourse of what teaching is all about because it examines the personal and social aspects of teaching. It is viewed by feminist educators as a means for undercutting the dominant position of male researchers by deemphasizing mathematical and symbolic skills (a male form of knowing) and elevating verbal skills and literary prose (in which females have usually excelled). It is viewed by the political left, sometimes referred to as "neo-Marxists," "critical pedagogists," "reconstructionists," and "constructivists," as a means of reducing the influence of traditional researchers who they often label "technocratic," overly rational or behaviorist, and politically biased or conservative. It is viewed by practitioners in general as a means for exposing the rhetoric of theoretical posturing, or at least reversing some of the previous silence teachers have had to endure because they were unable to understand the research and theoretical aspects of teaching.

Whether storytelling is more than rhetoric or folklore, whether it is more than surface descriptions of teaching activities, or whether it leads to any worthwhile generalizations or significance beyond the writer's portrayal is unclear. Nonetheless, it provides an opportunity for a new group of educators to introduce their own beliefs and strategies for purposes of constructing what they call "emancipatory knowledge," "critical inquiry," and "narrative modes of knowing" (simply put, new understanding and explanations) of the teaching-learning process, redesigning the power relations and discourse among teachers and students, and reforming teacher education.

Teaching is now seen as a "narrative in action," that is, an expression of personal "biography and history" (Connelly & Clandinin, 1990), whereby research and practice of teaching are integrated through stories. The new emphasis on teaching goes beyond what the teacher is doing and explores teacher thinking from the perspective of teachers and how teachers come to know their pedagogy. The teacher is depicted as one who copes with a complex classroom environment and simplifies it, mainly through experience, by attending to a small number of important tasks. The teacher is also viewed on a highly personal basis, sometimes as an expert and even in heroic ways. Experienced and expert teachers are considered to have knowledge of underlying principles, of knowing what they know, and their knowledge is considered crucial in defining how teachers come to know what they know and for constructing meaning for novice teachers. Teachers are viewed as having craft knowledge, and in cooperation with researchers who portray their stories, teachers are able to convey this knowledge about teaching to others in a helpful way.

The new research on teaching relies on language and dialogue, and not mathematical or statistical analysis, to provide the conceptual categories and to organize the data. It uses the approaches that journalists, reconceptualists, and critical pedagogists have advocated—metaphors, stories, biographies and autobiographies, conversations (with experts), exemplars, reflections, interviews, case studies, and voices (or narratives). It is research that has surfaced within the last ten years or so and looks at teaching "from the inside"; the personal and practical knowledge of teachers, the culture of teaching, and the language and thoughts of teachers.

Metaphors

Teachers' knowledge, and the way they speak about teaching, does not exist only in prepositional form, but also includes figurative language or metaphors. Teachers' thinking consists of personal experiences, images, and jargon, and therefore, figurative language is central to the expression and understanding of the teachers' knowledge of pedagogy.

Metaphors of space and time figure in the teachers' descriptions of their work (such as "pacing a lesson," "covering the content," "moving on to the next part of the lesson") (Clark, 1991; Munby, 1986). The studies on teacher style represent concepts and beliefs about teachers that can be considered as metaphors: the teacher as a "boss," "coach," "comedian," or "maverick." The notion of a "master" teacher, "lead" teacher, "star" teacher, "expert" teacher, and so on, are also metaphors, or descriptors, used by current researchers to describe outstanding or effective teachers.

Metaphors serve to organize a person's thinking by helping to describe, categorize, and conceptualize his or her knowledge and experiences. According to Kliebard (1982), language is the basis of metaphors and it is used to process thought, by which people make the complex and puzzling become more familiar and more readily understood.

In discussing metaphors, we are speaking of verbal concepts and abstractions. Most people use metaphors in everyday speech, without calling them or thinking about them as metaphors; they are merely called expressions, idioms, sayings, even slang. The various models and systems in this text that describe teaching and learning are verbal in nature, and to a large extent incorporate various metaphors. Teachers, also, rely on metaphors in their classrooms for transmitting learning experiences to students, and for describing their own teaching. Researchers constantly use metaphors, even though they often think they rely on and use mathematical models. The notions of teacher effectiveness, process-product research, special content knowledge, pedagogical knowledge or pedagogy, deep knowledge or thick knowledge, and critical thinking, are metaphors that help us conceptualize and uniquely describe our professional landscape (another metaphor).

In the final analysis, you might argue that all thought processes include metaphors; that is they act as templates or concepts that reflect how we conceive the world. When you or someone else describes your personally held system of beliefs and values, the words will have different meanings to different people, and idiosyncratic and figurative speech will be used to generate some of the descriptions. For those words or ideas that are not well specified, it will be the task of the researcher or narrator to assist the reader or other teachers to move from implicit language and private belief systems to explicit descriptions and agreed-upon cognitive frames of reference.

Stories

Increasingly, researchers are telling stories about teachers—their work and how they teach—and teachers are telling stories about their own teaching experiences. Most stories are narrative and descriptive in nature; they are rich and voluminous in language, and those about teachers make a point about teaching that would otherwise be difficult to convey with traditional research methods. The stories told reflect the belief that there is much to learn from "authentic" teachers who tell their stories about experiences we usually keep to ourselves or convey to others (Elbaz, 1991).

Stories told by teachers to researchers are considered more reliable and accurate, and tend to be codified and ordered into some form or pattern. These stories, however, tend to be modified or altered in character, stripped of some of the original meaning and vitality. Stories of teachers by teachers are suspect in terms of reliability and accuracy, for these stories tend to be autobiographical, self-serving, and grounded in ego.

Whether the stories are authored by researchers or teachers, they give an account of a place and action within the context of the person's individual history and that of a setting which is played out. Stories have an important social or psychological aspect as they evolve. Stories of teachers allow us to see connections between the practice of teaching and the human side of teaching; the stories of individual teachers allow us to see their knowledge and skills enacted in the real world of classrooms and appreciate their emotional and moral encounters with the lives of the people they teach.

Stories of teachers by teachers such as Bel Kaufman, Herbert Kohl, Johnathan Kozol, and Sylvia Ashton-Warner have become bestsellers because of their rich descriptions, personal narratives, and the way they describe the very stuff of teaching. These stories are aesthetic and emotional landscapes of teaching and learning that would be missed by clinically based process-product research studies of teacher effectiveness. Whether you wish to believe that the accounts of their own teaching and the work of other teachers are true descriptors, is another issue for researchers.

Stories of teachers by researchers are less descriptive, less emotional, and lesser known. Nevertheless, they are still personal and rich encounters of teachers, and they provide us with teachers' knowledge and experiences not quite on their own terms, but in an in-depth way of getting to know what teaching is all about. These stories provide unusual opportunities to get to know teachers as persons—and to respect them or fall in love with them—in a textual sense, of course. Most important, these stories represent an important shift in the way researchers are willing to convey teachers' pedagogy and understanding of teaching. Here, L. Schulman's (1991) point is worth noting: Observers and authors construct different realities so that different storytellers could write very different versions of the same teacher. Not only is the author a variable, but also differences in time, subject matter, students, and situation could lead sometimes to a striking contrast in portrayal and interpretation of the same teacher.

Biographies and Autobiographies

Stories written by researchers about teachers tend to be biographical, and stories written by teachers about themselves tend to be autobiographical. Both biography and autobiography encompass a "whole story" and represent the full depth and breadth of a person's experiences, as opposed to commentary or fragments. Unity and wholeness are found as a person brings past experience to make present action meaningful, and to better understand these experiences in terms of what a person has undergone (Barone, 1992; Butt & Raymond, 1987).

The essence of an autobiography is that it provides an opportunity for teachers to convey what they know and have been doing for years; what is inside their heads and unshaped by others. Whereas the biography is ultimately filtered and interpreted by a second party, the autobiography permits the author, in this case the teacher, to purport the information in his or her own way and on his or her own terms.

As human beings, we all have stories to tell; each person has a distinctive biography or autobiography in which is shaped a host of experiences and practices, and a particular standpoint or way of looking at the world. For teachers, this suggests a particular set of teaching experiences and practices, as well as a particular style of teaching and pedagogy.

Biographies and autobiographies of teachers may be described as the life story of one teacher who is the central character to a particular classroom or school—and of the classroom dynamics and school drama that unfolds. These types of stories are concerned with longitudinal aspects of personal and professional experiences that can bring much detailed and insightful information to the reader. They help us reconstruct teachers' and students' experiences that would not be available to us by reading typical professional literature on teaching (Grant, 1991; Solas, 1992).

Both biographies and autobiographies develop in a linear sequence, usually in temporal or chronological order: They are retrospective and deal with the life of the person. The accounts in biographies and autobiographies suggest that the author is in a position of "authority" with respect to the particular segment of the life being described; thus the thoughts and experiences of the author take on a sense of reality and objectivity not always assumed in other stories (Elbaz, 1991; Wood, 1992). But, when teachers write an autobiography about their own accounts in story form, as opposed to someone else writing the biography, they run the risk of being considered partial or writing slanted descriptions of their teaching prowess.

Thus Grumet (1987) suggests that researchers publish multiple accounts of teachers' knowledge and pedagogy, instead of a single narrative. The problem is, however, that this approach has a double edge: It suggests taking stories out of the hands of teachers. Joint publications between teachers and researchers, appropriate in some situations, are still another method for resolving this problem.

Perhaps the best example of this approach was executed by Smith (1968), a professor and psychologist, who studied the classroom of Geoffrey, a pseudonym for the teacher whose classroom was the center of the research. Although conducted more than twenty years ago, the idea of giving credit to the teacher/subject, even recognizing him as a co-author, still remains highly unusual today, even among so-called liberal, contemporary, or ethnographic researchers. Geoffrey never received full recognition, however, because his name was masked under the guise of anonymity. Although this remains the norm today, the question is: Should teachers be reduced to anonymity or pseudonymity; or even worse excluded from authorship?

The Expert Teacher

The term *expert* and the image of the expert teacher is now being applied to the current debate over teacher effectiveness. The concept involves new research procedures—such as simulations, videotapes, and case studies—and a flattering new language to describe the work of teachers and new prestige and authority for teachers (Welker, 1992). The research usually consists of small samples and in-depth studies (for example, complete lessons and analysis of what transpired), whereby expert (sometimes experienced) teachers are distinguished from novice (sometimes beginning) teachers. Experts are usually identified through administrator nominations, student achievement scores, or teacher awards (for example, Teacher of the Year). Novices are usually selected from groups of student teachers or first-year teachers.

Dreyfus and Dreyfus (1986) compare novices to experts across fields of study. The novice is inflexible and follows principles and procedures the way he or she has learned. The expert recognizes patterns and relationships and has a holistic understanding of the processes involved; he or she has the big picture in mind and responds effortlessly and fluidly in various situations. This view of the expert, as it relates to teachers, is depicted by Cushing, Sabers, and Berliner (1992), who point out that "expert teachers make classroom management and instruction look easy"; yet we know that teaching is a complex act, requiring the teacher "to do many things at the same time." Teaching consists of hundreds of interactions per hour, and the teachers' ability to control these interactions and maintain order and instructional flow "is testimony to their level of expertise" (p. 109).

Data derived from recent studies suggest that expert and novice teachers teach, as well as perceive and analyze information about teaching, in different ways. Whereas experts are able to explain and interpret classroom events on a macro level, novices provide detailed descriptions of what they did or saw, and refrain from making interpretations. Experts recall or see multiple interactions, and explain interactions in terms of prior information and events, whereas novices recall specific facts about students or what happened in the classroom. Novices provide literal and concrete descriptions of what occurred; they tend to report in step-by-step terms, like a radio announcer.

What experts (or experienced teachers) say or do about teaching is now considered important for building a science of teaching. The data derived from experts is rich in conversational and qualitative information, but limited in statistical analysis and quantifiable information. Studies of expert (experienced) teachers and novice (beginning) teachers show they differ in many specific areas of teaching and instruction.

1. *Experts tend to analyze student cues in terms of instruction, whereas novices analyze them in terms of classroom management.* Experts assess student responses in terms of monitoring student learning, providing feedback or assistance, and ways in which instruction can be improved. Novices fear loss of control in the classroom, to the extent that when they have

an opportunity to reassess their teaching on videotape, they focus on cues they missed that deal with students' inattentiveness or misbehavior. Although negative student cues appear to be of equal importance to experts and novices, positive cues figure more frequently in the discussion of expert teachers (Clark & Peterson, 1986; Kagan & Tippins, 1991a, 1991b).

2. *Experts make the classroom their own, often changing the instructional focus and methods of the previous teacher.* Novices tend to follow the previous teachers' footsteps, or are inclined to listen to experienced colleagues tell them how to teach. Experts talk about starting over and breaking old routines; they tell us about how to get students going and how to determine where the students are in terms of understanding content. Novices tend to begin where the previous teacher left off; they have trouble assessing where the students are, what their capabilities are, and how and where they are going (Cushing, Sabers, & Berliner, 1992; Livingston & Borko, 1989).

3. *Experts engage in a good deal of intuitive and improvisational teaching.* They begin with a simple plan or outline and fill in the details as the teaching-learning process unfolds, and as they respond to students. Novices spend much more time planning, stay glued to the content, and are less inclined to deviate or respond to students' needs or interests while the lesson is in progress (Sabers et al., 1991; Westerman, 1991).

4. *Experts continuously mediate between the objects of the lesson and the students' perceived understanding of the lesson.* Experts make more adjustments or alterations, what are termed "responsible elaborations," as they clarify and scaffold students' understanding of the content. Both experts and novices consider the students' preexisting knowledge about a topic, and that this provides a natural starting place for teaching. But experts are more inclined to and capable of correcting students' misconceptions so that they do not distort new learning (Borko & Livingston, 1989; Leinhardt, 1992).

5. *Experts seem to have a clear understanding of the types of students they are teaching and how to teach them.* In a sense, they seem to "know" their students before they meet with them. Novices do not have a well-developed idea of the students they are teaching. Whereas novices have trouble beginning the new term, experts routinely find out just what it is the students already know and proceed accordingly (Calderhead, 1992; Carter, 1990).

6. *Expert teachers are less egocentric and more confident about their teaching.* Novices pay more attention to themselves, worrying about their effectiveness as teachers and about potential discipline problems. Experts are willing to reflect on what they were doing, admit what they did wrong, and comment about changes they would make. Novices rarely alter their initial evaluations of what happened. Although they recognize mistakes

and contradictions in their teaching, they are defensive about their mistakes and seem to have many self-concerns and doubts about where and how to improve (Kagan & Tippins, 1991; Wildman et al., 1990, 1992).

The attempt to better understand teaching by comparing experts and novices is dominated by educational psychologists. It is based on knowledge stemming from theory, reflection, and experience. Proponents would probably call this "technical knowledge," similar to the information that experts in other fields possess and which separates them from the public. Critics would probably label this new information by expert teachers as nothing more than "folklore"—quaint, sentimental, and interesting—not scientific and with little chance for replicable and predictable results.

Exemplars

An exemplar is not merely an expert; he or she also exhibits a moral dimension that is vital for teaching students. When we look at our popular culture, there is widespread consensus that exemplar teachers have moral and ethical fiber. For example, in movies such as *To Sir with Love, Stand and Deliver*, and *The Karate Kid*, the virtues and methods portrayed are not so much those of pedagogical or technical expertise, as those of humanistic and moral references and beliefs.

Failure to consider this moral component in our teacher-effectiveness research and teacher-preparation programs suggests an inadequacy in our thinking and beliefs. We need only to remember that our great teachers of the past—Moses, Jesus, and Confucius—and our great teachers of the twentieth century—Mohandas Gandhi and Martin Luther King, Jr.—combined the pursuit of truth, kindness, and caring attitudes with their teaching.

These are the same virtues that many educators would argue today represent the real fiber of teaching. Because these traits are not easy to observe or measure, we tend to overlook them in our research paradigms. Humanistic and existentialist educators (Beane, 1990; Strike & Soltis, 1992; Zehm & Kottler, 1993), however, know that those who claim to be exemplars, or even "good" or "effective" teachers, must show not only pedagogical expertise but also moral expertise.

Exemplars are those whom other teachers may model in their teaching. Rather than zeroing in on their knowledge or pedagogy, we need to pay closer attention to their attitudes and feelings: what they do in the way of supporting and caring for their students, in the way they reach out and teach their students, how they build trust and mutual respect, how they engage and encourage their students to grow and become their best possible selves. In this connection, teaching is no longer confined to a set of goals, or only to some content and skills; rather it incorporates values and virtues that are somewhat oblique and hard to explain.

You may or may not agree: An expert teacher is a technocrat in terms of knowledge and pedagogy and exhibits excellent performance in the classroom; an exemplar teacher has a humanistic/moral framework that guides his or her teaching. Exemplar teachers seriously consider the meaning of their students' lives, as well as their social and psychological development. These teachers understand the need for caring and supporting behaviors.

A truly exemplary model of teaching would attempt to establish what Noddings (1984, 1992) calls a "caring" community, which she asserts coincides with a woman's natural and innate impulse to care for the young and coincides with the feelings of maternalism—which in turn gives rise to her self-esteem and acceptance in society. She contends that women usually build upon this basic feeling, whereas men often turn away from caring and view relationships in more intellectual and abstract terms. Noddings goes one step further and maintains that a feminine morality of caring is also linked to good taste, good manners, and refraining from harmful acts because they do not want to hurt their neighbors and because they want their respect.

Although it is politically incorrect to criticize or challenge feminist educators, Noddings' view of life is simplistic, and it is difficult to believe that such ways of knowing and acting cannot be found in the male's world. Not only does it suggest that only females can be moral mentors, but also that once we view the world in terms of gender we establish a mindset that closes our world in a set of blinders and biases—similar to the way people may perceive racial differences in simple dichotomies. How one respects and cares for others is not a sexual perspective, but probably more closely linked to prior experiences and a stage of development in a person's life that reflects self-assurance, self-actualization, and emotional maturity.

Of course, personal beliefs and values determine what people regard as exemplary, or even expertise. Practices or behaviors regarded as exemplary (or expertise) from one perspective or person may not be regarded as exemplary from another. This is keenly illustrated in the author's analysis of exemplary teachers in humanistic and moral terms; a different author might construct a different version of exemplary. Thus, researchers need to be clear on how they define exemplary, even expertise, and who they consider to exhibit these behaviors. Good teaching is not easily defined, even with all its scientific procedures and quantifiable data, so why should fuzzy metaphors such as exemplary teachers and expert or novice teachers be easier? These terms are packed with descriptive language and images that lead to striking portraits and interpretations.

Reflection

The term *reflection* refers to written or spoken comments that teachers make when recalling their thoughts while teaching or analyzing the performance of others. Reflective practices vary from reviewing or observing simple teacher behavior and pedagogy to complex aspects of teaching and learning.

One of the more sophisticated tools for analyzing teachers' reflective thoughts was developed by Ross (1989), who contends that reflection becomes increasingly complex depending on the individual's maturity and perception of safety in expressing one's views. The levels of complexity represent three levels: (1) describing a teacher's practice with little detailed analysis and little insight into the reasons behind teacher or student behaviors; (2) providing a cogent critique of a practice from one perspective but failing to consider multiple factors; and (3) analyzing teaching and learning from multiple perspectives and recognizing that teachers' actions have a pervasive impact beyond the moment of instruction.

In the later stages, you come to realize that behaviors (and feelings) are contextually based, and rather than dealing in absolutes or so-called objectivity you begin to deal in relative truths and points of view. In the third stage, you are open to more change and willing to admit that you don't always know the answer. However, the third stage suggests considerable experience and maturity; here, the inference is that beginning teachers operate at the lower levels of reflection, and therefore, are more closed minded and unwilling to accept other viewpoints about their teaching. This is only an educated guess, yet it does conform to research data that suggest that less than 25 percent of preservice teachers function above level 2 and only for particular topics (Ross, 1989).

Because of their inability to reflect upon and analyze their own classroom mistakes, many potentially talented teachers feel like failures and lose confidence in their abilities. Through "trial and error" some survive; however, more than 50 percent of beginning teachers leave the profession entirely within five years (Colbert & Wolff, 1992; Odell & Ferrano, 1992). More advanced levels of reflection among beginning teachers might be helpful for reducing teacher turnover.

It is through reflection that teachers focus on their concerns, come to better understand their own teacher behavior, and help themselves or colleagues improve as teachers. Through reflective practices, or forums, people learn to listen carefully to each other, and teachers are able to provide insight into their own work. By reflecting on their practices or what they do in the classroom, and the basis for it, teachers provide insights for researchers. The researcher is in the position to take the teachers' implicit knowledge and particular point of view and translate it into explicit knowledge and integrate it with other viewpoints.

Through reflection by teachers, followed by probing and further examining of specific teaching situations, a language of practice can emerge that allows us to better understand how teachers cope and deal with the complexity of their work. Here the key is to make sense of what teachers have to say, to clarify and elaborate on particular scripts or situations, and to delineate what meaning these reflections have for them and other professionals (Lasley, 1992; Yinger & Hendricks-Lee, 1992).

One might argue that too much emphasis is put on technical knowledge and skills in teacher preparation programs, which leaves beginning teachers poorly prepared to think about, make adjustments, and execute practice effectively. The novice teacher may be equipped with a host of theoretical and practical insights into teaching, but this knowledge is generic and does not apply to specific situations. The teacher must learn to reflect while teaching, what Schon (1983, 1991) called "reflection in action," to understand and think about events and phenomena as they unfold in the classroom. Teacher knowledge, what some of us call "pedagogy," no matter how sound or scientific, is specialized and context based. Therefore, the hunches, judgments, and behaviors of teachers must be continuously modified, as events evolve, through reflection.

How we reflect, in the final analysis, is based on how we perceive the world and how we construct knowledge and give meaning to events. This in turn is based on our professional knowledge base, prior experiences, and personal and social values. But the script or equation can go on and on: In order to reflect, we need to *care* about our students, we have to be *motivated* to teach, *flexible* to see the world in the eyes of others, *socially responsible* in our actions, and *conscious* of what we are doing. The list is endless, but when it comes down to it, it is humanistic or philosophical traits that count, not mathematical models or clinical descriptions. Reflection is a matter of listening to others, recounting experiences and events, dialoguing with others, and respecting other perspectives that differ from ours.

Interviews

Interviews have been used for many years to help participants recall or examine their thoughts and feelings about a host of topics. In eliciting a teacher's personal or practical knowledge through interviews, patterns of teacher thinking can emerge.

To explore in depth the meaning by which teachers acquire, develop, or use their expertise about teaching and learning, open-ended discussions can reveal more elaborate information and richer information than closed-ended questions. The assumption is that interviews permit teachers to draw on a variety of sources of knowledge, to deal with their teaching decisions, to clarify what they know, and to translate their "practical" knowledge into "professional" knowledge.

Prior to the researcher's intervention, the teacher's personally held systems of principles and values of teaching are typically not well specified or clear. The central task of the interviewer is to help the teacher move from implicitly held and private belief systems to explicit descriptions and to organize a frame of reference that can be used by other teachers.

Although interviews have contributed much to understanding teacher thinking and knowledge, they are not without problems. First, they are predicated on the assumption that teachers can articulate their otherwise tacit knowledge; second, interviews assume that what people say accurately represents their thought processes or what they actually do in practice; next, they presuppose that all participants in the interview process share the same vocabulary and perceptions; fourth, they fail to account for the difference between teachers who are often focused on immediate concerns and practical issues, and researchers who are more concerned with general concepts and theoretical issues (Solas, 1992).

Case Studies

Case studies originated at the Harvard Law School at the turn of the century, and were subsequently adopted by the Harvard Business School. The object was to present real-life situations, accompanied by relevant facts, and to generalize particular decisions into broad understanding during class discussions (Merseth, 1991). Drawing its inspiration from these two schools, the Harvard Graduate

School of Education adopted the case method approach to train teachers and administrators in the 1970s.

Although criticized by some for its lack of academic rigor and simplistic and sketchy situations, the case method has expanded to teacher preparation institutions with a "practical" or qualitative research orientation. Whereas in the past, case studies were written by textbook authors or professors who developed their own cases for class, today they are being told by teachers, in the role of "teacher-author," and developed in collaboration with researchers.

Many critics maintain that teachers cannot act as authors by themselves, and that they lack the theoretical background to write complex narratives to be used by other teachers. But they can express themselves in writing through several drafts with the help of professors or researchers who are actively involved in publishing teacher education materials. According to J. Schulman (1991, 1992), with teacher-researcher collaboration, the case study can become a compelling narrative and vivid tool for the individual teacher-author to reflect upon and to inform other teachers.

The worth of the case method is that it focuses on teaching problems and dilemmas that teachers face in the classroom. It is a narrative written by a teacher about a particular incident or event, including background details, feelings among people (teachers and/or students), and personal relationships. Careful analysis of cases among participants makes them aware of various meanings and interpretations of situations. Through discussion and reflection, they come to know their own personal biases and values, and learn to face themselves and how they can improve their own pedagogy through broad understanding of the principles and problems of teaching.

The case method provides the opportunity for teachers to "reframe" their thinking, that is a process described by Schon (1991) in which the practitioner comes to a new understanding in terms of practice or professional development. It also provides the opportunity for teachers to participate as members of a research team, to express their own thoughts and experiences, and to reject the traditional approach to teacher education that associates professional knowledge (specialized content and pedagogy) with only theoreticians, textbooks, and lectures. Based on the assumptions that storytelling is part of the human experience, and that there is much to be learned from stories, case studies today give the individual telling the story, as well as those listening to and discussing it, new insights and a chance to change their own practice.

THEORY INTO PRACTICE

The notion of *voice* sums up what I have been trying to convey about the aforementioned quantitative and linguistic tools for describing what teachers do, how they do it, and what they think when they are teaching. Voice corresponds with such terms as the "teacher's perspective," "teacher's frame of reference," or "getting into the teacher's head." It also infers teacher empowerment and the idea of teachers collaborating with researchers as equals in teacher effectiveness research and teacher preparation programs. The idea should be considered against the backdrop of previous teacher silence and impotence in deciding on issues and practices that affect their lives as teachers. As Elbaz (1991) asserts, the fact that researchers are now willing to give credibility to teachers' knowledge, teachers' practices, and teachers' experiences helps readdress an imbalance which in the past gave little recognition to teachers. The idea, now, is that teachers have a right and role to speak for teachers and about teaching.

Although there are some serious attempts to include teachers' voices, the key question is to what extent do these new methods permit the "authentic" expression of teachers to influence the field of teacher behavior research and teacher preparation programs. In the past, it has been difficult for teachers to establish a voice, especially a voice that commanded respect and authority, in the professional literature. The reason is simple: The researchers and theoreticians have dominated the field of inquiry and decided on what should be published. The invisible university, comprised of professional associations, informal professional networks, and professorial-editorial friendships, has also shut out teachers from print and power.

With the exception of autobiographies and stories written by teachers, teachers' voices are still filtered through the researchers' writings and publications. Thus, even today, most teachers' voices are co-opted and cannibalized by others, and thus their voices are altered or diffused. Although the language of research and the notion of voice treat teacher thinking and teacher experiences on the teachers' terms, and permit them to view themselves and their colleagues in the way they wish, we still have not recognized the importance of their role or input in determining the science of teaching.

For decades, as far as I can remember when I first began teaching some 30 years ago, teachers' experiences and wisdom, sometimes conveyed in the form of advice or recommendations, were written off as nothing more than "cookbook recipes" or a list of "do's and don'ts"—irrelevant to the world of research and theory of teaching. Now, under umbrella terms such as *teacher thinking*, *teacher processes*, *teacher knowledge*, *teacher practices*, and *practical knowledge*, it has become acceptable, even fashionable, to take what teachers have to say and adapt it and turn it into *professional knowledge*, *pedagogical knowledge*, or *teacher cognition*.

It is nice to know that some researchers are now collaborating with practitioners, and taking what teachers say as serious, but we are still not giving credit where credit is due: where researchers and practitioners are co-equals and where practitioners have real names and are accepted on similar terms with researchers as part of a research team or teacher training program. Here I am talking about a sense of community—of working together and sharing credit.

If one picks up the latest books on teaching, there is an emphasis on teachers' voices and such terms as *teachers' lives*, *teachers' visions*, and *teachers' realities* are used in the titles of these books—all in the name of creating a knowledge base from the perspective of teachers. The emphasis is on what and how teachers teach, the effect teaching has on teachers, and how teachers' experiences and thoughts influence the teachers' sense of self. The teacher is now seen as a person, not a statistic or factoid, as with prior research. The teacher has a voice and an important message to convey. He or she is not just one of 100 or more subjects—manipulated or controlled to produce a significant finding for some researcher who gets most, if not all, the credit. Instead of generalizing from large numbers of teachers, we have detailed analysis of a few teachers: narratives of teachers, by teachers, and for teachers.

Throughout the new paradigm on teaching the centrality and wisdom of the teacher is reaffirmed, which is welcomed and proper. But it would be more appropriate when practitioners get full credit as collaborators or co-authors—not referred to as "Nancy" or "Linda," as in one well-known recent case, or as "Stacey," "Sharon," and "Susan" in still another case, and so on. These are real people who should not be reduced to false names or obscurity. They need to be heard as real people with real and full names. The culture of teachers and professors as well as schools and universities should be close enough to bridge these differences.

SUMMARY

No research paradigm has an exclusive patent on how to generate knowledge. There are no be end-end all procedures or basis for saying "this is the appropriate way." Traditional research, with its emphasis on quantitative designs and methods, has dominated the scientific and theoretical framework in education and especially research on teaching. But many interesting and provocative publications are evolving from the qualitative approach, including a broader framework about teacher research that includes storytelling and narrative inquiry.

Although the new paradigm can be criticized for its research softness and political agenda, it represents new ideas and ways of presenting knowledge about teaching. It senses our prior difficulty in communicating with teachers, as well as their subsidiary role in research. Now the practitioner's role is enlarged to "teacher-author" and "expert" who interacts and collaborates with researchers. Rather than being mystified or disenfranchised by research jargon and methodology, teachers are now able to express their views in their own language and on their own terms and share their own knowledge and wisdom with others.

Alternative approaches for reporting, interpreting, and reinterpreting knowledge about teaching are used, such as dialogue and conversations, biographies and autobiographies, tapes, interviews, and case studies. The knowledge and thinking of teachers with a range of expertise are organized in narrative structures that teachers can fully understand, appreciate, and integrate into their professional experiences.

References

Barone, T. E. (1992). "A Narrative of Enhanced Professionalism." *Educational Researcher* 21: 15–24.

Beane, K. D. (1990). *The Task of Post-Contemporary Education.* New York: Teachers College Press, Columbia University.

Borko, H., and C. Livingston (1989). "Cognition and Improvisation: Differences in Mathematics Instruction by Expert and Novice Teachers." *American Educational Research Journal* 26: 473–498.

Butt, R., and D. Raymond (1987). "Arguments for

Using Qualitative Approaches in Understanding Teacher Thinking: The Case for Biography." *Journal of Curriculum Theorizing* 9: 62–93.

Calderhead, J. (1992). "The Nature and Growth of Knowledge in Student Teaching." *Teaching and Teacher Education* 4: 531–535.

Carter, K. (1990). "Teachers' Knowledge and Learning to Teach," in W. R. Houston, ed., *Handbook of Research on Teacher Education*. New York: Macmillan, pp. 291–310.

Carter, K. (1993). "The Place of Story in the Study of Teaching and Teacher Education." *Educational Researcher* 22: 5–12.

Clark, C. (1991). "Real Lessons from Imaginary Teachers." *Journal of Curriculum Studies* 23: 429–434.

Clark, C. M., and P. L. Peterson (1986). "Teachers' Thought Processes," in M. C. Wittrock, ed., *Handbook of Research on Teaching*, 3rd ed. New York: Macmillan, pp. 255–296.

Colbert, J. A., and D. E. Wolff (1992). "Surviving in Urban Schools." *Journal of Teacher Education* 43: 193–199.

Connelly, M., and J. Clandinin (1990). "Stories of Experience and Narrative Inquiry." *Educational Researcher* 19: 2–14.

Cushing, K. S., D. S. Sabers, and D. C. Berliner (1992). "Investigations of Expertise in Teaching." *Educational Horizons* 70: 108–114.

Cziko, G. A. (1992). "Perceptual Control Theory." *Educational Researcher* 21: 25–27.

Doyle, W. (1992). "Curriculum and Pedagogy," in P. Jackson, ed., *Handbook of Research on Curriculum*. New York: Macmillan, pp. 1–24.

Dreyfus, H. L., and S. E. Dreyfus (1986). *Mind over Machine*. New York: The Free Press.

Elbaz, F. (1991). "Research on Teachers' Knowledge: The Evolution of Discourse." *Journal of Curriculum Studies* 23: 1–19.

Fish, S. (1990). "Rhetoric," in F. Lentriccia and T. McLaughlin, eds., *Critical Terms for Literary Study*. Chicago: University of Chicago Press, pp. 203–222.

Grant, G. E. (1991). "Ways of Constructing Classroom Meaning." *Journal of Curriculum Studies* 23: 397–408.

Grumet, M. R. (1987). "The Politics of Personal Knowledge." *Curriculum Inquiry* 17: 319–329.

Grumet, M. (1988). *Bitter Milk: Women and Teaching*. Amherst, MA: University of Massachusetts Press.

Kagan, D. M. (1992). "Professional Growth among Preservice and Beginning Teachers." *Review of Educational Research* 62: 129–170.

Kagan, D. M., and D. J. Tippins (1991a). "Helping Student Teachers Attend to Student Cues." *Elementary School Journal* 91: 343–356.

Kagan, D. M., and D. J. Tippins (1991b). "How Teachers' Classroom Cases Express Their Pedagogical Beliefs." *Journal of Teacher Education* 42: 281–291.

Kliebard, H. M. (1982). "Curriculum Theory as a Metaphor." *Theory into Practice* 21: 11–17.

Lasley, T. J. (1992). "Promoting Teacher Reflection." *Journal of Staff Development* 13: 24–29.

Leinhardt, G. (1992). "What Research Tells Us about Teaching." *Educational Leadership* 49: 20–25.

Livingston, C., and H. Borko (1989). "Expert-novice Differences in Teaching." *Journal of Teacher Education* 39: 36–42.

Merseth, K. K. (1991). "The Early History of Case-based Instruction." *Journal of Teacher Education* 42: 243–249.

Munby, H. (1986). "A Qualitative Approach to the Study of Teachers' Beliefs." *Journal of Curriculum Studies* 18: 197–209.

Noddings, N. (1984). *Caring: A Feminist Approach to Ethics and Moral Education*. Berkeley: University of California Press.

Noddings, N. (1992). *The Challenge to Care in Schools*. New York: Teachers College Press, Columbia University.

Odell, S. J., and D. P. Ferrano (1992). "Teacher Mentoring and Teacher Retention." *Journal of Teacher Education* 43: 200–204.

Ornstein, A. C. (1990). "A Look at Teacher Effectiveness Research." *NASSP Bulletin* 74: 78–88.

Ornstein, A. C. (1991). "Teacher Effectiveness Research: Theoretical Considerations," in H. C. Waxman and H. J. Walberg, eds., *Effective Teaching: Current Research*. Berkeley, CA: McCutchan, pp. 63–80.

Peshkin, A. (1993). "The Goodness of Qualitative Research." *Educational Researcher* 21: 23–29.

Pinar, W. F. (1992). "Dreamt into Existence by Others." *Theory into Practice* 31: 228–235.

Ross, D. (1989). "First Steps in Developing a Reflective Approach." *Journal of Teacher Education* 40: 22–30.

Sabers, D. S., K. S. Cushing, and D. C. Berliner (1991). "Differences among Teachers in a Task Characterized by Simultanity, Multidimensionality, and Immediacy." *American Educational Research Journal* 28: 63–88.

Schon, D. A. (1983). *The Reflective Practitioner: How Professionals Think in Action.* New York: Basic Books.

Schon, D. A. (1991). *The Reflective Turn: Case Studies in and on Educational Practice.* New York: Teachers College Press, Columbia University.

Schulman, J. H. (1991). "Revealing the Mysteries of Teacher-written Cases." *Journal of Teacher Education* 42: 250–262.

Schulman, J. H. (1992). *Case Methods in Teacher Education.* New York: Teachers College Press, Columbia University.

Schulman, L. S. (1991). "Ways of Seeing, Ways of Knowing." *Journal of Curriculum Studies* 23: 393–395.

Sizer, J. (1988). "Daliness." *Educational Research* 17: 5.

Smith, L., and W. Geoffrey (1968). *Complexities of an Urban Classroom.* New York: Holt, Rinehart and Winston.

Solas, J. (1992). "Investigating Teacher and Student Thinking about the Process of Teaching and Learning Using Autobiography and Repertory Grid." *Review of Educational Research* 62: 205–225.

Strike, K. A., and J. F. Soltis (1992). *The Ethics of Teaching.* New York: Teachers College Press, Columbia University.

Welker, R. (1992). "Reversing the Claim of Professional Status." *Educational Horizons* 70: 115–119.

Westerman, D. A. (1991). "Expert and Novice Teacher Decision Making." *Journal of Teacher Education* 42: 292–305.

Wildman, T. M., et al. (1990). "Promoting Reflective Practice Among Beginning and Experienced Teachers," in R. T. Clift, W. R. Houston, and M. C. Pugach, eds., *Encouraging Reflective Practice in Education.* New York: Teachers College Press, Columbia University, pp. 139–162.

Wildman, T. M., et al. (1992). "Teacher Mentoring: An Analysis of Roles, Activities, and Conditions." *Journal of Teacher Education* 43: 205–213.

Wood, D. R. (1992). "Teaching Narratives: A Source for Faculty Development and Evaluation." *Harvard Educational Review* 62: 535–550.

Yinger, R. J., and M. S. Hendricks-Lee (1992). "A Pattern of Language for Teacher Education." *Journal of Teacher Education* 43: 367–375.

Zehm, S. J., and J. A. Kottler (1993). *On Being a Teacher: The Human Dimension.* New York: Teachers College Press, Columbia University.

Discussion Questions

1. How would you define worthwhile research on teaching?

2. Which type of research, quantitative or qualitative, is best for reaching generalizations about teaching? For generating theories about teaching?

3. In your view, what is the most acceptable format and language for presenting findings about teaching?

4. For those who prefer traditional research designs, why do the research designs of narrative inquiry suggest softness and fuzziness?

5. For those who prefer storytelling as a means of knowing, why do large-group based and hypothesis-driven research seem restrictive and atomistic?

6. If storytelling is based on language, which in turn is open to multiple meanings and interpretations, then how do we reach conclusions or generalizations about the people or events being discussed?

Robert E. Stake and Linda Mabry

Robert E. Stake

Linda Mabry

Robert E. Stake is professor of education and director of the Center for Instructional Research and Curriculum Evaluation at the University of Illinois, Champaign. This center is widely recognized in educational circles as a site for innovative designing of program evaluation and is widely visited by practitioners across the country. The author of five books on research and evaluation, Bob has directed several nationwide evaluative studies including science and mathematics in U.S. schools, art teaching in U.S. schools, teaching and sex equity, teaching the deaf, environmental education, and education for gifted students.

Bob is the leading proponent of what is called "naturalistic responsive" or "client-centered" evaluation, where inquiry is focused on problems of the clients or professionals in a particular program context. His techniques of research include ethnography, case studies, and investigative reporting, as well as traditional psychometric data gathering of testing, surveying, and attitude scaling.

Stake has been teaching and conducting research for thirty-five years. He received his Ph.D. in psychology at Princeton University in 1958. He has taught summers at the University of Connecticut, Harvard University, and the University of British Columbia, and he was a Fulbright Fellow in Sweden in 1973 and in Brazil in 1984. He takes pride in noting that he has held the highest office of two divisions of the American Educational Research Association: Division B, Curriculum and Objectives, and Division D, Testing and Research Design.

Bob enjoys keeping in contact with his former students, many of whom have become prominent in testing and curriculum analysis. He once expressed his view of epistemology like this:

> When any one person discovers something, billions of people become ignorant of one more thing.
>
> Each of us learners is a mouse gnawing at an exploding castle.
>
> Grading someone down for not understanding "a body of knowledge" is like faulting the mouse for not gnawing the entire castle.

Linda Mabry is assistant professor of educational psychology at Indiana University, a graduate of the University of Illinois, and former Spencer fellow. She conducts qualitative research and program evaluations, often regarding arts education innovative methods of student assessment. Subjects of this work have included the R.O.P.E. assessment program at Walden III High School in Racine, Wisconsin; Art Resources in Teaching (A.R.T.) in Chicago; and several arts education sites for a National Center for Arts Education Research study reported in *Custom and Cherishing: The Arts in Elementary Schools* co-authored with her mentor Bob Stake and Liora Bresler (Council for Research in Music Education, 1991).

An arts enthusiast, Mabry frequents dance, theater, and music performances, foreign films, museums, and folk and popular arts events. She enjoys literature, travel, and the outdoors.

Mabry taught in elementary schools, grades 3 to 8, for several years in Texas and Illinois and also served as director of religious education for a private school. She believes that much of the criticism of teachers is scapegoating, which, she says, "fails to recognize the difficulties of their milieu and their often laudable efforts and commitments." She continues, "I hope my research and that of others can be attuned to important issues and phenomena that promote understanding by the public of the realities of school." Mabry's concept of an ideal teacher is one who combines good content and methodology with respect and concern for students. She claims to be fortunate to have had several teachers herself who have fit this ideal.

17 ❧

Case Study for a Deep Understanding of Teaching

Robert E. Stake and Linda Mabry

Understanding is not only a matter of formal theories; it is also a matter of particulars: the details of instances and situations, the sequences and patterns of specific happenings (Polya, 1954; Campbell, 1966; Spiro, Vispoel, Schmitz, Samarapungavan, & Boerger, 1987). Do we come to an adequate understanding of teaching by forming theories of teaching and by observing teaching casually? We think not. This chapter advocates that what is to be known is partially found in the deliberate study of individual teachers—not only as exemplars, as types, as instances of some subclass of all teachers but as unique, nongeneralizable human beings. In this chapter, we will discuss some characteristics of *intrinsic* case study (Stake, 1994) to indicate a seldom apparent compatibility of uniqueness and generalization.

> Marilynn teaches history in a suburban high school; could have been Head of the Social Studies Department two years ago, had she campaigned for it. She has been nominated for Teacher of the Year. She prides herself on sticking to the syllabus, that is, the syllabus as she has modified it, and continues gradually to modify it, over the years. She drives half an hour to and from work each day with three other teachers, all female, all her age. Marilynn would have quit teaching in a minute, she confides, if the family had had any other way to make ends meet. (Stake, unpublished)

The less we know about Marilynn, the easier it is to pigeon-hole her. As we examine the things that get her nominated for honors, we discover a certain wavering between determination and inspiration. As we scrutinize her refusal to support trial of an innovative curriculum, we find her easily able to recognize and verbalize the importance of intellectual discipline for her students. The more we know, the more we realize Marilynn is not so easy to categorize. Under certain trying circumstances, she shows signs of burn-out but not under others. At what point do we stop learning about teachers in general and learn only about this one teacher? Or with every idiosyncratic nuance, do we move toward an understanding of teaching?

THEORIES AND PRACTICAL KNOWLEDGE

We know what we know about teaching much as we know anything of life. We know it partly through personal histories of being taught, partly through our experiences of teaching, and partly through the reports of others and our observations of them (Polanyi, 1958). We aggregate cases according to some intuitive sampling plan, some weighting system, and tease out what is common, deviant, typical, and archetypal. Often we find some bottom line, some moral of the story. We trust certain sources over others. Our cautiousness and our intellectual discipline cause us to scratch for countervailing evidence, to find the limits of the rule. But we are swayed by the telling anecdote, especially the one that casts our contentions in a favorable light. All too little of what we know is the product of formal reasoning or the gathering of best evidence. We pay attention to compelling moments, yet we attain deep and sophisticated pictures of what teaching is.

Even in our most professional moments, our style of learning is experiential. We are not indifferent to research literature, to allusions to teachers in the media, or to portrayals of teachers in staff development sessions. But we relate most formalisms about teaching back to our own experience. Such reliance on experience is neither all good nor all bad. It is the best intellectual system we have for understanding many things. It gives us grounds for examining extremely complex phenomena. But it closes our minds to some data and some interpretations. We should be more open. Still, we should put our talent for experiential learning to the best use we can.

The naturalistic case study researcher engages in research efforts that consciously promote experiential learning (Lincoln & Guba, 1978; Eisner, 1991; Feagin, Orum, & Sjoberg, 1991). Reports are designed for accessibility to many audiences, not just the research community. Teachers, administrators, and policy makers are invited to make practical use of the understandings to be drawn. A special strength of case study research is its amity with the world of schools (Simons, 1980).

VICARIOUS EXPERIENTIAL KNOWING

Naturalistic case studies provide experiential accounts of teachers, often in ordinary circumstances. With effective description of persons, places, and events, the researcher provides a vicarious experience that readers can attach to other knowledge about teachers and teaching (Glesne & Peshkin, 1992). If the new knowledge is persuasive, the old is mended, revised, or, on some occasions, thrown out. Theorists, researchers, teacher educators, and teachers—we all come to know in this way.

Most ballads, folk stories, and fables could be efficiently summed up in a moral or message. Ethnographic studies could be reduced to abstracts or findings.

But vicarious experience is telling, and so we tell it. Vignettes sink into our consciousness at a level deeper than linguistic coding. Scenes and nuances become background, prior knowledge, against which future perceptions will be framed. In the following reportorial narrative, for example, Tracy Kidder (1989) imparts a wrenching separation when a difficult child is reassigned to a behavior disorder classroom.

> The day was almost over. Felipe finished up the card. "Goodbye, Clarence. Good luck, Clarence," it read. It was elegantly lettered. "I could've made a better one if I had more time," Felipe said.
>
> Clarence grinned. He was washing the boards, his back to the class. Children gathered around Felipe's desk and signed their names.
>
> Robert, keeping to his own desk, piped up, "I ain't signin' it. I hate Clarence."
>
> Chris [the teacher] wheeled on him. "Robert, things that we do to others come back to hurt us twice as bad."
>
> Robert wore a faint grin.
>
> "Think about it." Her voice was low and fierce. "That's not a very generous or nice thing to do, and I'm extremely disappointed in you." . . . She glanced at Clarence, who was still washing the boards. She looked at the children signing the card. She grabbed her pocketbook and rummaged through her change purse. She grabbed the tape dispenser. Inserting herself into the crowd around Felipe's desk, Chris hurriedly taped seven quarters to the card, the children murmuring, "Ooooo." It was a bribe of sorts. She wanted to make sure that Clarence would accept the card . . .
>
> Felipe handed Clarence the card. Clarence studied it, standing over near the front table.
>
> From near her desk, Chris called, "Good luck, Clarence. We'll all miss you." She wasn't saying goodbye . . .
>
> Alice, in purple coat and beret, rubbed Clarence's back hard. "Bye, Clarence."
>
> Clarence put down the card and scowled. He shoved it across the front table, rejecting it. He went back to washing the boards. But he started grinning again as the bus students trooped past him, sweet female voices saying, "Bye, Clarence."
>
> Little Arnie said, in a voice too squeaky for the manly words, "So long, old buddy."
>
> Then only the walkers remained. They loitered around the front table. Clarence examined the card again . . .
>
> Judith, detaching herself slightly from the throng, said, "A dollar seventy-five."
>
> Clarence put the card in his pocket . . .
>
> "Mrs. Zajac. Mrs. Zajac," said Clarence.
>
> "What, Clarence?"
>
> "Arshhht."
>
> She laughed.
>
> "I got her," said Clarence to Jimmy . . .
>
> Julio said, "If you see my cousin up there, tell him he's a wimp."
>
> "Yes, Clarence. You have a real nice time. Okay? And you be a good boy there?" Chris grabbed him from behind, in a gentle head lock, and moved him around in front of her. In her faintly mocking voice, which made the children giggle, Clarence grinning in her embrace and looking off to one side, she went on, "Like I know you can be? And work real hard, like I know you can do?" She gave him one more squeeze— "And have fun?"—and let him go. (pp. 190–192)

TENSION BETWEEN CASE AND ISSUE

In a case study, the case is the sharp focus of attention. That is what defines it as a case study, the study of a case. People sometimes study cases because they care deeply about those cases, for example, the estranged Nicole, described by Linda Mabry in *Learning to Fail* (1991), or Mr. Goeffrey's urban classroom studied by Louis Smith and his student, the teacher (Smith & Goeffrey, 1969). When the primary purpose is to understand that particular case, we have called the study an *intrinsic case study.*

People often do case studies, formally or informally, to illustrate an idea or an issue. Wanting to elaborate on styles of teaching such as those described by Myron Lieberman (1956), Ann Lieberman (1986), and many others, they may, for example, portray a teacher as the epitome of pedanticism. Their interest in the teacher more or less starts and stops with the illustration; their interest is in the syndrome or prototype. Fellini so illustrated teachers several times in his film *Satyricon.* There, the case is instrumental to the issue; it enhances issue development. We have called these studies *instrumental case studies* (Stake, 1994).

We find it important to differentiate between the *intrinsic* and the *instrumental* because we find a figure-ground relationship between cases and issues. Both cannot be primary in a study. If the case is primary, the issues are secondary, examined because they serve the effort to understand the case. And if the issues are primary, the complexity of the case will be less fully explored. There is a tension, sometimes outright conflict, between the two. Keeping the intrinsic-instrumental difference in mind helps us to deal with the tension. Notice the dialectic relationship between issue and case in the following fictional account.

> "I am summoned to see the headmistress at morning break on Monday," said Miss Brodie. "I have no doubt Miss Mackay wishes to question my methods of instruction. It has happened before. It will happen again. Meanwhile, I follow my principles of education and give of my best in my prime. The word 'education' comes from the root *e* from *ex*, out, and *duco*, I lead. It means a leading out. To me education is a leading out of what is already there in the pupil's soul. To Miss Mackay it is a putting in of something that is not there, and that is not what I call education. I call it intrusion, from the Latin root prefix *in* meaning in and the stem *trudo*, I thrust. Miss Mackay's method is to thrust a lot of information into the pupil's head; mine is a leading out of knowledge, and this is true education as is proved by the root meaning. Now Miss Mackay has accused me of putting ideas into my girls' heads, but in fact that is *her* practice and mine is quite the opposite. Never let it be said that I put ideas into your heads. What is the meaning of education, Sandy?"
>
> "To lead out," said Sandy, who was composing a formal invitation to Alan Breck, a year and a day after their breath-taking flight through the heather. . . .
>
> "That is a Citroen," said Rose Stanley about a motor car that had passed by. "They are French."
>
> "Sandy, dear, don't rush. Take my hand," said Miss Brodie. "Rose, your mind is full of motor cars. There is nothing wrong with motor cars, of course, but there are higher things. I'm sure Sandy's mind is not on motor cars, she is paying attention to my conversation like a well-mannered girl." . . .

Miss Brodie said, "So I intend to point out to Miss Mackay that there is a radical difference in our principles of education. Radical is a word pertaining to roots—Latin *radix,* a root. We differ at root, the headmistress and I, upon the question of whether we are employed to educate the minds of girls or to intrude upon them. We have had this argument before, but Miss Mackay is not, I must say, an outstanding logician. A logician is one skilled in logic. Logic is the art of reasoning. What is logic, Rose?" (Spark, 1962, pp. 54–56)

Jean Brodie is the author's *case,* with special but not primary attention to her independence and ego-crafted pedagogy. The issue in the excerpt is the attachment and detachment of teacher and acolytes. The more that author Muriel Spark develops the issue, the less sharp can be our understanding of the whole of Jean Brodie's life, of course, including that beyond the world of her pupils. And the more Spark helps us understand the fully-rounded complexity of the heroine, the less we understand her engagement with Sandy and Rose and the other "Brodie girls."

In the research literature of education, we find too few intrinsic case studies of teachers. By postponing, or even foregoing, issues, the intrinsic case study gives the reader time for deeper understanding of an instance of teaching. Detailed accounts of teachers, including most of those we present in this chapter, are instrumental. Issues dominate. The research question organizes the study, not the characters. In literature, also, theme and story overshadow much of what could be known about particular teaching (Smith, 1994). Readers would not enjoy accounts of teaching presented without story and theme, but we are persuaded there are too few diversions, tangents, subplots—fuller accounts of teaching to deepen the understanding of the particular teacher and teaching in general.

MULTIPLE REALITIES

We shape understandings with our perceptions of reality. Our realities as well as our understandings are transient and inconsistent. It is useful to try to merge our experience into a common and reliable reality, but it is also useful to hang onto disparate perceptions, some of which open windows to deeper realization. Note the depth of understanding of an Atlanta principal's leadership to be gained from Sara Lawrence Lightfoot's (1981) offering of more than one viewpoint.

Despite the grim statistics and relentless poverty that appear unchanged in the [George Washington] Carver [High School] community, the high school has undergone a major transformation in the last four years [1977–1981]. Everyone speaks of the time before and after the arrival of Dr. Hogans [principal]. Norris Hogans, a dark-skinned black man in his late forties, has been the catalyst of change. A former football player, Hogans is powerful in stature and character. He dominates the school. . . .

Everyone agrees Hogans is powerful. Some view his power as the positive charisma and dynamic force required to turn an institution around and move it in a new direction. These enthusiasts recognize his abrupt, sometimes offensive style, but claim that his determined temperament is necessary to move things forward. They willingly submit to his autocratic decisions because they view his institutional goals as worthy and laudable. His detractors, on the other hand, tend to keep their complaints to themselves, forming a covert gossip ring, and passively resisting his attempts to make changes by preserving their own inertia. Many of these resistant faculty have been at Carver for twenty-five or thirty years and are threatened by the changes that Hogans has forced on them. They were used to an administrative policy that permitted more faculty autonomy. Some claim that these old-guard faculty were used to "sitting on their butts and not doing anything, . . . and Hogans makes them clean up their act." Although there must be a variety of responses to his leadership, Hogans seems to be a person that people feel strongly about one way or the other. He is despised or revered. (p. 20)

Our spotlights are trained on experience more than on objectivity or reliability. We casually mix what has been, what it seems has been, and what it seems could be, not because reality is without virtue but because reality has no common dominion in all minds. We seek what is experienced. In this advocacy, the two of us are making little distinction between fiction and fact. There is a difference, of course, but both serve our plea. Fiction is appealing to people not only because it goes beyond their experience but because it insinuates their experience. In D. H. Lawrence's (1989) *The Rainbow*, a beginning teacher idealistically confronts the bitterness of established colleagues. Such conflicting views are common for teachers, but the content of each succeeding conflict holds the promise of a new interpretive twist of reality.

> "If I were you, Miss Brangwen," [Mr Brunt] said, menacingly, "I should get a bit tighter hand over my class."
> Ursula shrank.
> "Would you?" she asked, sweetly, yet in terror. "Aren't I strict enough?"
> "Because!" he repeated, taking no notice of her, "they'll get you down if you don't tackle 'em pretty quick. They'll pull you down, and worry you, till [Mr] Harby gets you shifted—that's how it'll be. You won't be here another six weeks"—and he filled his mouth with food—"if you don't tackle 'em quick."
> "Oh but—" Ursula said, resentfully, ruefully. The terror was deep in her.
> "Harby'll not help you. This is what he'll do—he'll let you go on, getting worse and worse, till either you clear out or he clears you out. It doesn't matter to me, except that you'll leave a class behind you as I hope *I* shan't have to cope with."
> She heard the accusation in the man's voice, and felt condemned. But still, school had not yet become a definite reality to her. She was shirking against it. It was reality, but it was all outside her. And she fought against Mr Brunt's representation. (pp. 352–353)

CONTEXTUAL DETERMINATION

A teacher makes a point memorable with a joke in one class; in the next, the same joke falls flat. Why? A creationist teaches evolution. Why? Teachers at one school are encouraged to have students write for their portfolios, while those at another are encouraged to teach punctuation as it will be tested on standardized instruments. Why?

From multiple realities, classrooms emerge as contexts for complex social interactions. The multifaceted uniqueness of each child, the diversity among students, and the intricacies of each group's particular dynamics profoundly mark teaching. This complexity is intensified by the contexts in which classrooms are located—cultural, organizational, curricular, legal, professional, policy, and collegial. Inevitably, contexts shape and are shaped by teacher perceptions and behaviors.

Case study researchers recognize context as crucial to understanding teaching, crucial to understanding each teacher. Contexts not only extend the background but alter the meanings of teaching. Context teaches the deeper nature of teaching, making comprehensible, for example, from Susan Dichter (1989), the decision of a dedicated veteran to leave his profession.

> Truman High [in the Bronx, New York] began amidst great fanfare, and its teachers were all enthusiastic. . . . For Manuel Montalvo, who is Puerto Rican, the racially mixed school was a chance to give something back to his own neighborhood. He regarded the school with great hope and eagerly joined its staff.
>
> At Truman he helped create a new language program. . . . But, Montalvo said, the new program failed. The pressures from without—drug pushers who walked into the school to conduct business, violence that led Montalvo to carry a bat and patrol the basement, racial strife and community power struggles—were part of the reason.
>
> Another reason was that few people within the system backed Montalvo up. His school life was a bizarre rerun of an old fairy tale, "The Emperor's New Clothes." Though there was no thread on the loom, his school bragged of its new clothes—its better scores, lower truancy rates, and new programs.
>
> None was real. Better scores meant lower standards, and the truant rate only appeared to go down: attendance at homeroom was made a condition of graduation and that is when the school counted heads.
>
> Montalvo called it "passing off paper plates as Lenox china." He fought it as long as he could, and last fall, after 26 years as a teacher, he decided he could not continue the charade any longer and he left the classroom. (pp. 39–40)
>
> "I wanted to give the best education I could—not to be involved in social work. . . . It is better to stay away than make a promise I cannot keep. . . . The school implies that there is a referral system that works. It does not." (pp. 46–47)
>
> "Administration blames teachers for their students' lack of achievement. But I can give you all the books and all the papers and all the notes in the world, and if you don't study them, you go no place. . . . In desperation, education [has adopted] an 'I tried' attitude." (p. 43)
>
> "The public is being lulled into a complacency with these pronouncements that everything is going to be all right—you know, don't worry, it's *mandated.*" (p. 47)
>
> "The school reflects society. It reflects it so painfully that your hands are tied." (pp. 42–43)

Cliché, perhaps, but much about teaching cannot be understood out of context.

CONFIDENCE THROUGH TRIANGULATION

The case study researcher, as all researchers, establishes a confidence in the accuracy of observations and the trustworthiness of interpretations. Qualitative researchers follow a program of triangulation. As described in Norman Denzin's

The Research Act (1989), the researcher employs a number of tactics to confirm data and to reduce irrelevant bias and interpretation: tactics such as repeated observations, multiple observers and vantage points, multiple methods, and interpretation of events from alternative theoretical positions. The researcher deliberately challenges her own emergent findings, pursues rival explanations, and reinforces conclusions about what is learned.

The reader too wants confidence; often he or she wants to be privy to analysis and interpretation processes. Most naturalistic case study researchers provide extended descriptions, a body of relatively incontestable data, and a patterned account of durable and clear meanings. Not incidentally, readers are invited to generate their own interpretations and implications. The researcher acts as an agent of the reader, supporting alternative interpretations by offering data in detail—data that contradict as well as data that support the researcher's conclusions.

In the following excerpt, David Hansen (1993) describes Ms Walsh, an experienced high school English teacher. His issue is the relationship between her style and her values. Note Hansen's service to reader confidence through repetitive patterning of her teaching.

> In her Public Speaking class, she reins in a suddenly rambunctious debate by raising her voice: "Please! You're upperclassmen! I *like* upperclassmen! Please prove me right that upperclassmen are mature!"
>
> She enacts a personalized touch again when she goes from group to group in a class she has divided into foursomes to prepare for a whole-group discussion. Placing her hand on the back of a chair and leaning over a group, she asks "Do you need me? Are you okay?" And to another she asks: "You know what you're doing? Do I need to worry? Because I *do* worry."
>
> She prepares a class for her absence the next day by saying to them: "You don't really need a substitute, you can do the practicing [of speeches] yourselves. But I will be *crushed* if I hear any bad reports about you!"
>
> Ms Walsh enunciates these and many similar comments in a tone of voice tinged with urgency and emotion. She conveys the idea that she is personally concerned both with her students' work and with their conduct. Her remarks often seem to have the force of what Austin (1962) called "performatives," that is, expressions which influence the structure and content of social relations. (A classic example of a performative is the minister's statement, "I now pronounce you man and wife," which unites two persons who seconds before were unrelated formally.) Ms Walsh's exclamations help shape social life in her classroom. They help bring into being an environment in which she and her students share a personal relationship that forms a basis for obligations and responsibilities. (p. 403)

DETAIL AND DISTINCTION

In Hansen's continuing description, Ms Walsh can be stereotyped as compulsive, authoritarian, and ritualistic. But with layers of descriptive detail, the patterns become complex and the ease of pigeon-holing is lost. Her teaching becomes deeply understood as repetitive detail is added. The image is splintered and reassembled as additional data are provided. So the reader is invited to confidence, and doubts, just as with acquaintances in real life.

Details consume precious attention, time, and space. Our patience often demands abstracts and executive summaries and bottom lines. But understanding suffers when we succumb to compaction. For the constructivist researcher and reader, knowledge is not a construction of central details, but a pastiche of intricate experiences (Schwandt, 1994).

Tessellations of detail portray Ms Walsh as a distinct individual. They do the same for a classroom, where patterns of interactions woven over time create shared histories easily misinterpreted in synopsis. In our minds, these layers become interwoven among the other things we know, complementing, clarifying, and expanding.

GENERALIZATIONS

Oddly, simultaneous with the portrayal of uniqueness comes enhancement of generalization. Fitted in among our previous understandings, what we learn from case studies helps us apprehend phenomena we continue to confront. Our understandings emerge gradually from particular cases understood in detail through personal and vicarious experience.

Deep understandings gained from personal and vicarious experience present a caution for case study researchers. Researchers are pressed to distill conclusions from observations, interviews, and review of documents. The case study researcher dares not offer broad generalizations about teaching on the basis of a case study or two, and he or she cannot enter prior personal experience into formal records. Rather, a case study researcher can assist readers to generalize for themselves, to use gleanings from that reporting to appreciate other cases of personal or professional interest. Researchers' promotion of generalizations made by readers is the essence of *naturalistic generalization*, a form of individually generated implications for which case study research is ideally suited (Stake & Trumbull, 1982). Naturalistic case studies of teaching help the reader toward a deeper understanding of the teaching he or she encounters by adding to the reader's store of knowledge, and by adding to his or her experiential and interpretive base.

THEORY INTO PRACTICE

Case study research corresponds to a theory of knowledge which holds that human action is based less on formal or propositional knowledge and more on tacit or experiential knowledge. According to this view, people respond to deep, personal, unstated understandings. Research can enhance this deep understanding by providing accounts of complex phenomena that offer vicarious experience, detailed and holistic. Such accounts add to or refine readers' interpretive backgrounds, enhancing their capacity to make the generalizations that matter ultimately: those which inform current and future practice.

Deep understanding is the link between case study and practice. Practical decisions and actions are based on deep understandings that can be informed by case study research. In offering accessible, holistic accounts filled with vicarious experience in detail, in consciously promoting readers' generalizations, perhaps in addition to those of the researcher, case study is unrivaled by other research methods. This methodology does not direct practice but empowers educators to develop approaches responsive to their unique situations.

SUMMARY

We have returned to our opening oxymoron: the generalizable particularity of case studies. Our aim is a deeper understanding of teaching. Research on teaching is often too quick to analyze, hypothesize, or generalize. The profession also needs studies that dwell upon the particular, that ponder the uniqueness of the situation, and that stay focused on the individual case until there is little more to be learned. What remains is a comprehensive, comprehensible picture. There are no mirror images; still, each case reminds us of others. We think some more; we resume our generalizing, drawing conclusions slightly different from those based on the previous teaching we have known.

Education-based, naturalistically studied cases of teaching, including some we have excerpted, help us build personal knowledge from which we may sense and interpret classrooms generally. We have advocated the detailing of unique cases in context, believing that understanding grows from acquaintance with many perspectives of reality, with vicarious experience, and with repetitive patterns. Pointing out the special accessibility of case studies for natural ways of knowing and for practical use, we have urged readers as well as researchers to take confidence in triangulated evidence. In this chapter, we have shared our thoughts about theory as a competitor for attention. Theories help us organize our thinking, yet often draw us away from a deeper understanding of the particular.

References

Austin, J. L. (1962). *How to Do Things with Words.* Oxford, England: Clarendon Press.

Campbell, D. (1966). "Pattern Matching as an Essential in Distal Knowing," in K. R. Hammond, ed., *The Psychology of Egon Brunswik.* New York: Holt, Rinehart and Winston.

Denzin, N. (1989).*The Research Act.* Englewood Cliffs, NJ: Prentice Hall.

Dichter, S. (1989). *Teachers: Straight Talk from the Trenches.* Los Angeles: Lowell House.

Eisner, E. (1991). *The Enlightened Eye.* New York: Macmillan.

Feagin, J. R., A. M. Orum, and G. Sjoberg, eds. (1991). *A Case for the Case Study.* Chapel Hill: University of North Carolina Press.

Glesne, C., and A. Peshkin (1992). *Becoming Qualitative Researchers.* New York: Longman.

Hansen, D. T. (1993). "The Moral Importance of the Teacher's Style." *Journal of Curriculum Studies* 25: 397–421.

Kidder, T. (1989). *Among Schoolchildren.* Boston: Houghton Mifflin.

Lawrence, D. H. (1989). *The Rainbow* (Cambridge ed.). Cambridge, England: Cambridge University Press.

Lieberman, A. (1986). "Collaborative Work." *Educational Leadership* 43: 4–8.

Lieberman, M. (1956). *Education as a Profession.* Englewood Cliffs, NJ: Prentice Hall.

Lightfoot, S. L. (1981). "Portraits of Exemplary Secondary Schools: George Washington Carver Comprehensive High School."

Daedalus 110: 17–37.

Lincoln, Y., and E. Guba (1978). *Naturalistic Inquiry.* Beverly Hills, CA: Sage.

Mabry, L. (1991). "Nicole, Seeking Attention," in D. Strother, ed., *Learning to Fail: Case Studies of Students at Risk.* Bloomington, IN: Phi Delta Kappa.

Polanyi, M. (1958). *Personal Knowledge.* Chicago: University of Chicago Press.

Polya, G. (1954). *Mathematics and Plausible Reasoning.* Princeton, NJ: Princeton University Press.

Schwandt, T. (1994). "Constructivist, Interpretivist Approaches to Human Inquiry," in N. Denzin and Y. Lincoln, eds., *Handbook of Qualitative Research.* Newbury Park, CA: Sage.

Simons, H., ed. (1980). *Toward a Science of the Singular.* Norwich, England: Center for Applied Research in Education, University of East Anglia.

Smith, L. (1994). "Biographical Method," in N. Denzin and Y. Lincoln, eds., *Handbook of Qualitative Research.* Newbury Park, CA: Sage.

Smith, L., and K. Goeffrey (1969). *Complexities of an Urban Classroom.* New York: Holt, Rinehart and Winston.

Spark, M. (1962). *The Prime of Miss Jean Brodie.* Philadelphia: Lippincott.

Spiro, R., W. Vispoel, J. Schmitz, A. Samarapungavan, and A. E. Boerger (1987). "Knowledge Acquisition for Application: Cognitive Flexibility and Transfer in Complex Content Domains," in B. C. Britton, ed., *Executive Control Processes.* Hillsdale, NJ: Lawrence Erlbaum, pp. 177–199.

Stake, R. (1994). "Case studies," in N. Denzin and Y. Lincoln, eds., *Handbook of Qualitative Research.* Newbury Park, CA: Sage.

Stake, R. E., and D. Trumbull (1982). "Naturalistic Generalizations." *Review Journal of Philosophy and Social Science* 1: 1–12.

Discussion Questions

1. How can case studies help beginning teachers deal with common problems? How can case studies be used to help experienced teachers with their problems?

2. How do case studies provide contextual information about how teachers teach?

3. How much of the researcher's interpretation should be offered to stimulate (withheld to perfect) the reader's opportunity to analyze and generalize?

4. How can we make case studies more accessible to busy practitioners?

5. In what other ways can practitioners be helped in assessing their own weaknesses and strengths?

Thomas J. Lasley and Thomas J. Matczynski

Thomas J. Lasley

Thomas J. Matczynski

Thomas J. Lasley is professor and holder of an endowed chair in teacher education at the University of Dayton. Prior to his university experience, he completed his baccalaureate (1969), master's (1972), and doctoral degrees (1978) at The Ohio State University. He taught at the middle grade level for six years and served for another six years as a consultant and assistant director with the Division of Teacher Education and Certification, Ohio Department of Education. Since 1983, he has been on the faculty of the University of Dayton, and between 1984 and 1990 he was the editor of the prestigious *Journal of Teacher Education.*

Professor Lasley regularly conducts staff development sessions for teachers and administrators throughout the country. He attributes his extensive consultant work to his ability to encourage teachers to think beyond the routine classroom practice and to experiment with new strategies for teaching—strategies that expand their potential and their students' potential. He maintains, "I try to help teachers understand that there are a few new ideas in education, but there are a lot of new approaches to old problems."

Biographies of teachers' lives such as *Escalante* by Barry Matthews and *20 Teachers* by Ken McCrorie are his favorite educational "reads."

Tom is also a member of an all-male book club—where he gets to meet a good many warriors and wanderers—that reads a variety of fiction and nonfiction works. Author of more than fifty articles on teaching and staff development, he has just published a new book through Bergin and Garvey entitled *Teaching Peace: Toward Cultural Selflessness.* When Tom is not reading, teaching, or consulting, he is out on the golf course. He golfs "around 85 and hits the long one—about 250 yards on the average," although he also admits to having "a heck of a hook."

Thomas J. Matczynski is professor of educational administration at the University of Dayton. He completed his bachelor's in 1964 and master's in 1968 at the University of Dayton, and his Ph.D. in curriculum and supervision at Ohio University in 1971. He taught in junior and senior high schools for four years and was a professor at Wright State University and Ohio University, as well as dean of education at Clarion University (PA) for six years, before coming to Dayton in 1987.

Matczynski regularly conducts staff development sessions for teachers and administrators in such areas as organizational change, curriculum design and evaluation, and models of teaching. He travels the same "inservice" road with his co-author, Tom Lasley, and also golfs with him. Matczynski claims to average 82 or 83, but finds the game somewhat frustrating because, as he puts it, "I have trouble breaking 80." Poor Tom!

To alleviate his frustration, however, Matczynski regularly gardens. His favorite perennials are coneflowers, since "their colors are beautiful, they are tall and sleek, and last for more than a month." He also enjoys building homes and says it's "more fun and rewarding than writing educational articles," although he has written some twenty-five articles and text chapters on supervision of instruction, staff development, and curriculum.

18 🪶

Reflective Teaching

Thomas J. Lasley and Thomas J. Matczynski

Reflection is now considered both personally and professionally efficacious. To be reflective about classroom practice, especially among those concerned with teacher development, is viewed as a pedagogical imperative. Good teachers think before they act (reflection-for-action), think while they act (reflection-in-action), and think after they act (reflection-on-action). They embrace what Dewey (1904) referred to as a "habit of reflection."

Enhanced teacher reflection does not engender or even necessarily ensure higher student achievement—the *sine qua non* of education for the past couple decades. Although the two areas are not mutually exclusive, there is no empirical evidence to suggest a direct relationship between teacher reflection and student achievement. Teacher reflection relates more to the quality of a teacher's professional life than to the quantity of student learning. Reflection enables teachers to explore more fully both the routine and complex dimensions of classroom practice. That exploration is the essence of professional practice because it requires that teachers move beyond being ruled by tradition or circumstance.

THE NATURE OF REFLECTION

Although teacher reflection has conceptual and philosophical roots with Dewey (1904, 1933), the popularization can be more directly attributed to Schon (1983, 1987) and van Manen (1977). Donald Schon examined how individuals in different professions (for example, architecture, musical performance, law, medicine) help apprentices acquire reflective capacities. The reflective process for Schon was not a prescribed, rational process; scientific theories do not dictate a professional course of action. Rather, for Schon, reflection entailed cognitive constructions in which one often knows more than one states—it embraces, in Eisner's terms (1985), a combination of connoisseur-like and critic-like qualities. The connoisseur exhibits a capacity for private appreciation; the critic engages in public disclosure and judgment of an artistic form. Reflection requires both appreciation and disclosure of the teaching act.

Van Manen (1977) examined teacher reflectivity and identified three levels of reflective thought. These levels are not mutually exclusive but they do represent a conceptual progression. Although the hierarchical levels require different types of thought, it would be erroneous to consider one level as always more important than another. The importance of each level is dictated by the context and circumstance of the teacher. For example, *Level one* (technical) reflection addresses "effectiveness" questions such as: Are the techniques that a teacher uses effective in achieving specific goals or objectives? The techniques become ends in themselves without asking central questions concerning the purposes of schooling. Level one reflection often results in cosmetic pedagogical changes, which Cuban (1988a) refers to as first-order change—that is, improving the efficacy and effectiveness of what is currently being done, without altering the goals of teacher role performance. Reflection at the first level focuses on the means rather than the ends of schooling.

Level two (interpretive) reflection requires more complex thought. At this level the teacher begins to examine the consequences of personal actions and requires connecting principles and practices. That is, how do organizational structures match with principles of action? Level two reflection requires teachers to think beyond "how?" to "why?": How appropriate are the goals that the teacher has established for the students?

Level three (critical) reflection is the most conceptually and philosophically complex. At this level the teacher reflectively engages the ethical and political issues of teaching. The prominent question is not "how" or "why," but rather "should" a teacher teach in a certain manner? Professional practice is linked with larger social, political, and economic issues. The result of Level 3 reflection is often what Cuban (1988a) refers to as second-order change—altering the fundamental ways in which organizations are put together, including new objectives, structures, roles, and responsibilities. Level 3 focuses on changes that affect the culture and structure of not only the classroom but the school as well.

The reflection that Schon and van Manen refer to requires both *time* and *collaboration*. Reflection is not something that occurs "on the run" or in personal isolation. Reflective practitioners must have time to consider the consequences of professional action and use the ideas of a variety of significant others to determine the implications of personal decisions. Those ideas are shared in a climate that encourages dialogue, questioning, and creativity; teachers are empowered to think *beyond what is* to *what might be.*

Program Orientations toward Reflection

A great deal of the reflectivity literature focuses on how teacher education programs prepare prospective teachers to reflect on classroom practice (Valli, 1992; Bullough, 1989; Roth, 1989; and Gore & Zeichner, 1991). Some preparation programs are organized around reflective themes that encourage preservice teachers to think critically about different dimensions of a teacher's role. The amount of reflection encouraged within a program is often indicative of programmatic structure. Zeichner (1992) describes four program traditions (or implicit structures) within American teacher education—academic (content-oriented), social efficiency (teaching principle-oriented), developmentalist (student-oriented), and social reconstructionist (social structure-oriented). Institutions tend to favor one of these traditions in the preparation of preservice teachers.

The academic tradition, for example, emphasizes content understanding, with a heavy emphasis on different forms of disciplinary knowledge. Shulman (1986, 1987) and others, according to Zeichner (1992), advocate views of "reflective practice which emphasize the teacher's deliberations about subject matter and its transformation to pupils to promote understanding" (p. 163). The preservice teacher, in essence, is expected to learn more than the content of the discipline. He or she must not only think about how knowledge is derived, organized, and warranted, but must also be able to understand the nuances of how knowledge is communicated to students.

Each of Zeichner's traditions has the potential for both reflective or nonreflective embeddedness. It is quite possible for a preservice teacher to complete a preparation program and never critically reflect on the implications of what was learned within the program. A preservice teacher might complete a program embedded in the social efficiency tradition (one that emphasizes a discrete set of teaching principles) and begin practice with a repertoire of pedagogical techniques that putatively represent scientifically derived "right" ways of dealing with classroom curricular and instructional problems. Such an individual would possess the pedagogically correct tools of teaching but would not exhibit an equivalent ability to consider the limitations of when to use those tools. However, at another institution (where a developmentalist perspective is in place) preservice teachers might learn not only the skills of teaching (that is, those grounded in the effective instruction movement), but also acquire an understanding of how their personal intuition, experience, and beliefs should shape classroom practice. Prospective teachers in such programs might learn, for example, when to use direct instruction techniques (in teaching specific content skills), when to favor alternative teaching strategies, and when to abandon "prescribed" strategies because of overarching student needs.

Within social reconstruction programs, reflection is a more endemic part of the preparation structure. Preservice teachers in such programs are encouraged to assume the role of social change agent and to consider ways in which the social organization of schools potentially mitigates the human potential of students. The focus in such programs may be much more oriented toward critical reflection than technical reflection—the former proffers an orientation to social change; the latter focuses more on exhibiting skills that maintain the social system.

Not all teacher education programs automatically foster reflective dispositions at van Manen's technical, interpretive, and critical levels. Some programs espouse sufficiently singular pedagogical understandings that preservice teachers are not encouraged to assume a critically reflective posture relative to what they are learning. While this may be understandable in the early phases of a preparation program, it is less justifiable in advanced levels of preparation when more relativistic processing of information occurs and when the complexity of teaching begins to emerge.

In some cases the propensity toward different types of reflection is dictated by program theme. Programs oriented toward social efficiency may be more inclined toward technical reflection (because they tend to emphasize technical skills); those that emphasize social reconstruction are more prone to foster critical reflection in preservice teachers (because they tend to emphasize social criticism). The disposition to foster different levels of reflection within programs also may be a by-product of the faculty responsible for program design and implementation. Some faculty members may be more disposed to foster or discourage critical reflection based on their personal, psychological archetypes and professional needs (Lasley, 1992; Pearson, 1989). Faculty members who are insecure about personal circumstances or professional knowledge may be less inclined to encourage critical reflectivity among preservice teachers (Lasley, 1992).

Personal Orientations toward Reflection

The actual process of reflection—what it looks like—can be either a rational (developmental) or a nonrational (intuitive) process (Korthagen, 1993). Clearly, the propensity has been to favor rational approaches, partly because such approaches are more measured and scholarly and partly because of practicality. The dichotomy between the rational and nonrational is somewhat analogous to the use of information processing approaches (left brain) as compared to gestalt, intuitive approaches (right brain). The reflection literature favors an analytic, verbal bias, but the actual reflection that occurs is often a function of psychological as well as conceptual realities. Lasley (1992) described how teacher dispositions to reflection may be influenced by psychological archetypes.

Reflective potential is somewhat developmental and emerges as a result of each individual's particular psychological stage of development. Drawing on the work of Pearson (1989), Lasley examined how some personal archetypes foster a disposition toward rational, explicit approaches, while others enable more nonrational, tacit approaches. Such conclusions have implications for designing staff development programs for teachers, especially if one embraces the concept that teachers pass through different stages of professional development and concern in their journeys toward full professional maturity (Fuller & Bown, 1975).

Teachers who engage in rational reflective processes focus on a narrow range of questions that can be logically addressed and sequentially answered as part of a discrete problem-solving process. Practically, this might entail something similar to the University of Maryland's approach to reflection (McCaleb, Borko, and Arends, 1992):

> Operationally . . . [reflection] means (1) taking action (sometimes routine); (2) reflecting (thinking back, analyzing) upon that action (what happened, why, what it meant); if resolution is not reached, moving on to higher levels of reflective or critical thought (multiple causes, conflicting goals, larger moral or ethical conflicts); and (3) coming up with alternative actions and thus continuing the cycle. . . . A major task of the [University of Maryland] program . . . [is] to instill a common knowledge base as the

formulation of plans and as a primary consideration in the analysis and evaluation of action. (p. 51)

To accomplish a problem-solving approach to reflection, preservice teachers at the University of Maryland (1) observe university faculty role models make decisions relative to their own teaching; (2) engage in personal journalizing in which they write about their own experiences and receive "active listening" responses from faculty members; (3) participate in microteaching in which they teach, critique/reflect, reteach, and reflect again with peers and faculty members; (4) engage in action research and case study analysis in which they focus on specific "problems of practice"; and (5) examine classroom practice/lessons in a way that enables them to address a set of questions, such as:

> To what extent does . . . classroom teaching exemplify principles of effective teaching as identified in the body of research? What elements of effective teaching are evident in . . . [a] teacher's classroom? What elements of effective teaching are not evident? In what ways do findings from the research on effective teaching seem to be appropriate standards against which to judge . . . classroom teaching? In what ways do effective teaching strategies seem to be inappropriate? (p. 54)

Other researchers (Korthagen, 1993) treat reflection as a holistic, gestalt-like process. There are no linear, sequential steps to reflection. Instead, teachers process information based on the types of life experiences they have had both inside and outside the classroom setting. Korthagen describes how the aesthetics of reflection are more intuitive and nonrational. Reflective teachers utilize metaphors, pictures, and guided fantasies to think through the meaning of teaching episodes. Korthagen describes how one teacher, "Heleen," came to a new understanding of her classroom management skills as a result of metaphoric analysis:

> In the first few months of her teaching, Heleen had serious discipline problems. In the description of her situation she said that she felt like a "lion-tamer," a metaphor suggested by a colleague teacher. The supervisor discussed the use of this metaphor with her, which brought to light a number of implicit connotations. These were concerned not only with external things like giving her students detention work, which she interpreted as "using the whip," but also Heleen's inner reality (fears, hopes, etc.). For instance, she felt that the "cage" in which she was shut up with the "lions" was locked; she could not get out and had to cope with the situation as best she could. Moreover, she felt that, above all she had to hide her fear, because showing that you are afraid is extremely dangerous with lions. As a lion-tamer you must be constantly aware of the fact that the lions are stronger than you are. Heleen felt that if they ever jumped her, she would be torn to pieces.
>
> Heleen and the supervisor could have used many words in rational analyses of all aspects of the classroom situation without ever grasping the essence of Heleen's interpretation of her situation, as it was possible to do through the use of metaphors. (p. 322)

Heleen's example illustrates the complexity of the reflective process. Reflection is more than just thinking about teaching—it requires a focus that enables teachers to see in *new ways* the extant reality of the classroom. Teachers need to develop vocabularies and perspectives that engender an enhanced awareness of teaching; supervisors must, in turn, develop a repertoire of techniques that foster varied reflective perspectives within teachers. As we will point out later in this chapter, one barrier to teacher reflection is evaluation systems used by supervisors that myopically examine teaching episodes. The use of metaphors (as in Heleen's example) extends teacher thinking beyond the apparent to the real.

BARRIERS TO REFLECTION

Reflection continues to be a phenomenon that is more conceptually discussed than practically understood. Preservice teachers are often forced to reflect (technically or critically) by the nature of their circumstance—they are "captives" within a controlled program. Inservice teachers exercise more professional choice and possess more personal autonomy; they are less inclined to "feel the need" to engage in different types of reflection. A number of internal and external factors prevent teachers from engaging in reflective activities, some over which teachers have little control (for example, the structure of the school day). This is not to suggest that teachers cannot begin to exercise influence on structural issues, but rather that some decisions (for example, regarding how the school day is structured) are typically outside teachers' immediate control.

The same lack of control is not true for many of the professions studied by Schon (for example, architecture, music). Although architects do not exercise total control over professional and personal daily schedules—few professionals do—they can dictate, in a general way, how their day will be organized (when breaks occur). Put in terms of the culture of schools, teachers are less likely to come into contact with new ideas because they are confined to the classroom and have a limited network of ongoing professionally based engagements within their schools or with their colleagues outside of the school building (Fullan, 1991)—the school culture is not collaborative. Teachers do receive educational information from conferences and professional journals in their fields, but they do not have the opportunity for continuous contact with colleagues to reflect upon instructional research and practice, which is a necessary, though not sufficient, condition for becoming aware of and following up on concepts that influence classroom practice (House & Lapan, 1978; Huberman & Miles, 1984).

The following internal and external barriers influence teachers' abilities to engage in different forms of reflection.

Barrier 1: Organizational Structure and Culture

American teachers have limited nonteaching time available for reflection. In general, teachers are responsible for instructing classes for all but one hour each day (Stevenson & Stigler, 1992). The factory metaphor drives the conceptual vision of American education; it also drives the professional classroom life of teachers. Nonteaching time is "down" time, and what little "down" time teachers have is used to meet immediate personal classroom needs rather than to foster more practical or theoretical reflection.

Teachers consistently feel the shortage of time. As Crandal (1982) and Huberman (1993) describe it, this "lack of time to do anything" affects teachers in a number of debilitating ways: It isolates them from engaging with other adults, especially colleagues; it exhausts their enthusiasm and energy; it limits their planning focus to short-term, day-to-day activities; and it limits their opportunity for sustained reflection. For urban teachers, the problems are especially acute. They face the "new" demands of ethnic and language diversity, special needs children, dysfunctional families, and a myriad of social, political, and economic problems that children in urban environments bring to the teachers' classroom doors. Given the nature of schooling in most schools across this country, the educational enterprise gives back little in the time needed for acquiring a sense of professional composure.

The heavy teaching loads of teachers are particularly noteworthy when compared to the realities of classroom educators who function in other cultures (to which American teachers are often unfavorably compared). Stevenson and Stigler (1992) note:

> When we informed the Chinese teachers that American elementary teachers are responsible for their classes all day long, with only one hour or less outside the classroom each day, they looked incredulous. How could any teacher be expected to do a good job when there is no time outside of class to prepare. . . . Japanese elementary school teachers are in charge of classes only 60 percent of the time they are at school. In fact, Japanese law limits the amount of time a teacher may spend in front of a classroom to twenty-three hours for a six-day week—no more than four hours a day. (pp. 163–164)

The isolation of American teachers further exacerbates the potential for reflection. Not only are teachers not given time to reflect, they also are isolated from peers in a way that precludes reflection (Lortie, 1975). Lortie's research, which is corroborated by other researchers (for example, Clark & Yinger, 1977; House & Lapan, 1978; Huberman, 1978, 1983), provides documentation not only for the practical realities of the classroom but also the affective dimensions of what teachers face daily as professionals. Sizer (1985) describes how teachers are separated by classroom structures (compartmentalized room arrangements) and curricular arrangements (tracking) that diminish dialogue between different teacher and student groups. The existence of such structures limits collective teacher action toward consensus building and thoughtful reflection.

Schools in which teachers have a shared consensus (collaborative culture) about organizational goals are more likely to incorporate new conceptions about teaching directed at student learning (Rosenholtz, 1989). Likewise, schools in which teachers have low consensus (noncollaborative culture) provide little attention to collectively defining school mission and goals; they enhance isolation among teachers, provide limited staff development opportunities that are collectively empowering, foster teacher helplessness in terms of what and how to teach, and engender a low commitment to the work ethos and organizational climate of the school.

Teachers who are physically and organizationally separated from one another do not have the opportunity to reflect on the possibilities and problems of professional practice. Relationships with other teachers and interactions with administrators are crucial for thoughtful reflection and professional change. Peer relationships are an important element in the change process, especially where the goal is the creation of collaborative cultures that enable technical, interpretive, and critical reflection—where teachers support teachers in thinking about professional ideas. Change involves learning something new, and peer engagement is a primary tool for social learning. New beliefs, attitudes, behaviors, skills, and meanings are acquired through an exchange of ideas, supportive relationships, and loyalty to one's work and organization (Goodlad, 1984; Rosenholtz, 1989).

Barrier 2: Administrative Behavior

Almost all school districts emphasize the concept of instructional leadership within a principal's job description. This concept is defined as helping teachers work together, assessing and developing school improvement in terms of curriculum and instruction, facilitating the change process, and so on. How administrators spend their time often indicates whether principals and superintendents view their roles as instructional leaders or program managers. Martin and Willower (1981) found that the principal's day is fragmented and focused upon the "crisis of the moment." Principals "demonstrated a tendency to engage themselves in the most current and pressing situation. They invested little time in reflective planning" (p. 80). Because principals engage in limited reflection, their teachers exhibit little desire to reflect. Instructional leaders who engage in purposeful reflection are in the minority: They realize that reflection takes time, requires support, and has political, social, and educational implications. Cuban (1988b) conducted an historical analysis of the principal's role and found that "the managerial role, not instructional leadership . . . dominated principal behavior" (p. 84). This should not be a surprise given the emphases of most principal preparation programs around the country. They tend to be management-oriented and do not encourage examination of social transformation ideas.

Administrators and teachers must work together to institute a collaborative culture that fosters reflectivity. In fact, the only way to foster meaningful reflection, whether technical, interpretive, or critical, is through collaborative engagement. Little (1981) identifies four conditions that must exist for school improvement to occur; these same conditions are essential ingredients for the emergence of school cultures that foster reflection.

1. Teachers must be able to engage in frequent talk about teaching practice.

2. Teachers and administrators must have opportunities to observe and provide feedback to one another.

3. Teachers and administrators must be able to plan, design, and evaluate teaching materials and practices together.

4. Teachers and administrators must be able to teach each other the practice of teaching.

Barrier 3: Technical Evaluation Systems

During the past decade a number of educators proffered technical evaluation systems that administrators utilize to assess teacher performance. Many of these systems are an outgrowth of the process-product research emphasis of the 1970s. Technical evaluation systems identify discrete teacher behaviors that putatively engender student achievement. Technical evaluation processes rely heavily on low-inference category systems to assess whether teachers exhibit requisite pedagogical skills (Evertson & Green, 1986).

The result has been the emergence of evaluation instruments that analyze the classroom environment atomistically. The Florida Performance Measurement System (Smith, Peterson, & Micceri, 1987) and the North Carolina Teacher Performance Appraisal Instrument (Holdzkom, 1987) are but two examples. In both the Florida and North Carolina evaluation instruments, teaching is divided into a set of operationally defined discrete skills: The presence of the skills indicates positive professional performance and the absence suggests areas for professional development.

Technical evaluation systems are not inherently negative, especially if they are used within the framework of more holistic evaluation processes (Millman & Darling-Hammond, 1990). Technical evaluation, however, precludes interpretive and critical reflection when it is the only system of teacher assessment—as it is in many school districts. Technical evaluations (especially the heavy use of "sign" systems or checklists) at their best encourage technical reflection and encourage teachers to think of "what is" rather than "what might be," with pedagogically correct practices being informed by the applied science literature. Such evaluation systems tend to emphasize low-level skills (for example, the teacher has materials ready at the beginning of the lesson), which van Manen (1977) and others place at the "lowest" level of (technical) reflection, rather than higher-order thinking processes that deal with the ethical and ideological questions of educational practice.

Used appropriately, technical systems have utility and conceptual power. But when they are the only approach for enabling teachers to think about their teaching, they become a detriment to higher forms of reflection. Teachers begin to think of means, not ends; they begin to focus on student control, not student needs; and they begin to break the teaching act into a series of discrete (unrelated) parts rather than consider teaching practice as a conceptual whole.

THEORY INTO PRACTICE

The ability to reflect is not one that magically manifests itself. Reflection requires purposeful inquiry and perspicacity. Teachers who develop facility with different levels of reflection understand that appreciating the complexities of classroom practice occurs through a commingling of two factors—purposeful intrapersonalness and focused extracenteredness. Purposeful intrapersonalness entails self-examination and self-questioning; focused extracenteredness requires that teachers draw on the expertise of "selected" others to better understand the personal reality of their own teaching. The approaches highlighted below conceptually represent these two factors. They examine how certain structural and cultural elements are essential for teachers to fully acquire a reflective disposition that will engender growth. And, they indicate how individual teachers and building administrators must collaboratively work together to create an environment that values reflection.

Reflective Disposition 1: A Willingness to Set Forth Questions of Professional Significance

Teachers need to develop skill in creating questions that cause them to challenge current practice. Questions should be focused on several different levels of classroom practice, including the psychological and philosophical underpinnings of practice. Table 18.1 illustrates questions at three different levels of reflective potential: technical, conceptual (interpretive), and dialectical (critical). The three levels are a conceptual variation of van Manen's (1977).

Teachers who are neophytes, at Fuller and Bown's (1975) survival stage, are most preoccupied with technical questions (for example, How can I use conflict resolution strategies to handle severe misbehavior?) (Lasley, 1992). Experienced teachers should engage in more conceptual and dialectical professional questioning. Again, using the example of disciplinary practice: Are my discipline strategies consistent with my classroom management objectives (conceptual level)? Or, at the dialectical level: In what ways do my teaching strategies enhance or hinder the capacity for personal responsibility of my students?

Evans' (1991) Teacher-initiated Research Project relies on teacher self-defined questions as a starting point for professional growth. Evans describes the process:

> Every other week, to assist each other with their classroom investigations [of questions], the teachers hold a two hour meeting complete with a discussion leader. Four or five people present their work to the group at each meeting. The other members serve as an advisory board to help each presenter at each phase of the work—selecting a topic, stating explicitly what he or she already knows and wants to know in relation to the topic, designing ways to gather more information, and making sense of what is learned. (p. 11)

The teacher starts with questions of personal significance, but the group fosters an atmosphere of collective responsibility (a collaborative culture) for answering the questions. The goal is to enhance teachers' understanding of how classrooms function and how classroom life influences student growth. The collaborative school culture enables the teacher to become more reflective and enables "support" teachers to provide perceptions that foster teacher growth.

Reflective Disposition 2: A Willingness to Use the Questions of Others to Assess Personal Pedagogical Decision Making

Cognitive coaching fosters question diversity and requires that supervisors pose ideas that challenge teachers' thinking. Cognitive coaching brings together the

Table 18.1   Approaches to Teacher Reflection

Approach	Focus
Technical	*Emphasis on technique* • What practices are and are not effective in the classroom? • What problems require attention? • What approaches can be used by the teacher to correct problem situations? • Is the class organized and well managed?
Conceptual	*Emphasis on the basis for current practice* • What is the espoused philosophical or theoretical basis for current practice? • Are the teacher's classroom practices consistent with the teacher's espoused philosophy? • Does current practice appear to foster or diminish student attentiveness to assigned tasks and learning?
Dialectical	*Emphasis on what ought to be* • Is the philosophy of the teacher consistent with the needs of the students'? • What teacher practices enhance or diminish student growth? • What student needs are not addressed by current teacher (and school) practices? • How should schools be reordered and restructured? And what must teachers do to facilitate such restructuring?

Reprinted with permission, *Journal of Staff Development.*

research on teaching, namely the process-product studies on effective teaching, with the qualitative approaches of clinical supervision (Costa & Garmston, 1993). Cognitive coaches understand that explicit prescriptions for good teaching do not exist. The ecology of different classrooms, coupled with the diversity of human personalities within classrooms, ensures a multiplicity of approaches to effective teaching. Cognitive coaches, whether administrators or fellow teachers, are not evaluative; they are facilitative. Their focus, argue Costa and Garmston, is "to provide a collegial relationship that supports teachers in becoming critically self-reflective about their work" (p. 5).

Cognitive coaches use the steps in the clinical supervision process to encourage teacher reflection. The coach relies on Rogerian paraphrasing techniques and probing questions to cause teachers to think beyond what is actually occurring in classroom situations. The systematic questioning on the part of the administrator enables teachers to self-monitor and self-analyze in ways that traditional evaluation procedures (especially technical evaluation) do not permit. Costa and Garmston describe how one "teacher who has not been very reflective is . . . now watching himself teach, almost like he had a camera on himself, and that when he catches himself in old patterns, he now employs alternatives" (p. 7).

The clinical and peer supervision models foster active questioning strategies because they are based on an analytical conceptual foundation. Coaches, whether administrators or teachers, are encouraged to use questions as a way of helping teachers consider the implications of classroom practice. The questions are not standardized, rather they are idiosyncratically determined based upon each teacher's unique circumstance. Teachers need collegial support to develop a full appreciation of their teaching position.

The collaborative models not only stimulate enhanced awareness of the complexity of teaching, but also enable teachers to achieve a more sophisticated understanding of their own potential (Paquette, 1987; Sparks & Bader, 1987). Interestingly, whereas clinical processes may have efficacy for inservice teachers in fostering reflection, they may limit the reflective potential of preservice teachers (Gore & Zeichner, 1991). The reason for this circumstance relates to the absence of a broader collaborative community in terms of student teacher conferencing. Gore and Zeichner note: "As we have begun to look at whole schools rather than individual classrooms as sites for student teaching . . . we have started to think about the need to broaden the learning community for student teachers beyond that which exists in the clinical supervision conference" (p. 134).

Reflective Disposition 3: An Ability to Discover How Personal and Extrapersonal Ideas Influence Professional Practice

Reflection requires a combination of rational and nonrational processes. In Korthagen's (1993) terms, "it is the integration of rational analysis and the process of becoming aware of one's guiding gestalts . . ." (p. 324). Teachers who use the ideas of others are able to see beyond the blinders of personal experience. Those significant others may be a supervisor (a principal) or an external consultant from within the field. Regardless of role, the external ideas emerge as another perspective for understanding the ecology of a classroom. External ideas do not constitute truth; they are, instead, representations from significant others who help teachers think in new ways about old problems. For some teachers the only ideas they consider are those of an external authority who attempts, explicitly or implicitly, to impose a pedagogical schema on how they should construct lessons or organize the classroom: These teachers are not reflective, they are indoctrinated. Some other teachers are so self-assured that they disdain any attention to what others say; they arrogantly proclaim knowledge of the "right" answers.

Teachers who appreciate the value of ideas realize their potential significance, regardless of whether those ideas come from within (personal) or without (extrapersonal). Personal ideas are explored through journals and other aesthetic techniques (for example, drawing) that enable the teacher to better understand the situational nature of personal knowledge. Educators who reflect by writing begin to discover personal schema and how those schema influence the way they organize and structure classrooms. Writing not only distills ideas, it also clarifies thought. Wibel (1991) states: "Writing for reflection has propelled me through a series of revelations, crises, and thoughts that helped me grow. Without this exercise I would not see my environment very clearly" (p. 45). Korthagen (1993) describes how painting reflects a personal sense of vision: "When a teacher draws a picture of a classroom, it is interesting to see which students are portrayed and in what positions. Certain messages are sent out by colors or objects which at first sight seem to be there by chance" (p. 322).

Extrapersonal representations entail using the ideas and questions of others to examine the efficacy of personal classroom practice. The advantage of videotaping and microteaching is that teachers who use such approaches for self-assessment reflect on their teaching using the ideas and questions of others. The literature on reflection is replete with examples of how teachers use collegial approaches as part of videotaping and microteaching analysis (Cruickshank, 1987; Sparks-Langer & Colton, 1991). Of less prominence in the available knowledge base, but of equal significance in terms of extrapersonal ideas, is the use of fiction and nonfiction about teachers' lives (Tama & Peterson, 1991). Such literature helps teachers "cultivate richer insights into what it means to be a teacher" (p. 22). Those insights broaden the classroom view of teachers and cause them to rethink and reevaluate personal decisions and dispositions. Reading texts about teachers' fictional or real lives (for example, Robert Coles' *The Call of Stories: Teaching and the Moral Imagination* or Ken Macrorie's *20 Teachers*) enables teachers to consider new possibilities for themselves within extant classroom realities.

SUMMARY

Reflection is a personal process, but it occurs most efficaciously in a collaborative culture. Teachers who reflect need ideas; they also require support—from teachers who share a common mission and from administrators who understand how organizational and curricular structures influence professional decision making.

The psychological disposition of teachers is also an important but often overlooked dimension to teacher reflectivity. For some teachers, reflection, especially critical or dialectical reflection, creates discomfort—a discomfort that necessitates the possibility of change. Teachers who are personally insecure or professionally timid will not readily change to embrace a reflective disposition— they will continue to use routine practice to solve both new and old problems. Collaborative school cultures will not eliminate such teachers, but they can create conditions within which the risk of reflection becomes viable, and with that risk comes the possibility of personal and professional growth.

References

Bullough, R. V. (1989). "Teacher Education and Teacher Reflectivity." *Journal of Teacher Education* 40 (2): 15–21.

Clark, C., and R. Yinger (1977). "Research on Teacher Thinking." *Curriculum Inquiry, 7* (4): 279–304

Costa, A., and R. Garmston (1993). "Cognitive Coaching: A Strategy for Reflective Teaching." *Wingspan* 9 (1): 4–8.

Crandal, D. (1982). *People, Policies and Practice: Examining the Chain of School Improvement* (vols. 1–10). Andover, MA: The Network.

Cruickshank, D. (1987). *Reflective Teaching.* Reston, VA: Association of Teacher Educators.

Cuban, L. (1988a). "A Fundamental Puzzle of School Reform." *Phi Delta Kappan* 70 (5): 341–44.

Cuban, L. (1988b). *The Managerial Imperative and the Practice of Leadership in Schools.* Albany: State University of New York Press.

Dewey, J. (1904). "The Relation of Theory to Practice in Education," in C. A. McMurry, ed., *The Relation of Theory to Practice in the Education of Teachers* (Third Yearbook of the National Society for the Study of Education, Part 1). Chicago: University of Chicago Press, pp. 9–30.

Dewey, J. (1933). *How We Think.* Chicago: Henry Regency Co.

Eisner, E. (1985). *The Educational Imagination,* 2nd ed. New York: Macmillan.

Evans, C. (1991). "Support for Teachers Studying Their Own Work." *Educational Leadership* 48 (6): 11–13.

Evertson, C., and J. Green (1986). "Observation as Inquiry and Method," in M. C. Wittrock, ed. *Handbook of Research on Teaching,* 3rd ed. New York: Macmillan, pp. 162–213.

Fullan, M. (1991). *The New Meaning of Educational Change.* New York: Teachers College Press, Columbia University.

Fuller, F., and O. Bown (1975). "Becoming a Teacher," in K. Ryan, ed., *Teacher Education* (Seventy-fourth Yearbook of the National Society for the Study of Education). Chicago: University of Chicago Press, pp. 25–52.

Goodlad, J. I. (1984). *A Place Called School: Prospects for the Future.* New York: McGraw-Hill.

Gore, J., and K. Zeichner (1991). "Action Research and Reflective Teaching." *Teaching and Teacher Education* 7 (2): 119–136.

Holdzkom, D. (1987). "Appraising Teacher Performance in North Carolina." *Educational Leadership* 44 (7): 40–45.

House, E. R., and S. D. Lapan (1978). *Survival in the Classroom.* Boston: Allyn and Bacon.

Huberman, M. (1978). "Microanalysis of Innovation Implementation at the School Level. Unpublished paper, University of Geneva.

Huberman, M. (1983). "Recipes for Busy Kitchens." *Knowledge: Creation, Diffusion, Utilization* 4: 478–510.

Huberman, M., and M. Miles (1984). *Innovation Up Close.* New York: Plenum.

Jackson, P. (1968). *Life in Classrooms.* New York: Holt, Rinehart and Winston.

Korthagen, F. A. J. (1993). "Two Modes of Reflection." *Teaching and Teacher Education* 9 (3): 317–326.

Lasley, T. J. (1992). "Promoting Teacher Reflection." *Journal of Staff Development* 13 (1): 24–31.

Little, J. W. (1981). "The Power of Organizational Setting." Paper adapted from final report, *School Success and Staff Development.* Washington, D.C.: National Institute of Education.

Little, J. W. (1982). "Norms of Collegiality and Experimentation: Workplace Conditions of School Success." *American Educational Research Journal* 19: 325–340.

Lortie, D. (1975). *Schoolteacher.* Chicago: University of Chicago Press.

McCaleb, J., H. Borko, and R. Arends (1992). "Reflection, Research and Repertoire in the Masters Certification Program at the University of Maryland," in L. Valli, ed., *Reflective Teacher Education.* Albany, NY: State University of New York Press, pp. 40–64.

Martin, W., and D. Willower (1981). "The Managerial Behavior of High School Principals." *Educational Administration Quarterly* 17 (1): 69–90.

Millman, J., and L. Darling-Hammond (1990).

Teacher Evaluation. London: Sage.

Paquette, M. (1987). "Voluntary Collegial Support Groups for Teachers." *Educational Leadership* 45 (3): 36–39.

Pearson, C. (1989). *The Hero Within.* New York: Harper & Row.

Rosenholtz, S. (1989). *Teachers' Workplace: The Social Organization of Schools.* New York: Longman.

Roth, R. A. (1989). "Preparing the Reflective Practitioner: Transforming the Apprentice through the Dialectic." *Journal of Teacher Education* 40 (2): 31–35.

Schon, D. (1983). *The Reflective Practitioner.* New York: Basic Books.

Schon, D. (1987). *Educating the Reflective Practitioner.* San Francisco: Jossey Bass.

Shulman, L. (1986). "Those Who Understand: Knowledge Growth in Teaching." *Educational Researcher* 15 (2): 4–14.

Shulman, L. (1987). "Knowledge and Teaching: Foundations of the New Reform." *Harvard Educational Review* 57 (1): 1–22.

Sizer, T. (1985). *Horace's Compromise: The Dilemma of the American High School.* Boston: Houghton Mifflin.

Smith, B. O., D. Peterson, and T. Micceri (1987). "Evaluation and Professional Improvement

Aspects of the Florida Measurement System." *Educational Leadership* 44 (7): 16–19.

Sparks-Langer, G. M., and A. B. Colton (1991). "Synthesis of Research on Teachers' Reflectivity." *Educational Leadership* 48 (6): 37–44.

Sparks, G. M., and S. Bader (1987). "Before and After Peer Coaching." *Educational Leadership* 45 (3): 54–57.

Stevenson, H. W., and J. W. Stigler (1992). *The Learning Gap.* New York: Summit Books.

Tama, M. C., and K. Peterson (1991). "Achieving Reflectivity through Literature." *Educational Leadership* 48 (6): 22–24.

Valli, L. (1992). *Reflective Teacher Education.* Albany, NY: State University of New York Press.

van Manen, M. (1977). "Linking Ways of Knowing with Ways of Being Practical." *Curriculum Inquiry* 6: 205–228.

Wibel, W. (1991). "Reflecting through Writing." *Educational Leadership* 48 (6): 45–46.

Zeichner, K. (1992). "Conceptions of Reflective Teaching in Contemporary U.S. Teacher Education Program Reforms," in L. Valli, ed., *Reflective Teacher Education.* Albany, NY: State University of New York Press, pp. 161–173.

Discussion Questions

1. In what ways does the culture of a school foster or prohibit teacher reflection?

2. What level of reflection (technical, conceptual, or dialectical) characterizes the reality of reflectivity that occurs in most urban schools? Suburban schools? Rural schools?

3. To what degree does the emotional disposition and personality archetype of a teacher influence a capacity for critical reflection?

4. How do government policies and school board mandates influence teacher dispositions to engage in critical reflection?

5. If collaborative cultures that foster reflection are possible, what changes in teacher, administrator, and community attitudes must occur to make collaborative structures a reality?

Part IV

The Social and Political Dimensions of Teaching

Schools are one of several institutions expected to "socialize" members of society. They are designed by adults to help children and youth accept society, and to possibly improve it. Every individual lives his or her life in a society—within some social, cultural, and political context. In a very meaningful and powerful way, the social, cultural, and political world we live in spills over into our classrooms and schools—and teachers must learn to deal with it as they select and organize the content, skills, and experiences to achieve the aims and goals of the curriculum. In short, the teacher is an agent of society, trusted to socialize and educate students, to help them get along with people and take the roles expected of them.

In Part IV, we examine the society in which American children and youth grow up: It is diverse and full of different (and sometimes competing) ideas. It consists of many groups with various historical roots and ways of life, some who perceive themselves as minorities deserving special entitlement, and others who by social class have certain advantages in terms of social mobility and political power. These and other social and political forces influence the teacher-learning process, in particular the teacher's planning, intentions, and methods.

This part consists of five chapters. In the first of these, Robert Slavin examines the problems and prospects of "Teaching At-risk Students: What Works?". His emphasis is on "what works": What programs seem to be effective in reaching and teaching students with a number of risk factors that often result in school failure. Slavin describes various Chapter 1 programs and practices with emphasis on prevention and prompt remediation in the early grades when problems first appear.

Chapter 20 considers "Multicultural Teaching in the Real World" of classrooms and schools. Martin Haberman and Linda Post contend that teachers seeking to prepare children and youth from diverse cultural backgrounds for life in society need to have them examine their own cultures as well as the culture of the larger society. Before a multicultural curriculum can be implemented in schools, the teachers' perceptions, roles, and instructional methods need to be clarified. Ten issues related to such implementation are raised and discussed.

The next chapter, "Coeducational Teaching: Taking Girls Seriously," is written by Susan Laird. She explores the concept of coeducation, and the need for girls to be taken more seriously by teachers, to see themselves reflected in the curriculum, and to be encouraged to participate in school sports and leadership activities. The author aims for sex equality and the elimination of gender bias in the way schools are organized, to include more experiences of interest for young women, and to teach boys to welcome girls as equal partners in the challenges of school and the larger society.

In Chapter 22, Henry Giroux advocates the role of "Teachers as Public Intellectuals." He challenges teachers to become more socially responsive and politically active, to act with courage and dignity, to question dominant values that result in inequitable conditions or undercut the history and identity of individuals and groups. He asks teachers to raise questions in class: to consider social issues, to challenge parts of the existing social order that result in discrimination or oppression—and to teach students to do the same. The ultimate questions, for Giroux, are to examine what knowledge is worth having and why—why schools legitimize some knowledge and ignore others. Other questions and issues deal with culture, race, gender, and various political and ideological ideas that teachers must learn to deal with in an honest and critical way.

In the last chapter of the book, Gary Griffin presents an overview on "Learning to Teach in Schools: Framework for Clinical Teacher Education." The author focuses on a rationale and need for clinical education for both preservice and inservice teachers. He views the clinical experience as an essential component of teacher education and proceeds to discuss seven critical features of teacher education programs. The program must be (1) context sensitive, that is, embedded in a classroom and school context; (2) purposeful and clearly articulated; (3) participatory and collaborative; (4) knowledge-based; (5) on-going and include three stages—preservice, induction, and inservice; (6) developmental, or concerned with the growth and improvement of teachers; and (7) analytical and reflective, so that teachers can diagnose and evaluate important classroom activities and experiences. Griffin ends the discussion with an analysis of social and political factors shaping teacher education and concludes that a number of deeply entrenched practices (which he defines) need to be modified or discarded to improve teacher education.

Robert E. Slavin

Robert Slavin is currently director of the elementary school program at the Center for Research on Effective Schooling for Disadvantaged Students at Johns Hopkins University. His undergraduate degree is in psychology from Reed College in Portland, Oregon in 1972. He then went to graduate school at Johns Hopkins University in social relations, graduating and receiving his doctorate In 1975. He has been at Johns Hopkins in a federally funded research center ever since.

Over the years, Slavin has published fourteen books and some 150 articles, chapters, and research papers. These have primarily dealt with cooperative learning, race relations, mainstreaming, programs for students at risk, and research methodology. Among his most recent books are *Effective Programs for Students at Risk* (Allyn and Bacon, 1990), *Success for All: A Relentless Approach to Prevention and Early Intervention in Elementary Schools* (Educational Research Service, 1992), and *Preventing Early School Failure* (Allyn and Bacon, 1994). He is also the author of a popular textbook, *Educational Psychology: Theory into Practice* (Allyn and Bacon, 1994), currently in its fourth edition.

Robert spends most of his time directing two related programs. One is Success for All, a restructuring program for elementary schools serving disadvantaged students. The other is Roots and Wings, a project funded by the New American Schools Development Corporation to create a design for the elementary school of the twenty-first century. Both programs are built on the idea that every child can learn and that schools must be organized to see that children do not fall behind in the elementary grades, no matter what it takes.

His advice to a beginning teacher is: "never stop learning, from your students, your colleagues, your profession. Growing each year means being willing to experiment, to talk shop with other teachers, to visit others' classrooms and schools and to encourage colleagues to come see what you are doing." It means seeking opportunities to "participate in workshops or courses and to share what you learn in them with others."

As one of the youngest contributors to the book, Robert has no intention of slowing down for a long time. However, on Sundays he manages to put aside his suit and tie and put on some sweats and bike ride with his wife and three children along the old railroad trails through the Maryland forest preserves.

19 ❧

Teaching At-risk Students: What Works?

Robert E. Slavin

In every school there are students who may be at risk for school failure. A student who is at risk is in danger of failing to learn at an adequate level. Being at risk does not mean a student has failed or is certain to fail, but it means that a student has one or more risk factors that often lead to school failure. The practical meaning of *at-risk*, and associated risk factors, change according to the age of the child. For example, unless he or she has obvious retardation or developmental delay, it is difficult to know whether or not a four-year-old will ultimately learn adequately in school. For young children, therefore, the most important risk factors are group characteristics such as being from a poor family. In contrast, after students have entered school, their actual performance and behavior become much more important than family poverty; the major risk factors for ultimate school dropout, for example, are low achievement, retention in grade, poor attendance, and assignment to special education (Slavin, Karweit, & Madden, 1989; Natriello, McDill, & Pallas, 1990).

What can teachers do to help students who are at risk for school failure? Research on the relationship between teaching behaviors and student achievement has found that effective teaching behaviors for students at risk are essentially the same as those for students in general. At-risk students need engaging curriculum, active instruction, and good classroom management practices, just as all students do (see Knapp et al., 1992; Larrivee, 1989).

One particular characteristic of most at-risk students in the United States is that they qualify for additional services or resources to help them catch up with their peers. This assistance goes under the general heading of compensatory education. Compensatory education is discussed in the following sections.

COMPENSATORY EDUCATION

Compensatory education refers to programs intended to improve the school success of children from poor families. In concept, these programs offer federal or state funding to enable local school districts to provide services to poor children beyond those ordinarily provided to them, to "compensate" for the effects of poverty. In practice, however, compensatory education programs usually provide supplementary services to low-achieving or at-risk children who attend schools with many poor children, rather than being restricted to children who are themselves in poverty.

Compensatory education began as part of Lyndon Johnson's War on Poverty in the 1960s. From the outset it has been linked to the civil rights movement and has been a key element in federal attempts to address issues of race as well as poverty. While most compensatory education dollars are federal, many states also provide money to supplement federal funds. State compensatory education programs are usually patterned on the federal programs, simply extending the number of students who can be served.

The largest of all federal education programs in elementary and secondary schools is Chapter 1 (of the Elementary and Secondary Education Act, or ESEA). Before 1981, this program was called Title I. In 1991 to 1992, national Chapter 1 funding was approximately $6.7 billion annually. One in every nine students receives Chapter 1 services—a total of almost five million children. More than 90 percent of school districts receive Chapter 1 funds. Chapter 1 funds are given to schools on the basis of the number of low-income students they serve, but within schools they are used to serve students according to their educational needs, not their poverty level. Because of this, and because nonpoor students so outnumber poor ones, the majority (58 percent) of students receiving Chapter 1 services are not themselves from families in poverty. However, poor students are disproportionate recipients of Chapter 1 services, as are African-American and Latino students. The great bulk of Chapter 1 services go toward elementary schools (grades K–8). Most Chapter 1 funds provide instructional services to students in reading, mathematics, and/or language.

Models of Chapter 1 Service Delivery

Two guiding principles of delivery of Chapter 1 services are that only eligible low-achieving students may benefit from these services, and that the services must supplement, not supplant, local educational efforts. The first of these, which typically limits the use of Chapter 1 funds to students who score below a certain cut-off score on standardized tests (for example, below the 40th percentile), keeps most schools from using Chapter 1 funds to improve the school overall, for example by reducing class size or implementing more effective practices in the school as a whole (the exception is schoolwide projects, described below). The "supplement, not supplant" requirement generally keeps schools from using Chapter 1 funds to provide services that non-Chapter 1 students receive out of local funds. For instance, a district could not provide preschool or summer school programs for low-achieving or disadvantaged students out of Chapter 1 funds if it also provided similar programs for non-Chapter 1 students out of local funds. A small army of state regulators audit Chapter 1 programs to make sure that funds are spent only on eligible students and that these funds supplement local efforts.

There are five principal models of service delivery used under Chapter 1 funding: pullout, in-class, add-on, replacement, and schoolwide. In pullout, students are taken out of their homeroom classes for thirty- to forty-minute periods, during which time they receive remedial instruction in a subject with which they are having difficulty, usually from a certified Chapter 1 teacher and usually in a class of eight or fewer pupils. In in-class models, the teacher (or, more commonly, an instructional aide) works with eligible students within the regular classroom setting. Add-on programs provide services outside of the regular classroom, as in summer school or after-school programs. (An increasingly popular option, using Chapter 1 funds to provide pre-kindergarten programs or to extend kindergarten to a full day, might also be considered an add-on model.) Replacement models involve placing Chapter 1 students in self-contained classes in which they receive most or all of their instruction. These programs require school districts to provide additional local resources to supplement Chapter 1 funds. Schoolwide projects are those in which all students in a high-poverty school can benefit from Chapter 1 funds. Until recently, schoolwide projects have been rare, as they could be used only in schools in which at least 75 percent of students were in poverty and in which the district was willing to provide matching funds to supplement the Chapter 1 allocations. The 1988 Hawkins-Stafford Act removed the matching fund requirement, so schoolwide projects are becoming much more common among high-poverty schools.

Although use of in-class, add-on, replacement and schoolwide models has increased in recent years, Chapter 1 funds still overwhelmingly provide pullout programs. In elementary schools, pullout designs are used in 84 percent of all Chapter 1 reading programs and 76 percent of math programs—more than all other models combined. Part of the reason for this is that pullout models most clearly fulfill the "supplement, not supplant" requirement of Chapter 1 regulations; in in-class models, there is always concern about the possibility that teachers or aides present in the regular classroom will be helping ineligible as well as eligible students.

How Effective Is Chapter 1?

Chapter 1 has a very well-defined purpose: to increase the reading and mathematics achievement of low-achieving students within schools with concentrations of students from families of low socioeconomic status. How successful has it been?

The best national assessment of the effects of Title I is the now rather dated Sustaining Effects Study (Carter, 1984), which compared achievement gains made by Title I students in 1976 to 1977 to matched "needy" students and to a representative sample of nonneedy students. Title I students generally made greater gains in reading and math than other needy students, but these gains were not adequate to close the gap between Title I and nonneedy students. In comparing Title I and matched needy students, only in first grade were differences educationally significant.

It is of course possible that in the years since the Sustaining Effects data were collected (1976–77), improved practices within Chapter 1 may have led to markedly improved outcomes. However, early results from a longitudinal study of

Chapter 1 mandated by Congress have not yet shown such outcomes (Puma et al., 1993).

Perhaps the best indication of the effectiveness of Chapter 1 services is indirect. This is the fact that the achievement gap between African-American and Latino students and white students in performance on the National Assessment of Educational Progress (NAEP) has been steadily diminishing since 1971 (Mullis & Jenkins, 1990). While Chapter 1 services are not restricted to minority students, they do disproportionately serve minority students, and it is reasonable to assume that Chapter 1 is responsible for at least part of the steady improvement in minority achievement.

Effects of Instructional Practices in Chapter 1 Classes

Chapter 1 is only a funding mechanism, not a specific instructional program. Many programs and practices can be provided to students under Chapter 1 funding. There have been a few studies of practices associated with reading and language achievement gain in Chapter 1 schools and classrooms. The findings of these studies are presented in the following sections.

Setting for Instruction Compensatory education can be delivered within the regular classroom, outside the regular classroom, or partially inside and partially outside the regular classroom. Instruction delivered outside the regular classroom has been given the name pullout instruction, since recipients are removed or "pulled out" of their regular classroom and sent to another location. Usually, the location is within the same school building, and the instruction delivered there is usually provided by an instructional specialist working with smaller groups of children than there were in the classroom from which the Chapter 1 student was removed. Instruction delivered within the regular classroom is called in-class or mainstreamed instruction. One approach to mainstreaming is for the regular teacher to instruct Chapter 1 students while Chapter 1 personnel, either a specialist teacher or aide, provide supplementary assistance. Another form of mainstreaming occurs when a Chapter 1 staff person instructs Chapter 1 students while the regular teacher works with the other students in the class.

Most of the research on the setting for compensatory education focuses on the two predominant models: pullout and in-class. In general, the literature leads to the following conclusions: (1) in some cases compensatory education in a pullout setting results in higher student achievement than in-class instruction, in other instances in-class instruction has a more positive effect, and in still others (the majority of cases), the setting for instruction has no significant effect on student achievement; (2) findings on the cost-effectiveness of the approaches are also mixed; and (3) the type of instruction delivered within a particular setting is more important than the setting itself (see Archambault, 1989).

Process-product Research in Chapter 1 Classes A study by Crawford (1989) investigated the relationship between the instructional practices of Chapter 1 pullout teachers and the achievement gains made by their students. Participants in the study were seventy-nine Chapter 1 teachers. Forty-four of the teachers were in elementary grade classes and thirty-five were in fifth-year centers or middle schools.

Across all grade levels, there were several indications that active, task-oriented teaching was related to greater reading gain in Chapter 1 classes. For example, the total number of minutes allocated for academic activity and the number of academic teacher-student interactions were both significantly positively correlated with gain. In addition, the number of nonacademic contacts per minute was negatively correlated with gain.

Analysis of data from the full sample also indicated that a number of measures of the quality or nature of interactions were significant predictors of reading gain. A rating of seatwork difficulty was positively related to gains, suggesting that teachers with high gaining classes made relatively more use of challenging materials. Those same teachers were active monitors, circulating to students who needed help with their seatwork exercises. Across grades, results also suggested that teachers who asked relatively more opinion questions of Chapter 1 students tended to have higher gains.

Another major process-product study of schools containing many disadvantaged students (but not only Chapter 1 students) was conducted by Knapp, Adelman, Marder, McCollum, Needels, Shields, Turnbull, and Zucker (1992) in the Study of Academic Instruction for Disadvantaged Students. This study involved two years of observations in 140 grade 1 to 6 classes in fifteen elementary schools in six districts in three states.

Aspects of instruction, curriculum, and school organization were correlated with achievement gain. In reading, teaching strategies emphasizing comprehension generally produced higher comprehension performance, but did not improve basic skills (word attack and letter-word identification). Providing students with extensive opportunities to write extended text (for example, daily journal writing with extensive teacher assistance and feedback) had a consistently positive effect on writing performance.

EFFECTIVE PROGRAMS FOR DISADVANTAGED STUDENTS

In a major review of research on a wide range of programs designed to increase student reading and mathematics achievement in Chapter 1 elementary schools, Slavin, Karweit, and Madden (1989) examined the published literature, technical reports, government reports, and other sources to find information on programs that had solid evidence of effectiveness (that is, had been compared to control groups over periods of at least one year and produced effect sizes of at least 25 percent of a standard deviation).

The effective programs identified fell into two major categories: changes in curriculum, instruction, or special services, and comprehensive schoolwide change. In the first category were programs focusing on *prevention, early intervention,* and *remediation.* The comprehensive programs generally incorporated all three of these to various degrees.

Prevention

The easiest learning deficits to remediate are those that never occur in the first place. Given the limited capacity of Chapter 1 (and special education) programs to bring students up to an adequate level of performance, attention has increasingly turned in recent years toward strategies designed to give intensive (usually expensive) services in the early grades to reduce or eliminate the need for remedial services later on (see Slavin, Karweit, & Wasik, 1994). Prevention programs typically focus either on preschool, on kindergarten, or on first grade.

Preschool One of the most widely discussed preventative strategies in recent years has been the provision of preschool education for four-year-olds, particularly those from disadvantaged homes. Increasingly, Chapter 1 dollars are being used to provide preschool to disadvantaged children, and President Clinton has made increasing Head Start preschool programs a cornerstone of his education policies. Research on preschool tends to find strong effects on the language and IQ scores of disadvantaged children immediately after the preschool experience, but these effects diminish each subsequent year until they are undetectable by the second or third grade (Karweit, 1994a). However, the students involved in many of the early studies of preschool are now in their late 20s, and longitudinal data following them for many years has found positive effects of preschool participation on such outcomes as high school graduation and delinquency (Zigler & Styfco, 1993).

Kindergarten Another new use of Chapter 1 dollars is to extend kindergarten from a half-day to a full-day program for disadvantaged children.

A review of the literature by Karweit (1994b) found that the effects of full-day kindergarten (in comparison to half-day) are very similar to the effects of preschool. That is, positive effects of the full-day programs on first-grade readiness or performance are usually found, but by the second or third grade the effects have generally disappeared.

First-grade Prevention Programs There are several effective instructional programs built on the proposition that success in first grade, particularly in reading, is an essential prerequisite for success later in school. These programs apply intensive resources, usually including tutors or other additional staff, to attempt to make certain that every child will successfully begin reading.

All of the preventative first-grade models use tutoring and/or small group instruction, and all are extremely successful in increasing students' reading achievement (Wasik & Slavin, 1993). Only one, Reading Recovery, has data on the long-term effects of intensive reading instruction in the first grade. Students who received an average of sixty thirty-minute lessons from a specially trained Reading Recovery tutor were compared to matched control children. By the end of the first grade, Reading Recovery students substantially exceeded control on an individually administered test of "text reading levels." Much of this difference maintained into the third grade with no additional intervention (Pinnell et al., 1988).

Classroom Change Programs

One of the most effective ways to reduce the number of children who will ultimately need remedial services is to provide the best possible classroom instruction in the first place. Therefore, an essential element of an overall strategy to serve students at risk of school failure is to introduce classroom instructional methods with a demonstrated capacity to accelerate student achievement, especially that of students at risk.

Continuous Progress Programs   In continuous progress models, students proceed at their own pace through a sequence of well-defined instructional objectives. However, they are taught in small groups composed of students at similar skill levels (but often different homerooms or even different grades). For example, a teacher might teach a unit on decimals to third. fourth, and fifth graders who have all arrived at the same point in the skills sequence. Students are frequently assessed and regrouped based on these assessments (Slavin, Karweit, & Madden, 1989; Gutiérrez & Slavin, 1992).

Cooperative Learning   In cooperative learning methods, students work in small learning teams to master material initially presented by the teacher. When the teams are rewarded or recognized based on the individual learning of all team members, cooperative learning methods can be consistently effective in increasing student achievement in comparison to traditionally taught control groups (Slavin, 1990). While there are many cooperative learning methods that have been successfully applied in many subjects, those that have been particularly effective in long-term evaluations share two important elements. First, learning groups work over many weeks toward some sort of group goal. Second, success in achieving this goal depends on the individual learning performance of each group member, not on a single group product.

Supplementary/Remedial Programs

In contrast to classroom change programs, supplementary/remedial models are applied outside of and usually in addition to regular classroom instruction, and are usually remedial rather than preventative in focus. That is, they are most often used with students who are already behind their agemates in basic skills.

Remedial Tutoring Programs   As was the case with the first-grade prevention programs, the most effective supplementary/remedial models involve one-to-one tutoring. However, unlike the preventative tutorial models that use certified teachers or paraprofessionals, effective remedial tutoring programs tend to use older students and/or volunteers.

Computer-assisted Instruction   Research on the achievement effects of computer-assisted instruction in general is highly variable in quality and only inconsistently finds positive effects (see Becker, 1992). However, a few specific CAI models have been successfully evaluated.

Schoolwide Projects

Perhaps the most important change introduced in the 1988 Hawkins-Stafford bill was a loosening of restrictions on Chapter 1 dollars to serve all students in schools in which at least 75 percent of students qualified for free lunch. As a result of this legislation, there has been a movement toward schoolwide projects in many districts. Research evaluating schoolwide programs has generally found perception of improved outcomes, especially when schools use the opportunity to implement innovative programs (instead of to continue pullouts or reduce class size) (see Schenck & Beckstrom, 1993). In addition, a few specific schoolwide models have been developed and evaluated. These are as follows.

Success for All   Success for All (Slavin, Madden, Karweit, Dolan, & Wasik, 1992) is a schoolwide restructuring program designed to see that students begin with success in the early grades and then maintain success through the elementary years. It combines many of the successful approaches identified in the research cited earlier: research-based preschool, extended-day kindergarten, beginning reading programs, one-to-one tutoring for students experiencing difficulties in reading in grades 1 through 3, and cooperative learning approaches to intermediate reading, writing/language arts, and mathematics. It also provides family support services and a project facilitator to coordinate the many program elements. Research in seven districts in different states comparing Success for All to other Chapter 1 schoolwide projects has found strong positive effects on reading achievement as well as reductions in retentions and special education assignments (Slavin et al., 1994).

School Development Program   Another important approach to schoolwide restructuring is a model developed and researched by James Comer (1988). This program, called the School Development Program, emphasizes school-based mental health services, parent involvement, and teacher involvement in restructuring of the school's programs. Research on the Comer model has found it to increase student achievement over time.

THEORY INTO PRACTICE

The most important principle of teaching at-risk students is to hold high expectations for all students and then provide the curriculum, instruction, and extra assistance necessary to make these expectations come true. For example, research supports the idea that virtually every child can read, so skillful, strategic, and enthusiastic reading is a reasonable and appropriate expectation for every child, regardless of family background or other factors. However, many children will not read adequately unless their reading program has an appropriate balance of phonics and meaning (Adams, 1990). Many will need rich preschool and kindergarten experiences to give them the oral language, background knowledge, concepts about print, and phonemic awareness that are critical underpinnings for first grade reading. Speakers of languages other than English may need reading instruction in their home language before transitioning to English reading later in elementary school (Wong-Fillmore & Valdez, 1986). Some students will require one-to-one tutoring or other services to succeed in reading in first grade. Beyond first grade, use of strategies such as cooperative learning will help all students build on their success in reading. In other words, we can say in principle that every child can read, but it is up to us as educators to provide what is necessary to see that even the most at-risk students actually become confident readers.

Another critical principle of teaching at-risk children is that prevention and early, intensive intervention are far better than remedial or special education. Once students have fallen significantly behind, it is very difficult to remediate their deficits, in large part because a student who has experienced failure many times is likely to have poor motivation to learn. Student learning problems first must be prevented by giving them good quality preschool and kindergarten experiences and then by using the best possible curricula and instructional methods, involving parents in support of student success, and using effective classroom management methods. When students fall behind despite these preventive efforts, they must receive immediate, intensive assistance (such as tutoring) to enable them to catch up as quickly as possible. When a child is given such intensive assistance, he or she can then profit from regular classroom instruction, and may never need further remediation.

A serious policy of prevention and early intervention requires a major shift of funds from remediation and special education toward tutors and other services for young children. School districts almost invariably spend much more on secondary than on elementary education, and they spend staggering sums on special education for students with learning disabilities. Yet by shifting some of these funds to the early elementary grades, it may be possible to substantially reduce special education placements and to deliver to secondary schools students who are capable, motivated, and ready for whatever secondary schools can teach them.

In teaching at-risk students, two key requirements are relentlessness and flexibility. Relentlessness means sticking with a child until you find a way to meet his or her needs. It means refusing to give up on a child, no matter what. Flexibility means a willingness to try many approaches, to consult with others, to involve parents, to experiment, and to do different things with some children than you do with the rest of the class if this is what they need. Of course, there may be practical limitations to what an individual teacher can do without added resources or assistance, but teachers working together in collaboration with any special services (such as Chapter 1 or special education) can solve just about any problem.

SUMMARY

Research on programs for at-risk children finds that instructional effectiveness depends on how resources are used. Effects of such programs are greatest when schools invest in staff development to implement specific, well-designed programs, such as first-grade tutoring models or cooperative learning, or to implement schoolwide change models such as Success for All and the School

Development Program. Federal Chapter 1 programs and state programs built along similar lines make an important contribution to the educational success of disadvantaged students, but more attention must be paid to how such funds are used to improve instruction if these programs are to more consistently improve the achievement of all students. Teachers can ensure the success of all children if they work in collaboration with each other to find ways to prevent students from falling behind in the first place, to intervene intensively when students start to experience learning problems, and to work relentlessly and flexibly to find solutions to students' problems.

References

Adams, M. J. (1990). *Beginning to Read: Thinking and Learning About Print*. Cambridge, MA: MIT Press.

Archambault, F. X. (1989). "Instructional Setting and Other Design Features of Compensatory Education Programs," in R. E. Slavin, N. L. Karweit, and N. A. Madden, eds., *Effective Programs for Students at Risk*. Boston: Allyn and Bacon.

Becker, H. J. (1992). "Computer-based Integrated Learning Systems in the Elementary and Middle Grades: A Critical Review and Synthesis of Evaluation Reports." *Journal of Educational Computing Research* 8: 1–41.

Carter, L. F. (1984). "The Sustaining Effects Study of Compensatory and Elementary Education." *Educational Researcher* 13 (7): 4–13.

Comer, J. (1988). "Educating Poor Minority Children." *Scientific American* 259: 42–48.

Crawford, J. (1989). "Instructional Activities Related to Achievement Gain in Chapter 1 Classes," in R. E. Slavin, N. L. Karweit, and N. A. Madden, eds., *Effective Programs for Students at Risk*. Boston: Allyn and Bacon.

Gutiérrez, R., and R. E. Slavin (1992). "Achievement Effects of the Nongraded Elementary School: A Best-evidence Synthesis." *Review of Educational Research* 62: 333–376.

Karweit, N. L. (1994a). "Can Preschool Alone Prevent Early Reading Failure?" in R. E. Slavin, N. L. Karweit, and B. A. Wasik, eds., *Preventing Early School Failure: Research on Effective Strategies*. Boston: Allyn and Bacon.

Karweit, N. L. (1994b). "Issues in Kindergarten Organization and Curriculum," in R. E. Slavin, N. L. Karweit, and B. A. Wasik, eds., *Preventing Early School Failure: Research on Effective Strategies*. Boston: Allyn and Bacon.

Knapp, M. S., N. E. Adelman, C. Marder, H. McCollum, M. C. Needels, P. C. Shields, B. J. Turnbull, and A. A. Zucker (1992). *Academic Challenge for the Children of Poverty*. Washington, D.C.: U.S. Department of Education.

Larrivee, B. (1989). "Effective Strategies for Academically Handicapped Student in the Regular Classroom," in R. E. Slavin, N. L. Karweit, and N. A. Madden, eds., *Effective Programs for Students at Risk*. Boston: Allyn and Bacon, pp. 291–319.

Mullis, I. V. S., and L. B. Jenkins (1990). *The Reading Report Card, 1971-88*. Washington, D.C.: U.S. Department of Education.

Natriello, G., E. L. McDill, and A. M. Pallas (1990). *Schooling Disadvantaged Children: Racing Against Catastrophe*. New York: Teachers College Press, Columbia University.

Pinnell, G. S., D. E. DeFord, and C. A. Lyons (1988). *Reading Recovery: Early Intervention for At-risk First Graders*. Arlington, VA: Educational Research Service.

Puma, M. J., C. C. Jones, D. Rock, and R. Fernandez (1993). *Prospects: The Congressionally Mandated Study of Educational Growth and Opportunity*. Interim report. Bethesda, MD: Abt Associates.

Schenck, E. A., and S. Beckstrom (1993). *Chapter 1 Schoolwide Project Study*. Portsmouth, NH: RMC.

Slavin, R. E. (1990). *Cooperative Learning: Theory, Research, and Practice*. Englewood

Cliffs, NJ: Prentice Hall.

Slavin, R. E., N. L. Karweit, and N. A. Madden, eds. (1989). *Effective Programs for Students at Risk.* Boston: Allyn and Bacon.

Slavin, R. E., N. L. Karweit, and B. A. Wasik (1994). *Preventing Early School Failure: Research on Effective Strategies.* Boston: Allyn and Bacon.

Slavin, R. E., N. A. Madden, N. L. Karweit, L. Dolan, B. Wasik, S. Ross, and L. Smith (1994). "Whenever and Wherever We Choose . . . : The Replication of Success for All." *Phi Delta Kappan.*

Slavin, R. E., N. A. Madden, N. L. Karweit, L. Dolan, and B. Wasik (1992). *Success for All: A Relentless Approach to Prevention and*

Early Intervention in Elementary Schools. Arlington, VA: Educational Research Service.

Wasik, B. A., and R. E. Slavin (1993). "Preventing Early Reading Failure with One-to-One Tutoring: A Review of Five Programs." *Reading Research Quarterly* 28: 179–200.

Wong-Fillmore, L., and C. Valdez (1986). "Teaching Bilingual Learners," in M. C. Wittrock, ed., *Handbook of Research on Teaching,* 3rd ed. New Haven: Yale University Press.

Zigler, E., and S. J. Styfco (1993). *Head Start and Beyond: A National Plan for Extended Childhood Intervention.* New Haven: Yale University Press.

Discussion Questions

Imagine that the following at-risk children were in a class at the grade level you teach or supervise. For each child, answer these questions:

- What could have been done in previous years to have prevented the child's problem?
- What can you do now to help this child succeed?

1. James is a very poor reader. He reads very slowly, makes many errors, and has difficulty understanding what he has read. His parents are deeply concerned about him, but don't know what to do to help him.

2. Sara is doing poorly in all school subjects. She seems bright and verbal, but has long had an inconsistent pattern of attendance, and often arrives at school hungry, dirty, or sleepy.

3. Ronald is doing reasonably well in school, and when motivated he can perform well. However, he seems bored in school most of the time, never volunteers an answer, and does the minimum necessary to get by. His behavior in class is totally different from that on the playground, where he is active, enthusiastic, and popular.

4. Sherry is a child with very uneven performance in school. She transferred to the school recently, and is totally lacking in some skills while above average in others. For example, she has no idea how to subtract, but multiplies well; she is very poor at decoding reading, but comprehends well when she is read to.

5. Mack is a child with a chip on his shoulder. He is always getting in trouble, and especially likes to do things that annoy his teachers but make his peers laugh. He is doing poorly in school but seems to suffer more from "won't do" than "can't do."

6. Marta is a child from a Spanish-speaking family who came to kindergarten with very little English. Her English is now passable on the playground but she is hesitant to use it in class. As a result, she does poorly in most school subjects. The major exception is math, where she does well except on word problems.

Martin Haberman and Linda Post

Martin Haberman   Linda Post

"My most vivid memory of being raised in Brooklyn, New York, was our backyard," remembers Martin Haberman. "It abutted the subway tracks and every three or four minutes, a train would roar by. This taught me the lessons of behavioral conditioning early and well. No one in my family ever noticed that every few moments we couldn't hear the radio, or each other, or a telephone voice, or that everything jiggled."

Haberman graduated from James Madison High School (the school had 5,500 students) in 1949, and then from Brooklyn College at age twenty. During his college days, he worked full time, fifty-four hours per week, while carrying a full load of college courses. As he says, "I guess I bought into the work ethic early and have never been able to shake it."

While teaching at the elementary school level in New York City, he went on to complete a master's degree in sociology at New York University and another master's at Teachers College, Columbia University. Haberman continued at T.C. for his doctorate in education, where he worked with Florence Stratemeyer as his major advisor and supervised student teachers in the Harlem public schools. He says, "It was during this period that my personal, work, and educational experiences jelled and I realized that my life's work would be

preparing teachers for urban schools serving children in poverty."

After completing his doctorate, Haberman came to the University of Wisconsin, Milwaukee, where he has remained for more than thirty years. For eleven years, he was the dean of an urban outreach program trying to help the university address inner-city problems through research and service. He is currently a distinguished professor of curriculum and instruction, and he is the author of seven books and 150 articles.

Over the years, Martin has developed more teacher education programs than anyone else in history. Some of his more successful models include the well-known National Teacher Corp., which brought more than 100,000 teachers into urban schools and alternative certification programs for attracting more minorities into teaching and for resolving the continuing shortage of teachers for inner-city schools. His interview techniques for selecting successful urban teachers and principals is currently used in many urban school districts across the nation.

Martin's work leads him to conclude that most successful inner-city teachers share "an ideology or set of beliefs and commitments which guide their behaviors and make them effective." This ideology is learned through "life experiences which transcend what is learned in formal education." For this reason, he feels (as does his co-author) that selection is more important than training; given the right people, on-the-job training will occur naturally and with the help of mentors.

"My most vivid memories of childhood reflect the death of my mother when I was six, and growing up with an alcoholic father and a series of step-mothers. Until I reached twenty-eight, and left home, I was the 'parent' of my younger brother and sister." Throughout these experiences, Linda Post was labeled as an "at-risk" child by her teachers and other adults in her environment. Nonetheless, she was able to excel in high school and then work two jobs at the same time to pay for college. She graduated from La Moyna College in 1969 and returned to Syracuse, her place of birth, for her master's (1971) and doctorate degrees in urban education (1975).

Because of her childhood experiences, Linda made a decision early in her professional life to pursue a teaching career in the inner city. During these years she recalls, "I found a commitment to working with urban children and children in poverty." And since her graduate school days at Syracuse, some twenty years ago, Linda has been supervising and directing urban teacher education programs. Currently she is associate professor of education at the University of Wisconsin, Milwaukee, and co-directs with Martin Haberman the Metropolitan Multicultural Teacher Education Program at U.W.

Linda sums it up this way: "Throughout it all, my goal to make a difference in urban education has been a driving force. I believe that better teachers make better schools, and to get better teachers we need to make better initial teacher selections." For Linda, the best and brightest teachers should be paid extra money and be teaching in our inner cities. I think she may have a good point.

20 &

Multicultural Teaching in the Real World

Martin Haberman and Linda Post

Imagine reading a catalogue of spare parts for machines that have never been built. Imagine further that the technical writers describing these spare parts have used very few (or none) of these parts but have collected the descriptions from others or simply made them up. After examining current texts, handbooks, and source books on how to make schooling more multicultural, one has the clear impression of the difficulty in trying to read and derive a comprehensive understanding from such a catalogue. Complex and difficult issues about the nature of teachers and teaching, learners and learning, schools and the community, are dealt with in cursory ways or omitted altogether. It seems to us that these issues must be realistically addressed before programs for improving multicultural education can be implemented in any meaningful way in real schools.

We recognize that while these issues are prerequisite to understanding what is happening and what might happen, they are not readily resolvable. Nevertheless, we believe that it is incumbent on the various proponents of multicultural programs to be clear about their positions and assumptions so that readers and users of the material they advocate can have a context for understanding where they are coming from, what they hope to accomplish, and why. Without greater amplification and clarity, much of the how-to-do-it on multicultural teaching reads like recipes of jejune activities.

Following are some of the critical issues that advocates might at least address. To continue to ignore these issues and simply hand out advice on specific new content and ways of teaching that content, will ensure that the present state of affairs continues. We see this as a time when much is written and discussed about multicultural education, but what is actually done in classrooms is bits and pieces of odds and ends in fits and starts.

MULTICULTURAL ISSUES

Issue 1: Can the particular multicultural program being advocated be implemented within the existing curriculum, or must the curriculum be restructured? One of the truisms about school curriculum is that things are added but never subtracted. Practicing teachers complain constantly about the addition of content by federal statute, state mandate, local board policy, or the reports of national commissions of experts in various subject matters. In addition, forces outside of education pressure schools to add content related to health, the environment, career education, and countless other valuable forms of learning. In many districts the school curriculum is actually legislated and controlled down to the number of minutes per week of instruction in the particular content areas. It seems imperative that advocates for any multicultural program state in specific terms whether their content is an add-on or to be integrated. In the case of the former, how will room be made in the curriculum; in the case of the latter, precisely how and with what subjects will the new content be integrated? To explain anything less than this is to continue the pretense that classroom teachers are independent decision makers in complete control of what they teach, and that providing them with catalogues of interesting lessons and activities they can use in their classrooms is all that is necessary.

Issue 2: Is the particular multicultural program to become part of the elementary school program, the social studies program, or integrated throughout all grade levels and subjects? The question of implementation is more than a question of finding time and deciding whether to add or integrate studies. As difficult as those questions are, this issue refers to such questions as: Which teachers bear responsibility for teaching what? Is the curriculum conceived of as a series of prerequisites and discrete steps from easy to hard, or is the curriculum a continuing spiral in which content is retaught at several later grades on increasingly advanced levels? Some advocate strategies for making pupils more culturally sensitive by utilizing all subject areas including topics in music, physical education, literature, science, and arithmetic. Other approaches seek to interrelate these studies into multicultural problems or projects that cut across several content areas. Unless this issue is addressed directly, many multicultural advocacies are readily pigeon-holed as being limited to social studies, or, even more, to social studies in the elementary grades.

Issue 3: Can the multicultural program being advocated be implemented by teachers using any form of instruction, or are some forms of instruction more appropriate than others? It is common to find multicultural activities and materials being proposed to teachers on the assumption that instruction is generic; that it doesn't matter if the teacher typically uses direct instruction, cooperative learning, or any other form of instruction. Even the most cursory scanning of proposed multicultural lessons and activities reveals that some will require team work, others individual research skills, and others the ability to follow directions carefully. Our reading of the advocacy literature in multicultural education seems to reveal an emphasis on cooperative activity. While this may certainly be desirable, most teachers still use direct instruction most of the time. Why is it reasonable for advocates of multicultural education to not state the form(s) of instruction that will best teach their programs? Do they really believe that all teachers will immediately understand the types of instruction that will be needed and will simply implement those forms? A simple tour of classrooms in most schools reveals that such a belief is not based on reality.

Issue 4: Can teachers implement a particular multicultural program within their existing role, or will the scope and responsibility of the teacher's work have to be reconstructed in order to implement the program? It is clear that in specific multicultural advocacies the teacher will have to be more involved with the parents, the school community, and a range of out-of-school groups. The teacher may also have to become involved with other professionals serving their students. There are clearly out-of-school activities in homes, organizations, businesses, social institutions—even churches—implied by some multicultural advocacies. It seems reasonable to us that proponents of these programs should spell out the new or special role they envision for the teacher in relation to parents, members of the community, members of various culture groups, and all others with whom they expect teachers to interact and cooperate. This issue also involves subissues such as teachers' free time, paid versus unpaid activities, and a possible redefinition of in-class and out-of-class teacher activities. It is critical that proponents of these programs address the realities of contracts, negotiations, and bureaucracies. They also need to develop and advocate strategies for dealing with these realities.

Issue 5: Can teachers implement a particular multicultural program as individuals, or is it necessary that they work in teams, or is it required that the total faculty and staff of a school agree to work on a particular multicultural program? Many advocates of multicultural programs have strong opinions about these matters. It seems to us that it would be most helpful to practicing teachers if proponents could organize their advice in terms of what one teacher might do, what a few might do, what a total department or several grades might do, and so on. To simply call for or announce that the total environment of the school must be changed is less helpful than to be specific about what is feasible when the unit of analysis is the classroom, the grade, the school, or the district.

It is clear from the history of curriculum change that securing total agreement among teachers and others on these matters will not be easy and may not even be possible. Does the advocate of a multicultural program have a responsibility to also advise teachers, principals, parents, and citizens on how they might proceed with less than total consensus? Do we assume that if total consensus is not readily achievable then neither is any part of the multicultural program?

Issue 6: Is the new content needed by teachers things they can be expected to know right now, or material they can be expected to learn, or content they can teach without really knowing it themselves? While most would agree that you can't teach what you don't know, it is not uncommon to find advocacies that encourage teachers to move ahead and "teach" activities dealing with various culture groups about whom they know nothing. If this is the case, then proponents need to be clear about the teacher's role as a coordinator of resource people, or materials, or videotapes. Honesty should compel proponents to state that they believe teachers can be ignorant of selected materials and/or content but that if these resources are used in certain ways, then these procedures, people, or materials will lead to the desired student learning. If proponents are unwilling to take this position openly, they should be willing to lay out what teachers need to learn first and *how they might learn it* before they offer the particular multicultural program. This issue is of critical importance since it is quite likely that multicultural material—particularly content related to the ethnicity of the children a teacher may be working with right now—may not have been part of the teachers' preservice teacher preparation.

This issue is directly related to Issue 3. Teachers using direct instruction of the whole class as their primary mode of teaching may find it difficult to suddenly transform themselves into coordinators of resources. Proponents of multicultural programs have a responsibility to lay out what teachers need to know themselves, and if this knowledge is gained prior to, during, or after conducting the activities recommended for children and youth.

Issue 7: What is the nature of American society being advocated? What is the vision of diversity being taught? Does it include groups based on gender, age, and physical condition as well as on language, race, ethnicity, religion, and culture? Does the content to be learned emphasize goals related to self-concept, knowledge, awareness, skills, or the advocacy of equitable treatment for others? Different proponents have different visions of what they intend their multicultural programs to achieve. We have elsewhere spelled out ten options of such goals (Haberman & Post, 1993). In reading goal statements, proponents are likely to state their support for all goals. It has become characteristic of proponents for almost any curriculum change to claim that if their advocacy is adopted there will be multiple good results. This is not simply a distortion but a disservice to educators and others seeking a clearer vision of what the proponents mean by greater multiculturalism. For example, what would it mean for American society if the particular proponent's vision were actually achieved? This level of clarity is more than can be found in most advocacies that make the student or child the unit of analysis and provide a lengthy wish list of what will be learned. But what these learnings will add up to for the common good is generally omitted. The quip, "If you don't know where you're going any road will get you there" seems appropriate.

Issue 8: Does the particular multicultural program emphasize cultural diversity internationally, nationally, state-wide, district-wide, or by school building? Proponents of various approaches to multicultural education emphasize different levels and do so without being conscious of the shifts. There are clear implications for the role and work of the classroom teacher who is teaching a program based on beginning with the local community, understanding ourselves, and learning to live together. Traditionally, young children have studied their communities while older children study more encompassing units (for example, countries, continents, the world, and so on). Is this the intention of particular multicultural advocates or do they have a new view of what is appropriate content for all ages? They have an obligation, it seems to us, to relate their advocacies to the developmental ages of children and youth, or to state directly that their programs are so vital or universal that they transcend such distinctions.

Issue 9: Will the learnings gained in the particular multicultural program being advocated be assessed by traditional means of evaluation, or will new form(s) of evaluation be used? Classroom teachers are well aware of the dominance of the testing program over what they teach, or what's in the curriculum guides, or what the students actually learn. Much of the activities, lessons, and other things being advocated in multicultural programs—and the outcomes they are supposed to achieve—do not seem to us to lend themselves to current forms of assessment used in schools. It seems that proponents need to be direct and honest with teachers and others they ask to adopt their suggestions. How will these learnings be assessed? How might these learnings impact on current forms of assessment? The present climate in which schools operate makes it virtually impossible for them to adopt new curricula without being able to state how they intend to be accountable. This includes not only what students will learn but how they will be assessed; how, by whom, and at what cost in time, money, and human resources. To recommend substantial curriculum changes without such assessment schemes seems to us to be less than responsible.

Issue 10: Are practicing teachers merely ignorant of the particular multicultural program being advocated, or do they hold values that would actively prevent them from implementing new programs of multiculturalism? It seems naive for proponents of particular multicultural programs to proceed on the assumption that classroom teachers simply need new knowledge and skills to implement their programs; that the teachers simply have a void in this area that needs to be filled in. Our experience with experienced teachers is that they have a range of strongly held views on multicultural issues. Many believe, for example, that school curricula should only recognize individuals and the total society; that cultural subgroups should be gradually assimilated into the larger society and cease to exist. Others believe it is counterproductive to the general welfare to recognize, let alone seek to enhance, diverse culture groups. Some teachers seriously question the right or wisdom of groups to retain a second language. Many teachers reject the concept that it is necessary to fight group prejudice and societal discrimination. They believe that each child should learn to deal with and accept every other child, and if *individuals* are taught to respect *individuals* then the problems of prejudice and discrimination would fade away. They see interpersonal relations as a substitute for multicultural education.

Do proponents of new and particular approaches to multiculturalism have a plan for changing widely held and deep seated teachers' values? Do they assume that teachers will simply lay aside their lifelong belief systems? We have not seen curriculum materials which even recognize that what teachers currently believe is of any importance, or that what teachers believe will control the impact of any curriculum.

TEACHING IN THE MIDST OF PERSISTENT CONCEPTUAL CONFLICT

Thus far we have argued that writing and disseminating activity books or other forms of multicultural curricula to teachers will not accomplish much that is lasting or apparent in schools unless the ten issues related to how schools and teachers actually work are also addressed. In the interest of moving our analysis ahead, let us assume that proponents of various types of multicultural pro-grams begin to address and even answer these questions. What next? Would anything still be needed to actually implement multicultural curricula in schools?

It seems that the nature of teaching, particularly in culturally diverse, urban schools characterized by many students in poverty, is extremely stressful work. One of the many reasons for this stress is that experts in every area of the cur-riculum bombard policy makers, school leaders, and teachers with conflicting advocacies of how to best teach every subject. Reading and math are the most notable examples, but a serious examination of the school's total curriculum reveals that every subject matter is literally a battleground of competing experts' views. Every publisher of texts and software has a competing program for every subject matter. And, if these differences over content are insufficiently stressful, there are equally strong and divergent advocacies regarding the processes to be adopted. Proponents of differing methods of teaching, and various ways of group-ing, testing, and scheduling create a continuous climate of tension and conflict.

Enter proponents for various forms of multicultural curricula. This advocacy generates even more points of contention than diverse advocacies of subject matters. (It certainly has more "experts" with opposing points of view.) It is our contention, however, that if we begin by recognizing and understanding that school people *typically* function in an arena of conceptual conflict, we can ne-gotiate multicultural curricula through the normal stresses and tensions to the point of implementation. The analysis that follows will lay out five areas of con-ceptual conflict which school people should expect and prepare for in the pro-cess of implementing a more multicultural curriculum: goal setting, staff development, children/youth development, teaching strategies, and American values conflicts. By recognizing these conditions we can prepare for them in advance and principals, teachers, students, parents, and community members may be able to work through what might otherwise be perceived as unforeseen and overwhelming controversies.

Teaching in the Midst of Goal Conflicts

Schools run for approximately 180 days each year without much discussion, let alone consensus, as to why. Clearly, various constituencies have different goal priorities. Citizens, parents, and school people have learned to cope with this divergence by rarely discussing questions of purpose. Most of us pretend that we not only know why there are schools and why there are particular subjects taught but also that there is some sort of tacit agreement on the matter. When a new subject matter or body of content is introduced, however, the question of pur-pose is more difficult to ignore. Some "fool" will inevitably raise questions like, "Why do we need this?" "What will adding this to the curriculum accomplish?" "What is the problem we're trying to solve?" It is unfair but inevitable that subject matters already in the curriculum will never have to meet the hard tests of having a clear purpose and gaining widespread agreement about meeting that purpose. Because consensus cannot be easily reached, existing subject matters are safely ensconced beyond recall. There will never be the widespread agreement needed to drop them. New subjects and programs, however, will have to meet the high standards of laying out clear purposes and gaining widespread support before their programs will be adopted.

What is the vision of victory? What is expected to happen after a particular advocacy for a new multicultural program is adopted? Many business leaders support an education that would prepare high school graduates to work cooperatively in more diverse work environments. Others support greater multiculturalism as meeting the need for better citizenship education. ("All those who come out of schools full of hate can still vote and hold office.") Others intend that multiculturalism foster advocacy regarding equity issues and that their programs will foster the moral character to engage in such activities. Some proponents focus their intentions for multicultural programs on making the process of teaching more relevant to students' lives so that existing subjects are learned better. These competing visions are amplified elsewhere (Haberman, in press).

Classroom teachers are familiar with these controversies and usually proceed with their daily work by ignoring them. While there is no clear evidence, many teacher educators and students of teaching believe that when teachers can make thoughtful connections between their activities and why they teach what they do, a more powerful form of teaching and learning will occur. It is our contention that if a team of teachers were to agree on a set of purposes for adopting a multicultural program and its particular vision, then all the lessons and activities those teachers might offer would inevitably be infused with those purposes, and so too would the learning gained by their students.

Advocates of multicultural programs have a twofold purpose for being explicit about their vision: first to pass the hurdle of having their program adopted by the various constituencies that comprise the school community; and second, to generate the commitment of thoughtful teachers who will regard that vision as undergirding their day-to-day work with children and youth.

Multicultural Programs and Staff Development

The second conflict that must be raised and faced by advocates of multicultural programs deals with their approach to the teachers themselves. Are the teachers the problem or the solution? Some writers, in analyzing the present situation, point to the monolinguism, ethnocentrism, and parochialism of the teaching force. They argue that teachers lack cultural breadth and openness and then propose activities, lessons, and materials that must be taught by those same teachers. If teachers' cultural narrowness is the problem, then it would seem reasonable to propose engaging in staff development or getting new teachers rather than assume that some unexplained transformation will occur when the teachers are given new ways to teach Columbus or celebrate Martin Luther King's birthday. *In practice it is not the activities that change teachers but the teachers who bring the activities to life.* No curriculum is teacherproof and beyond the ability of teachers to render it meaningless. Conversely, no set of activities or piece of content is so remote or unimportant that some teachers can make it meaningful and vital for the students they teach.

The problem here is that only a fraction of 1 percent of school budgets are devoted to staff development and that it is unlikely that even an intensive inservice program would change the way white or black or brown teachers look at gender or race issues (Sleeter, 1992).

Inservice teachers tend to be fixed on denying the existence or usefulness of subgroups in American society. In a study of 227 experienced teachers, we had respondents identify what they perceived as the goal of multicultural education (Haberman & Post, 1993). Regardless of differences in years of experience, sex, elementary or secondary teaching, or level of educational training, the respondents overwhelmingly chose the first two levels in Table 20.1. They either denied the need for teaching about or being sensitive to cultural subgroups (Level 1) or perceived tolerance as the most appropriate goal for teachers and schools.

Fewer than 5 percent of the respondents perceived that Levels 3, 4, or 5 were either necessary or desirable. It seems that the goals of an inservice education for teachers would move them in the direction of Level 5. Further, inservice teachers need to see that all children and youth need three types of learning: learning related to themselves, their subgroups, and the larger society (Haberman & Post, 1990).

Either through initial selection of teachers or retraining subsequently, it seems that practicing classroom teachers can only be dealt with as part of the solution. In spite of the difficulties presented thus far, there are better ways to address these problems. While there are still no model school systems, there are numerous examples of model schools in which faculty have changed their perceptions and their programs.

Unless advocates of particular multicultural programs address this issue in a forthright manner, it will continue to be a source of conflict surrounding faculty relationships. While proponents cannot solve the problem by simply stating their views or preferences, it seems that they have a responsibility to admit

Table 20.1   Levels of Multicultural Perceptions Held by Teachers

Denial of subgroups	1. Children/youth would learn that all people are individuals—distinctive personalities—regardless of their backgrounds.
Toleration	2. Children/youth would learn that we all have to learn to live together in this world regardless of our differences. Cooperation and tolerance are vital.
Heterogeneity	3. Children/youth would learn that every person comes from some ethnic group and that all groups are equally fine.
Advocacy	4. Children/youth would learn that the United States is made up of many racial, ethnic, and religious groups and each must be protected and enhanced.
Change	5. Children/youth would learn that we all have a responsibility to change the discrimination and prejudice in our society against certain groups.

there is a need for continuous teacher development and to state how they would meet this need.

Conflicting Models of Development

Classroom teachers, particularly many who are highly successful with children in poverty from diverse backgrounds, do not perceive that the children they teach are represented in texts on learning and development. Indeed, teacher trainers, particularly those in educational psychology, tend to support the view that learning is based on generic principles, that developmental stages are universal, and that "kids are kids." In the multicultural literature, however, there is a continuous debate on different learning styles derived from differences in groups: sex, race, and culture. Some argue that culture exerts so much control over the development of learning style that teachers need to be aware of what works best for children from various backgrounds. Individual personality differences or stages of development that were once assumed to be universal are no longer accepted as universal, typical, or normal (Shade, 1982). Others argue that this approach is itself a form of stereotyping and is counterproductive when it contends that black males learn best if taught in ways that involve hands-on, interaction, and oral communication (Hilliard, 1989).

Those who argue that cultural experience controls much of how children in various groups develop and may best be taught contend that future teachers and practicing ones need to reconceptualize what they regard as normal—that the responses they see in children and youth every day are perfectly natural responses to the conditions under which they live.

What does this add up to for practicing teachers? Some have traced five themes that characterize the lives of many who live in urban poverty (Haberman, 1993). This is not to claim that all poor people or those from diverse backgrounds experience these forces to the same degree or that their children will all respond to these forces in precisely the same way. We have sketched typical forces that engender normal responses in both the adults and children who live under these conditions. What might these five forces add up to? How might they interact and influence a youngster growing up? What might be normal responses to these life conditions?

Lacking trust in any adults might naturally lead one to be suspicious of their motives and their actions. Appearing to be shy or withdrawing from adults might be a perfectly normal response. Not expecting or seeking safety or the solution to one's problems from adults might be another reasonable response. The second force cited was the violence typical of urban life today. If those around us are potentially dangerous and life threatening, then interacting with them is to be avoided whenever possible. The perception of "no hope" is the third force that characterizes urban life for those in poverty and is frequently mistaken for a lack of initiative. If one sees no viable options it seems useless to expend effort. The fourth force cited relates to the impact of living under mindless bureaucracies. It becomes natural, normal—even desirable—to give the bureaucracy what it wants rather than respond in sensible or honest ways. It is only by responding to the bureaucracy on its own terms that any benefits can be derived. This teaches children who grow up under such conditions to initiate and reveal as little as possible and only what is being asked of them as their normal response. The fifth force cited relates to the culture of authoritarianism. The giving and taking of orders becomes the normal way of life. One's power becomes one's self-definition.

Taken together, the outstanding attribute one can be expected to *normally* develop as a result of these and other forces is frustration. Feelings of deep frustration are characteristic of both adults and children who grow up and live with the experience of urban poverty. And the one result we can be certain to derive from this abiding frustration is some form of aggression. For some it is overt and clear. For many others it takes the form of passive resistance. And for many others it is turned inward on oneself, leading to suicide and to the multiple ways poor people demonstrate a reckless abandon for their own bodies.

The world children in poverty frequently begin school with is a wait and see attitude. Not being certain or trusting of adults, surrounded by family and friends being "done to," living with violence, and having learned how to give and take orders are some of their skills. How classroom teachers build on this set of students' expectations seems to us to be a responsibility of those advocating multicultural programs to explain. To not do so implies that the advocate assumes the "kids are kids" approach is correct and viable.

Conflicting Models of Teaching

Those advocating multicultural programs generally recognize that the students who need these programs include middle- and upper-class, white, suburban, monolingual constituencies typically referred to as "the majority." In practice, however, multicultural programs are typically being adopted most frequently in large urban districts serving large numbers of children of color, many of whom are in poverty.

Observing in urban classrooms it is possible to find examples of almost every form of pedagogy: direct instruction, cooperative learning, peer-tutoring, individualized instruction, computer-assisted learning, behavior modification, pupil contracts, media-assisted instruction, scientific inquiry, lecture-discussion, tutoring by specialists or volunteers, even the use of problem-solving units common in progressive education. In spite of this broad range of pedagogic options, however, there is a typical, modal form of teaching that has become accepted as basic. Indeed, this basic urban style, which encompasses a body of specific teacher acts, seems to become stronger each year. If, in urban schools of the 1990s, a teacher were to *not* engage in these basic acts as his or her primary means of instruction, he or she would be regarded as deviant. In most urban schools, *not* performing these acts for most of each day would be considered *prima facie* evidence of not teaching. The teaching acts that comprise the core functions of urban teaching are

- Giving information
- Asking questions

- Giving directions

- Making assignments

- Monitoring seatwork

- Reviewing assignments

- Giving tests

- Reviewing tests

- Assigning homework

- Reviewing homework

- Settling disputes

- Punishing noncompliance

- Marking papers

- Giving grades

This core of urban teacher functions, in varying combinations, characterizes all levels and subject matters. A primary teacher might "give information" by reading a story to children, while a high school teacher might read to the class from a biology text. (Interestingly, they both offer the same reasons for the act: "The students can't read for themselves" and "they enjoy being read to.") Taken separately, there may be nothing wrong with these activities. There are occasions when any one of the fourteen acts might have a beneficial effect. Taken together and performed to the systematic exclusion of other acts, they have become the pedagogic coin of the realm in urban schools. They comprise the pedagogy of poverty; not merely what teachers do and what youngsters expect, but for different reasons, what parents, community, and the general public assume teaching to be (Haberman, 1991).

It seems clear to us, therefore, that advocates of particular programs need to recognize and deal with this issue of overly directive teaching. The students have been conditioned to want and expect it. This form of instruction supports the condition of "being done to" described earlier. It also fits nicely with the brutalities, neglect, and mistreatment many of them have suffered and which is described in our preceding discussion of developmental differences experienced by children reared in poverty. Advocates of multicultural approaches need to first recognize that when they propose "sensitizing," "humanizing," or "creating awareness," they are proposing a form of teaching that will be new to many of these children and youth—and to their teachers. Advocates can demonstrate they understand the magnitude and depth of this issue when, in addition to proposing neat new, discrete activities, they show teachers and their children how to move from the direction-giving and control mechanisms which pass for teaching to forms of instruction that demonstrate genuine respect for children.

This need was recently recapitulated for us in a program we offer that trains resident teachers on-the-job in an urban school system. One of our residents, a young, strong African-American male, was placed in an Open Education Specialty

School. Many other teachers, outside of the school, told him, "That's not the way 'our' kids can learn!" His and his children's outstanding success in this school using *extremely* student-centered teaching strategies underscores our point. It is possible for teachers to grow and change—even extreme amounts in one year—but it is incumbent on the advocates of a particular multicultural approach to recognize the need for changing the pedagogy of poverty and to explain the means for accomplishing such change. In our case we provided a full range of human resources, including a mentor teacher and a support network. We also had the advantage of being able to select the teacher to be trained. For advocates of new forms of multicultural curriculum and instruction to ignore the very narrow, limited view of teaching which many of the children *and their teachers* begin with may well be an irreparable flaw.

Conflicting Views of American Society

Proponents of various forms of multicultural programs typically focus on the activities and materials they recommend teachers implement. This is understandable since practitioners are focused on things to do, what works, and specific techniques and materials. Occasionally, advocates of a particular approach will also include some rationale dealing with what the program will accomplish if implemented. Rarely is there any analysis of what the "majority" or general American society is or stands for. The assumptions are that (1) the dominant culture is oppressive and insensitive to the various culture groups and needs to be made more open and equitable; (2) the dominant general culture is some sort of monolithic system; and (3) everyone, including teachers, knows and agrees on the values which characterize our society. It is this last assumption that is the least accurate. We do not believe that most teachers understand the value structure of the general society. Typically they teach bits and pieces of it indirectly or by modeling with little self-analysis of their impact on children. Teachers behave like most others; by doing what they regard as right or proper or polite without much reflection or analysis of the values their behaviors are demonstrating.

It seems to us that proponents of multicultural programs that inevitably make assumptions about the general American society should clearly and directly state what this society is and what it stands for. To describe it as insensitive, oppressive, and in need of change is insufficient. To make any form of multiculturalism work, teachers must be prepared to educate their students as both members of the larger, general society and as participants in particular subgroups.

American society differs from others in several manifest ways. Following are some examples of themes that characterize our society. Our culture is one which values attempts at active mastery rather than passive acceptance. Our people are more interested in the external world of things than in some inner experience of meaning. There is a great emphasis on individual personality, property, and freedom of choice. For over half a century sociologists such as Myrdal (1944) have identified American culture as a society characterized by the following values:

- Achievement and success
- Activity and work
- Moral orientation for judging others
- Humanitarian mores
- Efficiency and practicality
- Emphasis on progress
- Material comfort
- Equality
- Freedom
- External conformity
- Science and secular rationality
- Nationalism-patriotism
- Democracy
- Individual personality
- Racism and related group superiority themes

The "American Dilemma" to which Myrdal (1944) referred is

... the conflict between ... the American Creed, where the American thinks, talks, and acts under the influence of high Christian precepts, and on the other hand, the valuations on specific planes of individual and group living, where personal and local interests; economic, social and sexual jealousies; considerations of community prestige and conformity; group prejudice against particular persons or types of people; and all sorts of miscellaneous wants, impulses and habits dominate his outlook. (p. 354)

THEORY INTO PRACTICE

For classroom teachers, then, the first need is to have some notion of the basic value patterns that distinguish the general American society from others. The second need is to recognize that imbedded in our system of values are some (for example, racism) which we do not aspire to pass on to future generations. Third, and this may be the most difficult, is the need for teachers and others who would socialize others into the larger society to recognize that many of our basic values conflict with and contradict each other.

Referring to the list of fifteen basic values cited previously, there are times when the value of freedom of choice conflicts with the value of patriotism. At other times the value of achievement and success conflicts with our moral orientation. Certainly, our humanitarian values conflict with our racism and the belief that some groups are superior to others. The outstanding classroom teachers who are sensitive to the conflicts and contradictions built into the fabric of our society realize the difficulty of socializing their students to it *before* they ever take on the additional task of teaching a multicultural program that emphasizes the various culture groups which make up the larger society. Children/youth need to understand that our total society is constantly torn between violence and peaceful compromise, between consensus and authoritarianism, between science and religion, between freedom and order, and between concern for self and enhancement of the common good. It is into this maelstrom that the multicultural teacher introduces the added conflicts and discontinuities of ethnic, language, and other culture groups which frequently espouse values at odds with the larger society.

The assumption that the job of the multicultural teacher is to relate various culture groups to a larger society that has internal logic and one way of looking at things is dangerous and misleading. Advocates of multicultural programs have an obligation to share, however briefly, what they believe this larger society to be. Thus far, they seem to be taking the easier road of pretending we all know what American society is and that it is not characterized by its own dislocations and contradictions. Focusing on the various culture groups as the new knowledge that teachers need is certainly necessary. Our contention is that it is not sufficient.

SUMMARY

It is clear that present programs of teacher education are not preparing teachers for cultural diversity (Zeichner, 1993). Given the inadequate level of support available from public schools, inservice staff development does not seem to be any more effective at achieving greater multiculturalism. It may be more reasonable, as well as easier, to select teachers with a multicultural ideology in the first place—before any level of training is offered. But obviously, this is not an adequate solution. Regardless of the high teacher turnover in poverty schools serving diverse populations—and the high retirement rate—there is still an overwhelming need to train and retrain the practicing teachers who remain the core of the staff who serve as teachers. This means that new multicultural programs will have to deal with the issues we have raised regarding the real conditions of teacher practice in schools. This requires that multicultural advocates do more than hire on with publishers interested in neat new lessons that are graded by level or divided by subject, if they are serious about what their advocacies might actually mean in the lives of children/youth. Similarly, using teacher committees or nonprofit organizations to compile handbooks of activities for classrooms without addressing the issues we have raised will maintain multicultural curricula at a superficial level similar to new ways of making turkeys, or a neat new way to make a volcano.

There is no way to pursue new curricula—particularly curricula as emotionally charged as multicultural ones—without simultaneously addressing the issue of on-the-job teacher education and the conditions under which teachers work. The opportunities in this challenge are well worth the effort. Teachers can be models for learners as they work to develop greater awareness themselves. Students and their families can become resources and not simply inadequate objects of input. There can be little question that future schools will change *in response* to the greater diversity of the "new majority." Without planning, these changes might very well create school climates of greater control and restriction. By dealing with issues we have raised, classroom teachers may be proactively involved in making *multicultural* a meaningful word in the effect schools have on children and not a euphemism for schools with more safety aides.

References

Haberman, M. (1991). "The Pedagogy of Poverty versus Good Teaching." *Phi Delta Kappan* 73: 290–304.

Haberman, M. (1993). "Diverse Contexts for Teaching," in M. J. O'Hair and S. J. O'dell, eds., *Diversity and Teaching*. Ft. Worth, TX: Harcourt Brace and Jovanovich, pp. 1–8, 84–90.

Haberman, M. (1994). "Visions of Equal Opportunity" (the top ten fantasies of school reformers). *Phi Delta Kappan* 74: 689–692.

Haberman, M., and L. Post (1990). "Cooperating Teachers' Perceptions of the Goals of Multicultural Education." *ACTION in Teacher Education* 12: 49–54.

Haberman, M., and L. Post (1993). "The Dominance of Craft: What Cooperating Teachers Believe Their Students Need to Learn." A paper presented to the Association of Teacher Educators, Los Angeles.

Haberman, M., and L. Post (1994). "Multicultural Schooling." *Peabody Journal of Education* 69: 101–115.

Hilliard, A. (1989). "Teachers and Cultural Styles in a Pluralistic Society." *NEA Journal* (January): 65–69.

Myrdal, G. (1944). *An American Dilemma* (2 vols). New York: Harper & Brothers.

Shade, B. (1982). "Afro-American Cognitive Style: A Variable in School Success." *Review of Educational Research* 52: 219–244.

Sleeter, C. (1992). "Resisting Racial Awareness: How Teachers Understand the Social Order from Their Racial, Gender and Social Class Locations." *Educational Foundations* 27: 7–32.

Zeichner, K. (1993). *Educating Teachers for Cultural Diversity*. National Center for Research for Teacher Learning, Office of Educational Research and Improvement. Washington, D.C.: U.S. Office of Education.

Discussion Questions

1. Why is it necessary for proponents of greater multiculturalism to address the ten issues raised in this chapter?

2. How might teachers' different views of the school's goals affect the implementation of a multicultural curriculum?

3. What is the relationship between teachers' perceptions of multiculturalism and the need for staff development?

4. What is the connection between the impact of growing up in poverty and the need for a multicultural curriculum?

5. Why is the pedagogy of poverty antithetic to offering a multicultural curriculum?

6. What is it about American values that make them difficult for classroom teachers to implement?

Susan Laird

Susan Laird gives this advice to beginning teachers: "Choose friends and colleagues who will open your eyes to the world in new ways. Read as much as you can, and have the courage to care about people whom most others don't want to spend time, money, and energy on."

She says that her life in education began in earnest when she was a secretary—albeit one with a B.A. from Vassar College (1973)—for a program that served disadvantaged college students. "Their courage and hard work to survive racism and overcome past educational deficits moved me to volunteer as a teacher in an evening high school equivalency program for adults who were seeking new lives, and to return to college for a master's in teaching at Cornell University."

Laird recalls her first regular teaching assignment in a high school that was considered to have an "excellent" reputation. "I was shocked at the girls' situation. Having attended a girls' high school, I found it so different from my own earlier experiences. The school I was teaching at offered few leadership roles and sports programs for girls." Even the bravest girls spoke less than boys, and few books about or by women were available.

Some other teachers shared her concern and decided to do something about it. "Ever since, I have been willing to call myself a feminist." Most graduate schools and programs seemed blind to what Laird saw, but Jane Roland Martin, who later became her mentor, was not, so she went to Cornell for a Ph.D. in philosophy of education.

Since graduating from Cornell in 1988, Laird taught at the University of Maine for four years, and then moved on to the University of Oklahoma in 1992, where she is currently associate professor of educational leadership and policy studies. Her scholarly work for the past several years has addressed gender and teaching issues and has appeared in prestigious journals such as the *Harvard Educational Review.* Laird is currently writing her first book on maternal teaching and adolescent coeducation.

Susan recently took up ballet. She reads fiction on a regular basis and loves to hike mountain trails. She recommends that all teachers read Ntozake Shange's *Betsey Brown,* a playful yet profoundly philosophical novel about the difference between schooling and education in the midst of racial, sexual, and class conflicts.

21 🕭

Coeducational Teaching: Taking Girls Seriously

Susan Laird

U.S. public schools have not always been coeducational, but today most of us take coeducation for granted. We have grown accustomed to speak and write of teaching, and lately even of teaching reform, as if coeducation made no difference for teaching practice: as if girls and boys were indeed equally benefiting from U.S. schools' efforts to teach them. However, major findings on girls and education summarized by the AAUW report, *How Schools Shortchange Girls*, indicate that educators need to take girls far more seriously than most of us presently do—across the curriculum and in the extracurriculum, from early childhood through late adolescence (Wellesley Center for Research on Women [WCRW], 1992). Among many other recommendations, the AAUW report advises policy makers that "Teachers must help girls develop positive views of themselves and their futures, as well as an understanding of the obstacles women must overcome in a society where their options and opportunities are still limited by gender stereotypes and assumptions" (WCRW, 1992, p. 85).

Of course, 72 percent of all school teachers were themselves once girls (WCRW, 1992, p. 7). Belonging to what historically has been known as "woman's true profession," they may have become symbols of precisely the same situation that the AAUW report is now asking them to help correct (Laird, 1988b). Nonetheless, particularly alarmed about the rate at which women and their children are swelling the poverty-stricken population in the United States, the AAUW report calls upon educational leaders to prepare, certify, re-educate, and evaluate teachers with improvement of girls' education specifically in mind. At the same time it notes that many educators do not yet understand gender issues, and

Author Note: I thank the University of Maine for generously accommodating my scholarly needs in summer, 1993, during my work on this project. I am also grateful to Catherine Peaden and Jane Martin for critical comments on earlier drafts of this chapter.

further documents that in 1990 only 27.7 percent of all principals, 4.8 percent of superintendents, 33.7 percent of local school board members, and in 1991 nine of the fifty chief state school officers were women (WCRW, 1992, p. 7). Therefore, the AAUW report urges schools to encourage teachers, especially women teachers, to do their own research and also exercise leadership in reform efforts, so that they can help make coeducational teaching more educative for girls.

I do not think such efforts can succeed unless teachers themselves, of both sexes, do the hard work of thinking seriously about how they should respond to that challenge, and why (Laird, 1991). In order to take girls seriously in public schools, we need to ask, What is **coeducational teaching**? What can make it educative or miseducative for girls? I have no full, final answers to such questions. Detailing how schools shortchange girls alone cannot answer them. But, informed by the AAUW report, we can respond thoughtfully to them. We will revisit both educational philosophers' and women teachers' thoughts about what **coeducation** and **teaching** could and should mean. We will ask ourselves how helpful their thinking may be for our own attempt to clarify what coeducational teaching would mean if we took girls seriously.

THE CONCEPT OF COEDUCATION

The practice of coeducation dates at least as far back as 387 B.C., when Plato's Academy was founded. Women went to study there in large numbers at a time when Greek law forbade them even to attend public meetings. In the late eighteenth century United States, both sexes attended rural common schools. But the term *coeducation* was not coined until the mid-nineteenth century, when the idea became controversial for U.S. urban school systems (Tyack & Hansot, 1990). However, one of coeducation's advocates, John Dewey, did later argue that it would be "absurd to treat the question of coeducation as one to be debated on theoretical . . . grounds" (1911, p. 22). Today we seldom hear the old tiresome questions his opponents raised about the rightness of educating girls as their brothers' equals beyond the elementary years. But perhaps thanks to him, the concept of coeducation has never yet had any theoretical importance (Laird, 1988a).

Coeducation and Educational Theory

Why should we care about this theoretical neglect of coeducation? Seeing it, we should not be surprised to learn from David Tyack and Elisabeth Hansot that "The story of coeducation in public schools is in part one of silent change, of unintended results, of unlikely causes, of unheeded criticisms, and of hidden benefits and costs" (1990, p. 12). And what about coeducation today? According to the AAUW report, teachers do not give girls as much attention as they do boys. Girls are less likely than boys to see themselves reflected in curriculum they must learn, to receive encouragement as students of mathematics and science, to receive needed special education, to train for nonclerical vocations, and to participate in student leadership and sports. Even while public schools tend to treat boys and girls differently, they also tend to ignore psychological evidence that girls develop differently from boys. And although girls generally receive better grades than boys, their self-esteem plummets as they progress through their school years. Girls are at significantly greater risk than boys of suicide, depression, eating disorders, sexual victimization, some sexually transmitted diseases, early parental obligations, and future poverty as single adults heading households. Despite such research findings, which do often detail significant differences among girls of different races, classes, and abilities, only four of thirty-five recent educational reform reports reviewed for the AAUW report even considered girls or gender (WCRW, 1990, p. 6).

Concerned about contemporary educators' failure to think about women and girls, Jane Roland Martin (1982) has called upon philosophers of education to analyze the concept of coeducation. To date, no one has responded to her call. Yet Adrienne Rich was surely right when she said, "If there is any misleading concept it is that of 'coeducation'" (1979, p. 241). For the concept's meaning is much more complex than our common-sense understanding of it suggests. The history of coeducation in the United States has seen

> many ways to educate boys and girls together under the same roof of the public school: to separate them in distinct rooms or on opposite sides of the classroom but give them the same course of studies; to offer them distinct curricula; or to mix boys and girls together in the classroom, teach them the same subjects, and subject them to the same set of rules and rewards. (Tyack & Hansot, 1990, p. 4)

Philosophers and theorists have not yet explored this variety of meanings that coeducation can convey. They routinely insist upon understanding and evaluating education in terms of teaching, learning, and curriculum—and often also social context or governance (Gowin, 1981). But they have not yet inquired into the meaning of coeducational teaching, of coeducational learning, or of coeducational curriculum. Deprived of such conceptual development, coeducation does not signify any difference, sameness, equality, mutuality, appropriateness, domestic or political economy, or multicultural complexities in the two sexes' education together. Coeducation conveys no special meaning to *curriculum* that girls and boys might need to learn to get along with each other as equals or partners in any facet or phase of life. It imparts no significance to the character of their *learning* together as distinct from their learning apart. Nor does it convey any special meaning to *teaching* that the two sexes' different circumstances, interests, needs, aptitudes, developmental patterns, and social powers as learners might demand. Now faced with a major report that schools are shortchanging girls in many ways, we need to get beyond our old shallow view of coeducation. We need a new theoretical understanding of coeducational teaching that can speak to the complexity of our practical attempts to take girls seriously in schools.

Coeducation, Sex, and Gender

A student's or teacher's *sex* is a simple biological trait. But *gender* refers to the ever-changing and culturally various, yet powerful social pressures that students and teachers both confront, and may place upon each other, to conform to certain ideas of what is properly "feminine" or "masculine." The AAUW report considers this conceptual distinction educationally important. For girls who drop out of school not only have much higher poverty rates than boys who drop out; they are also more likely to accept traditional gender stereotypes than are girls who graduate (WCRW, 1990). Tyack and Hansot (1990) have called coeducation "the central puzzle in the gender history of American public elementary and secondary schools" (p. 5). Yet coeducation is a shallow concept largely because it defines the social context of public schooling only in terms of sex—as two-sexed by law. However, it is blind to gender.

I call this shallow concept of coeducation *gender-careless.* Theoretically, it is nearly meaningless; it reflects an unthinking attitude toward coeducation. Gender-careless coeducation attaches no special significance to gender because it takes seriously neither what girls as learners have in common nor their differences from each other. Much (if not most) coeducation today is gender-careless. However, any attempt to take girls seriously while teaching them together with boys does raise the theoretical question of whether or not we should think about gender, and if so, how.

Prior to the AAUW report, educators who have taken girls seriously have considered different philosophical positions on this question (Ayim et al., 1985; Martin, 1985, 1992). Often at odds with each other, past thinkers have addressed numerous philosophical questions about gender and education. For example, What does it mean to be or become an educated woman? Are womanliness and manliness products of nature or of education? How are particular ideals of womanliness and manliness related to each other and to different ideals of the good life and the just society? What harm can such ideals do to real people? How and why do our answers to such questions vary when we think specifically of race, class, religion, disability, and other educationally relevant differences? Is any particular ideal of womanliness a reasonable and humane expectation to place upon all school girls in the United States today? In trying to respond appropriately to *How Schools Shortchange Girls,* we will inevitably face such difficult questions.

Different positions on gender's role in schooling can arise from such inquiry; they can also imply distinctively different theoretical understandings of coeducation's meaning. We will consider two such positions in this chapter. A *gender-bound* meaning of coeducation has taken girls seriously by prescribing for them an education which aims at an ideal of womanhood that renders them different from and usually also subordinate to educated men. By contrast, a *gender-sensitive* meaning of coeducation would take girls seriously by attending to gender's effects in both boys and girls, but only when such vigilant attention "can prevent sex bias or further sex equality" (Ayim et al., 1985, p. 367; Martin, 1985, 1992). Not all advocates of gender-bound education have favored coeducation. Nor have all advocates of gender-sensitive education favored coeducation. But, since public schools in the United States are today coeducational by law, we will set aside the many possible objections to coeducation for now. As we shall see, unlike gender-careless coeducation, both gender-bound and gender-sensitive ways of thinking about coeducation require us also to think somewhat differently about what teaching might mean.

GENDER-CARELESS COEDUCATION AND TEACHING

In Book V of Plato's *Republic,* Socrates claims, against his companions' objections, that sex is a difference which, like baldness, should make no educational difference. As a thought experiment, he envisioned a society whose women of the guardian (ruling) class enjoy equality with men of their own class; therefore, he proposed that women should be educated together with men, exactly the same as men. This Socratic view of coeducation as ideally *gender-blind* is common today. Yet the AAUW report has exposed a pervasive *gender bias* in contemporary coeducational practice. It cites research evidence suggesting that gender-blind coeducational teaching can fail to eliminate gender bias because gender bias often comes from sources other than teaching itself: from the social context, from a school's curriculum, from students' learning habits, and from hidden curriculum. Indeed, Barbara Houston (1985) has demonstrated philosophically that an attitude of gender blindness "is likely to cause us to miss, or even to reinforce, more subtle forms of gender bias" (p. 360). Thus gender-blind coeducation may just be a confusing misnomer for gender-careless coeducation.

The Social Context of Coeducation

Plato's Socrates proposed gender-blind coeducation for a particular social context of his own invention, quite different from ours: a society without family or motherhood. Most of us would probably not want to live in a society as rigidly classed and controlled as he imagined, no matter how much sex equality we would find there. Still, he does seem to have had a crucial insight: that the private institutions of family and motherhood could pose some serious practical obstacles to sex equality. In failing to heed that crucial insight, are contemporary advocates of gender-blind coeducation gender-careless? Does the ideal of gender-blind coeducation offer a means of taking girls seriously in a social context like ours?

According to *How Schools Shortchange Girls,* 37 percent of girls, compared to 5 percent of boys, cite "family-related problems" as reasons for dropping out of school (WCRW, 1992, p. 48). At home boys may face family demands for financial help, but they rarely face the family demands for help with caretaking responsibilities that girls frequently do. Meanwhile, pregnant teens and teen mothers in many high schools still find their educational opportunities more limited than teen fathers': an obvious gender bias. Is gender-blind coeducation the best way to correct that bias? If U.S. schools were gender-blind, they would not judge teen mothers more harshly than they do teen fathers. But gender-blind schools would also assume a teen parent's practical freedom from primary responsibility for a child's care. Is this a fair assumption to make about both teen mothers and fathers?

Coeducational Curriculum and Learning

Socrates' proposal for gender-blind coeducation assumed that girls learn in exactly the same ways as boys. Yet psychologists have recently found that girls' and women's development may differ profoundly from theoretical accounts of "human" development based on evidence from boys and men alone (Gilligan, 1982; Gilligan et al., 1988). Although development and learning are not identical processes, they are closely related and often overlap. If the two sexes do not learn in identical ways, girls may require different teaching even in order to learn the same things as boys (Martin, 1985). Girls' learning in coeducational settings may especially differ from boys'.

For example, the AAUW report cautions educators against assuming that the increasingly popular practice of "cooperative learning" will automatically benefit girls' learning. It has proven effective at increasing students' cross-race friendships, mainstreaming students with disabilities, boosting academic achievement, and developing mutual student concerns. But *How Schools Shortchange Girls* does cite research suggesting that "positive cross-sex relationships may be more difficult to achieve than cross-race relationships or positive relationships among students with and without disabilities" (WCRW, 1992, p. 72). In small mixed-sex groups, boys more often than girls enjoy leadership opportunities that increase their self-esteem and social dominance. At the same time, boys do not respond as readily to girls' requests for help as girls respond to boys' requests. Small wonder, then, that researchers have found girls' achievement actually to decrease in mixed-sex learning groups. Similarly disappointing results have come from a few unusual experimental attempts at gender-blind physical coeducation intended to take girls' physical learning seriously and boost their participation in school sports (Houston, 1985). Perhaps girls could learn well from physical coeducation or mixed-sex cooperative learning groups if teachers carefully structured them with difficulties of cross-sex student interactions in mind. But gender-blind physical education and cooperative learning have been shown to foster gender bias and limit girls' learning. Gender-blind teachers who ignore such research findings are practicing gender-careless coeducation.

Curriculum can also cause girls' learning to differ from boys'. Gender-blind coeducational teaching of any subject becomes gender-careless whenever curriculum reflects no effort to be inclusive, accurate, affirmative, representative, varied, and integrated; whenever school people fail to take girls' learning seriously enough even to try to understand what curriculum or teaching practices may limit or enhance it. But even in this era of widespread reform, "so far no major curriculum-reform efforts have used explicitly gender-fair approaches" (WCRW, 1992, p. 64). The AAUW report cites mathematics and science as subjects whose teachers often fail to investigate how girls best learn in boys' company; consequently, many girls are academically shortchanged. Most physical and vocational education departments fail to challenge sex-stereotyping of sports and occupations, so girls may bring limited expectations of themselves and their futures, along with passive learning habits, into all their other classes. The curriculum of other subjects also often exclude girls, stereotype both sexes, subordinate and degrade girls, isolate materials on women, pay only superficial attention to contemporary issues, and include cultural inaccuracies. Are not such practices likely to affect girls' attitudes toward their own learning as well as boys' attitudes toward girls and women?

Gender-careless coeducation also frequently occurs whenever gender-blind schools, policy makers, and teachers repeat the adage, "Boys will be boys!," rather than investigate the sources of some antisocial behavior in seemingly innocuous gender practices. For example, Raphaela Best's (1983) participant-observer study of elementary school life, *We've All Got Scars*, shows how the apparently unbiased sex-segregation of children's restrooms can cause hidden curriculum in gender and sexuality to develop. In the boys' restroom at the school she studied, second-grade boys bonded with each other against the "opposite" sex, including both teachers and classmates. Consequently, some boys did not readily learn to read, and the playground became a site of sexual intrigue and harassment. What teaching might such coeducational problems demand?

The Standard Concept of Teaching

The recent teaching reform movement has not yet called upon philosophers to clarify the concept of coeducation, but that movement has consulted philosophers about the concept of teaching. Small wonder, then, that this movement's ideal of teaching as a Socratic interaction echoes the standard philosophical analysis of teaching, which is gender-blind (Laird, 1988b). Despite some variations, that analysis does consistently propose that teaching cannot be taking place unless a teacher is engaging students in a Socratic process of reasoning. A process of giving and asking for reasons, not the reasonableness of a teacher's approach to helping a student learn, is the essence of the standard concept of teaching (Martin, 1982). This standard analysis, based upon Plato's account of Socrates teaching one slave boy a geometric theorem, takes coeducation for granted without consideration of its possible effects on learning (Laird, 1989a). Can teaching thus understood responsibly address *How Schools Shortchange Girls?*

Certainly, rational dialogue about gender may play an important part in coeducational teaching. Raphaela Best (1983) demonstrates this possibility when she teaches boys and girls to discriminate between stereotypes and reality, between sexual love and friendly liking. But she notes that girls and boys also have to do different kinds of "psychological work" in order "to have more options than hatred or—sexual—love" for each other (p. 129). The AAUW report recommends that "Classrooms must become places where girls and boys can express feelings and discuss personal experiences" (WCRW, 1992. p. 80). The teaching of empathy, caring, kindness, affectionate friendship, and self-respect may prove necessary if coeducation is not to foster gender bias. Yet an act of teaching a child to feel friendly love or self-respect may not count as an example of teaching at all, in the standard philosophical view, if the teacher is primarily engaging a student's emotions. Moreover, the emotionally detached rationality that characterizes the standard concept of teaching can actually mystify developing sexual attractions, antipathies, and underground games among students, which can undermine coeducational learning even during the elementary school years. Therefore, a broader understanding of teaching than the standard one may be crucial to co-education that takes girls seriously.

What would teaching mean if it included encouraging positive daily relationships with schoolmates of the other sex? If it included education for adult responsibilities and mature intimacies as parents and homemakers? If it included fostering students' ability to recognize, withstand, and resist various injustices and discouragements? Would Socratic rationality be sufficient to accomplish such coeducational aims? Advocates of gender-bound and gender-sensitive coeducation agree with the AAUW report that it cannot.

GENDER-BOUND COEDUCATION AND TEACHING

Gender-bound coeducation teaches girls to be womanly and boys to be manly. However, ideals of womanliness and manliness have not always or everywhere been the same (Martin, 1985). Although often justly cast as a villain in girls' education (Ayim, 1985), gender-bound coeducation need not belittle girls' capabilities and self-esteem; nor does it necessarily deny girls full access to educational opportunities offered to boys. For example, long before the AAUW published *How Schools Shortchange Girls*, Louisa May Alcott, a nineteenth-century school teacher, portrayed schools' inhospitality to girls in her popular novel, *Little Women* (1868). Its tomboy hero, Jo, founded a "happy, home-like school" of her own in its second part (1869). Alcott subsequently articulated a progressive philosophical vision of gender-bound coeducation in her popular novels about Jo's school, Plumfield: *Little Men* (1870) and *Jo's Boys* (1886). As Alcott's narratives demonstrate, gender-bound coeducation can discourage girls' coquetry and submissiveness. At Plumfield, both girls and boys learn to be intelligent, strong, competent, and gentle-tempered. Some girls learn at the same time to be happy within the limited and subordinate societal roles traditionally prescribed for women in a world organized by and for men, while other especially talented girls learn to chafe against them. But Jo's vision of coeducation at Plumfield suggests that schools cannot take girls seriously without educating boys to like, respect, and be considerate of them. Thus, it entails a gender-differentiated concept of teaching that departs from the philosophical standard sense of teaching which the recent teaching reform movement has embraced (Laird, 1991).

Plumfield's Coeducation

We will find no mention of teenage pregnancy and parenthood, nor even divorce, in Alcott's novels. But as a single mother, Mrs. Hummel in *Little Women* lacks the necessary material and mental resources to support and raise healthy, happy children. Both Beth and Amy in *Little Women* are school dropouts, and their father's absence makes their mother, Marmee, their only teacher. Nat and Dan in *Little Men* are both homeless orphans when they come to Plumfield; Nan is a neglected, motherless child, wild as any boy. Besides taking girls seriously, then,

Jo is a "most peculiar but public-spirited schoolma'am" (Alcott, 1947, p. 18) who addresses her teaching talents to family troubles and gender troubles that undermine both sexes' education even today: for example, parental absence from home, maternal poverty, homelessness, and the widespread phenomenon that we call "at-risk" youth. Plumfield also addresses other familiar social ills such as racial intolerance and educational insensitivity to physical and mental disabilities. Coeducational curriculum, learning, and teaching at Plumfield all reflect Jo's vision of "a new and charming state of society" (Alcott, 1947, p. 370). Nonetheless, *Jo's Boys* makes clear that coeducation at Plumfield still supports a not entirely charming gender-bound social scheme in which women and men unequally shoulder the burdens of menial domesticity:

> ". . . it takes three or four women to get each man into, through, and out of the world. You are costly creatures, boys; and it is well that mothers, sisters, wives, and daughters love their duty and do it so well, or you would perish off the face of the earth," said Mrs. Jo solemnly, as she took up a basket filled with dilapidated hose; for the good Professor was still hard on his socks, and his sons resembled him in that respect. (Alcott, 1949, p. 15)

When Jo and Professor Bhaer admit girls to Plumfield in *Little Men*, they welcome girls' participation in every aspect of Plumfield's life while exempting boys from participation in its menial domesticity, which Martin has named the "reproductive processes of society" (1985, p. 6). Besides regular classroom subjects, Professor Bhaer's curriculum in the "productive processes of society" includes cultural, economic, and political activities for both sexes (Martin, 1985, p. 6): gardening, sports, savings and investment, herbal medicine, and peacemaking. But Plumfield's boys do not always welcome girls' participation in their athletic games, and sometimes a boy endangers the life of the whole school community with his rough and wild ways. Therefore, Jo's curriculum in the reproductive processes of society emphasizes female distinctiveness as a source of pride and strength for girls; as an object of gratitude, respect, and emulation for boys. Jo's curriculum proves crucial to correct the boys' keen sense that they have a special right to be wild or to be mean to the girls. In classes apart from boys, girls learn from Jo expert skills and moral values of domesticity. Thus, girls learn to respect themselves without emulating boys' wildness and despite boys' meanness. In their own gender-bound ways, both boys and girls learn to "trust, understand, and help one another" (Alcott, 1947, p. 369).

Through both Professor Bhaer's curriculum and Jo's curriculum, Nan grows up with encouragement to pursue a medical career as an unmarried woman, while Bess and Josie find encouragement to pursue artistic careers even as married women. All of Plumfield's female graduates learn to exert their own "feminine" moral impact on private and public worlds hitherto dominated by men, in their own individual and transformative ways. Meanwhile, Plumfield's boy students learn to respect and humbly support such distinctively "feminine" exertions, just as Professor Bhaer does with his wife Jo. But boys do not learn to surrender either their own privileged exemption from "maternal" and other domestic responsibilities or their privileged entitlement to girls' and women's habitual solicitude.

Plumfield's Differentiated Teaching

Teaching practice at Plumfield falls into three separate categories, the last one of which is decidedly gender-bound: *Socratic teaching*, *practical teaching*, and *maternal teaching*. When Jo first establishes Plumfield as a school, her father seems to anticipate the contemporary standard philosophical sense of "teaching" embraced by the teaching reform movement. For he welcomes Jo's experiment as "a chance for trying the Socratic method of education on modern youth" in Professor Bhaer's classroom (Alcott, 1869, p. 303). Yet Professor Bhaer does "train and teach in his own way" both inside and outside the classroom (Alcott, 1869, p. 304). His teaching includes not just the detached give and take of reasons essential to Socratic teaching, but also much practical teaching in the form of intimate talks, storytelling, sermons, companionable walks, and other shared activities full of affectionate conversation. Thus he aims to educate the children's bodies and hearts no less than their minds for participation in the productive processes of society. Moreover, he teaches tomboyish Nan, prissy Bess, and sensible Daisy with as much eagerness and practical energy as he teaches the boys.

Meanwhile, Jo herself sees their "happy, home-like school" as a chance to "be a mother" to its students, "to feel their wants, and sympathize with their troubles" (Alcott, 1869, p. 303). To Jo, such mothering means not mere coddling, consoling, and socialization, but her own genderized version of practical teaching. The curricular split between productive and reproductive processes of society marked by Professor Bhaer's and Mrs. Jo's separate coeducational efforts produces a conceptual distinction between his practical teaching and hers. Whereas his practical teaching and curriculum explicitly assign the productive processes to both boys and girls, her maternal teaching and curriculum explicitly assign the reproductive processes to girls. Jo teaches boys to honor this gender distinction, not through Socratic dialogue, but through honest, peaceful expression of her own hurt and anger at their disrespect for girls. Thus boys learn to accept their privileged reward for mature gentleness, which is the girls' well-taught skill and generous service to their domestic needs and wants. For just as Marmee has taught Jo and her sisters to "play pilgrims" and carry their "burdens" cheerfully in *Little Women* (Alcott, 1868, ch. 1), Mrs. Jo now teaches Plumfield's girls to love their duty and do it well through fun-filled kitchen play and sociable sewing sessions from which boys are banished.

Plumfield's distinctively different concepts of Socratic, practical, and maternal teaching make its coeducational values paradoxical. For the ideal of gender equality and the reality of a gender-bound society are contradictory. Still, they are both simultaneously fundamental principles for coeducational teaching at Plumfield. The separation between Jo's maternal teaching and Professor Bhaer's teaching, her different expectations of girls' and boys' learning, and his gender blindness raise questions about how appropriate such differentiated coeducational teaching might prove for girls and boys today. Is Alcott's thought experiment excessively pessimistic about the possibility of boys' growing up to truly egalitarian manhood? Remember, too, how many girls today are dropping out of school to care for their families. Is Plumfield's gender-bound coeducation unfair to impose upon girls a hard choice between childless, single womanhood and the woman's double workday of dual-career marriage or single motherhood?

GENDER-SENSITIVE COEDUCATION AND TEACHING

Gender-sensitive coeducation is neither gender-blind nor gender-bound because it is a way of taking girls seriously that aims for sex equality and the eradication of gender bias. Although it is the exact opposite of gender-careless coeducation and rejects gender-bound ideals, it does entail deliberately ignoring gender sometimes and paying careful attention to it at other times. Jane Roland Martin's *The Schoolhome* and Nel Noddings's *The Challenge to Care in Schools* do not analyze the philosophical concepts of coeducation and teaching that immediately concern us in this chapter, but they have made perhaps the only thought experiments in schooling that we could interpret as gender-sensitive coeducation. Therefore, they may help us to understand what a gender-sensitive concept of coeducational teaching might mean. Yet, as innovator of the "gender-sensitive" concept, Martin (1992) does warn that

> In the best of all possible worlds we would have a rule at our fingertips specifying precisely when and where gender makes a difference. In this world, however, there is nothing self-evident about the difference gender makes to education. Enough work has been done by now, however, to make it clear that gender affects the temperature of the classroom and that a chilly one for girls and women lowers their confidence and self-esteem. (p. 117)

Thought Experiments Revising Plumfield's Coeducation

Neither text mentions Alcott's Plumfield, but both do present cases for remaking U.S. schools according to Jo's basic ideal of the "happy, home-like school" that is not chilly for girls or women. For example, Noddings (1992) invites us to think of children in schools as "a large heterogeneous family" and organize their curriculum "around centers of care" (p. xiii) so that "matters of interest to women and minorities could be included in a natural way" (p. 115). Expressing concern about the children left behind when both mothers and fathers leave home each day for work, Martin invites us to envision the "schoolhome" as a school that has become for its students a "moral equivalent of home in which love transforms mundane activities, the three C's take their rightful place in the curriculum of all, and joy is a daily accompaniment of learning" (1992, p. 40). Her three C's are care, concern, and connection, which in a culturally diverse society entail a multicultural curriculum. What do these two former school teachers' recent philosophical visions of multicultural schooling have to do with gender?

Well aware of research that the AAUW report has summarized, both Martin and Noddings embrace Plumfield's coeducational plan of taking girls seriously by expecting them as well as boys, and women as well as men, to work at learning to live together and to make the public world healthier, happier, and more hospitable to children, the poor, people with disabilities, people of color, those who choose never to marry, and women. What's more, both advocate that schools should also take more responsibility than the AAUW report indicates they do now: responsibility such as Plumfield claims for teaching boys to welcome girls as equal partners in worldly challenges and to respect women's cultural contributions. But both diverge from the gender-bound aspect of Plumfield's coeducational plan by expecting boys as well as girls, and men as well as women, to work at learning to care intelligently and capably for themselves, others, and their surroundings. Martin (1992) argues that this aim will entail explicit efforts to overcome our culture's "domephobia—its devaluation of and morbid anxiety about things domestic" (p. 155). Noddings does not mention Alcott's morbidly anxious Beth in *Little Women*, Jo's little sister who dropped out of school and became deathly ill because (like many dropouts today) she devoted her life entirely to her family's domestic needs and lacked any self-esteem. But she does warn that "Girls especially may need help in understanding and rejecting pathological forms of caring—forms characterized by continual self-denial" (p. 105).

Martin (1992) anticipates some possible concerns about gender-sensitive coeducation. If girls learn the virtues of courage, loyalty, and self-assertion, will they become unnaturally masculine? If boys learn the virtues of care, concern, and connection, will they become unnaturally feminine? They will not, she argues. She might have cited Alcott's characters to demonstrate her point. But to explain it conceptually, she does cite Aristotle's golden mean, the virtue of moderation. She theorizes that the schoolhome would teach students to moderate between excesses and deficiencies of both traditional manliness and traditional womanliness. For example, in learning the three C's, boys should learn to avoid both unmanly deficiencies and macho excesses: both cowardice and fearlessness, both betrayal and blind allegiance, both meek passivity and overaggressiveness. Meanwhile, in learning "to speak their minds and stand up for themselves" (p. 112), girls should learn to avoid both unwomanly deficiencies and often denigrated feminine excesses: both coldness and indulgence, both indifference to others and self-sacrifice, both total separation from others and loss of self, both neglect and smothering. In view of these different learning tasks, Martin argues that some "different educational experiences" for girls and boys may be necessary even though the two sexes will do many things together in the schoolhome and neither sex will be exempt from either domestic or worldly cares. Gender-sensitive coeducation poses the challenge of responding to girls' and boys' previously differentiated socialization "without replicating the old, stereotypical curricular divisions of shop and auto mechanics for boys, home economics and typing for girls . . ." (p. 118).

Teaching in a Different Sense

What concept of teaching might such gender-sensitive coeducation entail? Noddings suggests that the standard, Socratic concept of teaching will be insufficient to the task of caring in schools, even if occasionally useful. Martin (1992) moreover insists that the schoolhome must not enforce a "public-private split" in its teachers' minds and actions: She may have had in mind Plumfield's curricular split between productive and reproductive processes, which distinguished Professor Bhaer's practical teaching from Mrs. Jo's maternal teaching (p. 167). Consequently, she argues for an obliteration of those programmatic distinctions that schools usually make between the extracurriculum and the curriculum proper. In her view, students' extracurricular efforts should cease to be peripheral to their schooling. This curricular change requires a different concept of teaching in the schoolhome insofar as it must integrate intellectual, practical, and nurturant activity. Although *The Schoolhome* does not mention that activities like theater, newspaper, food preparation and service, household upkeep, and talking heart-to-heart become central organizers of teaching and learning within both Marmee's home and Jo's coeducational school, she does suggest that teaching in the schoolhome will centrally involve such activities in addition to critical reasoning.

Martin recounts many teaching episodes, both real and imaginary, that suggest her possible debt to Alcott's portrait of maternal teaching, which aims for children's learning love and survival despite their conflicts, pains, and troubles (Laird, 1989b). Alcott's narratives represent maternal teaching as distinct from coddling, humiliation, prissy feminine socialization, and ignorant neglect, activities that mothers and other adults working with children may engage in; gender-sensitive coeducational teaching is distinct from these also. For according to Martin (1992), the schoolhome's "object is to teach children to stand inside and keep in good repair a web of connection that includes all of us" and "to teach our young to treasure their own good red blood and that of everyone else" (p. 118). Thus her representation of gender-sensitive coeducational teaching preserves that basic concept of the maternal teaching achievement which I have drawn from my reading of Alcott (Laird, 1994). But she assigns such teaching to both sexes, integrates both reproductive and productive processes into its curriculum, and expands its context to embrace not just those near and dear at home or even at school, but also in the world. This new curriculum and context for boys' and girls' learning to live together make the teaching of love and survival not simply a personal act, but a political one as well. Teaching students to recognize and resist domephobia, to love across cultural barriers erected by their ancestors or national leaders, and to survive cultural dismissal, devaluation, distortion, or harassment is a task that implies more than mere academic achievement. Whereas maternal teaching can be gender-bound or gender-sensitive, gender-sensitive coeducational teaching entails critical consciousness raising about gender's power to undermine children's capacities for love and survival in home, school, and world.

THEORY INTO PRACTICE

In practice, coeducational teaching will itself be an act of extended theorizing since theorizing about it is still speculative and incomplete. Why is this so? Despite differences of view among theorists of coeducation, all cited here do suggest that taking girls' education seriously will require schools to be happy, homelike places. Thus, especially at the secondary level, the typical public school environment may not even be adequate to support individual teachers' efforts at coeducational teaching. We may also wonder how adequately certification programs prepare students for coeducational teaching. Most teacher preparation programs operate from the premise that students can learn the most about teaching from observing the classroom activities of certified teachers in public schools, schools which are now shortchanging girls. Rare is the teacher preparation program that requires students to observe schools critically for signals of this problem. Rarer still is the program that requires students to observe and help adults teaching in an extracurricular context that takes girls seriously inside or outside school—a setting where maternal teaching or "teaching in a different sense" is likely to occur. Girls might feel more "at home" learning at Girl Scouts, 4-H, YWCA, youth theaters, dance studios, and so forth than they do at school. Perhaps such contexts could teach us something about teaching girls.

Given the omnipresent gender-carelessness of schools and teacher preparation programs, teachers have to do whatever they can with each other to change their schools gradually, educate themselves, and experiment with their teaching. Teachers can put girl students at the center of their own webs of connection for purposes of self-education on this issue. For example, a teacher in a gender-careless school could attend girls' sports events in which his or her students are playing. Such students can indirectly help bring teachers together with other adults who take them seriously. In the process, such teachers will inevitably be making a more homelike school environment. With at least one other teacher, one could use the bibliography and discussion questions for this chapter to begin some elementary self-education on taking girls seriously. Teachers could keep coeducational teaching journals to respond to their reading and to plan and record experimental coeducational teaching efforts, or—like Jo—to record their own case studies of girls in their classes who most urgently need to be taken more seriously. They could observe each other's teaching and discuss their positive and negative effects on girls' learning, especially as those effects differ for girls of different races, classes, and abilities. In short, working with each other, in dialogue with culturally diverse girl students, they can start to fill in some of the gaps in their prior teacher education and make their own thought experiments in coeducational teaching that takes girls seriously.

Teachers who have thus attempted "extra" work on their coeducational teaching seem to have gotten far more from it than they ever expected. In Ithaca, New York, for example, in 1982 to 1983, "teachers, classroom aides, parents, librarians, students, professors, and others" came together to air their concerns about "sexism in public education" (Ithaca Feminist Education Coalition [IFEC], 1984, p. 14). Beginning small, they held support groups and informal curriculum seminars for themselves after school. Their group grew rapidly, and they undertook many projects. Local teachers of mathematics and science formed their own study group. Other groups worked with the New York Women's Studies Association and coordinated a Women's Studies Day at the high school. They organized a Title IX committee with help from a concerned district administrator, sponsored a district-wide celebration of National Women's History Week, organized inservice education programs, and wrote a proposal for funding from the Women's Educational Equity Act (WEEA).

Through this latter effort they encountered political disagreements within the district's central administration and school board. Their WEEA proposal needed district authorization, and taking girls seriously enough to apply for federal funds to buy books of likely interest to them was initially labeled "radical." If this at first seems odd, remember that they did not have the AAUW report at hand to confirm the legitimacy of their concerns. But the Ithacans report that, in the process of pursuing such simple educational fairness for girls, they "saw moderate people become boldly active" (IFEC, 1984, p. 15). They quickly learned much about how the board of education and school district administration worked, another topic on which their teacher preparation had apparently been deficient. Moreover, their narrative suggests that their collaboration, and even the politics surrounding it, did build a strong sense of community support for teachers who took girls seriously. Certainly, schools cannot develop a homelike ethos without such a sense of collaboration and community.

The American Association of University Women (AAUW), which published *How Schools Shortchange Girls*, has become in some states a forum for similar efforts to improve coeducation. However teachers realize the possibilities of gender-sensitive coeducational teaching, they must understand that teaching occurs outside classrooms as well as inside them, that getting to know girls well is the best way to start taking them seriously, that taking girls seriously may be perceived as a political rather than an educational effort, that some collegial support is therefore crucial, and that continuing self-education and thoughtful experimentation will also be necessary.

SUMMARY

Coeducation in the United States today shortchanges girls. Our shallow, atheoretical understanding of coeducation is gender-careless. It blinds us to the harsh realities of girls' schooling in boys' company, as summarized in the AAUW report. Yet, beginning with Plato's *Republic*, past and recent thought experiments in coeducation have taken girls seriously. All note that we must think about the institution of the family and its relationship to women's lives and children's education if girls and boys are to be educated as each other's equals. In a society fraught with family troubles and gender troubles, Socrates' teaching provides an insufficient, gender-blind foundation for understanding the full complexities and many possibilities of coeducational teaching.

In coeducational thought experiments that avoid gender-carelessness, the school becomes a place where girls as well as boys can feel at home away from home, homelessness, or home violence. Gender-sensitive coeducation educates boys and girls to recognize and resist gender's power to undermine their free and responsible mutual cooperation as equals in both domestic and worldly efforts. In gender-sensitive coeducational practice such as Martin envisions in the schoolhome, teaching takes on a different sense from both the philosophical standard sense and the differentiated senses evident at Alcott's Plumfield. Gender-sensitive coeducational teaching integrates intellectual and practical activities as it aims for children's growing capacity and responsibility for learning to live together as equals with cultural differences: without violence, domination, domephobia, or self-denial. Would schools continue to shortchange girls if coeducational teaching were rigorously guided and evaluated by such explicit moral aims? This is an awesome but invigorating challenge that some teachers have already accepted.

References

Alcott, L. M. (1868). *Little Women.* Middlesex, England: Puffin Books.

Alcott, L. M. (1869). *Good Wives: Little Women, Part II.* Middlesex, England: Puffin Books.

Alcott, L. M. (1947). *Little Men: Life at Plumfield with Jo's Boys.* New York: Grosset & Dunlap. (Original work published 1870.)

Alcott, L. M. (1949). *Jo's Boys: A Sequel to "Little Men."* New York: Grosset & Dunlap. (Original work published 1886.)

Ayim, M., K. Morgan, & B. Houston (1985). "Symposium: Should Public Education Be Gender-free?" *Educational Theory* 35: 345–369.

Best, R. (1983). *We've All Got Scars: What Boys and Girls Learn in Elementary School.* Bloomington: Indiana University Press.

Dewey, J. (1911). "Is Coeducation Injurious to Girls?" *Ladies' Home Journal* (June): 22, 60–61.

Gilligan, C. (1982). *In a Different Voice: Psychological Theory and Women's Development.* Cambridge, MA: Harvard University Press.

Gilligan, C., J. V. Ward, and J. M. Taylor, with Betty Bardige, eds. (1988). *Mapping the Moral Domain: A Contribution of Women's Thinking to Psychological Theory and Education.* Cambridge, MA: Harvard University Press.

Gowin, D. B. (1981). *Educating.* Ithaca, NY: Cornell University Press.

Ithaca Feminist Education Coalition (1984). "Making Our Way Up Another 'Down Staircase.'" *Women's Studies Quarterly* 12: 14–15.

Laird, S. (1988a). "Women and Gender in John Dewey's Philosophy of Education." *Educational Theory* 38: 111–129.

Laird, S. (1988b). "Reforming 'Woman's True Profession': A Case for 'Feminist Pedagogy' in Teacher Education?" *Harvard Educational Review* 58: 449–463.

Laird, S. (1989a). "The Concept of Teaching: *Betsey Brown* vs. Philosophy of Education?" in J. M. Giarelli, ed., *Philosophy of Education 1988.* Normal, IL: Philosophy of Education Society/Illinois State University, pp. 34–45.

Laird, S. (1989b). "Maternal Teaching and Maternal Teachings: Philosophie and Literary Case Studies of Educating" (Doctoral dissertation, Cornell University, 1988). *Dissertation Abstracts International* 49: 3653.

Laird, S. (1991). "The Ideal of the Educated Teacher: 'Reclaiming a Conversation' with Louisa May Alcott." *Curriculum Inquiry* 21: 271–297.

Laird, S. (1994). "Teaching in a Different Sense: Alcott's Marmee," in A. Thompson, ed., *Philosophy of Education 1993.* Urbana, IL: Philosophy of Education Society/Illinois State University.

Martin, J. R. (1982). "Excluding Women from the Educational Realm." *Harvard Educational Review* 52: 133–142.

Martin, J. R. (1985). *Reclaiming a Conversation: The Ideal of the Educated Woman.* New Haven: Yale University Press.

Martin, J. R. (1992). *The Schoolhome: Rethinking Schools for Changing Families.* Cambridge, MA: Harvard University Press.

Noddings, N. (1992). *The Challenge to Care in Schools: An Alternative Approach to Education.* New York: Teachers College Press, Columbia University.

Rich, A. (1979). *On Lies, Secrets, and Silence.* New York: W. W. Norton.

Tyack, D., and E. Hansot (1990). *Learning Together: A History of Coeducation in American Public Schools.* New Haven: Yale University Press.

Wellesley Center for Research on Women (1992). *How Schools Shortchange Girls: A Study of Major Findings on Girls and Education* (The AAUW Report). Washington, D.C.: American Association of University Women Educational Foundation.

Discussion Questions

1. How would you respond to the philosophical questions raised by the AAUW report?

2. How would (a) gender-bound, and (b) gender-sensitive coeducational teaching most likely affect each way that gender-careless schools now shortchange girls?

3. How might a gender-bound curriculum (a) for girls, and (b) for boys most likely differ from a gender-sensitive one? What would the two curricula for girls have in common? What would the two curricula for boys have in common?

4. How must a teacher's own sex affect gender-bound coeducational teaching? How do you think a teacher's sex might affect gender-sensitive teaching? Remember to consider the different challenges that boys and girls can pose for such teaching.

5. How would (a) gender-careless, (b) gender-bound, and (c) gender-sensitive approaches to coeducation most likely affect the practice of your own teaching specialty?

Henry A. Giroux

Henry Giroux is a former social studies teacher who taught at the secondary school level for nine years. He graduated from Hope High School in Providence, Rhode Island, in 1961 and in 1963 received a basketball scholarship to Gorham State College. He eventually received a master's degree from Appalachian State University in 1967, and after working a few years attended Carnegie Mellon University, from which he received a doctorate in 1977. Since graduating from Carnegie Mellon, he has taught at Boston University, Miami University (Ohio), Tufts University, and Penn State University. While at Miami University, he was awarded a Distinguished Professorship and served as the director of the Center for Education and Cultural Studies. Currently, he holds the Waterbury Chair Professorship in secondary education at Penn State University.

Henry has been deeply influenced by the work of Paulo Freire, especially his provocative book, *Pedagogy of the Oppressed,* which he recommends to all teachers because of the way in which it integrates a language of politics, pedagogy, and hope. "I strongly suggest that teachers read in a wide range of fields, and take up the challenge of defining their teaching through a vision of hope and transformative change. I have attempted to guide my own work through this position, and have done so through my teaching, public speaking, and writing."

Giroux has published over 200 scholarly articles and chapters in a wide-ranging number of journals and books, and he presently serves on the editorial board for fourteen professional journals. In addition, he has authored thirteen books and edited six. His most recent books include *Postmodern Education* (University of Minnesota Press, 1991), *Border Crossings* (Routledge, 1992), *Living Dangerously* (Peter Lang, 1993), *Between Borders* (Routledge, 1993), and *Disturbing Pleasures: Learning Popular Culture* (Routledge, 1994).

When Henry is not writing or teaching, he is at the gym running around the track and lifting weights. He considers himself a "health nut" and takes "tons of vitamins daily," including C, E, and a mix of antioxidants. He also recommends that all readers get a juicer and drink plenty of fresh juice. Henry is also a movie buff and particularly favors "Dead Poets Society" and "Slackers" for teachers to critically analyze for their social implications.

22

Teachers as Public Intellectuals

Henry A. Giroux

> The society in which we live is desperately menaced, not by [the cold war] but from within. So any citizen of this country who figures himself as responsible—and particularly those of you who deal with the minds and hearts of young people—must be prepared to "go for broke." Or to put it another way, you must understand that in the attempt to correct so many generations of bad faith and cruelty, when it is operating not only in the classroom but in society, you will meet the most fantastic, the most brutal, and the most determined resistance. There is no point in pretending that this won't happen. . . . [And yet] the obligation of anyone who thinks of him or herself as responsible is to examine society and try to change it and to fight it—at no matter what risk. This is the only hope society has. This is the only way societies change. (Baldwin, 1988, p. 3)

I read the words of the famed African-American novelist James Baldwin less as a prescription for cynicism and powerlessness than I do as an expression of hope. Baldwin's words are moving because he confers a sense of moral and political responsibility upon teachers by presupposing that they are critical agents who can move between theory and practice in order to take risks, refine their visions, and make a difference for both their students and the world in which they live.

In order to take up Baldwin's challenge for teachers to "go for broke," to act in the classroom and the world with courage and dignity, it is important for educators to recognize that the current challenge facing public schools is one of the most serious that any generation of existing and prospective teachers has ever had to face. Since the publication of *The Nation at Risk* in 1983, the United States has lived through twelve years of reforms in which teachers have been invited to de-skill themselves, to become technicians, or, in more ideological terms, to accept a role that transforms them into "clerks of the empire."

TRADITION AND THE PEDAGOGY OF RISK

We live at a time when state legislators and federal officials are increasingly calling for the testing of teachers and the implementation of standardized curriculum; at the same time, legislators and government officials are ignoring the most important people in the reform effort, the teachers. Within this grim scenario, the voices of teachers have been largely absent from the debate about education. It gets worse.

Economically, while the salaries of teachers have kept up with the rate of inflation, the overall working conditions of teachers, especially those in the urban districts with a low tax base, have badly deteriorated. The story is a familiar one: overcrowded classrooms, inadequate resources, low salaries, and a rise in teacher directed violence. In part, this is due to the increased financial cutbacks to the public sector by the federal government, the tax revolt of the 1970s by the middle class that has put a ceiling on the ability of cities and states to raise revenue for public services, and the refusal by wide segments of society to believe that public schooling is essential to the health of a democratic society. Compounding these problems is a dominant vision of schooling defined largely through the logic of corporate values and the imperatives of the marketplace. Schools are being treated as if their only purpose is to train future workers, and teachers are being viewed as corporate foot-soldiers whose role is to provide students with the skills necessary for the business world. In short, part of the crisis of teaching is the result of a vision of schooling that subordinates issues of diversity, equity, community, and social justice to pragmatic considerations that enshrine the marketplace and accountability schemes that standardize the social relations of schooling. The political and ideological climate does not look favorable for teachers at the moment. But it does offer prospective and existing teachers the challenge to engage in dialogue and debate regarding important issues such as the nature and purpose of teacher preparation, the meaning of educational leadership, and the dominant forms of classroom teaching.

I think that if existing and future teachers are willing to "go for broke," to use Baldwin's term, they will need to reimagine teaching as part of a project of critique and possibility. But there is more at stake here than simply a change in who controls the conditions under which teachers work. This is important, but what is also needed is a new language; a new way of naming, ordering, and representing how power works in schools. It is precisely through a more critical language that teachers might be able to recognize the power of their own agency in order to raise and act upon such questions as: What range of purposes should schools serve? What knowledge is of most worth? What does it mean for teachers and students to know something? In what direction should teachers and students desire? What notions of authority should structure teaching and learning? These questions are important because they force educators to engage in a process of self-critique while simultaneously highlighting the central role that teachers might play in any viable attempt to reform the public schools.

In what follows, I want to offer an alternative language for defining the purpose and meaning of teacher work. While I have talked about teachers as intellectuals in another context, I want to extend this analysis by analyzing what the implications are for redefining teachers as public intellectuals (Giroux, 1988a, 1988b; Aronowitz & Giroux, 1993). In part, I want to explore this position by drawing upon my own training as a teacher and some of the problems I had to face when actually working in the public schools. I will conclude by highlighting some of the defining principles that might structure the content and context of what it means for teachers to assume the role of a public intellectual.

THE POLITICS OF NOT KNOWING

My own journey into teaching was largely shaped by undergraduate education training and my first year of student teaching. While the content and context of these experiences shaped my initial understanding of myself as a teacher, they did not prepare me for the specific tasks and problems of what it meant to address the many problems I had to confront in my first job. In what follows, I want to speak from my own experiences in order to illuminate the shortcomings of the educational theories that shaped both my perceptions of teaching and the classroom practices I was expected to implement.

During the time that I studied to be a teacher, I mostly learned how to master classroom methods, read Bloom's taxonomy, and became deft at administering tests, but I was never asked to question how testing might be used as a sorting device to track and marginalize certain groups. Like many prospective teachers of my generation, I was taught how to master a body of knowledge defined within separate academic disciplines, but I never learned to question what the hierarchical organization of knowledge meant and how it conferred authority and power.

For example, I was never taught to raise questions about what knowledge was worth knowing and why, why schools legitimated some forms of knowledge and ignored others, why math and English were more important than art, or why it was considered unworthy to take a course in which one worked with one's hands. I never engaged in a classroom discussion about whose interests were served through the teaching and legitimation of particular forms of school knowledge, or how knowledge served to silence and disempower particular social groups.

Moreover, I was not given the opportunity to reflect upon the authoritarian principles that actually structure classroom life and how these could be understood by analyzing social, political, and economic conditions outside of schools. If a student slept in the morning at his or her desk, I was taught to approach the issue as a problem of discipline and management. I was not alerted to recognize the social conditions that may have caused such behavior: that is, to the possibility that the student may have a drug-related problem, be hungry, sick, or simply exhausted because of conditions in his or her home life. I learned quickly to separate out the problems of society from the problems of schooling, and hence became illiterate in understanding the complexity of the relationship between schools and the larger social order.

My initial teaching assignment was in a school in which the teacher turnover rate exceeded 85 percent each year. The first day I walked into that school I was met by some students hanging out in the lobby. They greeted me with stares born of territorial rights and suspicion, and one of them jokingly asked me, "Hey man, you're new, what's your name?" I remember thinking they had violated some sort of rule regarding teacher-student relationships by addressing me that way.

Questions of identity, culture, and racism had not been factored into my understanding of teaching and schooling at the time. I had no idea that the questions that would be raised for me that year had less to do with the sterile language of methods I had learned as an undergraduate than they did with becoming culturally and politically literate about the context-specific histories and experiences that informed where my students came from and how they viewed themselves and others. I had no idea of how important it was to create a meaningful and safe classroom for them so that I could connect my teaching to their own languages, cultures, and life experiences. I soon found out that giving students some sense of power and ownership over their own educational experience has more to do with developing a language that was risk taking and self-critical for me and meaningful, practical, and transformative for them. During that first year, I also learned something about the ways in which many school administrators are educated.

LEADERSHIP FOR BANALITY

During that first year, I rented movies from the American Friends Service Committee, ignored the officially designated curriculum textbooks, and eventually put my own books and magazine articles on reserve in the school library for my students to read. Hoping to give my students some control over the conditions for producing knowledge, I encouraged them to produce their own texts through the use of school video equipment, cameras, and daily journals.

Within a very short time, I came in conflict with the school principal. He was a mix between General Patton and the Encino Man. At six foot three, weighing in at 250 pounds, his presence seemed a bit overwhelming and intimidating. The first time he called me into his office, I learned something about how he was educated. He told me that in his mind students should be quiet in classrooms, teachers should stick to giving lectures and writing on the board, and that I was never to ask a student a question that he or she could not answer. He further suggested that rather than developing my own materials in class I should use the curricula packages made available through the good wishes of local businesses and companies. While clearly being a reflection, if not a parody, of the worst kind of teacher training, he adamantly believed strict management controls, rigid systems of accountability, and lock step discipline were at the heart of educational leadership.

I found myself in a secular version of hell. This was a school in which teaching became reduced to the sterile logic of flow charts. Moreover, it was a school in which power was wielded largely by white, male administrators further reinforcing the isolation and despair of most of the teachers. I engaged in forms of guerrilla warfare with this administration. But in order to survive I had to enlist the help of a few other teachers and some members of the community. At the end of the school year, I was encouraged not to come back. Fortunately, I had another teaching job back east and ended up in a much better school.

In retrospect, the dominant view of educational leadership has had a resurgence during the Reagan and Bush eras. Its overall effect has been to limit teachers' control over the development and planning of curriculum, to reinforce the bureaucratic organization of the school, and to remove teachers from the process of judging and implementing classroom instruction. This is evident in the growing call for national testing, national curriculum standards, and the concerted attack on developing multicultural curricula. The ideology that guides this model and its view of pedagogy is that the behavior of teachers needs to be controlled and made consistent and predictable across different schools and student populations. The effect is not only to remove teachers from the process of deliberation and reflection, but also to routinize the nature of learning and classroom pedagogy. In this approach, it is assumed that all students can learn from the same standardized materials, instructional techniques, and modes of evaluation. The notion that students come from different histories, experiences, and cultures, is strategically ignored within this approach. The notion that pedagogy should be attentive to specific contexts is ignored.

TEACHERS AS PUBLIC INTELLECTUALS

I want to challenge these views by arguing that one way to rethink and restructure the nature of teacher work is to view teachers as public intellectuals. But I want to begin by first making the case for applying the general category of *intellectual* to teachers.

The category of intellectual is helpful in a number of ways. First, it provides a theoretical basis for examining teacher work as a form of intellectual labor, as opposed to defining it in purely instrumental and technical terms. In other words, it points to the connection between conception and practice, thinking and doing, and producing and implementing as integrated activities that give teaching a sense of dignity, meaning, and empowerment. Within this perspective there is a critical foundation for rejecting those philosophies and management pedagogies that separate conceptualization, planning, and design from the nature of teacher work itself.

Second, the concept of teacher as intellectual carries with it the imperative to critique and reject those approaches to teacher work that reinforce a technical, caste, and gendered division of labor. That is, it makes visible not only issues regarding how teachers as a whole are increasingly de-skilled through the proliferation of management by objectives schemes, but also how teaching is inscribed with various forms of social discrimination that serve to disempower women at all levels of decision making in the school apparatus.

Third, the category of teacher as intellectual highlights the political and ideological interests that structure teacher work. Neither the knowledge that teachers teach nor the ways in which they teach are innocent; both are informed by values that need to be recognized and critically engaged for their implications and effects.

Fourth, it also makes problematic the institutional and practical conditions teachers need to function in their capacity as intellectuals. In this case, the what, how, and why of teaching cannot be separated from the basic conditions under which teachers work. This suggests that teachers must be able to shape collectively the ways in which time, space, and knowledge organize everyday life in schools. More specifically, in order to function as intellectuals, teachers must struggle to create the ideological and structural conditions necessary for them to write, research, and work with each other in producing curricula and sharing power.

The unease expressed about the identity and role of teachers as public intellectuals has a long tradition in the United States and has become the focus of a number of recent debates. On one level, there are conservatives who argue that teachers who address public issues from the perspective of a committed position are simply part of what they call the political correctness movement. According to Aronowitz (1993), there is a deep suspicion of any attempt to open up the possibility for educators to address pressing social issues and to connect them to their teaching. Moreover, within the broad parameters of this view, schools are seen as apolitical institutions whose primary purpose is to both prepare students for the workplace and to reproduce the alleged common values that define the "American" way of life.

At the same time, many liberals have argued that while teachers should address public issues, they should do so from the perspective of a particular teaching methodology. This is evident in Gerald Graff's (1992) call for educators to teach the diverse ideological conflicts in English studies. In this view, the struggle over representations replaces how a politics of meaning might help students identify, engage, and transform relations of power that generate the material conditions of racism, sexism, poverty, and other oppressive conditions. Moreover, some radical feminists have argued that the call for teachers to be public intellectuals promotes leadership models that are largely patriarchal and overly rational in the forms of authority they secure. While there may be an element of truth in all of these positions, they all display enormous theoretical shortcomings.

Conservatives often refuse to problematize their own version of what is legitimate intellectual knowledge and how it works to secure particular forms of authority by simply labeling as politically correct individuals, groups, or views that challenge the basic tenets of the status quo. Liberals, on the other hand, inhabit a terrain that wavers between rejecting a principled standpoint from which to teach and staunchly arguing for a pedagogy that is academically rigorous and fair. Caught between a discourse of fairness and the appeal to provocative teaching methods, liberals have no language for clarifying the moral visions that structure their views of the relationship between knowledge and authority and the practices it promotes. Moreover, they increasingly have come to believe that teaching from a particular standpoint is tantamount to imposing an ideological position upon students. This has led in some cases to a form of McCarthyism in which critical educators are summarily dismissed as being guilty of ideological indoctrination.

While the feminist critique is the most interesting, it underplays the possibility for using authority in ways that allow teachers to be more self-critical while simultaneously providing the conditions for students to recognize the possibility for democratic agency in both themselves and others. Operating out of a language of polarization, some feminist education critics essentialize the positions of their opponents, and in doing so present a dehistoricized and simplistic view of critical pedagogy. Most importantly, all of these positions share in the failure to address the possibility for teachers to become a force for democratization both within and outside of schools.

Teachers must bring to bear in their classrooms and other pedagogical sites the courage, analytical tools, moral vision, time, and dedication that is necessary to return schools to their primary task: places of critical education in the service of creating a public sphere of citizens who are able to exercise power over their own lives and especially over the conditions of knowledge acquisition. Central to any such reform effort is the recognition that democracy is not a set of formal rules of participation, but the lived experience of empowerment for the vast majority. Moreover, the call for schools as democratic public spheres should not be limited to the call for equal access to schools, equal opportunity, or other arguments defined in terms of the principles of equality. Equality is a crucial aspect of democratizing schools, but teachers should not limit their demands to the call for equality. Instead, the rallying cry of teachers should be organized around the practice of empowerment for the vast majority of students in this country who need to be educated in the spirit of a critical democracy.

This suggests another dimension in defining the role of public intellectuals. Such intellectuals must combine their roles as educators and citizens. This implies that they must connect the practice of classroom teaching to the operation of power in the larger society. At the same time, they must be attentive to those broader social forces that influence the workings of schooling and pedagogy. What is at issue here is a commitment on the part of teachers as public servants to extend the principles of social justice to all spheres of economic, political, and cultural life. Within this discourse, the experiences that constitute the production of knowledge, identities, and social values in the schools are inextricably linked to the quality of moral and political life of the wider society. Hence, the reform of schooling must be seen as a part of a wider revitalization of public life.

Teachers must be concerned about fostering both critical inquiry and understanding, and also about how power works in the interest of domination. It references a model of leadership and pedagogical practice that combines a language of possibility with forms of self and social criticism that do not require educators to step back from society as a whole, but only to distance themselves from being implicated in power relations that subjugate, corrupt, or infantilize.

This is criticism from within, it is the telling of stories that speak to the voices of those who have been silenced, it is the willingness to develop pedagogical practices and experiences in the interest of a utopian vision that is synonymous with the spirit of a critical democracy. This is not a call for teachers to become wedded to some abstract ideal that removes them from everyday life, that turns them into prophets of perfection and certainty; on the contrary, it represents a call for teachers to undertake social criticism not as outsiders but as public and concerned educators who address the most pressing social and political issues of their neighborhood, community, and society as individuals who have an intimate knowledge of the workings of everyday life, who make organic connections with the historical traditions that provide themselves and their students with voices, histories, and a sense of belonging.

This should not suggest that as public intellectuals, teachers represent a vanguardist group dedicated to simply reproducing another master narrative. In fact, it is important for teachers to link their role as critical agents to their ability to be self-critical of their own politics while constantly engaging in dialogue with other educators, community people, various cultural workers, and students. Teachers need to be aware of the limits of their own positions, make their pedagogies context specific, challenge the current organization of knowledge into fixed disciplines, and work in solidarity with others to gain some control over the conditions of their work. At the very least, this suggests that teachers will have to struggle on many different fronts in order to transform the conditions of work and learning that go on in schools. This means not only working with community people, teachers, students, and parents to open up progressive spaces within classrooms, but also forming alliances with other cultural workers in order to debate and shape educational policy at the local, state, and federal levels of government.

Moreover, teachers need to provide the conditions for students to learn that the relationship between knowledge and power can be emancipatory, that their histories and experiences matter, and that what they say and do can count as part of a wider struggle to change the world around them. More specifically, teachers need to argue for forms of pedagogy that close the gap between the school and the real world. The curriculum needs to be organized around knowledge that relates to the communities, cultures, and traditions that give students a sense of history, identity, and place. This suggests pedagogical approaches that do more than make learning context specific, it also points to the need to expand the range of cultural texts that inform what counts as knowledge.

As public intellectuals, teachers need to understand and use those electronically mediated knowledge forms that constitute the terrain of popular culture. This is the world of media texts—videos, films, music, and other mechanisms of popular culture constituted outside of the technology of print and the book. As West (1990) puts it, the content of the curriculum needs to affirm and critically enrich the meaning, language, and knowledge that students actually use to negotiate and inform their lives.

In addition, teachers need to make the issue of cultural difference a defining principle of curriculum development and research. In an age of shifting demographics, large-scale immigration, and multiracial communities, teachers must make a firm commitment to cultural difference as central to the relationship of schooling and citizenship. In the first instance, this means dismantling and deconstructing the legacy of nativism and racial chauvinism that has defined the rhetoric of school reform for the last decade. The Reagan and Bush eras witnessed a full-fledged attack on the rights of minorities, civil rights legislation, affirmative action, and the legitimation of curriculum reforms pandering to Eurocentric interests.

Teachers can affirm their commitment to democratic public life by struggling in and outside of their classrooms, in solidarity with others, to reverse these policies in order to make schools more attentive to the cultural resources that students bring to the public schools. At one level, this means working to develop legislation that protects the civil rights of all groups. Equally important is the need for teachers to take the lead in encouraging programs that open school curricula to the narratives of cultural difference, without falling into the trap of merely romanticizing the experience of otherness.

At stake here is the development of an educational policy that asserts public education as part of a broader ethical and political discourse, one that both challenges and transforms those curricula reforms of the last decade that are profoundly racist in context and content. In part, this suggests changing the terms of the debate regarding the relationship between schooling and national identity, moving away from an assimilationist ethic and the profoundly Eurocentric fantasies of a common culture to one which links national identity to diverse traditions and histories.

THEORY INTO PRACTICE

I want to stress that teachers need to understand more critically what they know and how they come to know in a way that enables them to presuppose a notion of democratic public life that is worth struggling for. In effect, I want to emphasize that prospective and existing educators be given the opportunity in both the sites where they work and in existing teacher education programs and schools to develop the following elements of a language of critique and possibility.

First, central to developing teachers as public intellectuals is the need to recognize the importance of reading the present through an analysis of the past. This is not simply about teaching educators how to engage in the process of historical recovery; more importantly, it refers to the critical and pedagogical attempt to understand how to read the past from the perspective of both its established traditions and its omissions. This suggests treating the past less as an object of reverence than as one of struggle and dialogue. It means rejecting the past as a linear progression, as the development of an ongoing master narrative. On the contrary, history in this sense becomes a shifting terrain that offers possibilities for rethinking the present less as a reflection of the past than as a critical appropriation of the most important and critical insights of history. For teachers, this type of inquiry means linking the notion of historical examination to the imperatives of moral and political agency. Such an inquiry suggests locating ourselves and our visions inside of rather than outside of the language of history and possibility. Moreover, such an inquiry does not simply look, for instance, at the history of teaching, testing, or curriculum, but analyzes how different aspects of the latter emerge out of specific crises and responses to history.

Second, teachers need to develop what West (1990) has termed "prophetic criticism." Such criticism refers to developing a range of critical skills that enable teachers to keep "track of the complex dynamics of institutional and other related power structures in order to disclose options and alternatives for transformative (actions); it also attempts to grasp the way in which representational strategies are a creative response to novel circumstances and conditions" (p. 105). This is a form of criticism which makes visible how meaning is produced, what kinds of social relationships it attempts to legitimate, and how it either supports or disrupts relations of domination. This suggests giving students the opportunity in their classes to develop the ability and skills to think in oppositional terms, to deconstruct the assumptions and interests that limit and legitimate the very questions teachers ask as educational leaders. Being immersed in the language of social criticism also means understanding the limits of our own language as well as the implications of the social practices we construct on the basis of the language we use to exercise authority and power. It means developing a language that can question public forms, address social injustices, and break the tyranny of the present.

Third, teachers need a language of imagination, one that both insists on and enables them to consider the structure, movement, and possibilities in contemporary society and how they might act to prevent forms of oppression and develop those aspects of public life that point to its best and as yet unrealized possibilities. This is a language of hope, one that links empowerment to the possibility to dream and struggle for the material and ideological conditions that expand those human capacities and social institutions that provide the conditions for creating critical citizens and spaces for social justice. As public intellectuals, teachers need to address what it means for schools to create the conditions for students to be social agents willing to struggle for expanding critical public cultures that make a democracy viable.

Fourth, if the concept of teachers as public intellectuals is to operate in the service of a project of possibility, pedagogy must be seen as a form of cultural politics; that is, a politics that highlights the role of education as it takes place in a variety of sites to open up rather than close down the possibilities for keeping moral responsibility and hope alive at a time of shrinking possibilities. This is a form of education that recognizes that the principles of diversity, dialogue, compassion, and tolerance are at the heart of what it means to strengthen rather than weaken the relationship between learning and empowerment on the one hand, and democracy and schooling on the other.

SUMMARY

In conclusion, I believe that questions concerning public education are often discussed as if they have no relation to issues of power, politics, and struggle. Central to my argument has been the assumption that public schools are a terrain of struggle and that teachers can neither understand the nature of the struggle itself nor the nature of the schooling unless one raises the question as to what the purpose of public schooling actually is. It is this question of purpose and practice that makes clear what the limits and possibilities are that exist within public schools at a given time in history. This is essentially a question of politics, power, and possibility. For as we know, the way in which knowledge, values, and classroom social relations are produced, organized, and legitimated within the public schools presuppose and legitimate particular forms of history, community, and authority. The question is, of course, whose history, community, knowledge, and voice prevails. Unless this question is addressed, the issue of how one should teach, function as an intellectual, or relate to students and the wider society becomes removed from the wider principles that inform such issues. I have argued that public schools should be seen as sites for educating students in the language and practice of democracy and critical citizenship.

As public intellectuals, teachers can advance the assumption that public schools be understood as democratic public spheres in order to educate students to find their own voices while learning how to both understand and connect such voices to the exercise of civic courage. That is, such voices can be understood and critically interrogated as part of a wider exercise of compassion and conviction aimed at both protesting and transforming the mechanisms of power, domination, and subjugation that operate at the level of everyday life and in the wider society.

Central to my argument has been the view that public schools do not merely teach subjects or generate particular pedagogical strategies—they also create social identities. In other words, they introduce students to particular ways of life, and they often do so by privileging the discourses and experience of the dominant culture. If teachers are to take the democratic imperatives of schooling seriously, they need to democratize the culture of the curriculum and school in order to open it up to the diverse students and traditions that are essential to a multiracial and multicultural democracy.

Finally, I argue that teacher work is a form of intellectual labor that can only be understood in terms of its wider connections to public life—and that teachers need to make clear the political and moral referents they use to legitimate the appeals to authority they make in teaching particular forms of knowledge, legitimating particular social relations, and acknowledging the importance of a particular vision of public schooling. In other words, teachers and administrators need to have a discourse of ethics and substantive vision. In effect, I argue that teachers should not be reduced to pedagogical clerks or to servants of the empire. Instead, teachers need to define their pedagogical roles, in part by addressing the many instances of human suffering, struggles, and social problems that are a growing and threatening part of everyday life in America. This suggests an obligation to push both history and our own lives and beliefs against the grain, to recover collective memories that testify to the struggle against forms of subordination, and to work to connect our own work as both teachers and educators to forms of self and social empowerment.

References

Aronowitz, S. (1993). *Roll Over Beethoven: The Return of Cultural Strife.* Hanover, MA: Wesleyan University Press.

Aronowitz, S., and H. A. Giroux (1993). *Education Still Under Siege.* Westport, CT: Bergin and Garvey.

Baldwin, J. (1988). "A Talk to Teachers," in R. Simonson and S. Waler, eds., *Multicultural Literacy: Opening the American Mind.* Saint Paul, MN: Graywolf Press, pp. 3–12.

Giroux, H. A. (1988a). *Teachers as Intellectuals.* Westport, CT: Bergin and Garvey.

Giroux, H. A. (1988b). *Schooling and the Struggle for Public Life.* Minneapolis: University of Minnesota Press.

Graff, G. (1992). "Teaching the Conflicts," in D. J. Gless and B. H. Smith, eds., *The Politics of Liberal Education.* Durham, NC: Duke University Press, pp. 57–73.

West, C. (1990). "The New Politics of Difference." 53: 93–109.

Discussion Questions

1. How does the traditional definition of what it means to be a teacher differ from the notion of teachers as public intellectuals?

2. What is Giroux's criticism of the dominant model of teacher training?

3. In what ways might teachers join in alliances with others in order to apply their teaching skills outside of schools?

4. How might the relationship between teaching and the creation of critical citizens serve to criticize calls for national testing and a national curriculum?

5. What classroom practices would be consistent with the role of teachers as public intellectuals?

6. How might the structure of the school be reorganized to give teachers more control over their work?

Gary A. Griffin

Gary A. Griffin is currently professor of education at the University of Arizona. His higher education experience includes positions as professor and director of the Division of Instruction at Teachers College, Columbia University; program director at the Research and Development Center for Teacher Education at the University of Texas; and professor and dean at the College of Education at the University of Illinois, Chicago. He earned his bachelor's, master's, and doctoral degrees at UCLA. He began his career as a teacher in the Santa Monica Schools, where he taught in elementary and middle schools for ten years and eventually became a school principal. He has published extensively on the topics of teacher education, staff development, school change, and curriculum theory and development—racking up as many as thirty-one book chapters and thirty-two books, reports, and monographs, as well as a host of articles.

Griffin is active in the American Educational Research Association, was a member of the founding Executive Board of the Holmes Group, is a member of the AERA National Commission on Research and Practice, and served as ongoing consultant to the NEA Mastery in Learning Project. His longstanding preoccupation is working with teachers to make sense of the intricacies of teaching and learning in public school classrooms and to use that sense to improve educational opportunities for students and create stimulating workplaces for educators.

Gary enjoys the life of a professor and wouldn't have it any other way. A seasoned traveler to more than five continents and fifty countries, it is not uncommon to find him during the summers in far-off places such as New Zealand or Nepal. To keep his calories in check, he explains, "I cook exotic Asian cuisines—Thai, Cambodian, and Vietnamese—for friends and a few colleagues." And to make sure he is fit to travel, Gary swims regularly.

His most memorable teacher, he remembers, was his seventh grade English teacher because of her enthusiasm, depth of knowledge, and for "her first comment to my parents on Back to School Night: 'Gary doesn't mean to be a bad boy.'"

23 ❧

Learning to Teach in Schools: A Framework for Clinical Teacher Education

Gary A. Griffin

Clinical teacher education, learning to teach in ongoing classrooms and schools, is the focus of this chapter. The proposals here grew out of a program of research begun in the 1980s. It was then that the Research in Teacher Education (RITE) program was created at the Research and Development Center for Teacher Education at The University of Texas at Austin. The RITE research team conducted a set of studies with the express intention of better understanding the nature and effects of clinical teacher education in the United States. The studies included three major efforts:

1. A comprehensive multimethod, multisite descriptive study of student teaching (clinical teacher education as a function of cooperative relationships between universities and elementary and secondary schools) (Griffin et al., 1983)

2. An experimental study of inservice teacher education and leadership (clinical teacher education as a function of the relationship between instructional leaders and teachers) (Griffin et al., 1984)

3. An analytic study of formal state-mandated teacher induction programs (clinical teacher education connected by state law and regulation to the certification and licensure of beginning teachers) (Edwards & O'Neal, 1985)

Although the three major studies differed in many ways, they were all concerned with contributing to understanding how clinical teacher education is carried forward, how participants and outsiders describe it, the influence of context on educational opportunities, and the effects of the programs on the participants and on the contexts where they were brought to life. The three studies, then, despite differences in intentions and participants, can be looked at in terms of common features of clinical teacher education that appear to be strongly related to positive outcomes.

During and after the period of the RITE studies, researchers in other parts of the United States were also studying teacher education programs. These studies often included the clinical components of teacher education, but their research questions, methodologies, and conceptualizations make them natural companions to the RITE efforts (see, for example, Tikunoff, Ward, & Griffin, 1979; Little, 1982; Little, 1993; Berman & McLaughlin, 1975; Purkey & Smith, 1983; Talbert, 1993; Griffin, Lieberman, & Jacullo-Noto, 1982).

The discussion of clinical teacher education in these pages is not meant to suggest that learning about how to teach occurs *only* in clinical settings. I believe that clinical education is but one aspect of a broader conception of teacher education. For preservice teachers, this more comprehensive program would include a strong general education component and systematic exposure to and testing of modes of instruction, curriculum planning models, and other professional concepts. For career teachers, clinical education should be embedded in a complex plan of professional growth that includes self-study, participation in advanced graduate degree programs, involvement with professional associations, and the like (Lieberman, 1992; Little & McLaughlin, 1993).

The features of clinical teacher education programs presented in the remainder of this chapter have been found to be consistently related to positive outcomes, according to the perceptions of participants in the programs and to expert judgments. It is believed that these features are critical in the planning and conducting of clinical teacher education, whether for preservice students, beginning teachers, or career professionals.

THE RITE CLINICAL TEACHER EDUCATION FRAMEWORK

The research and theory I have identified suggest one defining property and seven critical features of an effective clinical teacher education program. The program must be *embedded in a school context* (defining property), and be (1) *context-sensitive*, (2) *purposeful and articulated*, (3) *participatory and collaborative*, (4) *knowledge-based*, (5) *ongoing*, (6) *developmental*, and (7) *analytic and reflective*. There is an obvious conceptual difference between the defining property and the critical features. The defining property sets the boundaries within which clinical teacher education is to be envisioned, implemented, and monitored. The critical features are the program characteristics that must be present *within* the defining property. The defining property and each of the critical features are presented in turn, although the effectiveness of the framework is dependent upon the interaction of *all* of the features over time.

Defining Property: The Program Is Defined by Its Relations with a School Context

The hallmark of a clinical teacher education program is its relation to the context in which it is carried forward. In contrast to general education and professional studies—typical components of teacher education—clinical teacher education takes place in living classrooms and schools. These real-life contexts and the people in them give form and substance to clinical teacher education. It is commonly believed that learning about teaching and schooling in colleges and universities differs sharply from learning to do teaching and schooling in elementary and secondary schools. Currently, two views of the relation of context to the preparation and continuing growth of teachers prevail. One view holds that nothing of real importance is learned until a person is faced with the daily problems and possibilities posed by students in classrooms (Ayers, 1993). This idea is often expressed as the dichotomy between the "ivory tower" of the university and the "real life" of schools. According to this view, the university deals with theory, whereas the schools teach the more practical (and more highly valued) skills necessary to become effective as a teacher. Indeed, there are teacher education programs currently in operation that depend solely upon successful practice in schools for determination of teacher adequacy, even for the purpose of granting state certification (Hoffman & Defino, 1985).

There is another, more comprehensive, view of the role of context in the education of teachers. This view acknowledges that the person learns from the context but also gives attention to learning and acting beyond mere *accommodation* to the context (Noddings, 1992; Ward & Tikunoff, 1977). The teacher-context relationship is seen as a means by which the teacher learns about, from, in, and how to act upon the context. Rather than learning only how schools operate at a technological level, the teacher candidate or beginning teacher learns why the classrooms and schools look the way they do, what conditions constrain or promote teaching and learning activity, how schools come to develop their often very special characters, how to connect schools with disciplined inquiry and analysis, and, importantly, how to act upon school and classroom contexts for the purpose of improvement.

Clearly, in the first of these two views, teacher education is divorced from context and can have only limited import because it is "theory without practice." In the second, however, we see the potential for teacher education to provide essential theoretical foundations applied in such a way that practice will be better understood and subject to change *and* improvement.

Feature 1: The Program Is Context-sensitive Currently, teachers and other school personnel are expressing considerable concern about "conditions of work." This is another way of acknowledging the power of context to reward or discourage teachers. Many see unfavorable work conditions as the primary reason why some of the finest teachers leave teaching and some of the most promising young people choose not to enter the teaching force. Among the most detrimental conditions is the powerlessness felt by many teachers. They note that their professional authority is often questioned and thereby diminished, and they conclude that they are mere cogs in a wheel whose direction is beyond their control (Griffin, 1986).

A program of clinical teacher education can be especially effective in providing a teacher with the knowledge and skills necessary to become a powerful influence for change in a school; not a person who just accepts contexts and learns to live within sometimes narrowly conceived intellectual and practical boundaries, but a person who can analyze the realities of a classroom and a school with the goal of making powerful changes for the better (Tikunoff, Ward, & Griffin, 1979). Thus, the teacher-context relationship suggested here is directed toward the teacher's understanding and acting upon situations in which teaching and learning occur.

What this position implies, of course, is that the classrooms and schools of the nation are rich in information directly related to teaching and schooling. Furthermore, that information can be used in vitally important ways to prepare people to become teachers and to help new and career teachers grow and develop. The context feature of the framework raises to a central position the characteristics, regularities, relationships, behaviors, and effects of what happens in schools.

Sensitivity to context can be accomplished in a number of ways. Prospective teachers, for example, are typically required to spend time in classrooms. How that time is spent, however, will determine whether or not the context is central to the teacher candidate's movement toward professional status. A field experience that is unfocused, lacking in concurrent expert guidance, and unconnected to developing ways of seeing and understanding the classroom context would clearly not meet the standard set forth here. Similarly, opportunities for new and career teachers to become expert in teaching that either ignore the contexts in which teaching is to take place or that only sporadically give attention to the situation-specific nature of teaching would also fall outside the RITE framework's specifications.

Contexts as discussed here, then, are assumed to be positive environments for learning the important social and professional manifestations of teaching. It is in these exemplary settings that clinical teacher education should take place. However, contexts in the organizational forms of schools and classrooms become not just the places where one learns the conventions of these places as they are, but also serve as sources of information for understanding teaching and schooling, and provide opportunities for analysis and attempts at improvement.

Feature 2: The Program Is Purposeful and Articulated   Scholars have noted that the goals of education as seen in schools often overlap and conflict, and that these goals are themselves often ambiguous in nature (Miles, 1964). That is, although schools are designed by the culture to do something related to the education of children and youth, that something is not as clearly defined and articulated as expected.

Likewise, the education of teachers at preservice, induction, and inservice levels of activity is often lacking in clear purposes, and the rationales for such programs are seldom well articulated (Griffin et al., 1983). (Articulation here means a high degree of clarity of presentation of ideas. Another meaning related to relationships between parts of a whole is suggested in the section describing the developmental feature of the RITE framework.)

Research strongly demonstrates the positive effects of clear, public expressions of purpose in teacher education programs. Unfortunately, negative examples abound. Consider the confusion that occurs when student teachers, cooperating teachers, and university supervisors cannot recall, let alone agree upon, the purposes of their clinical experiences together. Most practicing teachers can tell anecdotes about so-called "inservice days" that appear to have been composed of disconnected events leading to no widely understood purpose. And orientations for new teachers are often devoted to so-called "administrivia" and unconnected to a comprehensive plan to help teachers in the induction phase of their development move successfully into teaching roles.

More positively, research and less formal observation of practice illustrate that some teacher education programs are characterized by conscious and public attention to clarity of purposes (Griffin et al., 1984). Furthermore, the greater and more widespread the understanding of the purposes, the more likely that they will be realized. Clear, specific statements of purpose provide participants with a sense of direction, an expectation that something will be accomplished. Participants who are not informed of well-formulated purposes are placed in the position of trying to second-guess (or outsmart) those responsible for teacher education programs (Edwards & O'Neal, 1984).

It should be understood that the attention to purpose is not put forth as yet another means to coerce prospective or practicing teachers into a conforming stance. Although one purpose of a teacher education program might be as narrow as "to plan lessons according to the sequence of objective, development, motivation, practice, seatwork, and evaluation"; another purpose might be as broad as "to identify a school problem, develop a means to act upon it, and teach others in the school ways to use the solution." In either case, highly prescriptive or broadly conceptualized, such statements offer teacher education participants a sense of what is expected, what is valued, and what will be supported.

Feature 3: The Program Is Participatory and Collaborative Clinical teacher education, as suggested in the discussion of context, is largely a set of interactions between classrooms and schools and the people in them. These interactions are believed to be most effective when characterized by participation and collaboration (Lieberman, 1985).

Participation here refers to active involvement, the give-and-take that characterizes the liveliest professional and intellectual discourse (Griffin & Edwards, 1982). Participation means active questioning, diligence in the search for reasonable solutions to unreasonable problems, persistence in discovering the most powerful resources for instruction, formulation of important problems for public attention, and so on (Maeroff, 1993).

Some researchers call this brand of participation professional collegiality (Little, 1982). (This is in contrast, but not contradiction, to personal or social collegiality.) The assumption is that teachers, like other professionals, are more effective, and more knowledgeable about that effectiveness, when they have regular opportunities to be actively involved in the advancement of their important work.

Collaboration is an oft-used and ill-understood term, particularly in relation to matters of teaching and schooling. Collaboration is related to ownership. The teacher who has had some hand in formulating and carrying forward the effort (as opposed to being only the recipient of a set of externally imposed specifications) very probably will feel a strong investment in bringing it to successful operation. Also, and perhaps more importantly, teacher education programs for new and experienced teachers are aptly concerned with giving participants more authority in their teaching roles. Although the role of the "expert" is not to be downgraded, isn't it reasonable to assume that teachers, as they grow in knowledge and experience, will have greater insights into the issues that need to be dealt with than those who are not teachers? Many believe that it has been too long since teachers had a significant hand in the determination of their own professional destinies (Griffin, 1983).

The increasing emphasis on teachers as recipients of prescriptions for practice, "users" of routinized curricula, and objects of mandates made at state and local levels of policy has significantly eroded the teacher's professional dignity in the eyes of the public and, in fact, in teachers' views of themselves. There appears to be a deficit model of professional development at work, a set of blanket generalizations about teacher skill and competence that leads to increased emphasis on correcting unforgivable deficiencies. This mindset has led, in many instances, to the paraprofessionalization of teaching, wherein teaching is considered a technical (rather than intellectual or substantive) activity, one that is easily taught, efficiently observed, and readily remedied (Griffin, 1985).

The depiction of schools and teaching in this worst-case scenario detracts from efforts to attract strong teacher candidates, hold promising new teachers, and gain professional commitment from career teachers. Collaboration, when it is authentic, ensures that teachers have individual and collective voices when important decisions are made and when those decisions are enacted in school and classroom practice. Collaboration places teachers in positions of status with administrators and policy-making colleagues such that their ideas and insights become part of the decision structure. Collaboration provides teachers with all-too-often-missing communication lines with others concerned about the quality of educational opportunity.

Feature 4: The Program Is Knowledge-based   As for several of the other features of this framework of clinical teacher education, the specification of a knowledge base to guide practice seems either simplistic or superfluous. Unfortunately, neither conclusion is warranted. A number of teacher education programs appear to be informed more by opinions or impressions than by verified and reliable knowledge (Griffin et al., 1983). This may be related to the problem often observed by the research community: namely, that teachers in large numbers are relatively unable to speak comprehensively about why they do what they do in classrooms. Instead of referring to common knowledge about best practice, many teachers talk only about what they have tried and what has happened as a consequence of those trials (Lieberman & Miller, 1991). This, of course, is a form of knowledge, but it does not serve as a distinguishing mark of the teacher as professional.

It is entirely possible that the lack of attention to the development and distribution of knowledge about teaching and schooling contributes significantly to teachers' observed unfamiliarity with known theory and practice (Newmann, 1993).

I must assert here that knowledge can take many forms and can be derived from a variety of different perspectives (Peshkin, 1993). Knowledge here means more than a set of discrete facts, lists, prescriptions, and "findings." By knowledge, I mean a coherent set of such facts and other information that together allow us to make judgments, come to informed decisions, suggest desirable practices, and ask important questions. This knowledge is codified, is connected in its particulars, and is the resting place for concepts and constructs that make sense.

Certainly, recent attention to a rational, empirical view of teaching and schooling has contributed to our understanding of processes and outcomes and the relationships between and among them (Hawley et al., 1984). The effort of the past twenty years devoted to understanding which teaching behaviors are associated with which student achievements is of value to teacher education programs. But total reliance upon this body of knowledge to make major programmatic decisions about teaching, schooling, and teacher education is probably insufficient for the development of the kind of ideal teacher presented earlier in this chapter. In fact, it seems that single-minded dependence upon the process-product teacher effectiveness studies leads to a narrower vision of teaching and teachers than is desired by most professional educators.

In this framework for clinical teacher education, *theoretical knowledge* is of major importance. I agree with the proposition that "theory without practice is futile and practice without theory is fatal," that theory is developed out of practical understanding, and in turn, that theory informs practical situations. Theory is particularly powerful in helping prospective and career teachers understand and make sense of their professional worlds. Theoretical formulations suggest and define connections between disparate pieces of the complex teaching and schooling puzzle, and thus lead thoughtful teachers to make their own discoveries as a consequence of increased understandings.

A difficulty with using *theory* as a term related to teacher education in general, and to the clinical component of teacher education in particular, is that the word and what it represents have been demeaned over the years by casual and misinformed use. Theory has come to mean for many teachers all of that "stuff" that colleges and universities teach and that teachers can see no meaning for in their practical worlds. What has happened, then, is that the word has come to stand for a good deal of nonsense that passes under the guise of teacher education. Theory, in its very real sense, can be practical, useful, and of enormous value to teachers and others in schools.

The issues that must be dealt with by teachers and others in schools are complex, highly interactive, often imbued with urgency, and increasingly related to societal pressures and influences. Typical responses to this complexity are founded in what can be termed *propositional knowledge*. Propositional knowledge here refers to those ideas for schooling activity that are put forth as proposals; suggestions for change that have yet to be given theoretical or empirical tests of effectiveness. It is important in this discussion to stress that propositional knowledge is appropriate for this framework in direct relation to its *promise* for making desirable changes in educational settings. Relative promise rests on the credibility of the person or persons making the proposal, the logical "fit" with the most highly regarded purposes and practices of schooling, and the degree of comprehensive endorsement from these experts on teaching and schooling.

Another conception of knowledge is what has come to be called *craft knowledge.* This body of information, coherent and connected and conceptually whole, emerges out of disciplined practical situations and is cumulative over time. Teachers, individually and collectively, discover that certain practices, certain ways of meeting with students, and certain materials of instruction "work" again and again. This cumulative evidence is, of course, empirical in nature, but it does not have the scientific character of the disciplined inquiries discussed earlier in this chapter. It is, in a large sense, a way of viewing the worlds of teaching and schooling from the vantage point of the practitioner who desires above all else that children and youth in schools learn (Carter, 1992). And when there is evidence that some conditions for learning are more powerful than others for inducing that learning, another piece of craft wisdom is accumulated.

Suffice it to say that knowledge can take a variety of forms and can serve a number of functions in learning about teaching, learning how to teach, and coming to be a meritorious teacher over a career. The essential point to be made is that the RITE framework demands a reliance on knowledge in the formulation and implementation of clinical teacher education programs. A program may provide suggestions for teachers to alter their pedagogy; a program may offer knowledge in a form useful for making decisions; a program might even cause teachers to think about what *isn't* known with any certainty and, thereby, promote inquiry. In any case, the attention to knowledge related to the expectations of a clinical program is in direct opposition to the oft-experienced "sink-or-swim" approach to attaining high achievement in teaching.

Feature 5: The Program Is Ongoing The position taken by the RITE team, and shared by a number of scholars and practitioners, is that teacher education is a continuum, a stream of activity that begins when a person decides to begin professional and academic study leading toward a teaching career, and ends only when the decision is made to end that career. For purposes of convenience as well as demonstrated usefulness, this continuum has been described as having at least three stages: preservice teacher education, induction, and inservice teacher education.

This conception of teaching suggests that ten years' experience is equal to more than one year taught ten times. It argues against the sameness of teaching activity. It promotes the notion that teachers grow and change, adapt and reconstruct their worlds, and accumulate and discard ideas and practices. When one views teaching activity over time, one is forced to consider that opportunities to learn more and to use that knowledge ever more effectively must somehow be related to one another. In short, teacher education and its clinical component must be ongoing, systematic, and adapted to the stages of the person's growth toward the status of career teacher (Fuller & Bown, 1975).

Currently, there are few conceptions of teacher education that take this proposition seriously. There is, however, evidence to suggest that clinical teacher education *within stages* ought to be an ongoing activity, rather than the fits and starts that characterize so many efforts in the field. It is not uncommon for the elements of a preservice teacher education program, for example, to be ideologically and practically unconnected to one another except by the student's presence while moving through the program: an educational psychology offering (with required classroom observations) here, a tutoring experience as part of a reading methods course there, and student teaching somewhere else.

In perhaps even more dramatic fashion, inservice clinical teacher education seems to be driven by the fad of the moment. Seldom seen are commitments to long-term, comprehensively envisioned inservice programs undergirded by principles and properties that frame the program over time. Instead, teachers are confronted with sets of workshops that bear little conceptual or practical relationship to each other. Unfortunately, when attempts are made to provide coherence, those attempts are often only umbrellas under which any number of concepts, prescriptions, recommendations, and "workshops" huddle together.

The RITE framework requires that there be a strand of intention and activity that, over time and with concerted effort, guides a set of cumulative experiences aimed toward an articulated purpose. To require such continuity is to demand that clinical teacher education programs be thought of as long-term investments in teachers, teaching, schooling, and the advancement of the society. It is also to demand that the program be conceptualized and put forward with consideration given to its appeal to teachers and the degree to which that appeal will sustain participation over time. Here, of course, lies the rub. For an idea or a procedure or a new way of viewing teaching to "stick," it must be (for teacher education) uncharacteristically powerful. We know that teachers, like most adults, can learn to do almost anything. But we also know that teachers are more attracted to some ideas and practices than others (Oja, 1991).

Feature 6: The Program Is Developmental   The term *developmental* has been used by psychologists to refer to what can be called naturally occurring stages of growth, alterations in the ways that mind and body work as a consequence less of intentions to change than of the usual order of events. The RITE framework of clinical teacher education uses the term differently. Because I am concerned with the professional growth and change of teachers, I use the word *developmental* to suggest an orderly progression toward advanced professional status (Sprinthall & Thies-Sprinthall, 1983). Although one can assume that young adults, for example, will grow in maturity as human beings, I take the view that teacher education programs can contribute to that growth in professional ways.

Naturally, the developmental feature of the RITE framework is aligned with the ongoing feature in its emphasis on a set of activities that, *over time,* are incremental, cumulative, and purposeful (McLaughlin, 1991). In contrast, repetitive, unsequenced, unconnected teacher education opportunities are out of alignment with this framework.

Three considerations are of particular importance in designing a program that is developmental (Buchmann & Floden, 1993). First, one must distinguish the various levels of professional growth. Second, teacher education programs should be designed according to these distinctions between levels. Third, developmental differences will affect appropriate sources of information for planning a teacher education program at every level.

The existence of levels or stages of professional growth has been well-documented (Fuller & Bown, 1975). We are aware of the distinctions that can be made between prospective teachers, new teachers, and career teachers. Recently, teacher education programs have begun to be guided by these distinctions, and perceptive observers of schools have helped to sort out conceptual and programmatic issues that clarify the various stages. For a number of years, the role of teacher and the acts of teaching have been viewed as relatively "flat" or uniform. That is, "a teacher is a teacher is a teacher." This position suggests that there are relatively few differentiators in quality or style. It promotes the notion that the new teacher should look, act, and think much like the career teacher, that student teachers should quickly make the transition toward that same look, and, importantly, that teachers should therefore be rewarded pretty much the same, although longevity and advanced degrees are typically used to provide greater rewards for the veteran than for the newcomer.

Research activity and political activity have made serious dents in that point of view. From a research perspective, we are more sharply aware of the distinctions between novices and experts, neophytes and long-termers, beginners and veterans (Schlechty, 1985). Furthermore, we are aware of qualitative differences *within* these groups. Some newcomers are different from other newcomers, some veterans are more expert than others, and so on. These distinctions have meaning for the ways we think about and conduct teacher education programs.

In terms of the developmental feature as a planning stance, the RITE framework requires that clinical teacher education programs be planned and implemented such that the various intentions and activities lead toward significantly more sophisticated consequences over time. For preservice teacher education, this might mean a reconsideration and strengthening of the "observe, tutor, teach small group, teach whole group, student teach, teach all day, and teach all week" sequence that is typically spread over a two-year or longer period of time. For beginning teachers, it might mean a systematic assessment of the new teacher's role in the system and a gradual set of events that lead the person through that role and into career teacher status. For inservice education, it might mean a school system commitment to a conception of excellence and then, in the same way that a sound curriculum for children is planned, the formulation of a program presenting increasingly complex ways of demonstrating that excellence.

Feature 7: The Program Is Analytic and Reflective   Naive observers of classrooms and schools often comment on the helter-skelter human activity they see. Children are moving; teachers are moving; materials are distributed and collected; whole groups shift from one place in the building to another. Although teachers and other educators may agree that the activity is purposeful, our patrons sometimes conclude that this is a confusing and uncertain state of affairs. There *is* a certain "busyness" about teaching and schooling. The students arrive more or less on cue, and the next five or six hours are characterized by a variety of interactions among the students as well as between students and their teachers. In fact, it is this "meeting with students" that is most often central to any characterization of teaching as a professional activity. Put another way, teaching is most often defined by teacher-student interaction.

There is, however, a more comprehensive view of teachers and teaching. According to this view, teachers engage in a number of important activities that take place apart from students. They plan; they diagnose; they evaluate; they learn from experts; they attend graduate school (Doyle, 1990; Griffin, 1984; Miller, 1990). The RITE framework of clinical teacher education requires of professional development programs that time and space be set aside for the purposes of analysis and reflection, important intellectual activities that affect how one carries out one's professional role (Cochran-Smith & Lytle, 1990).

This feature, analysis and reflection, may at first glance seem a departure from my stance regarding the centrality of context to the RITE framework. Such is not the case. Too often, it appears, the time that teachers spend away from classrooms and schools, physically and emotionally/psychologically, is time that is purposefully divorced from consideration of those workplaces (Schon, 1991). Teachers attend classes in colleges and universities frequently devoted to issues dramatically unrelated to the realities of their professional worlds. There is, in effect, a distancing of the analytic and reflective aspects of teachers' lives that dilutes the power of those activities to alter life in classrooms. (Of course, it *is* important to engage in topics other than classrooms and schools. But to almost completely divorce the objects of study from what teachers regularly *do* is, I think, a serious error in judgment.)

It has long been hypothesized that reflecting upon one's activities is a powerful way to increase professional authority and effectiveness (Dewey, 1944). Furthermore, reflection is believed to improve the professional's ability to characterize and thus influence his or her ways of thinking about and acting upon the self in relating to others he or she encounters. In fact, teachers often become so caught up in their work worlds that they either choose to avoid reflection or are forced to do so in deference to the demands of classrooms and schools. Yet, there is evidence that teachers who regularly analyze and think about their professional activity are more perceptive and influential teachers (Nicholls & Hazzard, 1993).

SOCIAL AND POLITICAL FACTORS

Obviously most readers have experienced or observed some of the clinical teacher education factors presented here as they have come into contact with teacher education, with ongoing elementary and secondary schools, and professional organizations. It is unlikely, however, that the features have been observed or experienced as an integrated whole, as is proposed here. Although the framework makes considerable sense, from a research and theory perspective, the organizational and social realities of schools as human organizations and political agencies must be recognized and acted upon in order for the clinical teacher education framework to be put into action. Among these realities that must be considered are the four discussed here.

First, the histories of schools and the biographies of teachers and teacher educators are powerful influences against making significant changes in teacher education practice. The traditions, memories, and ingrained experiences surrounding most of us offer little new light onto the work we do or, in fact, the ways we think of that work. These histories and biographies, in some cases, have been transformed into certification and licensure requirements (so many university-based hours of instruction in this), permanent certification requirements (a master's degree or equivalent hours in that), and, in some schools, career ladder requirements (attending a number of workshops in something else). Seldom are these expectations rationalized beyond the sense of "we've always done this," or "that's how I/we moved through teaching." Schools, like other organizations, and the professionals in them tend to be very difficult to change, often unwilling or unable to rethink longstanding practices. In order for the clinical teacher education framework outlined here to take hold with any integrity, it will be necessary that some of the central and deeply entrenched, though seldom discussed, regularities of schooling are reinvented and/or discarded.

Second, the organizationally convenient practice of sorting teachers (and teacher candidates) into large groups for purposes of preparation and ongoing professional education makes up a major barrier to the framework discussed in this chapter. As students of teaching, for example, move through their university-based programs of study, they are typically treated as a coherent group, as people who are much like one another. As they read text, discuss, perform teaching tasks, engage in student teaching, and so forth, procedures and standards and expectations are pretty much the same. The RITE framework, it will be remembered, has several features that deny the wisdom of this broadscale and undifferentiated treatment. Similar to teacher preparation programs, professional development opportunities in schools also herd practicing teachers together for undifferentiated experiences in workshops, institutes, minicourses, or whatever. These practices do not take into account the importance of each teacher's context in terms of continuing to learn to teach, the integrity of each teacher's different teaching history, or the developmental variations among new, experienced, and veteran teachers.

Third, the politically expedient route of aiming low and hitting the mark in terms of setting standards for teacher performance does little service to teachers in their journey toward expert status or to the students who are with teachers on part of that journey. Although standards for teachers are being given greater attention by policy makers, teacher educators, and teachers themselves, there is little evidence that this attention is aimed at ensuring "best practice" rather than "safe practice." The framework proposed here rests on a set of understandings about teaching as complex intellectual activity that requires thoughtfulness as well as skill, dispositions to act in certain ways rather than by-the-book responses to teaching-learning situations, and reflection and analysis instead of robot-like demonstration of certain prespecified "behaviors." Unfortunately, when one examines expectations for teachers and expectations for teaching, one finds what might be termed lowest common denominators of knowledge, skill, and disposition. The persistence of the view, expressed in teacher education policy, that teaching is relatively mindless and undifferentiated persists. Aiming high and hitting the mark is hard. The framework here is meant to assist us in overcoming the difficulty of such a task.

Fourth, the unwillingness to raise the economic stakes in teacher education, of course, will continue to be a root cause of persistence in unexamined practice, expressed inability to make significant changes in current (and historical) practice, and few exemplary programs that demonstrate all or even some of the features of the framework proposed here. Obviously, it is expensive to differentiate instruction according to some concept of developmentalism. It is also expensive to identify and nurture exemplary contexts for learning to teach. And paying serious attention to reflection and analysis requires time, and time is money. Naturally, there are possibilities associated with reallocation of existing resources, redefining how those resources are to support teacher education. But these possibilities, I suspect strongly, will make few if any major inroads on teacher education innovation until significant changes are made in resource availability. We need to make convincing cases for the complex relationships between preparation for teaching and teaching, for continuing the education of novice teachers and providing ongoing professional opportunities for expert teachers. These cases must rest, ultimately, on conceptions of teaching and teacher education that capture rather than conceal the intellectual and practical complexity of the work.

THEORY INTO PRACTICE

This clinical teacher education presentation has included a number of examples of how the theories that were developed from the research on teacher education can be put into place. Of particular importance, given the defining feature of context, is the necessity that teachers learn their craft initially in exemplary elementary and secondary classrooms. For the theory to affect teacher education practice, it will be necessary to pay considerably more attention to the school and classroom contexts that surround and strongly influence how teachers come to understand and act out their work. The current practices associated with teacher education practice and student teaching, particularly in programs preparing large numbers of teachers, need to be re-examined, revitalized, and strengthened.

Professional Development Schools, it seems to me, can serve well the linked intentions of school improvement and enhanced teacher education. These schools, as proposed in a number of forums, are designed as companion institutions to colleges and universities and are meant to provide demonstrations of outstanding teaching and schooling *and* provide contexts for learning to teach that are challenging, supporting, and educative. I can think of few current proposals that are as closely aligned to the clinical teacher framework discussed here as are professional development schools.

A major issue in transforming the framework of theory into teacher education practice is the conception of teaching and teachers that drives teacher education. As long as there is credibility to the view that teaching is a relatively unsophisticated, by-the-numbers activity rather than complex sets of interactions rooted in solid understanding of the nature of knowledge, the problems of society, and the nature of students, this framework has little possibility of enactment. Why engage in ensuring the presence of the framework features in all their complexity if teachers are to be turned out in cookie cutter fashion? Only when prevailing views of teaching in many higher education institutions and school systems shift dramatically will this framework make sense as desired practice.

Clearly, for this quasi-theoretical set of features (and their interactions) to become practice, much greater attention than is usual must be paid to clarifying what knowledge is, how it is expressed in teaching-learning situations, and how meaning is to be made by teacher educators, teacher candidates, and experienced teachers. The view that knowledge is a commodity to be handed from an expert to a novice simply does not fit this framework that rests on making meaning out of the interaction of context, activity, biography, and expectations. Meaning (and supporting knowledge) are products of intricate interactions and sense-making opportunities, sometimes alone and sometimes with others. The interplay of these theoretical views, the framework and making sense of teaching, must be supported and celebrated for the framework to have any chance of success.

SUMMARY

This chapter has suggested a framework for clinical teacher education that may be put to use in programs designed for prospective teachers, beginning teachers, and career teachers. The framework proposes context as a defining property and a set of seven critical features that I believe are central to the enactment of sound clinical teacher education. Furthermore, the framework is based upon the strong belief that the best clinical teacher education programs will give attention to the defining property and all of the critical features in interaction.

Using this framework would cause teacher educators, preservice and inservice, to develop programs with clearly stated and public purposes. Such programs would be based on a conception of teacher growth and improvement that is grounded in an understanding of the issues and problems of teachers' relationships in their classrooms and schools, guided by a conception of cumulative experience and power over time, rooted in a substantial and verifiable knowledge base, and sensitive to the ways that participants think about and reflect upon both the programs and the places in which the teachers do their work.

The nation, it has been said, is "at risk" (National Commission on Excellence in Education, 1983). I am not certain that this general conclusion is warranted by the assumptions that led to it in some commission reports, scholarly pronouncements, and studies of schools. I am, however, concerned about the "at-risk" status of the nation in special terms of its teachers and their work in schools. If we want to move from a nation of "knowers of facts" to a nation of "problem solvers," from a conception of educational opportunity based on opportunism to one that leads citizens to discover the "good life," from a culture that undervalues our significant experiment in universal education to one that supports that enterprise, then we must work toward the intellectual and practical empowerment of teachers. One part of that important endeavor is the enactment of improved opportunities for teachers to become what we all know they want to be: thoughtful, effective, *excellent* professionals.

References

Ayers, W. (1993). *To Teach: The Journey of a Teacher.* New York: Teachers College Press.

Berman, P., and M. McLaughlin (1975). *Federal Programs Supporting Education Change, Vol. 4.* Santa Monica, CA: Rand Corporation.

Buchmann, M., and R. Floden (1993). "Coherence, the Rebel Angel." *Educational Researcher* 21 (9): 5–9.

Carter, K. (1992). "The Place of Story in the Study of Teaching and Teacher Education." *Educational Researcher* 22 (1): 5–12.

Cochran-Smith, M., and S. Lytle (1990). "Research on Teaching and Teacher Research: The Issues That Dive." *Educational Researcher* 19 (2): 2–11.

Dewey, J. (1944). *Democracy and Education.* Toronto: Macmillan.

Doyle, W. (1990). "Themes in Teacher Education," in R. Houston, ed., *Handbook of Research on Teacher Education.* New York: Macmillan, pp. 1–24.

Edwards, S., and S. O'Neal (1984). *Effective Supervision of Student Teachers.* Austin, TX: The University of Texas at Austin, Research and Development Center for Teacher Education.

Fuller, F., and O. Bown (1975). "Becoming a Teacher," in K. Ryan, ed., *Teacher Education (Seventy-fourth Yearbook of the National Society for the Study of Education).* Chicago: University of Chicago Press.

Griffin, G. (1983). "Toward a Conceptual Framework for Staff Development," in G. Griffin, ed., *Staff Development (Eighty-second Yearbook of the National Society for the Study of Education).* Chicago: University of Chicago Press.

Griffin, G. (1984). "Why Use Research in Preservice Teacher Education: A Proposal." *Journal of Teacher Education* 35 (4): 36–40.

Griffin, G. (1985). "The Paraprofessionalization of Teaching." Paper presented at the annual meeting of the American Educational Research Association, Chicago.

Griffin, G. (1986). "Thinking About Teaching," in K. Zumwalt, ed., *Improving Teaching.* Alexandria, VA: The Association of Supervision and Curriculum Development.

Griffin, G., S. Barnes, R. Hughes, S. O'Neal, M. Defino, S. Edwards, and H. Hukill (1983). *Clinical Preservice Teacher Education: Final Report of a Descriptive Study.* Austin, TX: The University of Texas at Austin, Research and Development Center for Teacher Education.

Griffin, G., S. Barnes, S. O'Neal, S. Edwards, M. Defino, and H. Hukill (1984). *Changing Teacher Practice: Final Report of an Experimental Study.* Austin, TX: The University of Texas at Austin, Research and Development Center for Teacher Education.

Griffin, G., and S. Edwards (1982). *Student Teaching: Problems and Promising Practices.* Austin, TX: The University of Texas at Austin, Research and Development Center for Teacher Education.

Griffin, G., A. Lieberman, and J. Jacullo-Noto (1982). *Interactive Research and Development on Schooling.* New York: Teachers College, Columbia University.

Hawley, W., S. Rosenholtz, and H. Goodstein (1984). *Good Schools: What Research Says About Improving Student Achievement.* Nashville, TN: Vanderbilt University.

Hoffman, J., and M. Defino (1985). "State and

School District Intentions and the Implementation of New Teacher Programs." Paper presented at the annual meeting of the American Educational Research Association, Chicago.

Lieberman, A. (1985). "Educational Policy and Leadership." Paper presented at the Allerton Symposium on Institutional Collaboration, Monticello, IL.

Lieberman, A. (1992). "The Meaning of Scholarly Activity and the Building of Community." *Educational Researcher* 21 (6): 5–12.

Lieberman, A., and L. Miller, eds. (1991). *Staff Development for Education in the '90s: New Demands, New Realities, New Perspectives.* New York: Teachers College Press.

Little, J. (1982). *School Success and Staff Development: The Role of Staff Developer in Urban Desegregated Schools.* Boulder, CO: Center for Action Research.

Little, J. (1993). "Professional Community in Comprehensive High Schools: The Two Worlds of Academic and Vocational Teachers," in J. Little and M. McLaughlin, eds., *Teachers' Work: Individuals, Colleagues, and Contexts.* New York: Teachers College Press, pp. 137–163.

Little, J., and M. McLaughlin (1993). *Teachers' Work: Individuals, Colleagues, and Contexts.* New York: Teachers College Press.

McLaughlin, M. (1991). "Enabling Staff Development," in A. Lieberman and L. Miller, eds., *Staff Development for Education in the '90s: New Demands, New Realities, New Perspectives.* New York: Teachers College Press, pp. 61–82.

Maeroff, G. (1993). *Team Building for School Change.* New York: Teachers College Press.

Miles, M., ed. (1964). *Innovation in Education.* New York: Teachers College Press.

Miller, L. (1990). "Teacher as Researcher." Paper presented at the annual meeting of the American Educational Research Association, Boston.

National Commission on Excellence in Education (1983). *A Nation at Risk: The Imperative for Educational Reform.* Washington, D.C.: Government Printing Office.

Newmann, F. (1993). "Beyond Common Sense in Educational Restructuring: The Issues of Content and Linkage." *Educational Researcher* 22 (2): 4–13.

Nicholls, J., and S. Hazzard (1993). *Education as Adventure: Lessons from the Second Grade.* New York: Teachers College Press.

Noddings, N. (1992). *The Challenge to Care in Schools: An Alternative Approach to Education.* New York: Teachers College Press.

Oja, S. (1991). "Adult Development: Insights on Staff Development," in A. Lieberman and L. Miller, eds., *Staff Development for Education in the '90s: New Demands, New Realities, New Perspectives.* New York: Teachers College Press, pp. 37–60.

Peshkin, A. (1993). "The Goodness of Qualitative Research." *Educational Researcher* 22 (2): 24–30.

Purkey, S., and M. Smith (1983). "Effective Schools: A Review." *Elementary School Journal* 83 (4): 427–452.

Schlechty, P. (1985). "Teaching as a Profession: What We Know and What We Need to Know." Paper presented at the annual meeting of the American Educational Research Association, Chicago.

Schon, D. (1991). *The Reflective Turn.* New York: Teachers College Press.

Sprinthall, N., and L. Thies-Sprinthall (1983). "The Teacher as an Adult Learner: A Cognitive-developmental View," in G. Griffin, ed., *Staff Development (Eighty-second Yearbook of the National Society for the Study of Education).* Chicago: University of Chicago Press.

Talbert, J. (1993). "Constructing a Schoolwide Professional Community: The Negotiated Order of a Performing Arts School," in J. Little and M. McLaughlin, eds., *Teachers' Work: Individuals, Colleagues, and Contexts.* New York: Teachers College Press, pp. 164–184.

Tikunoff, W., B. Ward, and G. Griffin (1979). *Interactive Research and Development on Teaching: Final Report.* San Francisco: Far West Laboratory for Educational Research and Development.

Ward, B., and W. Tikunoff (1977). "Why Consider Context?" Paper presented at the annual meeting of the American Educational Research Association, New York City.

Discussion Questions

1. Select a classroom for observation (or recollection) and imagine that you know nothing about "why" the classroom and the events in it are as they are. Describe what the classroom is like, what happens in it, and who does what. What characteristics of classrooms are difficult to understand, rationalize, and support when prior knowledge is not used?

2. What are the most important features of classrooms for the novice teacher to know about? Why?

3. Select a topic or issue from the educational literature (for example, cooperative learning) and design a plan, incorporating the clinical teacher education framework features, to prepare teachers to deal with the issue.

4. Describe a teacher education program (preservice or inservice) and analyze it in relation to the features of the clinical teacher education framework.

5. Using the framework presented in the chapter, provide examples of how the features were or were not present in your own program of studies. How might the program have been different if the features *were* present?

6. Which features of the framework are most desirable? Why? Which are least desirable? Why? Examine the reasons, intellectual and practical, that you think influenced your reaction to the features.

Index